Inclusion of Students With Autism

Using ABA-Based Supports in General Education

Joel Hundert

pro·ed
An International Publisher

8700 Shoal Creek Boulevard
Austin, Texas 78757-6897
800-897-3202   Fax 800-397-7633
www.proedinc.com

© 2009 by PRO-ED, Inc.
8700 Shoal Creek Boulevard
Austin, Texas 78757-6897
800/897-3202   Fax 800/397-7633
www.proedinc.com

Library of Congress Cataloging-in-Publication Data

Hundert, Joel.
    Inclusion of students with autism : using ABA-based supports in general
education / Joel Hundert.
        p. cm.
    Includes bibliographical references and index.
    ISBN 978-1-4164-0390-6
    1. Autistic children—Education.   2. Inclusive education.   3. Behavioral
assessment.   I. Title.
    LC4717.H86 2009
    371.94—dc22   2008028335

Art Director: Jason Crosier
Designer: Vicki DePountis
This book is designed in Fairfield LH and Agenda.

Printed in the United States of America

2   3   4   5   6   7   8   9   10   18   17   16   15   14   13   12   11

Contents

Chapter 1
Introduction to Students With Autism, Applied Behavior
Analysis, and Supported Inclusion   1

Chapter 2
Assessment and Supported Inclusion   21
Appendix 2A: *Data Collection Forms for Assessing Readiness
for Inclusion   45*

Chapter 3
Planning For and Accommodating a Student With Autism   53
Appendix 3A: *Five Recommended Commercially Available
Curriculum Programs   75*

Chapter 4
Principles of Instruction   81

Chapter 5
Facilitating the Communication of a Child With Autism
in a General Education Setting   101

Chapter 6
Promoting Peer Interaction in General Education Classrooms   113
Appendix 6A: *Social Script for the Ball and Pipe Game   137*

Chapter 7
Following School Routines Independently   141

Chapter 8
Teaching Thinking Skills   153

Chapter 9
Preventing and Dealing With Problem Behaviors   171
Appendix 9A: *Data Collection Forms for Assessing Problem Behaviors*   *215*

Chapter 10
Working Collaboratively With Families   235
Appendix 10A: *A Person-Centered Approach to Supported Inclusion*   *249*

Chapter 11
Preparing Staff for ABA-Based Supported Inclusion   253
Appendix 11A: *Adaptive Classwide Plan*   *273*

References   275

About the Author   295

Index   297

1

Introduction to Students With Autism, Applied Behavior Analysis, and Supported Inclusion

Chapter Topics

- Autism

- Early intensive behavioral intervention

- Applied behavior analysis

- Inclusion of children with developmental disabilities in general education

- Supported inclusion of children with developmental disabilities in general education

- Instructional targets in supported inclusion

The emphasis of this book is to describe how specific procedures based on principles of applied behavior analysis (ABA) can be used to support children with autism in general education classrooms. There has been a considerable amount written on how to develop and deliver applied behavior analytical therapy for young children with autism, typically on a one-to-one basis, in a highly structured environment such as a clinic (e.g., Leaf & McEachin, 1999; Lovaas, 2003; Maurice, Green, & Luce, 1996). Similarly, there is a considerable amount of literature regarding the inclusion of students with autism in general education settings (e.g., Kluth, 2003). There has, however, been very little written on how to apply interventions based on the principles of applied behavior analysis to assist children with autism in general education settings.

This book starts with a brief introduction to children with autism, applied behavior analysis, and supported inclusion. Then, it describes how to assess a child with autism's readiness for inclusion. The majority of the book describes ABA-based interventions to assist in the adjustment of children with autism who are in an inclusive school setting.

Autism

For convenience, the term *children with autism* will be used to refer to three subgroups of children described under the *Diagnostic and Statistical Manual of Mental Disorders* (DSM IV–TR; American Psychiatric Association, 2000) category of Pervasive Developmental Disorders (PDD): Autistic Disorder, Pervasive Developmental Disorders–Not Otherwise Specified (PDD-NOS), and Asperger's Syndrome. Because these three subcategories include groupings of children with autism that differ mainly in the severity, not the type, of symptoms children in each grouping display, the term *Autism Spectrum Disorders* (ASDs) is also used in the field to refer to children who fall along the same continuum of autistic symptoms (Wing, 1988). The symptoms that characterize children with Autistic Disorder are shown in Table 1.1. Although the symptoms in Table 1.1 describe autism in general, individual children have varying degrees of each symptom, from mild to severe.

Autism is a complex, lifelong neurodevelopmental disorder that affects approximately 3 in every 1,000 children (Yeargin-Allsopp et al., 2003), with about 4 times more boys than girls affected (Fombonne, 2003).

Although there is growing evidence that autism has a genetic component (Bailey, Le Couteur, Gottesman, & Bolton, 1995) and is a neurodevelopmental disorder (Wing, 1988), there is still no identified cause of the disorder and, therefore, no known means of preventing the onset of autism. Until lately, the long-term outcome for children with autism tended to be pessimistic, with follow-up studies indicating that most children with autism would require lifelong supports (Howlin, Goode, Hutton, & Rutter, 2004).

When reaching adulthood, most children with autism continue to show significant deficits in communication and ritualized, compulsive behaviors and social skills. They tend not to live independently, to obtain competitive employment, or to have many close social relationships (Billstedt, Gillberg, & Gillberg, 2005).

Table 1.1
Summary of Core Symptoms Characterizing Children With Autistic Disorder

Impairment in Social Interaction

- Impairment in the use of nonverbal behaviors to regulate social interaction
- Failure to develop peer relationships
- Lack of spontaneous seeking to share activities with others
- Lack of social or emotional reciprocity

Impairment in Communication

- Delays in spoken language
- Impairment in the ability to initiate or sustain conversation
- Stereotypic or repetitive use of language
- Lack of social imitation

Repetitive and Stereotyped Patterns of Behavior

- Preoccupation with stereotyped interests
- Adherence to nonfunctional routines
- Preoccupation with parts of objects

Source: American Psychiatric Association (2000).

Early Intensive Behavioral Intervention

Over the past decade, there has been an explosion of interest in early intensive behavioral intervention (EIBI). This interest can be traced to two significant influences. First, Catherine Maurice, a mother of two children with autism, described her struggles in locating and obtaining effective treatment for her sons. Her children made remarkable gains with EIBI, and her description of her struggles and the positive outcomes for her sons fuelled interest in ABA treatment. The second impetus for the widespread interest in EIBI is a growing body of outcome research studies showing positive effects of EIBI with young children with autism. One of the first outcome studies examining the effectiveness of EIBI was completed by Ivar Lovaas (1987). In this study, three groups of children with autism, approximately 3.5 years of age, were followed over (approximately) a 2-year period. One group of 19 children received an average of 40 hours per week of EIBI. A second group of 19 children received an average of 10 hours of EIBI. Finally, a third group of 22 children received an intervention other than EIBI. A number of measures were taken before the start of treatment and again about 2 years later, including children's performance on intelligence tests, a test of language functioning, and the amount and type of help required when they entered elementary school.

Nine of the 19 children receiving 40 hours a week of EIBI increased their IQ score into the average range and did not require special education support to pass Grade 1. This result was in contrast to the finding that none of the 19 children in the 10-hour-a-week group functioned in the average range of intelligence on posttest and passed Grade 1 without special education assistance. Similarly, only 1 of the 22 children in the no-EIBI group achieved similar gains.

A follow-up study was conducted on the continued gains of these same children when they reached about 11 years of age (McEachin, Smith, & Lovaas, 1993). No further EIBI was provided to these children, beyond the 2 years they initially received. The no-EIBI group was discontinued in this follow-up study because it was difficult to locate the children. The results indicated that 9 of the 19 children in the 40 hours of EIBI group continued to pass grades without special education support and scored within the average range in IQ, compared to none of the 19 children who had received only 10 hours of EIBI a week.

A review of the literature on child outcomes associated with EIBI is beyond the scope of this book and can be found in the published conclusions of a number of consensus panels that were established to examine this body of research and form conclusions about treatment for young children with autism (National Research Council, 2001; New York State Department of Health, 1999). Several other studies have replicated the early research of Lovaas and his colleagues and are summarized in Table 1.2. The original studies by Lovaas (1987) and by McEachin et al. (1993) indicated that only children with autism who received EIBI showed large gains in adjustment with continued positive effects 4 years later. These studies did not systematically compare the outcome of EIBI to another intervention. It is possible that, for this study, the obtained superior effects of EIBI were due to the high number of treatment hours, not to the form of treatment (i.e., EIBI) provided.

A more recent study by Eikeseth, Smith, Jahr, and Eldevik (2002) compared the effectiveness of two interventions that were both delivered about 30 hours a week. One intervention was behavioral treatment similar to that described by Lovaas (1987). The second intervention consisted of a mixture of different treatments. Even though the two interventions were implemented with about the same number of hours per week, children receiving the behavioral treatment showed a 17-point gain in IQ, compared to about a 4-point IQ gain for children receiving the eclectic treatment. It should also be pointed out that the two groups differed in the amount of supervision each therapist received and in the background of the supervisor for the two groups. Supervisors of behavior treatment were trained in that intervention; supervisors of the eclectic intervention were not. Howard, Sparkman, Cohen, Green, and Stanislaw (2005) also found that about 30 hours a week of behavioral treatment produced many more gains in children with autism than did a comparable amount of eclectic treatment. These studies suggest that it is not just the number of hours of treatment by itself that is the critical component to the effectiveness of EIBI, but also the type of treatment (behavioral) and the supervision provided.

Methodological limitation of this body of research has been described (Kasari, 2002). The evidence in support of the effectiveness of EIBI for young children with autism is compelling, but not unquestionable. It does suggest that applied behavior analysis should be a central component to early intervention effects for young children with autism, as recommended by a New York State consensus panel (New York State Department of Health, 1999).

Early intensive behavioral intervention typically consists of the provision of one-to-one treatment with a young child with autism held in a controlled environment, free from distractions. As the child shows improvement in adjustment, more naturalistic ways of teaching the child are introduced (Lovaas, 1987; Smith, Groen, & Wynn, 2000). In part because of their involvement with ABA with their young child with autism, many families have come to expect that similar forms of interventions based on ABA are available to children when they enter general education settings (Jacobson, 2000). In many cases, high-quality EIBI is available for children with autism in school. In other cases, families have had to fight to obtain the needed treatment (Yell & Drasgow, 2000).

(text continues on p. 9)

Table 1.2
IQ Gains for Outcome Studies of Early Intensive Behavioral Intervention (EIBI)

Study	Design	Groups	Setting of intervention	Interventionists	Supervisors	Results on IQ gain Pre-	Post	ES
Lovaas, 1987	• Unmatched groups • Pre–post assessment over 2 years	EIBI, N = 19, about 40 hr/wk over 2 yrs	Home	Trained student therapists	Trained university supervisors	53	83.3	UNK
		Parent training, N = 19, about 10 hr/wk	Home	Trained student therapists	Trained university supervisors	46	52.2	UNK
		No-ABA control, N = 22, eclectic	UNK	UNK	UNK	UNK	57.5	UNK
McEachin, Smith, & Lovaas, 1993	• Unmatched groups • Pre–post assessment over 7 years	EIBI, N = 19, about 40 hr/wk over 2 yrs	Home	Trained student therapists	Trained university supervisors	53	84.5	UNK
		Parent training, N = 19, about 10 hr/wk	Home	Trained student therapists	Trained university supervisors	46	54.9	UNK
Sheinkopf & Siegel, 1998	• Matched groups • Pre–post assessment interval = 20 mo.	Intensive behavioral treatment, N = 11, 19.4 hr/wk over 15.7 mo.	Home	UNS	UNS	62.8	89.7	1.0
		No treatment, N = 11	NA	NA	NA	61.7	64.3	0.1
Smith, Groen, & Wynn, 2000	• Matched-pair randomized groups • Follow-up 7–8 yrs later • Average age = 36 mo.	EIBI, N = 15, 24.52 hr/wk for 1 yr then lessened over the next 1 to 2 yrs	Home then school	Trained university student therapists	Trained student therapists who met additional criteria	50.5	66.5	1.4
		Parent training, N = 13, 5 hr/wk, over 3–9 mo.	Home	Trained university student therapists	First author	50.7	50.0	0.0

(continues)

Table 1.2 *Continued*

Study	Design	Groups	Setting of intervention	Interventionists	Supervisors	Results on IQ gain		
						Pre-	Post	ES
Eikeseth, Smith, Jahr, & Eldevik, 2002	• Assigned to behavioral or eclectic treatment based on availability of supervisors • 4–7 yrs old	Behavioral treatment, N = 13, 28.0 hr/wk, over 1 yr	Local schools	Teachers and aides who received 10 hr/wk of supervision	Met UCLA model supervision criteria	61.9	79.1	1.5
		Eclectic treatment, N = 12, 29.1 hr/wk, over 1 yr	Local schools	Teachers and aides who received 2 hr/wk of consultation	Nonbehavioral supervisor	65.0	69.5	0.4
Howard, Sparkman, Cohen, Green, & Stanislaw, 2005	• Nonrandomized groups • 30–37 mo. old	Intensive behavior analytic treatment, N = 29, 25–40 hr/wk, over 14 mo., operated by private agency	Home, school, & community	Trained and supervised paid college students who followed supervisors' programs	Master's degree in psychology	58.5	89.9	1.7
		Intensive eclectic intervention, N = 16, 30 hr/wk, over 14 mo.	Public special education classrooms for children with autism	Special education teachers and aides	UNS	53.7	62.1	0.6
		Nonintensive public early intervention programs, N = 16, 15 hr/wk, over 14 mo.	Public early intervention classrooms	Special education teachers and aides	UNS	59.9	68.8	0.6

(*continues*)

Table 1.2 Continued

Study	Design	Groups	Setting of intervention	Interventionists	Supervisors	Results on IQ gain		
						Pre-	Post	ES
Sallows & Graupner, 2005	• Randomly assigned to groups • About 34 mo. old • Measured over 4-yr period	Clinic-directed EIBI, N = 13, 39 hr/wk for first yr, 37 hr/wk for second yr, 6–10 hr/wk in-home supervision, weekly consultation	Home	Trained therapists	Met UCLA model supervision criteria	50.8	73.1	2.1
		Parent-directed EIBI, N = 10, 32 hr/wk in first yr, 31 hr/wk in second yr, 6–10 hr/mo. in-home supervision, only consultation	Home	Trained therapists	Met UCLA model supervision criteria	52.1	79.6	3.1
Cohen, Amerine-Dickens, & Smith, 2006	• Age- and IQ-matched children assigned to groups based on parental preference • About 34 mo. old • Measured over 3-yr period	EIBI from a community agency, N = 21, in home then in school, parent training, 35–40 hr/wk	Home, then school	Trained therapists	Met UCLA model supervision criteria	62	87	UNK
		Parent-directed EIBI, N = 10, 32 hr/wk in first yr, 31 hr/wk in second yr, 6–10 hr/mo. in-home supervision, only consultation	Mixture of locations	UNK	UNS	59	73	UNK

(continues)

Table 1.2 Continued

Study	Design	Groups	Setting of intervention	Interventionists	Supervisors	Results on IQ gain Pre-	Post	ES
Zachor, Ben-Itzchak, Rabinovich, & Lahat, 2007	• Nonrandomized groups matched by age; 22–33 mo. old • Measured over 1-yr period	ABA, N = 20, 35 hr/wk, 1:1, discrete trial teaching	Center	Trained behavioral therapists	Behavior analyst	UNK	UNK	UNK
		Eclectic-developmental, N = 19, 35 hr/wk	Center	Preschool special education teacher, various therapists	UNK	UNK	UNK	UNK
Eikeseth, Smith, Jahr, & Eldevik, 2007	• Assigned to behavioral or eclectic treatment based on availability of supervisors • Average of 5.5 yrs old at start and 8.0 at follow-up	Behavioral treatment, N = 13; 28.0 hr/wk over 2.5 yrs	Local schools	Teachers and aides who received 10 hr/wk of supervision	Met UCLA model supervision criteria	61.9	86.9	2.2
		Eclectic treatment, N = 12, 29.1 hr/wk, over 2.5 yrs	Local schools	Teachers and aides who received 2 hr/wk of consultation	Nonbehavioral supervisor	65.0	71.9	0.5
Reed, Osborne, & Corness, 2007	• Nonrandom assignment to high-intensity (30 hr/wk) or low-intensity behavioral approach • Measured over 9–10 mo. 2 yrs 6 mo. to 4 yrs 0 mo.	Behavioral approach, N = 14, 20–40 hr/wk	Home	UNK	UNK	57.2	about 72.5	0.8
		Behavioral approach, N = 13, 10–20 hr/wk	Home	UNK	UNK	49.3	about 56.3	0.5

Note. ABA = applied behavior analysis; ES = effect size (the mean of the prescore subtracted from the postscore, divided by the prescore standard deviation); NA = not applicable; UCLA = University of California, Los Angeles; UNK = unknown; UNS = unspecified. An effect size of +1.0 is equivalent to a gain of 1 standard deviation.

Applied Behavior Analysis

This book focuses on implementing applied behavior analytic interventions for children with autism in general education classrooms. Since its start, ABA has been associated with interventions in schools. In fact, the very first article that appeared in the *Journal of Applied Behavior Analysis* was a study by Hall, Lund, and Jackson (1968), which demonstrated that having teachers pay attention to elementary-school students when they were studying, and not when they were off task, increased the amount of time these students spent studying in the classroom. Several other studies on the effect of teacher behavior on the appropriate behavior of students in general education classrooms appeared in the first volume of the *Journal of Applied Behavior Analysis*.

It is important to have an appreciation of the history and principles of the field of applied behavior analysis, particularly as it applies to children with autism. Arguably, its greatest contribution to the field of treatment intervention in general is its adoption of a scientific methodology for understanding and changing human behavior. It is important to understand what a significant impact a scientific approach to psychology could have on our understanding of human behavior. To illustrate this point, consider how ancient Greeks explained why objects fell to the ground. Aristotle (384–322 BCE) proposed that all matter is composed of five elements: fire, earth, air, water, and aether (substance of the heavens). The first four elements had natural realms where they existed. Aristotle stated that the natural state of all matter is at rest in a location determined by the types of elements of which it was composed. An apple falls off a tree because of the force of the "earth" elements inside of the apple trying to reach its natural resting place, the ground.

In our modern age, this explanation for falling bodies seems ridiculous, but really, what is wrong with it? Yes, it is inconsistent with what we now know about the forces of gravity, but more fundamentally, the explanation is inconsistent with the methods of science. Aristotle's explanation attributes the cause for the observed phenomenon of falling bodies to events that cannot be directly observed or, in some other way, measured.

Empirical discoveries in science are based on identification of functional relationships between at least two observable events. One event is the dependent variable—the event that is being manipulated and whose impact on a second event is being measured. For example, one may study the relationship between room temperature and the length of an aluminum rod. The independent variable is the temperature of the room and the dependent measure is the length of the aluminum rod. In science, knowledge progresses through discovery of functional relationships between changes in one event (independent variable) and changes in a second event (dependent variable).

The difficulty of the ancient Greeks' explanation of falling bodies is that although a body falling can be observed and its speed can be measured, there is no way of measuring the presence or composition of "elements" within objects. Since the independent variable cannot be observed, its relationship with the dependent variable can never be confirmed or rejected. In other words, the explanation for falling bodies does not lend itself to the conventions of scientific inquiry.

So, what do falling bodies have to do with applied behavior analysis? Up until the 1920s, explanations for human behavior were attributed to human states of consciousness. John Watson (1913) proposed that a study of human behavior should be based on the observation of changes in behavior and factors that influence those changes. B. F. Skinner (1938) was influenced by Watson and argued that the understanding of human behavior should be based on an analysis of the functional relationship between observable events and changes in behavior. A person eats because it has been a number of hours since the individual last ate. A child with autism is aggressive because of events that preceded and/or followed the aggression. For instance, the frequency of aggression may increase because, following the aggression, the child obtained a desired activity or event.

The field of behavior analysis first began with the study of animal behavior, through which general principles of behavior were identified. Skinner and colleagues conducted thousands of studies between the 1930s and 1950s using initially rats and then pigeons to identify these general principles. The field of experimental analysis of behavior emerged into a field of applied behavior analysis—the application of the behavior analytic methodology to the understanding and changing of socially significant behaviors.

In the inaugural issue of the *Journal of Applied Behavior Analysis*, Baer, Wolf, and Risley (1968) wrote a paper entitled "Some Current Dimensions of Applied Behavior Analysis," which has been instrumental in defining the field. They suggested that there are a number of characteristics of an applied behavior analytic study. First, it needs to deal with an applied issue—one that is socially significant to participants and to society. In other words, ABA deals with real problems and with bringing about changes to those problems, rather than collecting information only to form a theory. Second, the phenomenon being studied must be measurable. That is, in most instances, the dependent variable being examined is quantifiable changes in behavior. A third feature is that ABA is analytical in that it studies the functional relationship between manipulated events (independent variable) and the resultant changes in behavior (dependent variable) through experimental design. A fourth characteristic is that ABA is technological, meaning that all of the procedures used to bring about behavior change are precisely described so that the procedures can be replicated in future studies.

As indicated earlier, at the turn of the 19th century, psychology was characterized by a focus on mental processes through careful attention to one's own consciousness. Watson (1913) posed that human behavior can be studied using scientific methodology. Skinner (1938) developed the field of experimental analysis of behavior and, through it, identified principles of behavior. The field of applied behavior analysis emerged in 1968 with the Baer et al. (1968) article. The Association of Behavior Analysis was formed in 1978, and the Behavior Analysis Certification Board was started in 1998. There also have been significant events in the use of applied behavior analysis with children who have autism. Lovaas (1987) published an initial research study on the outcomes of EIBI. This led to a number of replication studies that continue on today. Catherine Maurice (1993) published a book describing the success of ABA with her two sons with autism (*Let Me Hear Your Voice*). A summary of these key events can be found in Figure 1.1.

As can be seen, the field of ABA is relatively new—about 40 years old—and its widespread application with children with autism is only about 20 years old. It has been only in the past few years that ABA has had an extensive presence in supporting children with autism in general education classrooms.

Now, with the success of early intensive behavior intervention, there is growing interest in the use of applied behavior analysis to support children with autism in general education classrooms. Up until now, much of the focus of ABA for students with autism has been conducted in special education classrooms. Parents of children with autism who have been receiving EIBI prior to their child's reaching school age have argued that their child should continue to receive ABA when he or she enters school (Yell & Drasgow, 2000). In such an environment, schools are pressured to claim that they are using ABA to support children with autism in general education settings. The chal-

1913 – J. B. Watson publishes *Psychology as the Behaviorist Views It*

1938 – B. F. Skinner publishes *The Behavior of Organisms*

1958 – First issue of the *Journal of Experimental Analysis of Behavior* published

1968 – First issue of the *Journal of Applied Analysis of Behavior* published

1978 – Formation of the Association for the Analysis of Behavior, International

1987 – O. I. Lovaas publishes research on the outcome of early intensive behavior analysis for young children with autism

1993 – Catherine Maurice publishes her book, *Let Me Hear Your Voice,* about the success of ABA with her sons with autism

1998 – Formation of the Behavior Analyst Certification Board

Figure 1.1. Important events in the history of applied behavior analysis and autism.

lenge will be for consumers to ensure that what is being described as applied behavior analysis in schools for children with autism is, in fact, being well implemented.

Figure 1.2 shows suggested critical features of ABA programs that should be in place when applied behavior analysis is being used.

Inclusion of Children With Developmental Disabilities in General Education

Today, it is common for children with disabilities to be educated in community schools just like any other child. In 1998, over 75% of children with disabilities attending preschools in Southern Ontario were in settings with typically developing children, rather than in self-contained specialized settings (Hundert, Mahoney, Mundy, & Vernon, 1998). The percentage of children with disabilities who attend a general education classroom for at least part of the school day has increased dramatically for the past 10 years. From the 1989/1990 school year to the 1999/2000 school year, the percentage of students in the United States with mental retardation who were placed in general education classrooms for some or much of the school day increased from 27.3% to 44.7% (Williamson, McLeskey, Hoppey, & Rentz, 2006). A similar emphasis in special education for the inclusion of children with disabilities into general education classrooms can be found in other countries, such as Canada (Dworet & Bennett, 2002) and Great Britain (McLaughlin et al., 2006).

Guralnick (2001) described four models of preschool inclusion: full inclusion, cluster inclusion, reverse inclusion, and social inclusion. In full inclusion, children with disabilities are full participants in the general education classrooms. They participate in all activities, and, where necessary, there is adaptation to promote the participation of the child with autism and the implementation of their Individualized Education Programs (IEPs). In a "cluster" model of inclusion, a class of children with disabilities

- All interventions have a written objective that identifies the desired performance, the outcomes for the child, the conditions under which those outcomes are to occur, and the criteria that would be expected (e.g., "During lessons conducted in classroom without the assistance of a paraprofessional, Jack will complete his seatwork assignment on time and with at least 80% of items correctly answered").

- Program interventions are based on an initial assessment of the child's behavior and/or skills.

- All interventions are written in sufficient detail to allow procedures to be readily followed and subsequently replicated.

- The instructional methods used have been established to be effective in research and/ or are consistent with accepted principles of learning in the field of applied behavior analysis (e.g., prompting, reinforcement, chaining).

- Methods are in place to ensure the fidelity of the implementation of the interventions to the developed plan and consistency of implementation across those who are implementing the intervention.

- Direct and frequent measurements of the behavior change of the child's target behaviors are taken, and the data are used to determine program direction.

- Interventions focus on the acquisition of new behavior, as well as on generalization of those new behaviors to natural environments.

- Staff who are implementing applied behavior analytic interventions are trained and supervised by a Board Certified Behavior Analyst.

Figure 1.2. Suggested critical features of applied behavior analytical programs.

and a class of children without disabilities are joined to form one classroom with teachers co-teaching. All planning and teaching responsibilities are determined by the two teachers. In a reverse inclusion model, a small group of typically developing children joins a special education class of children with disabilities. In a social inclusion model, children with disabilities are educated in the same location as typically developing children are but within separate classrooms. Children with disabilities receive different curriculum programming and supports. There may be periodic times when the children with disabilities are present with typically developing children, such as during recess, lunch, and art or music activities.

Inclusion has not always been the predominant model of educating children with disabilities. In 1967, the widely applied model of special education for children with disabilities was self-contained special education classrooms. At the time, the use of segregated, self-contained classes for children with developmental disabilities was challenged in a seminal article by Dunn (1968). Special education classrooms and schools originally started in the early 20th century because many jurisdictions passed legislation compelling all children to stay in school until the age of 16 years (Holingsworth, 1923). Previously, parents could remove their children from school to work, or schools could exclude children because of learning and/or behavior problems. After compulsory education legislation was in effect in North America, children needed to stay in school until age 16 years. Self-contained classrooms and self-contained schools were developed to accommodate children with learning and/or behavior problems who would otherwise be excluded. It is important to note that self-contained special education classrooms were created to provide a setting that reduced the pressures for children with disabilities to meet the expectations of general education classrooms and make what was believed to be greater progress in the special education setting.

Dunn (1968) argued that there was little justification for self-contained special education classrooms because of the following: (a) There was research at the time suggesting that students with mental retardation could make as much progress in general education settings as in special education settings; (b) the process of identifying students for special education classrooms resulted in inadequate and harmful labeling of students; and (c) general education classrooms were better able to accommodate individual differences in teachers during the 1960s. Dunn made several suggestions for alternatives to self-contained special education classrooms for students with mild mental retardation and suggested revamping the special education system in the United States.

This and other articles with a similar focus, combined with litigation about the discriminating nature of special education, challenged traditional models of special education. In 1975, the U.S. Congress passed the Education for All Handicapped Children Act (P.L. 94-142), which guaranteed that all students with disabilities would be provided a free and appropriate public education. This act also mandated that children be placed in the "least restrictive environment" to receive that education. That legislation evolved into the Individuals With Disabilities Education Act (IDEA) in 1990, which has since been amended, most recently into the Individuals With Disabilities Education Improvement Act of 2004.

Similar support for inclusion of students with disabilities can be found in Western countries outside of the United States. For instance, in Canada, responsibility for education is the jurisdiction of each individual province. Almost all provinces in Canada have legislation specifying the following: (a) Students with special needs should be identified; (b) identified students with special needs should receive a special education plan; and (c) there is a process for parent input into student identification and placement (Dworet & Bennett, 2002). The legislation in Canadian provinces tends not to prescribe either the need to use the least restrictive environment (although in practice, the least restrictive environment is typically used to consider placement options) or a way of completing an IEP. Despite differences in legislation and educational policy across jurisdictions, there is a general embracing of inclusion of children with disabilities into the general education system.

There are compelling arguments for the inclusion of children with developmental disabilities in classrooms, based on laudable beliefs about the rights of children with developmental disabilities to be educated in a normalized setting alongside their typically developing peers. In addition to philosophical and ethical arguments for children with disabilities to be included in general education, there are particular assumptions about the benefits of doing so. It has been argued that including children with disabilities in general education classes will produce improvement in their social adjustment by being exposed to the positive models of typically developing children (Richarz, 1993). Unfortunately, there are few empirical studies showing that exposing children with disabilities to typically developing children, by itself, produces gains in the social skills of the children with disabilities (Hundert et al., 1998). Moreover, as compared to typically developing children, children with disabilities in general education classrooms tend to be behind their peers academically (Kamps, Walker, Maher, & Rotholz, 1992), pay attention to the teacher less often (Koegel, Koegel, Frea, & Fredeen, 2001), be more disruptive (Koegel, Koegel, Hurley, & Frea, 1992), be more demanding on teachers' time (Hundert, Mahoney, & Hopkins, 1993), and interact with peers less often (Guralnick, 1990). The movement for the inclusion of children with disabilities in general education has been driven by social, political, and legal forces (Yell & Drasgow,

2000) without a strong procedural foundation. Although practitioners are generally clear about *why* it is important to include children with disabilities in general education, they are less clear on *how* to structure classrooms and to prepare children with autism to make such a placement in general education successful. The central issue is no longer why inclusion should occur, but how to make the arrangement work.

Although there have been a number of research studies examining the effective use of EIBI, there have been no large-scale, controlled research studies describing school programs that have produced substantial gains in children with autism through supported inclusion. There have been a few studies that have described impressive adjustment of children after leaving specialized, but inclusive, preschools. Strain and Cordisco (1994) reported that the majority of children with autism leaving the Learning Experiences. . . An Alternative Program for Preschoolers and Parents (LEAP) program had functional communication skills and transitioned into typical school settings. The Toddler Center of the Walden Early Childhood Program also reported excellent outcomes (McGee, Morrier, & Daly, 1999). On exit from these programs, 82% of children with autism used spoken words and 71% exhibited an increased play proximity to peers.

Although such reports of the positive adjustment of children with autism upon leaving specialized inclusion programs is encouraging, these studies did not use standardized measures to track pre–post changes in child adjustment. Stahmer and Ingersoll (2004) reported gains of children under age 3 years with autism who attended the Children's Toddler School for an average of 9.5 months. Gains in language ability and in adaptive behavior were found and were greater than what would be expected by the passage of time alone. Because the study by Stahmer and Ingersoll did not include a comparison group of children with autism who received a different program, it is difficult to interpret those results. Harris, Handlemen, Kristoff, Bass, and Gordon (1990) directly compared the gains in language development of five children with autism who attended a specialized inclusive classroom for preschoolers at the Douglas Developmental Disabilities Center to those of another five children who attended a segregated classroom at the same center. Children were not randomly assigned to the two programs. A measure of language development was administered to children on entry to their respective programs and then again 5 to 11 months later. Data from a group of four typically developing children attending the individual program was used for comparison. As would be expected, Harris et al. (1990) found that the language scores of both groups of children with autism were lower than those of typically developing peers both before and after interventions. More importantly, though, they found that both the group of children in the inclusive program and the group of children in the segregated setting showed significant growth in language development, but there was no difference in the amount of gain between the two groups. No comprehensive and controlled studies on the developmental gains of children with autism in general education classrooms have been completed.

Supported Inclusion of Children With Developmental Disabilities in General Education

As indicated by the studies discussed in this chapter, placement alone in a general education classroom without additional intervention is unlikely to produce improvement in the social or academic adjustment of children with autism. The term *supported inclusion* conveys that successful inclusion of a child with disabilities in a general education setting requires the availability and systematic deployment of additional resources to support that child. Strain, McGee, and Kohler (2001) defined *supported inclusion* as "the provision of resources needed to ensure maximum learning in the context of natural environments" (p. 345).

Obviously, the type and amount of resources depends on the needs of a child with autism and on the features of the general education class. There seem to be at least four types of resources that would frequently be needed to support a child with autism in a general education setting. One is the potential need of additional personnel to assist the general education classroom teacher in educating the child with autism. For example, a paraprofessional may be needed to assist a child with autism in following classroom routines, completing class assignments, and understanding instructional exercises. There are at least two significant challenges to the use of paraprofessionals to help children with autism in the classroom. The first is that when a paraprofessional is present, there may be a tendency for the classroom teacher to be less involved with the child with autism. Marks, Schrader, and Levine (1999) found that when a paraprofessional was involved in supporting a child with disabilities in a general education classroom, the majority of responsibility for that child's education fell to the paraprofessional, not to the general education classroom teacher. Moreover, in a survey of their view of their job, paraprofessionals reported that an important function of their job was to free the classroom teacher from having to spend extra time helping the child with disabilities (Giangreco & Broer, 2005). The second, and perhaps related, challenge is for the child with autism to make gains with the assistance of a paraprofessional without developing a dependency on that help. A child with autism must be able to function successfully when the paraprofessional is absent. To achieve this outcome, a child with autism needs to learn to orient to the classroom teacher and his or her classmates rather than to the prompts delivered by the paraprofessional. The resource of a paraprofessional to assist a child with autism in a general education classroom may be important, but likely more important is how the paraprofessional works with the classroom teacher to bring about gains in the child with autism.

A second potential resource in supported inclusion is time for involved educators to prepare and plan for the inclusion of a child with autism. Team meetings and the development of interventions involve time that may not be readily available to educators unless they are freed up from other duties to complete these activities.

A third resource is specialized equipment (e.g., a visual timer) and materials (e.g., instructional workbooks) that may be needed to support the child with autism. Programming materials such as visual schedules (Mesibov, Browder, & Kirkland, 2002), curriculum modifications (Kern & Dunlap, 1998), and contingent reinforcement (Charlop-Christy & Haymes, 1998) have all been shown to be effective for children with autism in general education classrooms.

A fourth potential resource needed for supported inclusion is knowledge of how to develop and implement interventions for the child with autism. As suggested by Eikeseth et al.'s (2002) study, consultants knowledgeable of ABA and experienced in supported inclusion for children with autism would be needed to supervise or at least consult on planning for children with autism in general education classrooms. Realistically, supported inclusion requires the formation of a team that includes the child's parent(s), the school principal, a consultant with expertise in practical and effective strategies for children with autism in a general education classroom, a paraprofessional to assist the child with autism, and the classroom teacher. Even with such a team, there is a seemingly inherent dilemma in planning for the inclusion of children with autism. If one were concerned only about arranging an optimal learning environment for children with autism, it would ideally be characterized with the features shown in the left-hand column in Table 1.3.

The difficulty is that the features associated with optimal learning for many children with autism do not correspond to how learning is typically arranged in general education classrooms, as listed in the right-hand column of Table 1.3. Hence, the dilemma. If educators structure learning to be optimal for a child with autism in a general education class setting, the child with autism may be learning his or her own curriculum on a one-to-one basis, perhaps in a location other than in his or her classroom. If this is the instructional arrangement, the child with autism's learning has little to do with being in the general education classroom setting. Granted, the child with autism may at times be physically *in* the classroom, but because the learning activities for the child with autism occur in isolation from everyone else, he or she would not be one *of* the class. On the other hand, teaching the child with autism along with the rest of the class may be unsuitable for many children with autism. The child's skill level is unlikely to be at the same level as that of the rest of the class, or the child with autism may not be able to respond to the looser structure inherent in most classroom settings. In the latter situation, a child with autism may flounder in a general education class and not receive the needed supports to learn.

If the two options, of placing a child with autism in a general education class and hoping for the best or removing the child with autism from the general education classroom for one-to-one instruction, will not work, what should be done? One choice is to educate some children with autism out of the mainstream. Krantz and McClannahan (1998) argued that it is not in the best interest of a child with autism to be placed in a general education classroom without (a) supports in place in the general education classroom to accommodate the child with autism and (b) the child possessing a particular set of skills to be successful in that setting. They described that schools may not be able to provide the intensive one-to-one assistance that sometimes is needed to accommodate a child with autism who shows significant behavior needs, and they commented on the limited training of paraprofessionals to help these children. They indicated that the types of ratio enhancement and staff preparation that would be necessary to successfully accommodate a child with autism may exceed available financial resources. They proposed the alternative strategy of "specialized science-based intervention programs" to prepare children with autism for the transition into general education. They reported that of the 41 children who had been served at the Princeton Child Devel-

Table 1.3
Hypothetical Features Associated With Optimal Learning of Children With Autism and Typical Learning Arrangements of General Education Classrooms

Optimal learning arrangement for children with autism	Typical learning arrangement in general education classrooms
Taught on a 1:1 basis or in a small group	Taught as a group
Taught at child's own pace	Taught via lockstep progression
Taught at child's own level	Taught at class level
Uses individualized materials	Uses class materials
Uses individualized instruction	Uses group instruction
Has frequent and direct measurement	Has infrequent and indirect measurement

opment Center before 60 months of age, 14 (34.1%) were successfully transitioned into schools.

A contrasting position was offered by Strain et al. (2001), who described a number of myths associated with inclusion of children with autism, including the myth that children with autism must be ready *before* they are placed in a general education class setting. They argued that there is no compelling evidence to support the "readiness" assertion and described examples of self-control, language, and peer-mediated interventions that have been introduced for children with autism in general education classrooms without initially teaching children readiness skills.

The truth about the suitability of supported inclusion of children with autism may fall somewhere in between these two positions. There has been little or no evidence supporting a full inclusion model for children with autism (Johnson, Meyer, & Taylor, 1996), nor have there been studies indicating that children with autism will not be successful in general education classrooms unless they first have been prepared in a specialized setting (Strain et al., 2001).

It may be that not all children with autism can be successfully included in a general education classroom with the typical teacher–student ratios, level of teacher and paraprofessional preparation, and quality of consultation available. If supported inclusion is seen as one possible arrangement to produce optimal development of a child with autism among other possible arrangements, then supported inclusion may not be the intervention of choice for all children with autism. In fact, there is some evidence that children with more severe disabilities may show greater gains in a segregated, rather than in an integrated, class (Buysse & Bailey, 1993; Freeman & Alkin, 2000; Mills, Cole, Jenkins, & Dale, 1998). However, the danger of precluding a child with autism's placement in a general education classroom based on level of disabilities or degree of functioning is that it may prevent consideration of an inclusive option that might be effective for that child. One reasonable position is to plan for the inclusion of all children with autism unless there is compelling evidence for why such a placement would not be effective and then to provide those children with more specialized learning arrangements, at least initially.

Another option to bridge the gap between the structured conditions associated with optimal learning of children with autism and the teaching features common in many general education classrooms is to embed the teaching of children with autism into routines of the general education classroom. As stated by Johnson, McDonnell, Holzwarth, and Hunter (2004), "it seems unlikely that inclusion will succeed unless general educators have strategies available to them in assuming a direct teaching role in meeting the educational needs of students with developmental disabilities in their classes" (p. 226). Much of the emphasis of this book is on describing ABA-based procedures that can be embedded into the routines of general education classrooms.

Instructional Targets in Supported Inclusion

The success of placing children with autism into general education classrooms may depend on the fit between the skill set of children with autism in key areas associated with positive outcomes in that setting and the quantity plus quality of the available supports.

Several studies have surveyed elementary-school teachers for their opinion of the competencies of potential children with disabilities that would be necessary for the children to achieve positive outcomes in their class (Byrd & Rous, 1990; Chandler, 1992; Kemp & Carter, 2005). The theme that emerges from this literature is that teachers place a higher emphasis on the ability of children with disabilities to follow classroom routines than they do on their achievement of specific academic goals. Based on these studies and our own experiences supporting children with autism in general education classes, my colleagues and I have identified seven areas of functioning that we typically target for children with autism in general education classrooms. Each is described below.

1. The ability to participate and learn in a group—One of the important goals of inclusion is for a child with autism to be able to learn as much as possible within a group format. A child with autism in a general education classroom needs to be able to attend to a teacher presentation of a lesson, answer questions posed, and follow instructions directed to the entire class. The child needs to be able to raise his or her hand when appropriate and to answer questions correctly. Without some ability in these skill areas, a child with autism would be limited in his or her ability to participate actively in group instruction.

2. The ability to initiate and sustain reciprocal peer interaction—One of the purposes of placing a child with autism in a general education classroom is for opportunities to learn how to interact with typically developing peers. It would be important for a child with autism to respond to peer play invitations, to sustain reciprocal interaction, and to initiate these interactions.

3. The ability to complete seatwork assignments independently—One of the expectations in a general education classroom is for children to be able to understand what is needed when given a seatwork assignment and to complete the assignment accurately and on time. Seatwork assignments may be modified to fit the needs of the child with autism.

4. The ability to communicate needs clearly and independently—It would be desirable for children with autism to communicate their needs to others with little or no assistance. This communication may be made orally, by signing, or by using a pictorial communication system or some other form of communication.

5. The ability to follow classroom routines independently—Children in general education classrooms learn most general routines, such as how to line up for recess, to hang up their coats, and to leave the classroom to go to the school washroom. The ability to follow general routines is an important skill for children with autism to learn.

6. Reduction of problem behaviors that interfere with learning—There are a number of problem behaviors that a child with autism may exhibit that might interfere with his or her learning. These problem behaviors include aggression, stereotypy, and off-task behavior.

7. The ability to self-regulate, make inferences, and take the perspective of others—It may be possible to set up environmental conditions that help children with autism to display the type of behaviors described above. However, unless children with autism develop the ability to regulate their own actions, they will always be dependent on someone to guide their actions.

If the seven targets just described are, in fact, important for the success of a child with autism in a general education classroom, then teaching one or more of these skills should result in measurable outcomes for that child, such as increased active engagement on task or more frequent and correct communicative responding. Empirical adjustment of children with autism in general education classrooms needs to be undertaken.

Study Questions

1. Why is there an interest in the use of applied behavior analysis for children with autism in schools?

2. What is some of the history of inclusion of children with disabilities in general education?

3. What are Guralnick's (2001) four models of preschool inclusion?

4. What does *supported inclusion* mean and what are four potential types of supports?

5. Discuss both sides of the issue of readiness of children with autism before they are included in general education.

6. List the seven target skills associated with the success of a child with autism in an inclusive setting.

2 Assessment and Supported Inclusion

Chapter Topics

- Norm-referenced assessment

- Criterion-referenced assessment

- Assessment of inclusive classroom skills (on-task behavior, peer interaction, responding to questions during lessons, independent seatwork, and problem behavior)

- Inter-observer reliability

- Data summary

The process of identifying a child with autism's strengths and needs for supported inclusion starts with collecting information about the child's skills and behaviors in relevant areas. To draw conclusions about the results of a child's assessment, the data obtained must first be compared to some form of performance expectations. Differences between the child's actual and expected performance suggest areas for intervention. Two types of comparisons for interpreting the results of a child's assessment include the following: (a) A child's results are compared to norms reflecting the performance of other children of the same age or in the same grade, and (b) a child's results are compared to the expectation of the specific general education class into which the child with autism will be or has been placed. Each of these two types of expectations can be used to plan the supported inclusion of a child with autism.

Norm-Referenced Assessment

Tests of cognitive skills, adaptive behavior, academic achievement, and many other areas can be administered to a child with autism to provide information on how that child compares in the tested area to children on whom the test was normed. Typically, a child with autism scores significantly lower on these tests than his or her typically developing peers do. Therefore, confirming this point through the administration of norm-referenced tests would not add helpful information to an assessment. However, in many situations, it might be beneficial to use norm-referenced data to track changes in the development of a child with autism relative to the general level of performance of typically developing children.

Figure 2.1 illustrates the hypothetical growth trajectory of children with developmental disabilities compared to the hypothetical growth trajectory of typically developing children (Ramey & Ramey, 1998). A child's chronological age is plotted on the x axis, which in Figure 2.1 shows the age span from 1 to 7 years. (Note: It is possible to depict longer age spans than this.) A child's developmental age is plotted on the y axis, which also depicts an age span from 1 to 7 years.

By definition, as a typically developing child ages 1 year, his or her development (be it cognitive, language, etc.) also progresses 1 year. This hypothetical growth trajectory of typically developing children is represented as a dashed diagonal line. In contrast, the hypothetical growth trajectory of children with autism tends to slow in a decelerating curve, as represented by the solid curved line in Figure 2.1. Since one does not know the pattern of developmental growth of the child with autism, the decelerating curve and the diagonal line are both hypothetical. A comparison of the child's current functioning in an area with the hypothetical growth trajectory of children with autism would indicate an estimate of how the child would develop from that point in time forward if the child were to receive little or no intervention. A comparison of the child with autism's results with the hypothetical growth trajectory of typically developing children would indicate how much growth would need to occur if the child with autism would approximate the development of that child's age peers.

Using the graph in Figure 2.1, one may be able to make a gross estimate of the hypothetical growth trajectory of an individual child with autism, as illustrated in Figure 2.2. First, locate the chronological age of the child with autism and an age-equivalent score for the child from a norm-referenced test, such as an intellectual test, a language test, or an academic achievement test. For each measure to be depicted, a different trajectory is drawn on the chart. Data point A shown in Figure 2.2 represents an

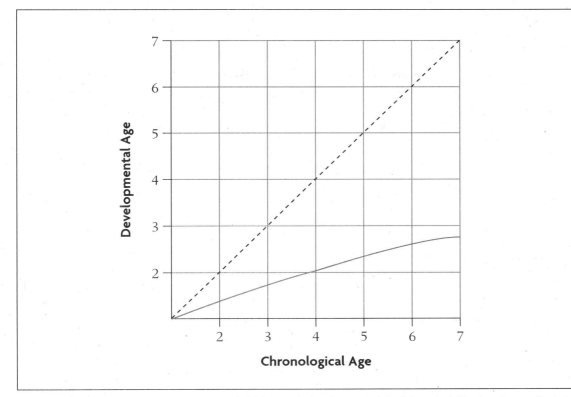

Figure 2.1. Hypothetical growth trajectory of children with developmental disabilities (solid line) and typically developing children (dashed line). *Note.* From *Early Intervention and Early Experience,* by C. T. Ramey and S. L. Ramey, 1998, *American Psychologist, 53,* p. 112. Copyright 1998 by the American Psychological Association. Adapted with permission.

initial IQ score result for a child. At the time, this child was 3 years 11 months and was tested in cognitive abilities at an age equivalent of 2 years 0 months. At the same time, the child's score in language development was an age equivalent of 2 years 7 months, as shown by data point B in Figure 2.2.

A decelerating growth curve is drawn to intersect with both the bottom left-hand corner of the chart and data point A for one growth curve to represent growth in intellectual development. A second growth curve is created in the same way to intersect with data point B to depict the child's growth in language development. These decelerating growth curves represent a hypothetical trajectory of the development of a child with autism who would receive limited or no intervention.

Over a 2.5-year span, this child was tested two more times (at age 5 years and at age 6 years 6 months), with the results shown in Figure 2.2. At age 5 years, the child scored at about an age equivalence of 2 years 5 months in intellectual development and an age equivalence of 4 years 1 month in language development. When the child was 6 years 6 months of age, the child scored at an age equivalence of 3 years 0 months and 4 years 11 months in intellectual and language development, respectively. Based on these data, the child made gains in both IQ and language development greater than the predictions of each of the hypothetical growth curves intersecting through points A and B. The data shown in Figure 2.2 suggest that although there has been gain in the IQ scores of the child with autism, more substantial gain has occurred in the child's language development. It appears that in the area of language, the child with autism is closing the gap with his typically developing peers. However, the child's development in

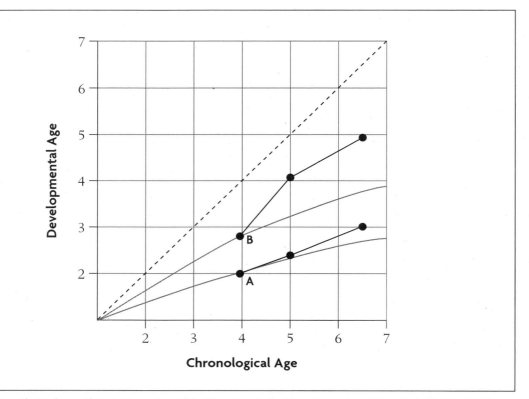

Figure 2.2. Hypothetical growth trajectory of a child with autism indicating age-equivalent scores in IQ (A) and in language development (B) when tested at age 3 years 11 months, 5 years, and 6 years 6 months.. *Note.* From *Early Intervention and Early Experience,* by C. T. Ramey and S. L. Ramey, 1998, *American Psychologist, 53,* p. 112. Copyright 1998 by the American Psychological Association. Adapted with permission.

cognitive skills, although improving, is not catching up to that of his typically developing peers.

Creating graphs like these allows those currently working with a child to monitor his or her development in relation to a possible decelerating growth trajectory depicting likely outcome if the child receives limited or no intervention and in comparison to the growth trajectory of typically developing children (i.e., the dashed line). Such graphs may be helpful in planning interventions and in reviewing a child's gains.

In summary, the steps of creating a hypothetical developmental trajectory are as follows:

1. For each relevant developmental area, locate the earliest assessment results that have age-equivalent scores for the child with autism. Locate the child's chronological age at the time of testing and the age-equivalent result of testing. Plot the point where these two intersect on the growth chart.
2. Adjust the decelerating growth curve line to intersect with the point plotted in step 1. A curved line can be drawn by hand or by using a computerized drawing program, such as the curved line option on the drawing toolbar found with Microsoft Word.
3. Add any subsequent test results in the same developmental area, and connect data points depicting test results for a child in the same domain.
4. Fill in new assessment results as they occur.

Criterion-Referenced Assessment

A second type of assessment that may be helpful in identifying areas of need for a child with autism in an inclusive class is to determine how that child's skills compare to expectations of critical skills for success in *that* particular class. In other words, how do the skills and behaviors of a child with autism compare to expectations of skills associated with success in that classroom? Because every classroom is likely unique in its composition of students, teacher expectations, adult–child ratio, and so on, the assessment of the skills and behaviors of a child with autism associated with success in an inclusive setting needs to be conducted in relation to a particular classroom, rather than to a particular grade in general. Such assessment information would also serve as a baseline from which future gains could be determined.

Although norm-referenced measures may be helpful to depict the developmental growth of a child with autism compared to that of age peers, they do not provide information of the child's precise academic skills in relation to the performance standards of a particular class. On the other hand, a curriculum-based measurement (CBM; Deno, 1985) probes a child's performance on a hierarchy of skills selected directly from the class curriculum area. The first step in the development of a CBM is to identify the hierarchy of learning outcomes associated with the curriculum in a given subject area. The breakdown of the components of a curriculum may be found on the Web site for the school board or the state/province. For example, a breakdown of the content of the mathematics curriculum for New York State can be found at http://www.emsc.nysed.gov/ciai/mst.html.

The next step is to develop a means of probing a child's skills in each of the areas of the curriculum. For example, one skill in a math curriculum may be that children at a particular grade would be able to solve "double-digit addition without carrying" problems. A probe of the child's skills may consist of selecting five items that represent the universal set of all possible double-digit-addition-without-carrying problems, such as shown below.

$$24 + 35 = \underline{\qquad} \qquad \begin{array}{r} 61 \\ + 10 \\ \hline \end{array} \qquad \begin{array}{r} 88 \\ + 11 \\ \hline \end{array} \qquad 53 + 35 = \underline{\qquad} \qquad \begin{array}{r} 24 \\ + 43 \\ \hline \end{array}$$

It is important to ensure that the selected items truly represent the skills being taught in class. In the example above, it is relatively easy to select items to include in the CBM since arithmetic has a definable set of problems that can be readily determined. However, consider the more ambiguous task of probing if a child is able to read from a reader used in the class with adequate accuracy and fluency. This skill can be probed only by presenting a child with progressive sections of a particular reader and measuring the child's reading performance. For example, suppose the child is expected to read from a reader consisting of 13 separate stories in a book that totals over 150 pages. One way of probing the child's skills is to select brief reading passages from the reader approximately every 15 pages. A reading passage of about 100 words that ends in a complete sentence could be selected. With each reading passage, there would be three reading comprehension questions formulated. The child's accuracy and fluency (number of correctly read words per minute) in oral reading would be measured for each selected passage. A performance criterion would be set for each probe level to define whether the child showed acceptable performance at each probe level and therefore if the material at that level needed to be taught. A failure to meet the performance criterion at a particular skill level would suggest that the child required instruction on the material at that skill level. In the above example of double-digit arithmetic, a mastery criterion may be for the child to solve four of the five presented items at each skill level. In the case of reading, the mastery criteria for each selected reading passage may be for the child to read at least 90% of the words correctly, at a rate of at least 80 correct words per minute, and to answer all three reading comprehension questions correctly. If the child scored less than the mastery criteria (e.g., less than 80% correct at 75 words per minute), the child would be considered not to have met the criteria for that particular level of the probe and further instruction would be warranted on the material at that level.

Results for a CBM of reading may look as shown in Table 2.1. This table shows hypothetical results for a child with autism on 6 of 10 reading samples taken from a 10-page interval from the class reader, *Basal Reading Series, Level 2.* The child met the criteria for levels 1, 2, and 3, but not for 4, 5, and 6. After three consecutive reading passages on which the child failed to meet criteria, further probes were stopped.

A similar method can be used to complete a CBM of arithmetic. Table 2.2 shows 10 probes of early arithmetic skills, ranging from testing if the child with autism can rote count, to testing if the child with autism can complete double-/single-digit addition with carrying (e.g., $25 + 6 = $ _____). In this example, the mastery criterion for each level is set at 80% correct or higher and the hypothetical child was able to demonstrate mastery of skill levels 1 to 5, but not 6 or above. Which skill would you start to teach a child if the child's results were as depicted Table 2.2? The answer is skill level 6: adding pictures of marks to five, such as adding three vertical lines to one vertical line.

In the examples in both Tables 2.1 and 2.2, the child passed each level at the beginning of the probes. The child then failed to pass a more advanced probe level and thereafter did not pass any higher probe levels. These results of the assessment are clear and easy to understand. Sometimes, however, a child's results are not as clear as this. Consider the following set of results for a hypothetical child:

Level 1 – passed

Level 2 – passed

Level 3 – passed

Level 4 – failed

Level 5 – failed

Level 6 – passed

Level 7 – failed

Level 8 – failed

Level 9 – failed

It is necessary to set rules for where to begin probing a child in a skill hierarchy and also where to stop the probing sequence. For example, one may estimate the level of the child's skills, based on teacher report, and start probing the child slightly below that skill level. In arithmetic, there may be indication that the child should be able to solve single-digit addition problems to five at criterion (skill level 7 in Table 2.2). When probed, however, the child correctly answered three of the five presented problems and therefore did not meet the performance criterion of that skill. The assessor should then probe the next lower skill in the sequence—in this case, adding arrays of marks (skill level 6 in Table 2.2). If the child is not able to demonstrate mastery on this skill, then the child is probed on the next lower level. This would continue until the child passes three consecutive skill levels.

Table 2.1
Sample Results of a Curriculum-Based Measure of Reading
(Using the Reader Basal Reading Series, Level 2)

Level	Page	# Words	# Correct words	# Errors	Accuracy (%)	Minutes	Fluency (words/min)	Comprehension	Met criteria
1	15	97	92	5	94.8	1.07	86.0	3/3	Yes
2	25	105	96	9	91.4	1.13	85.0	3/3	Yes
3	36	95	81	14	85.3	1.08	75.0	3/3	Yes
4	46	111	91	20	82.0	1.29	70.5	3/3	No
5	55	97	76	21	78.4	1.33	57.1	2/3	No
6	66	98	64	34	78.4	1.62	39.5	0/3	No
7	73	103	—	—	—	—	—	—	—
8	85	99	—	—	—	—	—	—	—
9	96	89	—	—	—	—	—	—	—
10	105	109	—	—	—	—	—	—	—

Note. Dashes mean that since these levels of the curriculum-based assessment were not administered to the child, no results are available.

Table 2.2
Sample Results of a Curriculum-Based Measure of Arithmetic

Level	Skill	# Items presented	# Correct	% Correct	Met criteria
1	Rote count to 10	5	5	100	Yes
2	Rote count with 1:1 touching objects	5	5	100	Yes
3	Count out objects to 10	5	5	100	Yes
4	Receptive discrimination of numerals 1 to 10	5	5	100	Yes
5	Match numerals 1 to 5 to arrays of marks	5	4	80	Yes
6	Add array of marks to 5	5	1	20	No
7	Single-digit addition to 5	5	0	0	No
8	Single-digit addition to 10	5	0	0	No
9	Double- and single-digit addition without carrying	5	0	0	No
10	Double- and single-digit addition with carrying	5	0	0	No

Suppose that the child can demonstrate mastery on skill levels 4, 3, and 2 in Table 2.2. There is no need to probe the child on any lower levels. Next, it would be important to establish the uppermost limit of the child's skills in the area. Probes are administered to the child starting at level 5 and progressing higher until the child fails to demonstrate mastery on three consecutive skills. If the results are as shown above, then instruction would start at skill level 4.

If a child does not demonstrate mastery on three consecutive levels, easier levels are added at the beginning of the skill hierarchy until the child does demonstrate mastery on three skill levels in sequence. Similarly, if the child does not reach a ceiling of performance by failing to pass three consecutive levels, then additional levels are introduced at the upper end of the skill hierarchy until the child fails to meet probe criteria for three consecutive skills.

How should one establish at what level, within a possible hierarchy of skills representing the content of curriculum, to begin to teach a child with autism? For academic skills, one develops a skill hierarchy in each curriculum area of interest and directly probes the child on tasks that represent each skill. The results of a child's performance are compared to a mastery criterion for each skill level. A child is then taught the lowest skill on which mastery was not demonstrated. After the child has later demonstrated mastery of the taught skill, it is prudent to probe the child on higher skills before providing any more instruction. If the probe indicates that, for whatever reason, the child is now able to meet the mastery criterion of a level two ahead of the one just mastered, then jump to teach that level and omit teaching the skill at the next level. Again, instruction is provided on the lowest skill in the sequence on which mastery was not demonstrated. This method of probing ahead after a child has met the criterion on a lower skill continues until the child has progressed through the targeted skill areas.

Assessment of Inclusive Classroom Skills

Not all potential instructional targets for a child with autism in an inclusive classroom consist of increasing the child's skills in an academic area. Sometimes, instructional targets for a child with autism consist of teaching the child behaviors that are important for success in an inclusive classroom, such as staying on task, interacting with peers, responding to questions during lessons, completing seatwork assignments independently, or controlling problem behaviors. Assessment strategies for each of these areas are described in the sections that follow. In addition, Appendix 2A (see the end of this chapter) includes blank, reproducible data collection forms that may be used to assess these five areas of a child's behavior associated with successful supported inclusion. All five measures have the same following components:

1. Each behavior to be measured is described in measurable detail to allow for reliable counting of the occurrence of that behavior.
2. A method for recording data is described allowing the quantification of occurrences of the behavior.
3. A data sheet is used for recording occurrences of behavior.

The assessment of a child's behaviors in these types of areas is conducted in a manner significantly different than the method described for assessing a child's academic skills. The assessment of a child's behavior typically consists of observing the child with autism in a situation in which the behavior to be taught is expected.

On-Task Behavior

If one is interested in measuring the degree to which a child with autism is on task during a class lesson, the following steps are usually followed:

1. A response definition of the target behavior is written so that it can be easily and reliably quantified (e.g., "On-task behavior is defined as a child being oriented to the task assigned by the classroom teacher, including observing the teacher when the teacher is talking, observing another student when he or she is answering a question, or being engaged in another action directed by the teacher").

2. A method of sampling the child's behavior is selected from those available in the field (see Cooper, Heron, & Heward, 2007). In this case, a momentary time sampling procedure may be selected in which the child is observed on regular intervals (e.g., every 20 seconds using a stopwatch or another signaling device, such as audio signals recorded on an audiotape played on an audiotape machine via earphones). The child is observed at the instant of the signal, and the observed behavior is coded as being on task or not, based on the response definition.

3. A data sheet is created on which the observer can count and then tally the child's target behavior. Figure 2.3 is an example of a data sheet for observing a child's on-task behavior. The data are summarized as the percentage of occurrences on which the child was on task. A reproducible version can be found in Appendix 2A.

4. The number of observations (e.g., three) and the situations in which the observations should be completed (e.g., all during class lessons) are decided. The results of each observation are averaged.

Suppose the on-task behavior of a child with autism is recorded on three occasions and averaged to be 20%, as shown by X in Figure 2.4. It is difficult to make sense of this result without some comparison of what other students in the same situation were doing under the same circumstances. The results of the occurrence of a target behavior for a child with autism may be easier to understand if viewed in relationship to the performance of the class. Since it is typically not feasible to track the behavior of every other student in a class, one may ask the classroom teacher to nominate one student who represents an average-performing child in that classroom in the areas being assessed (e.g., on-task behavior). Similarly, to get an estimate of the lower range of the class performance, one may ask the teacher to nominate a child, other than the child with autism, who in his or her estimation would perform the lowest in the class on that measure. The names of the children selected do not need to be revealed.

Figure 2.5 shows how this information can be used to anchor the child with autism's performance to the rest of the class. It depicts the mean occurrence of on-task behavior during a fourth-grade language lesson. The results also depict scores for two other children in the class. The X represents the performance of the child with autism. The circle represents the results of the child whom the classroom teacher estimated is at the class average in on-task behavior. The horizontal line represents a child nominated by the teacher as having the greatest difficulty in the class with on-task behavior other than the target child with autism. The vertical line connecting the score of the average student to that of the lowest student other than the target child in on-task behavior suggests the range of children's performance in on-task behavior for the bottom half of the children in the class. In Figure 2.5, the level of on-task behavior shown by the child with autism is considerably behind that of the rest of his or her classroom peers.

The addition of the results for the two other children gives a very gross indication of where the child with autism may fit in the class on this indicator. Averaging across a number of observations makes it more likely that the data reflect the true occurrence of the behaviors or skills being measured. The more observations that contribute to the summary, the more represented the data are, but there is a trade-off of an increased time to complete the assessment.

Repeated measurement would allow for examination of changes over time in the performance of the child with autism in comparison to peers. For example, one might start by completing three separate observations of children's on-task behavior in the manner described above. A few days later, specific intervention could be introduced (e.g., the child's paraprofessional could provide prompts and reinforcement for the child with autism to increase active engagement on task) to increase the on-task behavior of the child with autism. A second block of three probes of the on-task behavior of the three children (i.e., the child with autism, a teacher-selected average child, and a teacher-selected next lowest child) could then be completed. Results for this hypothetical situation are shown in Figure 2.6. Here, there was a slight increase in on-task behavior shown by the two children nominated by the classroom teacher, but a more substantive increase in on-task behavior shown by the child with autism.

Peer Interaction

To assess a child's peer interaction, one could measure the child's interactions with other children during a free play session in a preschool setting and during recess at an

On-Task Behavior

Child's Name: __Tom Mouhot__   Date: __February 28__

Time: __11:15__   Coder: __JH__   Teacher: __Mrs. Garcia__

School: __Riverside Public School__   Lesson: __Language__

Instructions: Using a stopwatch, observe the child for an instant every 20 seconds. Put a circle around the letter *O* if the child is on task (see definition below) or the letter *N* if the child is not on task. If it is unclear to whom the child should be attending or if the teacher is out of the room, circle the letter *X*. Continue recording the child's behavior for 15 minutes.

	20 sec	40 sec	60 sec
Min 1	Ⓞ N X	Ⓞ N X	O Ⓝ X
Min 2	O Ⓝ X	O Ⓝ X	O Ⓝ X
Min 3	Ⓞ N X	Ⓞ N X	Ⓞ N X
Min 4	O N Ⓧ	O Ⓝ X	O Ⓝ X
Min 5	Ⓞ N X	Ⓞ N X	Ⓞ N X
Min 6	Ⓞ N X	O Ⓝ X	Ⓞ N X
Min 7	O Ⓝ X	O N Ⓧ	Ⓞ N X
Min 8	Ⓞ N X	Ⓞ N X	Ⓞ N X
Min 9	Ⓞ N X	Ⓞ N X	O Ⓝ X
Min 10	O Ⓝ X	O Ⓝ X	O Ⓝ X
Min 11	O Ⓝ X	Ⓞ N X	O N Ⓧ
Min 12	Ⓞ N X	Ⓞ N X	Ⓞ N X
Min 13	Ⓞ N X	O Ⓝ X	Ⓞ N X
Min 14	O Ⓝ X	Ⓞ N X	Ⓞ N X
Min 15	Ⓞ N X	Ⓞ N X	O Ⓝ X

Count the number of *O*s: __26__
Count the number of *N*s: __16__
Count the number of *X*s: __3__

Divide the number of *O*s by the number of *O*s and *N*s and multiply by 100: __61.9%__

Response definition = On-task behavior is defined as a child being oriented to the task assigned by the classroom teacher, including observing the teacher when talking or another student when answering a question, or being engaged in classroom participation directed by the teacher.

Figure 2.3. Example of a completed data collection form for measuring on-task behavior.

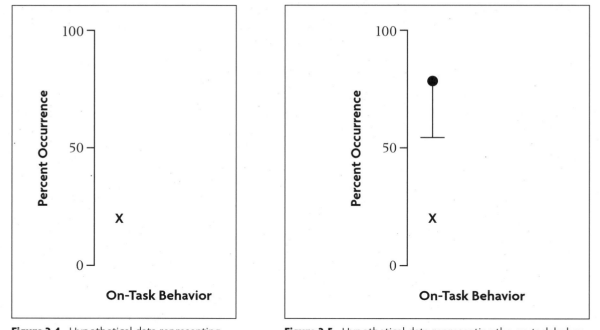

Figure 2.4. Hypothetical data representing the on-task behavior of a child with autism (*X*) occurring at about 20% of observations.

Figure 2.5. Hypothetical data representing the on-task behavior of a child with autism (*X*) in a class with a teacher-selected average child (solid circle), showing on-task behavior on about 80% of occurrences and a child selected by the teacher as next lowest to the child with autism (vertical line), showing on-task behavior at about 60% of occurrences.

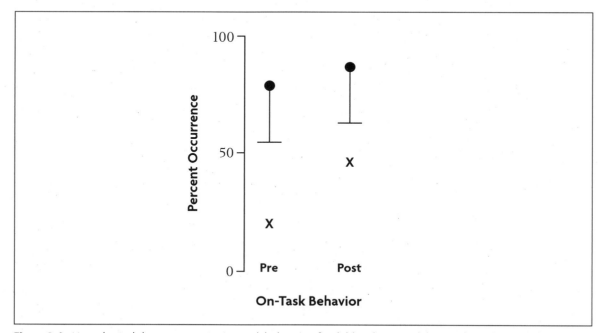

Figure 2.6. Hypothetical data representing on-task behavior of a child with autism (*X*), a teacher-selected average child (solid circle), and a child selected by the teacher as next lowest to the child with autism (vertical line) before and after an intervention. The child with autism showed a gain in on-task behavior from about 20% at pretesting to about 47% at posttesting. During that same period, the on-task behavior of the average child and the next lowest child in the class increased from about 80% to about 85%, and from about 60% to about 70%, respectively.

elementary school using a behavior recording procedure such as momentary time sampling. The peer interaction of a child with autism would be compared to that of a student in the class identified by the teacher as being about average and compared to a student in the class identified by the teacher as being the lowest functioning next to the child with autism. First, the observer needs to learn the behavioral definition described on the observation form and, if using a 10-second momentary time sampling method of behavior recording, to prepare an audiotape with an audio signal (e.g., the sound of a bell) that occurs every 10 seconds. The observer watches one child while listening to the audiotape via earphones. When the observer hears the audio cue, he or she records whether or not the child is displaying interactive play at that instant. If interactive play is observed to occur at the instant of observation, the recorder then circles the code of IP (interactive play) on the data collection form. See Figure 2.7 for a completed example of a data collection form for tracking peer interaction. A blank, reproducible version of this form can be found in Appendix 2A. If the child is engaged in any behavior other than interactive play (e.g., playing near other children, not playing, interacting with an adult), then NIP (no interactive play) is crossed out for observation one. On the next audio signal, the observer records the behavior of the next child (either the child nominated by the teacher as average or the child nominated by the teacher as the next lowest functioning child in play) in the same way. The order of observing the three children is determined at random each observation session. During a 15-minute observation session, each of the three children would be observed twice a minute, for a total of 30 observations for each child. The total number of IP episodes is tallied for each child, divided by the total number of observations (typically 30), and then multiplied by 100, to give a percentage score. This observation is repeated two more times, and the data are averaged over the three observations.

Responding to Questions During Lessons

This measure tallies occurrences of the child with autism and two comparison children raising their hands when the classroom teacher asks a question directed at the class or at a child individually during a class lesson. It also tracks if the child raised his or her hand to answer a class-directed question and, if called upon individually by the teacher to answer, whether the child answered correctly. One child is observed for 1 minute, then the second child and the third child are each observed for 1 minute, with the order of observing the three (child with autism, teacher-selected average child, and teacher-selected next lowest functioning child) randomly determined each session. Observation continues until 10 minutes of data are collected for each child, even if the observation is carried over to a subsequent class lesson. Figure 2.8 shows a completed example of a data collection form used to track whether a student responds to questions during lessons. A blank, reproducible version of this form can be found in Appendix 2A.

The observer records every question asked by the teacher and codes if the teacher's question was directed to the class in general or to the child (i.e., the student being observed) individually. If the question was directed to the class, the observer notes if the target child raised his or her hand or not and, if so, if the hand-raising was prompted (e.g., the child's arm was nudged by a teacher assistant) or not. Finally, for either a class-directed or an individually directed question, the observer records if the child answered the question correctly independently, correctly but with a prompt (e.g., the teacher pointed to the correct answer on the blackboard), or incorrectly. Failure of the observed child to respond to an individually directed question would be considered an incorrect response. At the end of the session, the observer calculates (a) the percentage of

Peer Interaction

This data collection form is used for assessing the occurrence of interactive play of a child with autism. Select a 15-minute period when you would be able to observe the child with autism, a child in the same class selected by the teacher as being average in peer interaction, and a third child in the same class selected by the teacher as being the next lowest in peer interaction to the child with autism.

Use a 10-second momentary time-sampling method of behavior observation. Observe one child, then the second, and then the third. Over the 15 minutes, each child should be able to be observed 30 times. The response definitions are as follows.

Interactive Play (IP): The child is engaged in a play activity (e.g., pushing a toy truck, coloring), within 2 minutes of at least one other child and is interacting verbally (e.g., talking about a play activity) or nonverbally (e.g., allowing another child to take turns playing with a toy, listening when another child is talking specifically to him or her) with another child.

No Interactive Play (NIP): Any other play behavior (e.g., not playing, interacting with an adult, playing by him- or herself).

Peer Interaction

Child's Name: __Tom Mouhot__   School: __Riverside Public School__

Date: __February 28__   Time: __10:15__   Observer: __JH__   Setting: __Playground__

IP = interactive play   NIP = no interactive play

	Tom	Child 2	Child 3			Tom	Child 2	Child 3
1	IP (NIP)	IP (NIP)	(IP) NIP		16	(IP) NIP	(IP) NIP	(IP) NIP
2	(IP) NIP	(IP) NIP	(IP) NIP		17	(IP) NIP	(IP) NIP	(IP) NIP
3	(IP) NIP	(IP) NIP	(IP) NIP		18	(IP) NIP	(IP) NIP	(IP) NIP
4	IP (NIP)	IP (NIP)	(IP) NIP		19	IP (NIP)	IP (NIP)	(IP) NIP
5	(IP) NIP	(IP) NIP	(IP) NIP		20	(IP) NIP	IP (NIP)	(IP) NIP
6	IP (NIP)	IP (NIP)	(IP) NIP		21	IP (NIP)	(IP) NIP	(IP) NIP
7	(IP) NIP	(IP) NIP	IP (NIP)		22	IP (NIP)	(IP) NIP	(IP) NIP
8	IP (NIP)	(IP) NIP	(IP) NIP		23	IP (NIP)	IP (NIP)	(IP) NIP
9	IP (NIP)	IP (NIP)	(IP) NIP		24	IP (NIP)	(IP) NIP	(IP) NIP
10	(IP) NIP	(IP) NIP	(IP) NIP		25	IP (NIP)	IP (NIP)	(IP) NIP
11	(IP) NIP	(IP) NIP	(IP) NIP		26	IP (NIP)	(IP) NIP	(IP) NIP
12	(IP) NIP	(IP) NIP	(IP) NIP		27	IP (NIP)	(IP) NIP	(IP) NIP
13	(IP) NIP	(IP) NIP	(IP) NIP		28	IP (NIP)	IP (NIP)	(IP) NIP
14	IP (NIP)	(IP) NIP	IP (NIP)		29	IP (NIP)	(IP) NIP	(IP) NIP
15	IP (NIP)	(IP) NIP	(IP) NIP		30	IP (NIP)	IP (NIP)	(IP) NIP
					#	12 18	20 10	28 2
					%	40%	67%	93%

Figure 2.7. Example of a completed data collection form for tracking peer interaction.

Responding to Questions During Lessons

This data collection form is used for recording the frequency of children raising their hands for questions and, if called upon by the teacher, the percentage of questions answered correctly. Observe the child with autism, a teacher-selected average student, and a teacher-selected next lowest functioning student in a random order for 1 minute each. During that interval, for each teacher question directed to the class, record if the child raised his or her hand or had to be prompted (i.e., an adult provided a physical, gestural, or some other form of a prompt for the child to raise his/her hand). Record if the child answered correctly if called upon. For a question the teacher directed specifically to the child, record if the child answered correctly. Continue until ten 1-minute observations are taken of each child.

Responding to Questions During Lessons

Child With Autism: ___Tom Mouhot___   Teacher: ___Mrs. Garcia___

Date: ___Feb 29___   Start Time: ___2:05___   End Time: ___2:35___   Length in min: ___30___

Lesson: ___Social Science___   Coder: ___JH___

N = no hand raised   H = hand raised   P = prompted to raise hand

+ = answered correctly without prompt   p = prompted to answer and was correct

– = not prompted to answer and was incorrect

Child 1: Tom		Child 2: Michael		Child 3: Andrew	
Class-directed question	Individual-directed question	Class-directed question	Individual-directed question	Class-directed question	Individual-directed question
Ⓝ H P | + p –	+ p –	N Ⓗ P | + p –	+ p –	Ⓝ H P | + p –	+ p –
Ⓝ H P | + p –	+ p –	N Ⓗ P | + p –	+ p –	Ⓝ H P | + p –	+ p –
Ⓝ H P | + p –	+ p –	Ⓝ H P | + p –	+ p –	N Ⓗ P | + p –	+ p –
N H Ⓟ | + ⓟ –	+ p –	Ⓝ H P | + p –	+ p –	N Ⓗ P | ⊕ p –	+ p –
Ⓝ H P | + p –	+ p –	N Ⓗ P | + p –	+ p –	N Ⓗ P | + p –	+ p –
N H Ⓟ | + ⓟ –	+ p –	Ⓝ H P | + p –	+ p –	Ⓝ H P | + p –	+ p –
Ⓝ H P | + p –	+ p –	N Ⓗ P | + p –	+ p –	N Ⓗ P | + p –	+ p –
Ⓝ H P | + p –	+ p –	N Ⓗ P | ⊕ p –	+ p –	N Ⓗ P | + p –	+ p –
Ⓝ H P | + p –	+ p –	N H P | + p –	⊕ p –	N Ⓗ P | ⊕ p –	+ p –
N H P | + p –	+ Ⓟ –	Ⓝ H P | + p –	+ p –	Ⓝ H P | + p –	+ p –
Ⓝ H P | + p –	+ p –	N Ⓗ P | + p –	+ p –	Ⓝ H P | + p –	+ p –
N H Ⓟ | + p ⊖	+ p –	N Ⓗ P | + p –	+ p –	Ⓝ H P | + p –	+ p –
N H P | + p –	+ p ⊖	Ⓝ H P | + p –	⊕ p –	N Ⓗ P | + p ⊖	+ p –
N H Ⓟ | + ⓟ –	+ p –	N Ⓗ P | + p –	+ p –	N H P | + p –	+ p ⊖
Ⓝ H P | + p –	+ p –	N H P | + p –	+ p –	N H P | + p –	+ p –
N H P | + p –	+ p –	N H P | + p –	+ p –	N H P | + p –	+ p –
N H P | + p –	+ p –	N H P | + p –	+ p –	N H P | + p –	+ p –
N H P | + p –	+ p –	N H P | + p –	+ p –	N H P | + p –	+ p –
# 9 0 4 | 0 2 2	0 1 1	5 8 0 | 1 0 0	2 0 0	6 7 0 | 2 0 1	0 0 1

Figure 2.8. Example of a completed data collection form used to track whether a student responds to questions during lessons.

(continues)

	Child 1	Child 2	Child 3
Percentage of class-directed questions for which the child raised his or her hand independently (Divide the total number of times the child raised his or her hand [H] by the total number of class-directed questions)	0%	61.5%	53.8%
Percentage of class-directed questions that the child answered correctly without a prompt (+) (Divide the total number of times the child answered a class-directed question correctly [+] by the total number of times the child answered a class-directed question)	50.0%	100%	66.7%
Percentage of individual-directed questions that the child answered correctly (+) (Divide the total number of times the child answered an individual-directed question correctly [+] by the number of times the child answered an individual-directed question)	0%	100%	0%

Figure 2.8. *Continued.*

class-directed questions for which a child raised his or her hand and (b) the percentage of class- and individually directed questions answered correctly without prompts.

Independent Seatwork

It may be important to measure the ability of the child with autism to complete seatwork independently. As with previous areas of measurement, the teacher selects an average student in the class for completing seatwork independently and the lowest student in completing seatwork independently other than the child with autism. The observer notes the type of seatwork assignment given (e.g., mathematic problems, questions to answer in a text), the number of items assigned, the number of items the child attempts, and the number of items that were correctly answered. Using a stopwatch, or preferably recorded signals on an audiotape listened to through an audiotape machine, the observer records a child's engaged on-task behavior using a 10-second momentary time sampling method. The definition of *engaged on-task behavior* is written on the data collection form. At the 10-second signal, the observer codes the task engagement of the second child. At the 20-second signal, the observer codes the task engagement of the third child. This repeats for a total of 15 minutes, making 30 observations per child. At the end of the session, the observer tallies the percentage of occurrences of engagement on task, the percentage of items attempted, and the percentage of items attempted that were answered correctly. Figure 2.9 shows a completed example of a data collection form used to track a child's completion of independent seatwork. A blank, reproducible version of this form can be found in Appendix 2A.

Independent Seatwork

This data collection form tracks the amount of time that a child spends working on a seat-work assignment, the percentage of items attempted, and the percentage of items answered correctly over a 15-minute period. Observe the child with autism, a teacher-selected average student, and a teacher-selected next lowest functioning student in a random order. Note the type of seat work assignment given. At the end of the time period, note the number of assigned items; the number of attempted items, the number of correct items; and, of the number of attempted items, the percentage that were correct. Use a 10-second momentary time-sampling method to code engagement on task; put a line through *E* for engaged or *N* for not engaged. *Engagement on task* is defined as the child looking at his or her work and being engaged in an activity appropriate for the task (e.g., reading, writing).

Independent Seatwork

Child: **Tom Mouhot**   Setting: **In class**   Date: **March 1**

Assigned Task: **Math**

E = engaged   N = not engaged

	Child 1 Tom	**Child 2**	**Child 3**		**Child 1** Tom	**Child 2**	**Child 3**
1	Ⓔ N	Ⓔ N	Ⓔ N	16	E Ⓝ	E Ⓝ	Ⓔ N
2	E Ⓝ	Ⓔ N	Ⓔ N	17	Ⓔ N	Ⓔ N	Ⓔ N
3	E Ⓝ	Ⓔ N	Ⓔ N	18	Ⓔ N	Ⓔ N	Ⓔ N
4	E Ⓝ	Ⓔ N	Ⓔ N	19	E Ⓝ	Ⓔ N	Ⓔ N
5	Ⓔ N	Ⓔ N	Ⓔ N	20	E Ⓝ	Ⓔ N	Ⓔ N
6	E Ⓝ	Ⓔ N	Ⓔ N	21	Ⓔ N	Ⓔ N	Ⓔ N
7	Ⓔ N	Ⓔ N	Ⓔ N	22	Ⓔ N	Ⓔ N	Ⓔ N
8	E Ⓝ	Ⓔ N	Ⓔ N	23	E Ⓝ	E Ⓝ	Ⓔ N
9	E Ⓝ	Ⓔ N	Ⓔ N	24	Ⓔ N	Ⓔ N	Ⓔ N
10	E Ⓝ	Ⓔ N	Ⓔ N	25	E Ⓝ	Ⓔ N	Ⓔ N
11	E Ⓝ	Ⓔ N	Ⓔ N	26	E Ⓝ	Ⓔ N	Ⓔ N
12	E Ⓝ	Ⓔ N	Ⓔ N	27	E Ⓝ	Ⓔ N	E Ⓝ
13	E Ⓝ	Ⓔ N	E Ⓝ	28	E Ⓝ	Ⓔ N	Ⓔ N
14	Ⓔ N	Ⓔ N	Ⓔ N	29	E Ⓝ	Ⓔ N	Ⓔ N
15	Ⓔ N	Ⓔ N	Ⓔ N	30	Ⓔ N	E Ⓝ	Ⓔ N
Total *E*s					11	27	28
% *E*s					36.7	90.0	93.3
# of assigned items					8	20	20
# of attempted items					4	20	20
# of correct items					2	17	20
% of attempted items that were correct					50.0	85.0	100

Figure 2.9. Example of a completed data collection form for tracking completion of independent seat work.

Problem Behavior

The last example of a data collection form is one used to track the occurrence of problem behaviors that interfere with the child's learning—including, typically, stereotypic behavior, aggression, and/or disruptive behavior. A stock response definition for each of the three behaviors can be found on the completed example of the data collection form in Figure 2.10. However, the specific definition needs to be adjusted to fit the particular problem behaviors displayed by the target child. A blank, reproducible version of this form can be found in Appendix 2A.

Problem behavior would be tracked on an event-recording basis for half a day. In other words, an observer would tally the number of times a problem behavior occurred. If the problem behavior of interest occurs at high frequency, then a shorter observation period (e.g., 1 hour) would be selected. The data collection form breaks the observation time into half-hour intervals. In the column labeled Activity, the observer enters a description of the assigned activity (e.g., math, recess, music) during each half-hour interval. The observer enters a tick mark for every aggressive behavior, stereotypic behavior, or disruptive behavior that the child displays during each 30-minute interval. At the end of the observation, the observer tallies the number of occurrences of each problem behavior for each 30-minute interval. An observation is repeated two more times. Results are analyzed to derive the mean number of each problem behavior per hour and to examine if higher frequencies of problem behaviors occur during certain activities and/or time intervals than others. Because the desired occurrence of aggressive, stereotypic, and disruptive behaviors of students in classrooms is zero, there is no need to compare the target student with autism to other students in the classroom.

Inter-Observer Reliability

How does one know whether any of the above measures are reliable? In other words, would someone else measuring the same behavior at the same time get the same results? To satisfy standards of measurement, there should be a periodic check of the reliability of measurements. Inter-observer reliability is arranged by having a second observer observe the same behavior of the same child at the same time. A Y-adaptor with a second set of earphones is attached to an audiotape machine so that a second observer can hear the same audio cues that the first observer can hear. No discussion would occur between the two observers while data were being collected.

Inter-observer reliability is calculated by tallying the number of times the two observers agreed on the *occurrence* of the target behavior divided by the total number of observations and then multiplied by 100. Inter-observer agreement on the *frequency* of behaviors would be derived by dividing the lower of the two frequencies of observer data by the higher frequency and then multiplying that number by 100. For observations to be considered to have acceptable reliability, inter-observer agreement should be 80% or higher (Hawkins & Dobes, 1975).

Training of observers typically consists of presenting written information on the response definition of the behavior being observed and information about the method of observing behaviors. Observers would then practice observing by using a video of the behavior of interest or by practicing observing in a different classroom. Practice in observation methods should continue until the observers can demonstrate high

Problem Behaviors

This data collection form is for measuring the occurrence of problem behaviors of a child with autism in an inclusive setting. There are three problem behaviors that will be counted on an event basis: aggression (hitting, biting, kicking, scratching, head butting, throwing objects at others, spitting at others), stereotypic behavior (repetitive actions such as body rocking, hand flapping, jumping, finger flicking), and disruptive behavior (actions that would disrupt the rest of the class, including screaming, throwing objects, ripping paper, flopping on the floor, running around the room). However, the specific definition needs to be adjusted to fit the particular problem behaviors displayed by the target child.

Count each occurrence of any of the three behaviors during each 30-min interval. At the end of the interval, also write in the activity(ies) that occurred during that time period. Add up the total number of problem behaviors for each 30-minute interval at the end of the row, and calculate the total for each of the problem behaviors at the bottom of the columns. Divide the total number of behaviors by the number of hours of observation. Repeat for a second day. Average the results for the two days.

Problem Behaviors

Child: _Tom Mouhot_   Date: _Feb 26_

School: _Riverside Public School_   Class: _Mrs. Garcia_

Time Started: _8:45_   Time Finished: _12:00_   Total Minutes: _195_   Total Hours: _3.25_

Definitions

Aggressive Behavior: _throwing objects, hitting_

Stereotypic Behavior: _repetitive action (e.g., jumping, hand-flapping)_

Disruptive Behavior: _out of seat_

Time	Activity	Aggressive behavior	Stereotypic behavior	Disruptive behavior	TOTAL
8:30–9:00	Arrival at school	///			3
9:00–9:30	Reading				0
9:30–10:00	Reading/Math		/	/	2
10:00–10:30	Math/Recess			//	2
10:30–11:00	Music			////	4
11:00–11:30	Phys. Ed.	//	#####		7
11:30–12:00	Phys. Ed.	///	//		5
	TOTAL	8	8	7	23
	Mean number of behaviors per hour (divide the totals by the number of hours)	2.5	2.5	2.1	7.1

Figure 2.10. Example of a completed data collection form for problem behaviors.

(e.g., 90%) agreement with one another. It is at this point that observers would be asked to score the behaviors of children with autism in supported inclusion environments.

Data Summary

Results of a child with autism on each of the five measures included in Appendix 2A are shown in Figure 2.11. The child whose data are shown in Figure 2.11 is in a regular Grade 3 class. His mean on-task behavior appears to be lower than that of the child selected as average in the class (mean of 82%), but slightly higher than that of the child selected by the class teacher as being the second lowest. A similar result occurred for independent seatwork, with the results of the child with autism falling between those of the children selected to represent an average and the second lowest child. Based on this information only, on-task behavior and independent seatwork may not be identified as areas of high need for this child with autism.

In contrast, it appears that interventions may be needed to target improvement in the other three areas measured. The child with autism interacted with peers at a mean of 11% of the time, in contrast to 23% and 41%, respectively, for the children selected to be the second lowest child and the average child in the class. During class lessons, the child with autism normally answered group-directed questions at a mean average of 30%, considerably lower than the two comparison children did. The child with autism exhibited either disruptive behavior or stereotypic behavior an average of about 14 times an hour. A reassessment of the children on these same measures would help to indicate if the interventions were effective.

These data indicate that the child with autism is below the rest of the class in active engagement on task, peer interaction, the frequency of communicative responses, and raising hand to group-directed questions. This hypothetical child, however, is within the class range for percentage correct to individually directed questions and the amount of time spent completing seatwork assignments. Reassessment would indicate if the child with autism improved in skill areas.

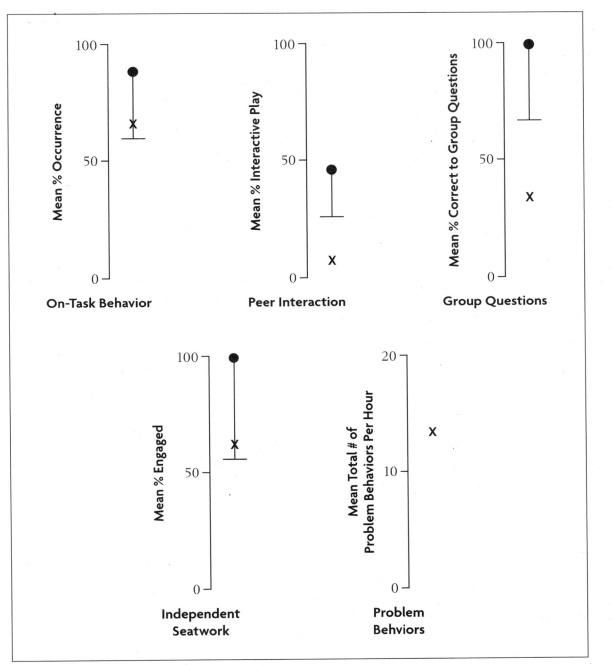

Figure 2.11. Hypothetical data representing the performance of a child with autism (*X*) in the areas of on-task behavior, peer interaction, responding to group questions, independent seatwork, and problem behaviors, compared with a teacher-selected average child (solid circle) and a child selected by the teacher as being next lowest to the child with autism (vertical line).

Study Questions

1. An intellectual test was completed for a child with autism, aged 4 years 7 months. The results of the testing suggested that the child scored at the 2 years 2 months level. Place a dot on the chart below to depict this result, and draw a curved line to depict a hypothetical growth curve ranging from the child's birth to age 7 years.

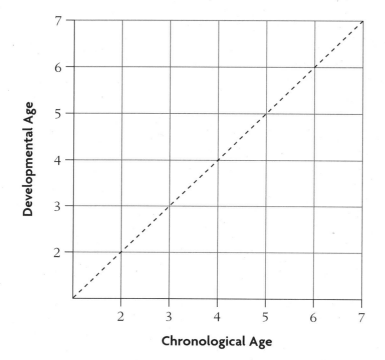

2. Describe how a criterion-referenced assessment can be used to assess a child's skills in an area in which there is a finite and known set of answers, such as in math.

3. Describe how a criterion-referenced assessment can be used to assess a child's skills in an area in which there is not a finite set of known assessment criteria, such as reading accuracy and comprehension.

4. How does one use the criterion-referenced assessment results to identify the level to begin teaching a child?

5. Describe how one can assess a child's behavior, such as on-task behavior.

6. Interpret the following results (Figure 2.12).

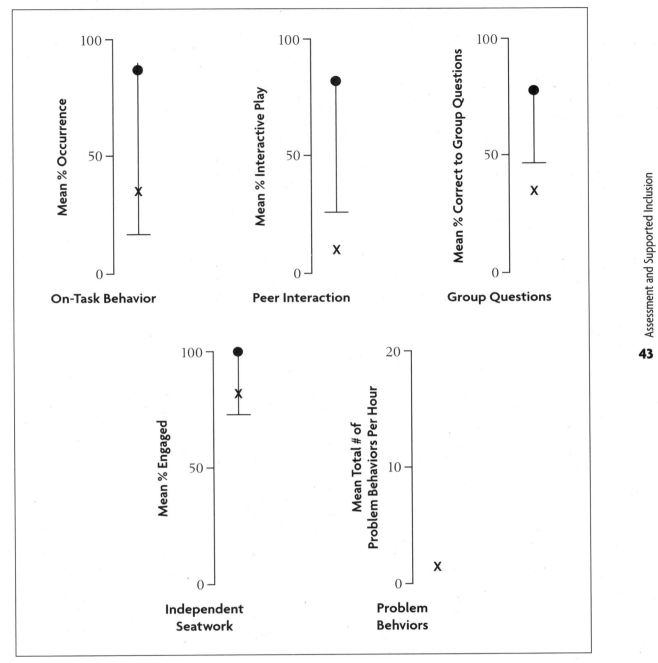

Figure 2.12. Study Question #6.

Data Collection Forms for Assessing Readiness for Inclusion

On-Task Behavior   46

Peer Interaction   47

Responding to Questions During Lessons   48

Independent Seatwork   50

Problem Behaviors   51

On-Task Behavior

Child's Name: _____ Date: _____

Time: _____ Coder: _____ Teacher: _____

School: _____ Lesson: _____

Instructions: Using a stopwatch, observe the child for an instant every 20 seconds. Put a circle around the letter O if the child is on task (see definition below) or the letter N if the child is not on task. If it is unclear to whom the child should be attending or if the teacher is out of the room, circle the letter X. Continue recording the child's behavior for 15 minutes.

	20 sec	40 sec	60 sec
Min 1	O N X	O N X	O N X
Min 2	O N X	O N X	O N X
Min 3	O N X	O N X	O N X
Min 4	O N X	O N X	O N X
Min 5	O N X	O N X	O N X
Min 6	O N X	O N X	O N X
Min 7	O N X	O N X	O N X
Min 8	O N X	O N X	O N X
Min 9	O N X	O N X	O N X
Min 10	O N X	O N X	O N X
Min 11	O N X	O N X	O N X
Min 12	O N X	O N X	O N X
Min 13	O N X	O N X	O N X
Min 14	O N X	O N X	O N X
Min 15	O N X	O N X	O N X

Count the number of Os: _____
Count the number of Ns: _____
Count the number of Xs: _____

Divide the number of Os by the number of Os and Ns and multiply by 100: _____

Response definition = On-task behavior is defined as a child being oriented to the task assigned by the classroom teacher, including observing the teacher when talking or another student when answering a question, or being engaged in classroom participation directed by the teacher.

Peer Interaction

This data collection form is used for assessing the occurrence of interactive play of a young child with autism. Select a 15-minute period when you would be able to observe the child with autism, a child in the same class selected by the teacher as being average in peer interaction, and a third child in the same class selected by the teacher as being the next lowest in peer interaction to the child with autism.

Use a 10-second momentary time-sampling method of behavior observation. Observe one child, then the second, and then the third. Over the 15 minutes, each child should be able to be observed 30 times. The response definitions are as follows.

Interactive Play (IP): The child is engaged in a play activity (e.g., pushing a toy truck, coloring) within 2 minutes of at least one other child and is interacting verbally (e.g., talking about a play activity) or nonverbally (e.g., allowing another child to take turns playing with a toy, listening when another child is talking specifically to him or her) with another child.

No Interactive Play (NIP): Any other play behavior (e.g., not playing, interacting with an adult, playing by him- or herself).

Peer Interaction

Child's Name: _____ School: _____

Date: _____ Time: _____ Observer: _____ Setting: _____

IP = interactive play   NIP = no interactive play

			Child 2		Child 3					Child 2		Child 3	
1	IP	NIP	IP	NIP	IP	NIP		16	IP	NIP	IP	NIP	IP	NIP
2	IP	NIP	IP	NIP	IP	NIP		17	IP	NIP	IP	NIP	IP	NIP
3	IP	NIP	IP	NIP	IP	NIP		18	IP	NIP	IP	NIP	IP	NIP
4	IP	NIP	IP	NIP	IP	NIP		19	IP	NIP	IP	NIP	IP	NIP
5	IP	NIP	IP	NIP	IP	NIP		20	IP	NIP	IP	NIP	IP	NIP
6	IP	NIP	IP	NIP	IP	NIP		21	IP	NIP	IP	NIP	IP	NIP
7	IP	NIP	IP	NIP	IP	NIP		22	IP	NIP	IP	NIP	IP	NIP
8	IP	NIP	IP	NIP	IP	NIP		23	IP	NIP	IP	NIP	IP	NIP
9	IP	NIP	IP	NIP	IP	NIP		24	IP	NIP	IP	NIP	IP	NIP
10	IP	NIP	IP	NIP	IP	NIP		25	IP	NIP	IP	NIP	IP	NIP
11	IP	NIP	IP	NIP	IP	NIP		26	IP	NIP	IP	NIP	IP	NIP
12	IP	NIP	IP	NIP	IP	NIP		27	IP	NIP	IP	NIP	IP	NIP
13	IP	NIP	IP	NIP	IP	NIP		28	IP	NIP	IP	NIP	IP	NIP
14	IP	NIP	IP	NIP	IP	NIP		29	IP	NIP	IP	NIP	IP	NIP
15	IP	NIP	IP	NIP	IP	NIP		30	IP	NIP	IP	NIP	IP	NIP
								#						
								%						

Responding to Questions During Lessons

This data collection form is used for recording the frequency of children raising their hands for questions and, if called upon by the teacher, the percentage of questions answered correctly. Observe the child with autism, a teacher-selected average student, and a teacher-selected next lowest functioning student in a random order for 1 minute each. During that interval, for each teacher question directed to the class, record if the child raised his or her hand or had to be prompted (i.e., an adult provided a physical, gestural, or some other form of a prompt for the child to raise his/her hand). Record if the child answered correctly if called upon. For a question the teacher directed specifically to the child, record if the child answered correctly. Continue until 10 1-minute observations are taken of each child.

Responding to Questions During Lessons

Child With Autism: _____   Teacher: _____

Date: _____   Start Time: _____   End Time: _____   Length in min: _____

Lesson: _____   Coder: _____

N = no hand raised   H = hand raised   P = prompted to raise hand
+ = answered correctly without prompt   p = prompted to answer and was correct
− = not prompted to answer and was incorrect

Child 1:		Child 2:		Child 3:	
Class-directed question	Individual-directed question	Class-directed question	Individual-directed question	Class-directed question	Individual-directed question
N H P + p −	+ p −	N H P + p −	+ p −	N H P + p −	+ p −
N H P + p −	+ p −	N H P + p −	+ p −	N H P + p −	+ p −
N H P + p −	+ p −	N H P + p −	+ p −	N H P + p −	+ p −
N H P + p −	+ p −	N H P + p −	+ p −	N H P + p −	+ p −
N H P + p −	+ p −	N H P + p −	+ p −	N H P + p −	+ p −
N H P + p −	+ p −	N H P + p −	+ p −	N H P + p −	+ p −
N H P + p −	+ p −	N H P + p −	+ p −	N H P + p −	+ p −
N H P + p −	+ p −	N H P + p −	+ p −	N H P + p −	+ p −
N H P + p −	+ p −	N H P + p −	+ p −	N H P + p −	+ p −
N H P + p −	+ p −	N H P + p −	+ p −	N H P + p −	+ p −
N H P + p −	+ p −	N H P + p −	+ p −	N H P + p −	+ p −
N H P + p −	+ p −	N H P + p −	+ p −	N H P + p −	+ p −
N H P + p −	+ p −	N H P + p −	+ p −	N H P + p −	+ p −
N H P + p −	+ p −	N H P + p −	+ p −	N H P + p −	+ p −
N H P + p −	+ p −	N H P + p −	+ p −	N H P + p −	+ p −
N H P + p −	+ p −	N H P + p −	+ p −	N H P + p −	+ p −
N H P + p −	+ p −	N H P + p −	+ p −	N H P + p −	+ p −
N H P + p −	+ p −	N H P + p −	+ p −	N H P + p −	+ p −
#					

(continues)

	Child 1	Child 2	Child 3
Percentage of class-directed questions for which the child raised his or her hand independently			
Percentage of group-directed questions that the child answered correctly			
Percentage of individual-directed questions that the child answered correctly			

Independent Seatwork

This data collection form tracks the amount of time that a child spends working on a seatwork assignment, the percentage of items attempted, and the percentage of items answered correctly over a 15-minute period. Observe the child with autism, a teacher-selected average student, and a teacher-selected next lowest functioning student in a random order. Note the type of seatwork assignment given. At the end of the time period, note the number of assigned items; the number of attempted items; the number of correct items; and, of the number of attempted items, the percentage that were correct. Use a 10-second momentary time-sampling method to code engagement on task; put a line through *E* for engaged or *N* for not engaged. *Engagement on task* is defined as the child looking at his or her work and being engaged in an activity appropriate for the task (e.g., reading, writing).

Independent Seatwork

Child: _____   Setting: _____   Date: _____

Assigned Task: _Math, Reading, Language Arts, Social Studies, Other_ _____

E = engaged   N = not engaged

	Child 1	Child 2	Child 3		Child 1	Child 2	Child 3
1	E N	E N	E N	16	E N	E N	E N
2	E N	E N	E N	17	E N	E N	E N
3	E N	E N	E N	18	E N	E N	E N
4	E N	E N	E N	19	E N	E N	E N
5	E N	E N	E N	20	E N	E N	E N
6	E N	E N	E N	21	E N	E N	E N
7	E N	E N	E N	22	E N	E N	E N
8	E N	E N	E N	23	E N	E N	E N
9	E N	E N	E N	24	E N	E N	E N
10	E N	E N	E N	25	E N	E N	E N
11	E N	E N	E N	26	E N	E N	E N
12	E N	E N	E N	27	E N	E N	E N
13	E N	E N	E N	28	E N	E N	E N
14	E N	E N	E N	29	E N	E N	E N
15	E N	E N	E N	30	E N	E N	E N

	Child 1	Child 2	Child 3
Total *E*s			
% *E*s			
# of assigned items			
# of attempted items			
# of correct items			
% of attempted items that were correct			

Problem Behaviors

This data collection form is for measuring the occurrence of problem behaviors of a child with autism in an inclusive setting. There are three problem behaviors that will be counted on an event basis: aggression (hitting, biting, kicking, scratching, head butting, throwing objects at others, spitting at others), stereotypic behavior (repetitive actions such as body rocking, hand flapping, jumping, finger flicking), and disruptive behavior (actions that would disrupt the rest of the class, including screaming, throwing objects, ripping paper, flopping on the floor, running around the room). However, the specific definition needs to be adjusted to fit the particular problem behaviors displayed by the target child.

Count each occurrence of any of the three behaviors during each 30-min interval. At the end of the interval, also write in the activity(ies) that occurred during that time period. Add up the total number of problem behaviors for each 30-minute interval at the end of the row, and calculate the total for each of the problem behaviors at the bottom of the columns. Divide the total number of behaviors by the number of hours of observation. Repeat for a second day. Average the results for the 2 days.

Problem Behaviors

Child: _____ Date: _____

School: _____ Class: _____

Time Started: _____ Time Finished: _____ Total Minutes: _____ Total Hours: _____

Definitions

Aggressive Behavior: _____

Stereotypic Behavior: _____

Disruptive Behavior: _____

Time	Activity	Aggressive behavior	Stereotypic behavior	Disruptive behavior	TOTAL
8:30–9:00					
9:00–9:30					
9:30–10:00					
10:00–10:30					
10:30–11:00					
11:00–11:30					
11:30–12:00					
	TOTAL				
	Mean number of behaviors per hour (divide the totals by the number of hours)				

3 Planning For and Accommodating a Student With Autism

Chapter Topics

- Using embedded instruction
- Using individualized group instruction
- Adapting the general education class curriculum
- Adapting a commercial curriculum

As stated in earlier chapters, the planning and implementation of interventions associated with the inclusion of a child with autism requires a team of individuals who come together to plan for the needs of the child. This team would typically consist of all those who are critical to ensuring the success of a support plan for the child, including those who can develop interventions, those who can implement the interventions, and those who can provide additional resources (e.g., teaching materials, administrative support, planning time) to the interventions, as well as those who are the guardians of the child. An approach that is often taken to guide the sequence of steps taken by the support team is person-centered planning (Fox, Dunlap, & Philbrick, 1997; Singer, Goldberg-Hamblin, Peckham-Hardin, Barry, & Santarelli, 2002), described in more detail in Chapter 10.

One of the first steps in the planning process for a child with autism is to clarify the roles and responsibilities of the team members to ensure that the actions of one team member are complementary to the actions of other team members in moving the child's plan along. Problems are likely to occur on a team if members do not have clearly defined roles. For example, a team may include a speech–language pathologist (SLP) from a school system and an SLP from outside of the school system. The team would need to define which of the two SLPs should take responsibility for which components of the child's plan. They would also need to clarify the steps to be followed in planning and executing the support plan, as well as the roles taken by each member of the team in relation to everyone else on the team.

In the left-hand column of Table 3.1 is a list of the common steps taken in planning for a child with autism. For example, typically, the first step is to determine what information would be helpful in identifying the child's strengths and needs from which an intervention plan could be developed. One needs to ensure that the steps listed in the left-hand column match the steps to be followed in the planning for the child. The names and positions of each individual who will be part of the team are entered in the top row. At the initial meeting, there should be a discussion to clarify the roles of each individual in planning and implementing each of the steps listed in the left-hand column. For each step, the potential roles are as follows: lead (provides the main direction for the step), assists (assists in the execution of the step), input (has input into the plan), and informed (is informed of what occurs in the step). For example, for the design of the assessment plan in the first step, the school psychologist might take the lead, with assistance in data collection from the classroom teacher, and the rest of the team are kept informed. When it comes to the fourth step, the formulation of the interventions, the special education teacher may take the lead with help from the school psychologist and a behavior analyst involved with the child outside of school. This plan forms the blueprint for how the team will work together. Obviously, the specifics of the plan would be individualized to the needs of the child, and the particulars to those who are involved.

Although the assessment of skills of children with autism is important for establishing a profile of a child's current level of functioning, it is only through the careful design of interventions and the consistent implementation of these interventions that gains in the development of children with autism can occur. A richness of information about applied behavior analysis (ABA)-based intervention can be found in such journals as the *Journal of Applied Behavior Analysis* and the *Journal of Positive Behavioral Interventions*, as well as in numerous books.

Much of the research that has been conducted on the use of ABA procedures for children with autism has been carried out in clinical settings, special education classes, or some other specialized setting in which someone other than a teacher implements an intervention, such as an experimenter or someone under the close supervision of the experimenter. Such studies suggest that ABA intervention is effective with young

Table 3.1

Example of a Plan to Clarify Roles and Responsibilities of a Team Planning Assessment and Intervention for a Child With Autism in a School Setting

Planning steps	Parent(s):	Classroom teacher:	Para-professional:	Principal:	Special education teacher:	School psychologist:	Behavior analyst:
1. Designs assessment plan	F		F	F	I	L	I
2. Implements assessment		L	A				
3. Defines problems, identifies strengths	I	I	I	I	A	L	A
4. Formulates intervention	I	I	I	I	L	A	A
5. Secures resources	F			L	A		
6. Implements intervention		L	A		A		
7. Ensures fidelity of program implementation					L	A	A
8. Collects data on child outcome		L	A		I	I	
9. Analyzes data					A	L	A
10. Makes adjustments to program	I	A	A		L	A	A

Note. L = leads; A = assists; I = has input; F = is informed.

children with autism when implemented under optimal conditions. There are a number of ABA interventions that have been tested under more natural conditions in general education classes. Some of the interventions that have been used in an inclusive setting with children who have autism are described in the sections that follow.

Using Embedded Instruction

Overview

Embedded instruction consists of injecting teaching opportunities within the routines of the school day to teach a child the targeted skill or behavior. Embedded instruction is 1 of 27 interventions that have been identified as having sufficient scientific support to be included in child-focused practices recommended by the Division of Early Childhood of the Council for Exceptional Children (Wolery, Anthony, Caldwell, Snyder, & Morgante, 2002).

The study by Hoyson, Jamieson, Strain, and Smith (1998) was one of the first to describe how to embed learning opportunities for children with autism into preschool activities. In the Learning Experiences . . . An Alternative Program for Preschoolers and Parents (LEAP) program, eight individual objectives were identified for each child with autism. For each of these eight objectives, staff planned three learning opportunities that occurred during natural activities in the school day (for 24 learning opportunities per day, per child with autism). For example, an objective of a child with autism may be to learn how to respond to familiar actions, such as "give me," "find the," and "push." When the child is in a "manipulative" play area in preschool, his or her teachers attempt to create situations in which the child with autism can respond to "give me" requests by his or her peers. A similar strategy of embedding instructional opportunities into the regular class has also been described by McGee, Morrier, and Daly (1999). Wolery, Anthony, and Heckathorn (1998) used transition times to provide embedded instruction. While a child with autism moved from one activity to the next in the regular classroom, the child was presented with an opportunity to practice a skill.

Design Recommendations

The first step in the development of embedded instruction is to select objectives from the child's Individualized Education Program (IEP) that could be taught within the routines of the school day. It may be difficult for staff in general education programs to focus on more than three objectives for each child with autism at one point in time. The example that follows illustrates how objectives may be selected.

Brian: Example Objectives for Embedded Instruction

Brian is an 8-year-old boy with autism attending a general Grade 3 class with the help of a full-time paraprofessional. Brian is able to read first-grade material at 80% accuracy and at 75 words per minute. He is able to correctly solve double-digit arithmetic problems without carrying, spell most words at a first-grade level, and write simple sentences without assistance. It is difficult to comprehend Brian's speech, particularly when he gets excited. He does request desired objects and activities in complete sentences. The three objectives selected by Brian's team were:

> Brian will state the correct definition for each of five vocabulary words on three consecutive occasions.
>
> Brian will be able to subtract single-digit numbers and state the answer at 90% accuracy without prompts.
>
> Brian will be able to write a complete sentence that contains a subject, a verb, an object, an adjective, and an adverb with no spelling or syntax errors.

After the objectives have been selected for the child with autism, the next step is to identify when, in the course of an instructional day, one can embed opportunities for the child to practice the targeted skills. (For the example above, at least three practice sessions are planned each day for each of the three selected instructional targets for Brian.) A specific plan would be developed for how to teach the child each instructional target. For example, Polychronis, McDonnell, Johnson, and Jameson (2004) provided the general education teacher with a script describing how to practice an instructional set of five items with a child with autism (e.g., a set of five pictures of clock faces set at 15 minutes past the hour). This practice session was held with the child with autism individually during a lesson given to the entire class. Teachers present the instructional set for each instructional target three times during a 30-minute lesson. Polychronis et al. (2004) used a set procedure for teaching an instructional target, including the following:

(a) The teacher presents the stimulus (e.g., paper clock face set at 15 minutes past the hour) with an instruction (e.g., "What time?").

(b) The teacher immediately (0-second delay) gives the correct response (e.g., "2:15").

(c) The child is reinforced for repeating the correct response. The type of reinforcement used would be determined by the child's preferences.

(d) If the child with autism fails to answer within 3 seconds or answers incorrectly, the teacher ensures that the child is attending (e.g., touches the child), points at the stimulus, says the correct response, and re-administers the instruction.

(e) This teaching continues until the child's performance satisfies a mastery criterion (e.g., 100% accuracy on 3 consecutive days).

(f) Once the mastery criteria are achieved, steps (a) to (e) are repeated with a 3-second delay between the presentation of the stimulus (clock face) and the prompt for the correct response.

The teacher would identify when, in the course of the day, the three practice opportunities could be held for each of the three objectives. In Polychronis et al. (2004), the three opportunities were held during the same 30-minute session. In other cases, the three practice opportunities were spread over an entire day.

Johnson, McDonnell, Holzwarth, and Hunter (2004) demonstrated that general education teachers and paraprofessionals could successfully implement embedded instruction during breaks, transitions, and opening/closing activities for three children with developmental disabilities. They found that children were able to learn skills selected from the child's IEP objectives in the general education classroom. Teachers rated embedded instruction as both effective and acceptable.

Select Instructional Items From Actual Errors

In the Johnson et al. (2004) study and the Polychronis et al. (2004) study, children with autism received between 10 and 15 embedded instruction trials each school day. My colleagues and I have made four modifications to this procedure for delivering embedded instruction. First, we select a child's instructional targets for embedded instructions from the child's IEP objectives, but we pick the specific items to teach by keeping track of errors the child makes in the course of the day in the area of each objective. This method ensures that the items taught are ones that the child with autism may be able to use in everyday situations. From the log of potential instructional targets, we select five items for each of three instructional areas selected for each participating child.

Increase the Number of Embedded Instruction Trials

A second modification that our team has made is to increase the number of embedded instruction trials that a child with autism receives in a school day, with the assumption that more trials will result in faster acquisition of the selected instruction targets. Polychronis et al. (2004) presented trials at the rate of about one every 2 minutes under a 30-minute distributed trial condition (15 trials per day in total) and one every 8 minutes in a 120-minute distribution trial condition (15 trials per day). They found that children with autism learned faster when the same number of embedded instruction trials was distributed over 30, rather than 120, minutes.

We attempt to provide children with autism with more practice on instructional targets than described by Polychronis et al. (2004). We try to conduct at least three instructional sessions of embedded instruction for each child, each school day, when the child is engaged in an activity into which the instruction is embedded. During these 30-minute lessons, a child typically receives between 2 and 0.2 embedded instruction trials per minute, depending on the skill being taught to the child. This amounts to a total of between 18 and 180 trials per day.

Use a Two-Part Mastery Criterion

Another modification we have made is to use a two-part mastery criterion for each instructional item. The child with autism first needs to answer an item correctly twice in a row. At this point, the instructor stops teaching that item, but continues with the remaining items. For the second part of the mastery criterion, the item that the child correctly answered twice in a row is re-administered at the next instructional session, and the child is expected to answer the item correctly on the first presentation. This second part of the performance criteria helps to ensure that the child is able to maintain his or her performance over time and in some situations, to a different instructor. If the child makes an error during this initial trial, then continued instruction is provided using a 3-second constant time delay prompt. In constant time delay, the instructor presents a question for the student to answer (e.g., a math problem printed on a flash card, an orally presented factual question about science) and then waits a fixed period of time—in this example, 3 seconds. If the student does not answer the question correctly or does not respond before the selected interval of time is completed, then the instructor delivers a model of the correct answer—in essence an error correction. If the student does answer the presented question correctly, then the instructor does not deliver a model.

Teach in Sets of Five

The fourth modification is that we construct instructional sets of five items, three of which are novel and two of which are review, selected at random from all previously learned items. The ratio of review to new items ranges from 3:2 to 1:4, depending on the child. For example, suppose the following three areas were selected to use embedded instruction for a child with autism: (a) knowledge of everyday situations (e.g., "Why do you need to put an address on envelopes that you mail?"), (b) antonyms, and (c) single-digit addition. A group of five items to teach would be composed of one untrained item from each of the three instructional areas (from the five identified in the log) and two items selected at random from previously learned items. The five items are taught as a set. Novel items are introduced using a 0-second constant time delay prompt until the child achieves two consecutive correct responses for the same instructional item. At that point, instruction changes to a 3-second constant time delay prompt.

Use Index Cards

Each item to be taught using embedded instruction is placed on an index card. On one side of the card is the instruction to be presented to the child and what would be considered a correct response for the child. On the other side of the index card is a form on which results of the child's performance can be recorded trial by trial. An example of a card for embedded instruction is shown in Figure 3.1. The child is taught the five

---

Embedded Instruction

Instructional Area: Opposites

Example Question: "What is the opposite of *enter?*"

Expected Response: "Exit" or equivalent

Mastery Criteria: (a) 2 consecutive correct and (b) correct response on initial presentation for subsequent session

Date	May 3	May 3	May 3							
0 sec	✓ Ⓧ	Ⓥ X	Ⓥ X	✓ X	✓ X	✓ X	✓ X	✓ X	✓ X	✓ X
Date	May 3	May 3	May 3	May 3	May 4					
3 sec	Ⓥ X	✓ Ⓧ	Ⓥ X	Ⓥ X	Ⓥ X	✓ X	✓ X	✓ X	✓ X	✓ X
Date										
Review	✓ X	✓ X	✓ X	✓ X	✓ X	✓ X	✓ X	✓ X	✓ X	✓ X
Date										
Review	✓ X	✓ X	✓ X	✓ X	✓ X	✓ X	✓ X	✓ X	✓ X	✓ X
Date										

Key: ✓ = correct; X = incorrect

Figure 3.1. Example of a card for embedded instruction of one item. The instructions are located on one side of the index card and data are recorded on the reverse.

items as a set. As previously stated, typically, two of the items being taught are ones that the child had already mastered. The set of five items are shuffled to be presented in a random order each time. A child is presented with the instruction as described on the index card, and whether or not the child was correct is entered on the reverse side of that card in the section that corresponds to whether the item is being taught using a 0- or a 3-second constant time delay or whether the item has already been mastered and is now on review.

The results shown in Figure 3.1 represent the results for one instructional item as it was taught as part of a set of five items. The item was first presented using a 0-second constant time delay. On the first trial, the child answered incorrectly (the X was circled), but the child was correct on the subsequent two trials (the checkmarks are circled). The child met the mastery criteria for 0-second constant time delay. When the item was presented at a 3-second constant time delay, the child answered the item correctly on the next trial, incorrectly on the following trial, and correctly on the following two trials, satisfying the first part of the mastery criterion (2 consecutive correct). Finally, the next trial was presented with a different person and a new session (on May 4). The child answered correctly, satisfying the second part of the mastery criterion. At this point, the item was placed in the pool of items to be used for review.

The following is an illustration of how embedded instruction can be used in the previously described example of Brian. An instructional strategy would be created for each of the three objectives selected, as shown in the example below.

Brian: Example Instructional Strategies for Embedded Instruction

Objective #1: Brian will define correctly each of five vocabulary words on three consecutive occasions.

Instruction: Get Brian's attention and ask, "What does _____ (one of his vocabulary words) mean?" See the embedded instruction card for a definition of the correct response. If the child is correct, deliver a confirmatory statement (e.g., "Yes, that is correct") and then praise (e.g., "Wow, what a great answer"). If the child does not respond within 3 seconds or gives an incorrect response, model the correct response, and then ask the question again. A correct response at this point is reinforced with mild praise.

Mastery Criteria: 5/5 correct on two consecutive trials.

Objective #2: Brian will complete sheets of five problems of subtraction from 20 (e.g., 18 − 12 = _____) without prompts.

Instruction: Present a sheet with 10 arithmetic problems, half of which are presented in a vertical format (e.g., $+\frac{2}{2}$) half horizontally (e.g., 2 + 2 = _____). Brian is given 1 minute to answer the sheet, and then he scores his own answers using a red pencil. For each subtraction error, Brian copies the subtraction problem onto a flash card with the answer written on the reverse side. Brian practices the problems on the flash cards by himself and raises his hand when he feels that he can solve all 10 problems without errors. Brian is then given a new sheet of 10 subtraction problems selected at random from the set of possible subtraction problems from 20. His answers are scored, and he is reinforced for correct performance.

Mastery Criteria: two consecutive sheets of at least 9/10 correct.

Objective #3: Brian will write complete sentences that contain a subject, a verb, and an object.

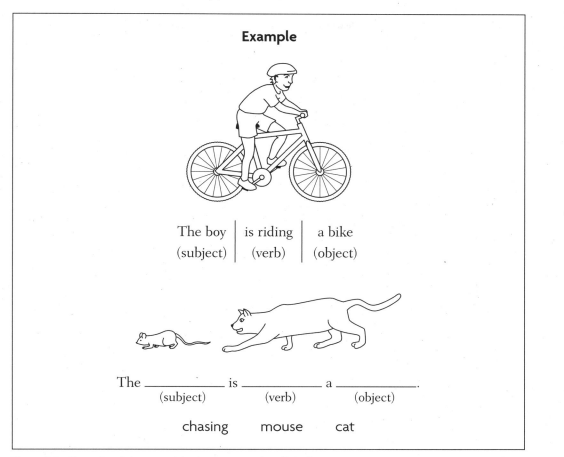

Example

The boy | is riding | a bike
(subject) | (verb) | (object)

The _____ is _____ a _____.
(subject)   (verb)   (object)

chasing   mouse   cat

Figure 3.2. Example of the materials given to a student (Brian) to compose a sentence containing a subject, a verb, and an object.

Instruction: Present a picture under which is a place for the child to compose a sentence that describes the picture. The sentence should have written prompts to assist the child in writing the subject, verb, and object, as shown in Figure 3.2. First, explain that the top of the page contains an example. Next point to the sentence *The boy is riding a bike* with the parts of the sentence labeled below. Tell the child that he or she is to write in the missing words in the sentence that describes the second picture. Point out the choice of words shown below the picture. Let the child answer, and then immediately score.

Criterion: All three components correct for three consecutive sheets, and then present figures that show the blanks for completing a corresponding sentence, but exclude the three words from which the child is to choose. The child would need to fill in the three blanks for three consecutive worksheets without seeing the words to be selected.

To assist in the planning for embedded instruction, the teacher indicates on a planning sheet which activities could be used during the course of each school day to practice each of the child's three objectives for at least three sessions each day. A weekly planner is developed, such as the one shown in Figure 3.3, and times when each objective could be practiced are inserted into this weekly planner. Figure 3.3 depicts a

Weekly Planner

Student: _____ Week of: __November 22_____

Objectives	1	2	3
	B1: Brian will give the definitions of each of five vocabulary words on three consecutive occasions	B2: Brian will complete sheets of five subtraction problems from 20 (e.g., 18 − 12 = _____) without prompts.	B3: Brian will write complete sentences that contain a subject, a verb, and an object.

Time	Activity	Monday	Tuesday	Wednesday	Thursday	Friday
8:40	Entry bell	B1: _3/5_	B1:_____	B1:_____	B1:_____	B1:_____
8:45–9:05	Art					
9:05–9:45	Language: Writing	B3: _3/3_	B3:_____	B3:_____	B3:_____	B3:_____
9:45–10:00	Recess (15 minutes)	B1: _4/5_	B1:_____	B1:_____	B1:_____	B1:_____
10:00–10:40	Social Studies	B3: _3/3_	B3:_____	B3:_____	B3:_____	B3:_____
10:40–11:20	Math	B2: _4/5_	B2:_____	B2:_____	B2:_____	B2:_____
11:20–12:25	Lunch	B2: _3/5_	B2:_____	B2:_____	B2:_____	B2:_____
12:25–1:05	Phys Ed					
1:05–1:45	Language: Reading	B3: _3/3_	B3:_____	B3:_____	B3:_____	B3:_____
1:45–1:55	Recess (10 minutes)	B1: _4/5_	B1:_____	B1:_____	B1:_____	B1:_____
1:55–2:35	Science		B3:_____	B3:_____	B3:_____	B3:_____
2:35–3:15	Math	B2: _4/5_	B2:_____	B2:_____	B2:_____	B2:_____
3:15	Dismissal					

Figure 3.3. Weekly planner for scheduling a student's (Brian's) Individualized Education Program objectives into the class timetable with hypothetical data illustrated for Monday.

plan for embedding instruction during a school week. Activities and the time of their occurrence are shown in the left-hand column. To simplify the illustration, Figure 3.3 shows the same schedule of activities in the class occurring 5 days a week. In reality, each school day would tend to have a different schedule of activities from the other school days.

Brian's three objectives are shown at the top of Figure 3.3, with the codes B1, B2, and B3. These codes are placed into activities to plan when the child will be given practice in each of the three objectives. For example, when Brian first comes into the room in the morning, the teacher assistant would ask Brian to define each of the five target vocabulary words. To ensure three practice sessions per day for each objective, Brian will also be asked to practice defining those same five words before going out for morning and afternoon recesses. A schedule for practicing the other two objectives (B2 and B3) is shown in Figure 3.3.

The same planner is also used to record the results of the practice. Figure 3.3 shows Brian's results for embedded instruction on Monday, with the remaining days left blank, until Brian is able to practice his three objectives on those days as well. Data are then examined to determine if the child has demonstrated mastery of an instructional target or if revisions to the instructional plan need to be made.

Using Individualized Group Instruction

Hoyson et al. (1998) described a way to embed the individualized objectives of a child with autism into a lesson presentation—a method that they referred to as "individualized group instruction." In this method, a teacher would determine how a child with autism in the class could practice at least one of his or her instructional objectives as part of a lesson presented by the teacher. The lesson is planned so that the child with autism in the group receives a minimum of four opportunities to respond to his or her individual objectives within the lesson. To organize the lesson, the teacher creates an index card that contains the name of the lesson on the front and the individual objective for the child with autism on the back. The teacher would also write a script of the teacher's instructions to the child with autism during the lesson. For example, the teacher may be presenting a lesson on parts of a sentence to a second-grade class that contains a child with autism for whom that content would be much too difficult. That child with autism may be working on using adjectives when describing presented pictures. Accordingly, the teacher would plan to have three different pictures shown during the lesson and call on the child with autism to describe the picture using color, size, and/or or quantity as adjectives (e.g., *The big black cat sat on the fence*). The spoken sentence by the child with autism would be written on a blackboard and used by the rest of the class to identify parts of a sentence.

Although the outcome of the LEAP program has been evaluated (Strain & Hoyson, 2000), there appears to have been no specific evaluation of the effectiveness of individualized group instruction specifically. Our team uses individualized group instruction in each of our two "preparatory" classes to transition children with autism from small-group instruction to supported inclusion in a general education classroom. All of the six or so children in a preparatory class had previously received instruction through discrete trial teaching. In the preparatory class, children are taught academic skills (e.g., reading, spelling, writing, mathematics) and nonacademic skills (e.g., peer interaction, conversational skills, independent seatwork) as a group. As depicted in Figure 3.4, the children are seated in a semicircle around a lead teacher, who presents a 15-minute lesson on a topic. There are typically a number of support teachers seated behind the children with autism to deliver prompts and reinforcement and to deal with a child's problem behavior if it occurs. Over time, the amount and type of prompting is systematically faded for individual children.

As shown in Figure 3.4, children with autism are seated on cushions placed on a rug, with the lead teacher and two or three support teachers situated behind the

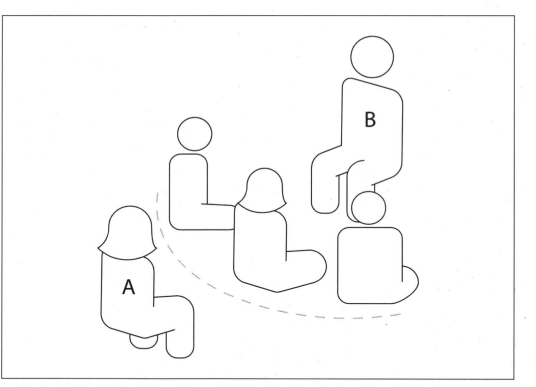

Figure 3.4. Illustration of the position of the support teacher (A) behind the children in the preparatory class who are being taught by the lead teacher (B).

children. A support teacher is located behind the child with autism so that the child is focused on the lead teacher who is presenting the lesson, rather than on the support teacher.

The lead teacher is responsible for presenting the lesson, and the support teachers facilitate the participation of the children in the lesson. There are five types of instructional statements that the lead teacher may deliver to the group:

- *Individual-directed questions*—The teacher directs a question toward an individual child (e.g., "Josh, what is 5 + 7?").
- *Individual-directed action*—The teacher requests a specific action from an individual child (e.g., "Amanda, put the small pencil in the red cup").
- *Group-directed questions*—The teacher poses a question to the group as a whole (e.g., "Who knows the name of an oak tree seed?").
- *Group-directed action*—The teacher requests a particular action from the group (e.g., "Stand up if you are wearing white socks").
- *Group choral responding*—The teacher cues the group to respond in unison (e.g., "OK, I want you to tell me the sound this letter makes. Ready?" In a sweeping motion, the teacher touches the letter).

My colleagues and I attempt to maintain a particular distribution of teacher instruction across types of instruction based on our experience. This distribution may change depending on the composition of the children in the group and the subject matter being presented. The distribution is typically as follows: individual-directed questions—20%; individual directed actions—10%; group-directed questions—20%;

group-directed actions—10%; and group choral responding—40%. The particular mix of teacher instruction to produce optimal learning for children is an empirical question that needs to be tested.

When the teacher directs questions to an individual child, the other children have nothing to do other than to wait. In fact, the other children do not need to respond in any way as the single child answers the teacher's question. Somewhat better participation may result from group-directed questions, since initially each child has the possibility of being called on to answer. However, once one child is selected to answer, the other children have no opportunity to practice the skill. Only group choral responding and group-directed actions require all children to respond to a teacher instruction at the same time. Increased child responding is associated with better child learning (Morrison, Sainato, Benchaaban, & Endo, 2002).

Adapting the General Education Class Curriculum

In any elementary-school class, there is a range of abilities of the students who compose the class. For example, in an average third-grade class, the range in students' ability in reading may be between plus or minus two grade levels (Greenwood, Carta, Kamps, & Arreaga-Mayer, 1990). That is, there would be at least one child with a reading ability at a first-grade level and at least one child with a fifth-grade reading ability in most third-grade classes. Teaching a class of children who have such variability in skill level would be a challenge for any teacher. The inclusion of a child with autism in a general education classroom would likely increase that challenge.

It may not be too much of a stretch for a teacher to include a child with autism whose skills are close to those of the rest of the class. For instance, the child who is 6 months to 1 year behind grade level in a third-grade class may be able to learn using the same instructional materials and the same teaching materials as the rest of the class, perhaps with some assistance and/or adaptation of the class objectives.

However, a general education teacher would have considerably more difficulty accommodating the learning needs of a child with autism whose skills are very much lower than those of the rest of the class. For instance, how would one teach a child in a sixth-grade class whose skills in most academic subjects fall at a second-grade level or lower? If one were planning for a child with autism on a totally individualized basis, that child would likely receive a tailor-made curriculum with perhaps no overlap of instructional materials or objectives with his or her classmates. In essence, the child with autism would be physically in the same room, but would not function with the rest of the class. In such an arrangement, the purpose of inclusion would be restricted to the possibility of social benefits. But, as will be discussed in Chapter 6, even this possibility may be wishful thinking.

It would be equally inappropriate to expect that this child with autism would be able to complete the same work as the other children in the class. The work may be far too difficult for the child with autism. It is not accommodation of the child to fit the curriculum that is needed, but rather accommodation of the curriculum to fit the child. In the former, efforts may be made for the child with autism to participate in class lessons to some degree or to complete part of class assignments. The difficulty is that the altered expectations may not have anything to do with the individual objectives set for the child with autism. The child may be in the same class and complete modified activities with his or her peers, but those activities are not moving the child toward goals that were established as being important for the child. Schuster, Hemmeter, and Ault (2001) found that only one third of a group of children with developmental disabilities in kindergarten to Grade 3 general education classrooms received *any* instruction on their IEP objectives each day. The rest (two thirds of the group) received instruction on less than half of their IEP objectives.

Unless the modifications to the learning activities in a general education class for a child with autism address important objectives for that child, the instruction provided may have little value for the child with autism.

Anderson, Jablonski, and Knapp (2003) described four types of adaptations that can be made to the general curriculum to accommodate children with autism:

- *General curriculum*—The child with autism follows the regular classroom curriculum without modification.

- *Supplementary curriculum*—The child with autism participates fully in the general curriculum but with some assistance.

- *Simplified curriculum*—The child with autism learns the general curriculum, but there is a modification of the difficulty of the work and/or the child with autism is expected to achieve fewer objectives; or work difficulty may be simplified by reducing the amount of work the child with autism is expected to complete. Alternatively, the curriculum can be simplified by adding visual prompts to the material so that it becomes easier to complete.

- *Alternative curriculum*—The child with autism is taught using a different curriculum than the rest of the class uses.

Using information from Anderson et al. (2003), my colleagues and I have created a planning form (see Figure 3.5) with an example plan written in. This form is used to plan how to adapt the curriculum for a child with autism. The ways in which the curriculum can be adapted are shown at the top of the form, with letters A to I for reference. As shown in Figure 3.5, Robert receives math instruction on Mondays, Wednesdays, and Fridays from 10:30 to 11:15 A.M. He also is provided with math remediation in the resource room on Tuesdays and Thursdays, 2:00 to 2:40 P.M. Moreover, when Robert is given a math assignment or test to complete, he is expected to answer only the computation problems, not the math problems presented in sentences that are presented to the rest of the class. In addition, the computation problems that are presented to Robert are modified to contain a visual model of how to complete the assigned problems and visual prompts to assist in solving the problems. Similar plans are made for adapting language arts for Robert, as shown in Figure 3.5. In language arts, Robert also received remediation twice a week in the resource room and has modified expectations for written work. He dictates his answers to the teacher assistant, who writes them out. Robert then types the hand-written copy on a computer.

The goal of curricular adaptation is to modify the work activities to address the child's individual objectives. So how does one adapt the curriculum to ensure that the level is suitable for a child with autism? Kern and Dunlap (1998) identified a number of curricular variables that have been shown to improve the performance of children with developmental disabilities on learning activities. One variable is modifying the difficulty level of the work for the child with autism. For example, where I work, we arrange material for children with autism so that the child *begins* learning the work with answering at least 50% of items correctly and increases response accuracy from

Curriculum Adaptation Plan

Child With Autism: _Robert_   Class Teacher: _Mrs. Jones_

School: _Bending Oak_   Date: _September 27, 2009_

Modifications

A. Alternative Curriculum—Provide different instruction/materials and alternate activities to meet a student's individual outcomes.

B. Alternate Expectations—Adapt the goals/expectations while using the same materials.

C. Level of Support—Increase the amount of personal assistance.

D. Participation Level—Adapt the extent to which a learner is actively involved in the task.

E. Difficulty—Adapt the skill level, problem type, or rules about how the student may approach the work.

F. Amount—Adapt the number of items that the student is expected to learn or to complete.

G. Time—Adapt the time allotted for learning, task completion, or testing.

H. Input—Adapt the way instruction is delivered to the student.

I. Output—Adapt how the student can respond to instruction.

Days: Time	Subject	Modification	Adaptation
M W F: 10:30–11:15	Math	A	Resource room for remediation on M W F 10:30–11:15
		B	Expected to complete computation problems only
		E	Visual model is provided on how to solve computations; visual prompts added to problems
T Th: 2:00–2:40	Language Arts	A	Resource room for remediation T Th 2:00–2:40
		B	Expected to tell ideas to teacher assistant, who will write them for later computer entry
		C	Has a teacher assistant
		I	Uses computer to write answers

Figure 3.5. Hypothetical plan describing the modifications of the curriculum in math and language arts for a child with autism (Robert).

that point. Difficult work is associated with poor academic performance and also an increase in problem behaviors (e.g., Weeks & Gaylord-Ross, 1981). There are a number of strategies that can be used to make work in the general curriculum less difficult for children with autism: (a) Lessen the amount of work, (b) intersperse reviews of previously learned material when presenting new material, (c) increase pacing, (d), provide a choice, and (e) add prompts. Each of these strategies is described below.

- ***Lessen the amount of work***—A child with autism may be assigned the same learning activities as the rest of the class, but be expected to complete less of it. For example, rather than completing six questions assigned from a spelling workbook, the child with autism may be asked to complete only the first three questions. Similarly, if a child with autism in a Grade 1 class has difficulty sitting during a 30-minute lesson, he or she may be expected to participate only for the first 15 minutes of a lesson and then return to his or her desk to begin completing a seatwork assignment.

• **Intersperse reviews**—The difficulty of an activity may be lessened by interspersing a review of previously learned material into that new activity (Harrower & Dunlap, 2001). For example, if a child is about to be presented with single-digit division (e.g., 8 ÷ 2 = _____), the assignment may be modified so that half of the problems consist of single-digit multiplication questions that the child has previously mastered. A study using a similar strategy was described by Neef, Iwata, and Page (1977), who found that interspersing known words with unknown words facilitated the acquisition and retention of spelling and reading for six adolescents with developmental disabilities.

• **Increase pacing**—A child's performance in an activity may be affected by the pace at which the information is presented. For instance, Dunlap, Dyer, and Koegel (1983) found that when the interval between instruction was brief (4 seconds or less), there was an increase in correct responding and a decline in stereotypic behavior for a group of children with autism, aged 6 to 11 years, compared to their behavior under slower paced conditions.

• **Provide a choice**—Children with autism have been shown to improve their performance on tasks when they are given choice over which activities to complete from a limited set of options (Dyer, Dunlap, & Winterling, 1990). Typically, my team gives students with autism a choice over two matters when providing instruction: (a) the order in which they will attempt the work activities that we have prepared and (b) what will be used as backup reinforcement for their work performance. The work is divided into small units and a one- to three-word description is written on a label. The labels for the upcoming week are shown on a display with a column labeled To Do and another labeled Done. The child is shown the labels for the three or four upcoming work units that are displayed under the To Do heading attached by Velcro and asked to pick which work he or she wants to do. The child then removes that label and places it on the work table. After that work is finished, the child places the text label on the display under the heading Done and then picks the next work unit from those remaining under To Do. This pattern continues until the child completes the three or four work units, and then the child typically receives a brief break.

• **Add prompts**—Another strategy to make the instructional material easier is to add prompts. A prompt is a cue introduced to a learning situation that increases the likelihood that the child will respond correctly (Cooper, Heron, & Howard, 2007). More on prompting procedures and prompt fading will be discussed in the next chapter. Visual prompts can be embedded in the instructional material. For example, in *Teach Your Children to Read Well* (Maloney, Brearley, & Preece, 2001), the appearance of the letter *a* is modified to assist children in learning that *a* can make different sounds, depending on the word in which it appears. For example, the letter *a* in the word *late* would be written as "ā." The letter *a* in the word *and* would be written as "a." Later, the visual prompt of the bar above the letter *a* in some words is removed.

Another prompting procedure that can be used to assist children with autism is to learn the sounds associated with individual letters and digraphs if they are already able to label the beginning sounds of words when presented with the corresponding picture. For example, if the child is able to say the sound /h/ when shown a picture of a hat, then line drawings of common objects that begin with that sound are superimposed on letters as visual prompts to assist the child in learning letter–sound associations. The child is asked to pronounce the corresponding sound when presented with the letter *h* with a line picture of a hat superimposed on the letter. The letter *t* would have a picture of a tiger with arms extended over the letter. As the child learns to pronounce correctly the sound equivalent to letters with superimposed pictures, sections of the picture are systematically removed. For example, Figure 3.6 shows a picture of a hat superimposed over the letter *h*. A child would already know how to pronounce the beginning sound associated with this picture. After the child demonstrates that he or she can consistently make the sound /h/ when shown the picture on the far left in Figure 3.6, the child is then shown the next picture to the right, which has the letter *h* superimposed over a picture of the hat. As the child responds correctly to the superimposed stimuli, the picture is systematically removed in sections, as illustrated in Figure 3.6.

Larry: Example Modifications to a General Education Class Curriculum

Larry, who has autism, was attending a fourth-grade class and was about one grade behind the rest of the class, based on results of a standardized measure of academic achievement. He was having difficulty learning how to solve double-digit multiplication problems that involved carrying of digits. He was, however, able to complete multiplication problems to 20 and double-digit multiplication problems that did not involve carrying. The class expectation was to solve a page of multiplication problems from a math textbook. He was to copy each problem into his exercise book and to answer each problem on his own. His accuracy on this task was near zero.

The following adaptations were made:

Several multiplication problems were placed on a separate sheet with 10 problems to a sheet. A series of equivalent sheets were developed.

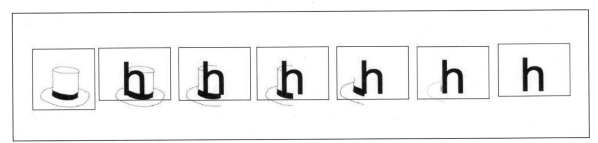

Figure 3.6. Example of a within-stimulus prompt sequence for teaching a child to say the sound associated with the letter *h*.

A mastery criterion of at least 9 out of 10 correct on a sheet without assistance was used. In addition, problems needed to be completed within 10 minutes.

The sheet contained a line drawing of an arrow showing where to start on the page. At the bottom right-hand corner of the page was a line drawing to cue the child to raise his hand when he finished the sheet.

Visual prompts were added to each problem to assist in the sequence of solving the multiplication with carrying, as shown in Figure 3.7.

The visual prompts guided Larry in the steps used to solve multiplication problems. His instructor modeled each step. She began with the multiplication of 7 × 6 with the answer placed in the first row below the problem. Then she did the multiplication of 7 × 3 and placed the answer in the second row. The numerals embedded in the arrows showed the sequence of steps for Larry to follow. Larry then was asked to add the two numbers together to derive the sum. Once Larry demonstrated mastery of this addition step, he was presented with the last step (summing the numbers) and the second-to-last step (multiplying the bottom number and the number in the tens column and placing the result in the second row. Over time, Larry was expected to complete more steps of solving these problems independently. At this point, the problems presented to Larry looked like the one shown in Figure 3.8. As can be seen, the results of each multiplication were removed. Larry was expected to follow the steps shown by the arrows: to multiply 7 × 6, write in the product, then multiply 7 × 3 and write in that product. Larry was then expected to add the two numbers together.

Backward chaining (Cooper et al., 2007) consists of teaching a task that is broken into a series of steps by performing or assisting the student with the initial steps and then teaching the student to perform the last step. Once mastered, the student is then taught the second-to-last step, and so on. For Larry, backward chaining was continued until he was able to solve a multiplication problem on his own.

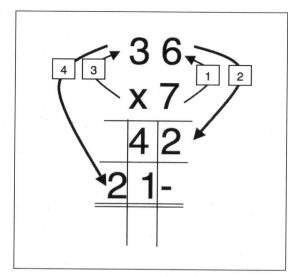

Figure 3.7. Example of visual prompts to help a child with autism to solve a multiplication problem with carrying.

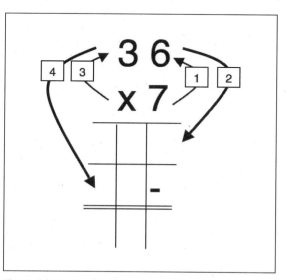

Figure 3.8. Example of Step 1 in fading the visual prompts to help a child with autism to solve a multiplication problem with carrying.

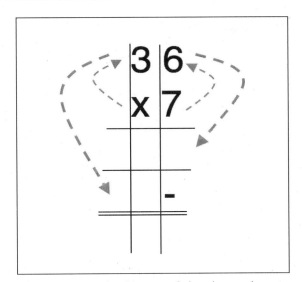

Figure 3.9. Example of Step 2 in fading the visual prompts to help a child with autism to solve a multiplication problem with carrying.

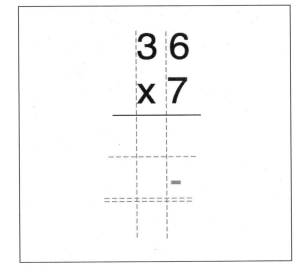

Figure 3.10. Example of Step 3 in fading the visual prompts to help a child with autism to solve a multiplication problem with carrying.

Next, the numbers embedded in the arrows to show Larry the sequence of steps were removed and the arrows were made fainter, as shown in Figure 3.9. The final step was to remove the arrows and to fade the lines that indicated the ones and tens columns, as shown in Figure 3.10. Subsequently those lines would be removed completely.

At each step, Larry was presented with a sheet of 10 problems selected at random from all possible double-digit multiplication problems with carrying. When Larry finished the page and raised his hand, he was given an answer sheet and red pen to self-correct. Each correct response was reinforced by receiving a point, which was accumulated and exchanged for preferred objects (e.g., snacks, trinkets) during breaks in the school day.

If Larry scored at least 90% of the problems on the sheet correctly within 8 minutes, he moved on to a more difficult step. If he failed to meet the mastery criterion on the worksheets, he would receive an equivalent version of the same type of problem (i.e., another set of multiplication problems with carrying selected at random from the universal set). If Larry failed to master this skill after four sheets, revisions to this strategy were introduced.

Adapting a Commercial Curriculum

A considerable amount of effort is needed to design a curriculum around a child with autism and to develop the associated instructional materials. In some circumstances, it might be easier to purchase a commercially available curriculum series than to develop the curriculum materials for a child with autism. In Appendix 3A, there is a description of five commercially available programs that I have found to be well designed.

The programs were selected because they had the following features considered critical for good programs:

- There is peer-reviewed research evidence supporting the effectiveness of the program or the general approach used in the program (e.g., direct instruction; Carnine, Silbert, Kameenui, Tarver, & Jong, 2006).
- The method of teaching is clearly laid out and includes how to deliver instructions, how to correct errors, and how to pace material.
- The scope and sequence of the instructional material is clearly laid out.
- The actual material is clear and appropriate for the objectives.

Yet, all of the five programs selected were lacking in some areas important for teaching a child with autism. All but one did not include mastery or revision criteria for a lesson. A child should not progress to the next instructional material until that individual child is able to demonstrate that he or she has mastered the objectives of the lesson (e.g., demonstrates a particular level of accuracy and/or fluency). Similarly, child performance criteria should be used to indicate when revision to the instructional program is needed. Another limitation found in all five of these instructional programs is that each was structured so that after initial placement in the series, a child would start at the beginning of the program material and progress to the end. There was no easy way of eliminating particular content if it was judged to be irrelevant for the child or if the child already possessed the skill being taught.

A second feature absent in all five programs was a way of quantifying and displaying a child's performance. A visual display of child performance would allow one to easily discern whether a child was learning at an acceptable rate. Thus, our team added a way for instructors to keep track of the child's performance every session. An example of the recording form we used for *Teaching Your Child to Read Well* is shown in Figure 3.11. The recording form has two sections. The first is the results of the child's rate of reading sounds, letters, words, and the story (i.e., number of correct responses per minute). We modified the mastery criteria to be easier for children with autism. For example, story-reading fluency was reduced to 125 words per minute, rather than the 200 words per minute suggested in the program. The second area on each recording form is for displaying data on the length of time it took a child to master each lesson. As shown in Figure 3.11, we recorded the number of 30-minute sessions that it took for the child to master each lesson. The first two lessons were mastered after one session; the third lesson took the child two sessions to master; the fourth lesson took five sessions to master, and so on.

In some of the programs, my colleagues and I have also had to simplify the language of instruction given to children with autism. For example, when an 11-year-old child with autism was learning *SRA Thinking Basic* (McGraw-Hill), we found that the program contained relatively complex verbal instructions, which the child's instructors were following word for word. Because this boy had difficulty understanding what the instructions meant, he began to throw the instructional material and hit the instructors. After simplifications to the instructions were made, no further aggression occurred.

The following is a list used to assist in selecting appropriate commercially available programs:

- There is peer-reviewed research evidence indicating that the program or the approach taken in the program is effective.
- The scope and sequence of the curriculum is appropriate for the child with autism.

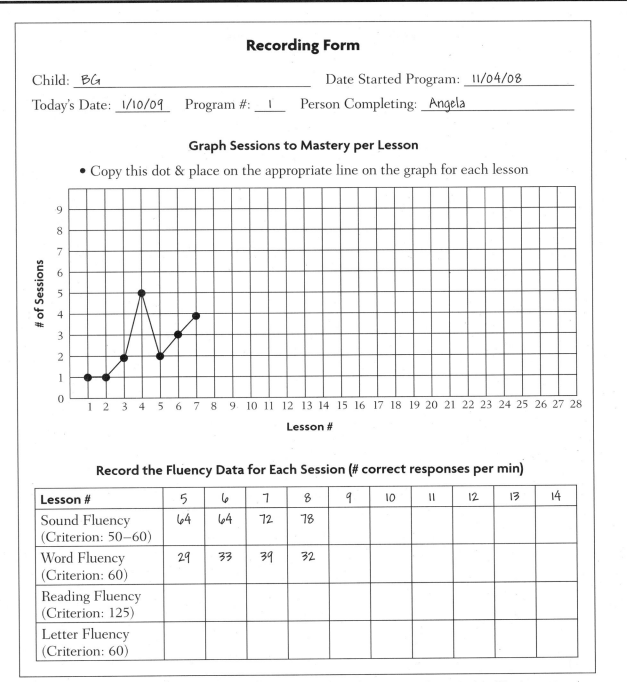

Recording Form

Child: BG   Date Started Program: 11/04/08

Today's Date: 1/10/09   Program #: 1   Person Completing: Angela

Graph Sessions to Mastery per Lesson

• Copy this dot & place on the appropriate line on the graph for each lesson

# of Sessions (y-axis, 0–9)

Lesson # (x-axis, 1–28)

Record the Fluency Data for Each Session (# correct responses per min)

Lesson #	5	6	7	8	9	10	11	12	13	14
Sound Fluency (Criterion: 50–60)	64	64	72	78						
Word Fluency (Criterion: 60)	29	33	39	32						
Reading Fluency (Criterion: 125)										
Letter Fluency (Criterion: 60)										

Figure 3.11. Recording form for tracking a child's performance on *Teaching Your Child to Read Well* (Maloney, Brearley, & Preece, 2001).

- There is an objective for each lesson.
- Mastery and revision criteria are set for each lesson.
- The sequence of material progresses in small steps and is logical.
- The content matches the curriculum expectations of the school.
- The method of teaching is clearly described, indicating how to deliver instructions, make corrections, and pace the material.
- The material is clear and appropriate for the curriculum.

Study Questions

1. What are embedded instructions?

2. Describe how you would design embedded instructions to teach a child with autism to solve single-digit addition problems who is attending a Grade 3 class.

3. How can the number of embedded instruction trials per day be increased to more than 15 per day?

4. Record the following results for the embedded instruction of telling time to 15 minutes: The child is presented with five different clock faces and is expected to name the correct timer. These are the results for one of the clock faces. Training started on May 22 with 0-second constant time delay. The child answered the first two trials incorrectly and then the next two correctly. Later that same day, the child was presented with the clock face with a 3-second constant time delay. The child was correct on the first trial, made an error on the second trial, and correctly answered the following two trials. On the following day, the same clock face was presented by a different person and the child answered correctly. Enter the results on the recording form below.

Date											
0 sec	✓ X	✓ X	✓ X	✓ X	✓ X	✓ X	✓ X	✓ X	✓ X	✓ X	✓ X
Date											
3 sec	✓ X	✓ X	✓ X	✓ X	✓ X	✓ X	✓ X	✓ X	✓ X	✓ X	✓ X

5. Describe individualized group instruction and contrast it with embedded instruction.

6. What are the four types of adaptations described by Anderson et al. (2003)?

7. Describe how one can use the amount of work, interspersed review, pacing, choice, and prompting to adapt a curriculum for a child with autism.

8. Describe how commercial curricula can be adapted for children with autism.

Five Recommended Commercially Available Curriculum Programs

Teach Your Child to Read Well   76

Saxon Math   77

Spelling Mastery   78

Thinking Basics   79

Reasoning and Writing   80

Program #1: *Teach Your Child to Read Well*

Author(s):	Michael Maloney
Publisher:	QLC Education Services, Belleville, Canada www.teachyourchildrenwell.ca
Instructional Materials:	Instructor manual, student workbook, student reader
Approximate Cost:	$74.95 Canadian for instructor manual, student reader, and student workbook
Series:	**Level 1A:** Grade K–Grade 2 (phonics and blending skills) **Level 1B:** Grade K–Grade 2 (beginning reading series) **Level 2:** Grade 3–Grade 4 **Level 3:** Grade 5–Grade 6 **Level 4:** Grade 7–Grade 8
Skills Taught:	Oral reading, spelling
Placement Test:	Yes
Scripted Lessons:	Yes
Described Scope & Sequence:	Yes
Format:	60 lessons to each level
Evaluation:	Fluency checks
Mastery Criteria:	None for the lessons; standards of 50–60 sounds/min, 60 words/min in word lists, and 200 words/min in story reading suggested
Revision Criteria:	None specified
Reinforcement Procedure:	Points based on rated performance at the end of each lesson
Error Correction Procedure:	Model–lead–test–repeat
Visual Display of Student Performance:	Fluency charts
Other Features:	Based on direct instruction Carefully worked out scope and sequence of curriculum Scripted teacher lessons

Program #2: *Saxon Math*

Author: Nancy Larson

Publisher: Saxon Publishers, Orlando, FL
http://saxonpublishers.harcourtachieve.com

Instructional Materials: Lesson materials, teacher's materials, workbook, classroom materials

Approximate Cost: $180 U.S. for teacher's manual; $30 U.S. for student workbook

Series: Grades K–3
Grades 4–5
Middle school
High school

Skills Taught: Mathematics

Placement Test: Yes

Scripted Lessons: Teacher behavior only

Described Scope & Sequence: Yes

Format: The meeting, the lesson, class practice, and written practice

Evaluation: None specified

Mastery Criteria: 80%

Revision Criteria: None specified

Reinforcement Procedure: None specified

Error Correction Procedure: None specified

Visual Display of Student Performance: None specified

Other Features: Covers elementary and secondary education

Program #3: *Spelling Mastery*

Authors:	Robert Dixon & Siegfried Engelmann
Publisher:	SRA McGraw-Hill, Columbus, OH www.sraonline.com
Instructional Materials:	Teacher presentation book, student workbook
Approximate Cost:	Teacher presentation book is about $111; student workbook is about $46 U.S.
Series:	Levels a–f
Skills Taught:	Approaches to spelling
Placement Test:	Yes
Scripted Lessons:	Yes
Described Scope & Sequence:	Yes
Evaluation:	End-of-program mastery test
Format:	Series of exercises for each lesson, student workbook
Mastery Criteria:	None specified
Revision Criteria:	None specified
Reinforcement Procedure:	A point system is described, but not built into the program
Error Correction Procedure:	Model–lead–test–delayed test
Visual Display of Student Performance:	None specified
Other Features:	• Based on direct instruction • Uses three approaches to spelling: whole-word, phonemic, and morphemic • Skills are taught in "tracks" • Web provides information on background research

Program #4: *Thinking Basics*

Authors:	Siegfried Englemann, Phyllis Haddox, Susan Hanner, & Jean Osborn
Publisher:	SRA McGraw-Hill, Columbus, OH www.sraonline.com
Instructional Materials:	Teacher materials, student book
Approximate Cost:	Teacher materials are about $180 U.S.; student book is about $48 U.S. for five
Series:	Level A of "Corrective Reading Comprehensive"
Skills Taught:	Recitation behavior, deductions, analogies, basic information, divergent reasoning skills, statement–inference skills, rule application skills, vocabulary skills. For children with at least Grade 4 level of academic skills in reading.
Placement Test:	Yes
Scripted Lessons:	Yes
Described Scope & Sequence:	Yes
Evaluation:	Mid-program and end-of-program Mastery Test
Format:	65 lessons Series of exercises for each lesson, student workbook
Mastery Criteria:	None specified
Revision Criteria:	None specified
Reinforcement Procedure:	Points awarded for performance
Error Correction Procedure:	Model–test–retest–delayed test
Visual Display of Student Performance:	None
Other Features:	Uses direct instruction

Program #5: *Reasoning and Writing*

Authors:	Siegfried Engelmann, Ann Brown Arbogast, & Karen Lou Seitz Davis
Publisher:	SRA McGraw-Hill, Columbus, OH www.sraonline.com
Instructional Materials:	Teacher presentation book, teacher's guide, answer key book, student workbooks
Approximate Cost:	$200 U.S.
Series:	Levels A–F
Skills Taught:	Story grammar, sequencing and spatial orientation, classification, following instructions and writing instructions, constructing deductions and drawing conclusions, clarity, time, rate and distance, perspectives, writing
Placement Test:	No
Scripted Lessons:	Yes
Described Scope & Sequence:	Yes
Format:	30–35 minutes for teacher-directed activities, 10–15 minutes for independent work
Evaluation:	7 test lessons
Mastery Criteria:	None specified
Revision Criteria:	None specified
Reinforcement Procedure:	None specified
Error Correction Procedure:	None specified
Visual Display of Student Performance:	None specified
Other Features:	• Provides suggestions for organization of the class • Specifies objectives

4 Principles of Instruction

Chapter Topics

- Prompts (types, hierarchies, and fading)
- Reinforcers (selecting reinforcers, using token systems)
- Error-correction procedures

Amy: Example Prompt, Reinforcer, and Error Correction Procedure

Amy is a 6-year-old girl with autism who attends a general education first-grade classroom and has the help of a paraprofessional. A number of learning activities have been developed for her. One is to work on her ability to pronounce printed words of three color names: *red, yellow,* and *blue.* Amy is already able to name these colors when presented with colored objects. To make the task easier for Amy, the paraprofessional printed the names of the colors in their corresponding color on index cards. The paraprofessional presents each card individually in a random order. If Amy reads the presented word correctly, she is praised enthusiastically and is given a one-half-inch-square picture of her favorite cartoon character to place on a 10-item token strip. (Amy has learned that when she accumulates 10 pictures, she will be able to exchange them for five small sour candies just before recess or lunch. Earlier in the day, Amy was given choices among three activities or objects she could earn when learning to read color words. She selected sour candies.) The paraprofessional then presents the next color word for Amy to read: *green.* Amy is somewhat distracted and does not give an answer. After 3 seconds with no response, the paraprofessional says, "Green," waits 2 seconds, and then says, "What is the name of this word?" while pointing to the word *green.* Amy then repeats, "Green." To be sure that Amy has attended to the word and is not just responding with imitations to the paraprofessional's model, the paraprofessional switches tasks and asks Amy questions about her age and where she lives. The paraprofessional then returns to present the word *green* for Amy to read. Amy reads the word correctly. The paraprofessional then praises Amy and moves on to presenting the word *blue* for Amy to read.

Sands, Kozleski, and French (2000), defined *curriculum* as the "what" of teaching and *instruction* as the "how" of teaching. The above illustration of Amy's learning of color words describes "how" she is being taught. The "what" of her teaching would include the instructional objective this program addresses and the sequence of instructional targets that led up to the current step, three-color words presented on index cards.

The "how's" of teaching can be analyzed into common components of instructional programs used with children with autism. The teacher's use of different colored markers to write the letters of the printed words presented to Amy is an example of a **prompt.** Amy was assisted in labeling the word correctly with the additional cue that she had previously learned—to name the color of objects. It is likely that at the beginning of this task, Amy was attending to the color of the words rather than to the letters themselves. However, over time, the color prompt would be gradually removed as Amy continued to read words correctly.

A prompt is presented before a child responds. If the response is correct, the child receives a preferred object or activity that increases the likelihood that the child will use that response in the future. Such items are called **reinforcers.** In the example above, Amy received small pictures that were later exchanged for a previously selected backup reinforcer (i.e., sour candies).

A third component of teaching illustrated in the example about Amy was the use of an **error correction procedure** after Amy failed to answer an item within

3 seconds. The paraprofessional modeled the correct response, asked Amy to copy that response, switched to a different activity, and then re-administered the same item again.

Prompts

Prompt Types

There are a number of different types of prompts that can be used in a teaching situation. Some are more effective than others for particular instructional targets and are presumably more effective with particular children. Some types of prompts are delivered directly by the instructor, rather than being built into the stimulus-discriminations that the child is making (e.g., *b* vs. *d* visual discrimination, adding numbers). Here are six types of prompts that may be helpful to use when teaching a child with autism:

- *Physical prompt*—The use of manual guidance to assist the child in correct responding
- *Gestural prompt*—The use of pointing to assist the child in correct responding
- *Verbal prompt*—The use of verbal response to assist the child in a correct response (e.g., saying the initial sound of a letter [saying, "rrrr"] as the teaching assistant points to a red object and expects the child to label the color)
- *Visual prompt*—The use of visual information to assist the child in a correct response (e.g., writing the printed color words in their respective colors to help Amy learn to name the color words)
- *Positional prompt*—The positioning of items in a way to assist the child in identifying the response (Typically, the correct item is positioned closer to the child, making it more likely the child would select it.)
- *Modeling*—The modeling of a correct response to the child prior to the child responding

In the example of teaching Amy to label color words, rather than the use of visual prompts, one could have used a verbal prompt, such as the paraprofessional saying the beginning sound of the word. Alternatively, a model of the correct response could have been used. Here, the paraprofessional would show the printed word, read it, and then ask Amy to read the presented word.

Physical and gestural prompts are most suited to learning motor tasks (e.g., shoe tying, handwriting, dressing) and are less suited for learning conceptual tasks (e.g., naming colors, completing math problems on a sheet). Children with autism have a tendency to overfocus on one feature of a stimulus in a multiple-stimulus presentation. This phenomenon is referred to as stimulus "over-selectivity" (Lovaas, Koegel, & Schreibman, 1979). When a child with autism is presented with a complex stimulus (e.g., a picture of a bird and a picture of a fork), the child will learn to discriminate that complex stimulus based on only one of the components (i.e., either the picture of the bird or the picture of the fork). In contrast, typically developing children tend to discriminate complex stimuli by attending to multiple stimuli. For example, a child with autism might be taught receptive discrimination of *big* and *small* by being presented with pairs of pictures showing two identical objects (e.g., balls), one bigger than the other. The instruction would be to touch either big or small. Successful learning of this task requires the child to attend to the relative size of one picture in the pair as compared to the other. In overselectivity, a child with autism might attend to only one of the two pictures in the pair and, as a result, fail to learn this discrimination.

Suppose one were to teach a child with autism to touch a picture of a pencil, when also presented with pictures of an airplane and a pair of scissors. If, as illustrated in Figure 4.1, the picture of the pencil were positioned closer to the child (positional prompt), the child would be more likely to touch the pencil when the instructor showed him or her a pencil. For the next trial, the order of the presented items would be randomized and a second of the three items would be presented. As the child continued on the task, the relative physical proximity of the target stimulus to the child would be gradually reduced until the positional prompt was entirely removed. The child with autism would likely correctly touch the picture of the pencil as long as its position was relatively closer to him or her than the other pictures were. However, once the positional prompt is completely removed, it is unlikely that the child will continue to respond correctly. Why would this be? In this situation, the correct response of the child with autism was likely under the stimulus control of the physical proximity of the pencil, rather than its visual properties. The child was likely attending to the physical proximity of the target stimulus, which, when removed at the end of the fading sequence, left the child at a loss of how to make a discrimination.

When teaching children with autism a similar task, as in matching one pencil to another pencil, Schreibman (1975) found that children with autism learned a discrimination task more easily if the prompts built into the stimulus presentation exaggerated the relevant component of the training stimulus, as opposed to having the prompt be external to the stimulus, such as the use of a gestural prompt, or a visual prompt that is not part of the stimulus presentation (e.g., a gesture from the instructor). An example of a within-stimulus prompt for teaching a child to match numerals 1 to 4 to an array of marks is shown in Figure 4.2. A child would be shown numerals 1, 2, 3, and 4 on cards placed faceup on a table and one of the arrays (e.g., two) of the smaller numerals. (Having the mark of the arrays composed of the target numeral would assist the child in answering correctly.) It would be likely that, initially, the child would match the small numeral on the array to the larger numeral presented on one of the four cards in front of him or her. The shape of the small numeral on the array would then be gradually

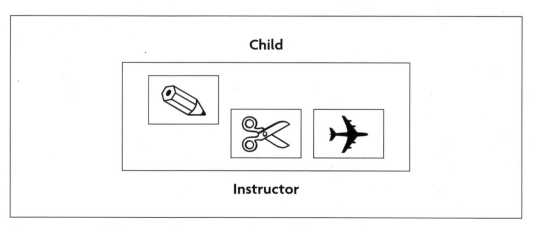

Figure 4.1. Example of a positional prompt in teaching a child receptive discrimination of *pencil, scissors,* and *airplane.* The picture of the pencil is positioned closer to the child than the pictures of the other two objects are.

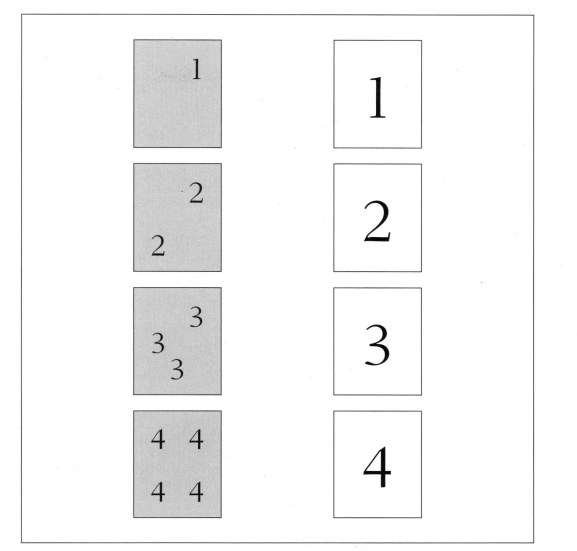

Figure 4.2. Example of stimulus shaping in teaching a child to match arrays of marks to the corresponding numerals.

changed over three steps to become a circle, as illustrated in Figure 4.3. The shapes of the markings on the other three cards would be faded in the same way. Please note that the position of the markings on the page change as well so that the child does not learn to make the discrimination by the position of the markings on the arrays.

Bailey and Wolery (1992) described two types of within-stimulus prompts: stimulus shaping and stimulus fading. **Stimulus shaping** consists of selecting a critical feature of the target stimulus that is necessary for the discrimination and then exaggerating it in the initial presentations. For example, in discrimination of circles from ovals, the shape of the stimuli is critical for the learning. In stimulus shaping, the circle is presented, but initially, instead of an oval, the child is shown a square to differentiate from the circle, with the assumption that it would be easier for the child to discriminate between a circle and a square than to do so when presented with a circle and an oval. Over time, as the child correctly responds, the shape of the square is gradually modified to appear closer and closer to that of an oval, as shown in Figure 4.4

Stimulus fading consists of exaggerating a feature of the target stimulus that is irrelevant for the discrimination. In the same example of circle–oval discrimination,

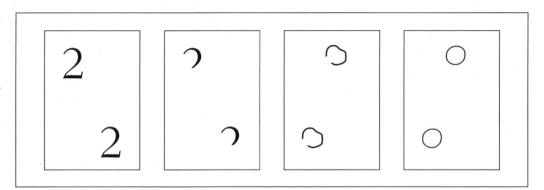

Figure 4.3. Example sequence of fading the form of the visual prompt from a numeral to a circle.

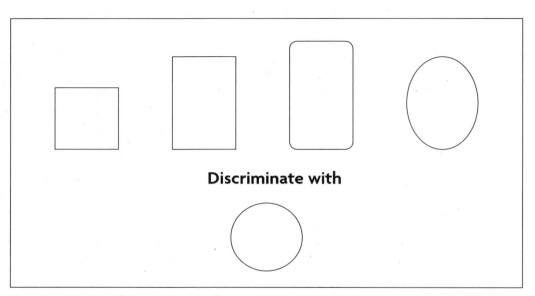

Discriminate with

Figure 4.4. Example of stimulus shaping of a square to an oval.

one can make the oval larger and gradually reduce its size. The size of the oval is an irrelevant feature for the discrimination—the shape of the figure is what is critical. Alternatively, one can add color and texture to the oval, and once the child responds correctly, gradually fade out the colors.

The example used in Figure 4.2 is an example of stimulus shaping. The prompting strategy consisted of manipulating the critical feature (i.e., the number of marks) that distinguished the stimuli. This example used a task that involved matching one visual stimulus (i.e., a number array) to a second visual stimulus (i.e., a printed numeral).

How would one plan the use of within-stimulus prompts for matching a spoken word to a picture? For example, suppose you have already taught a child with autism to touch one picture of his father, mother, and brother with another picture of the same person. Next, you would introduce a task in which the child would touch a picture of a relative when the person is named. The challenge in moving from a visual–visual matching task to matching an auditory stimulus (e.g., "Mommy") to a visual stimulus (e.g., a picture of the child's mother) is for the child with autism to attend to the auditory information and then point to the corresponding picture. At this point in the child's learning, errors would not likely be due to a confusion of the visual discrimination of one picture from the other since this skill was already mastered by the child prior to teaching auditory–visual discriminations. The errors are more likely to be found in the connection between the sound of the word *mommy* and the picture of the child's mother. A prompt, if used, would help the child discriminate among the sounds of the words rather than the visual properties of the pictures.

Digitized auditory recordings can be made of each of the three relatives pronouncing their identity (e.g., the child's father would say, "Daddy"). The child would first learn to match the sound of the family member saying his or her name with the corresponding picture. The unique sound of the person saying his or her own identity would serve as a within-stimulus prompt in learning to touch the picture corresponding with the label. Our team has used computer software to teach this type of task. Once the child has learned to match the sound of a relative pronouncing his or her identity with its corresponding picture, the instructor would present the same task by first stating the label followed 3 seconds later with the audio recording of the family member. The family member sound would also be presented more faintly. Gradually, the interval between the instructor's delivered label and the digitized sound of the relative's name would increase. Eventually, the learner would hear the sound of the instructor labeling the picture without the presentation of the family members' voices.

Prompt Hierarchies

In general, physical and gestural prompts may be the most appropriate types of prompts to use when teaching motor responses that do not require a high degree of stimulus discrimination (e.g., shoe tying, dressing, handwriting). Within-stimulus prompts may be the most effective type of prompt to use when teaching discrimination (e.g., matching lowercase to uppercase letters, pronouncing the sounds of letters, computing addition problems). The selection of the type of prompts is determined by the nature of the activity being taught and the responsivity of the child. But how do you know how much of a prompt to use and how to organize the delivery of prompts?

Two other important decisions about prompting must be made: Within a hierarchy of possible prompts, how do you know (a) where to start prompting with a child and (b) how to fade prompts? One approach is to develop a prompt hierarchy that progresses in intensity. For example, one can develop the following hierarchy of physical prompts to assist a child to put on his or her coat independently:

1. *Full physical prompt*—Hand-over-hand assistance
2. *Partial physical prompt 1*—Lighter force; the physical prompt consists of guiding the child's elbow rather than the child's hand
3. *Partial physical prompt 2*—Lesser degree of prompts with less force, and guidance given to the child's upper arm
4. *Partial physical prompt 3*—A light nudge to the elbow
5. *Gestural prompt*—Pointing to the article of clothing

This hierarchy of physical prompts is also referred to as *graduated guidance* (Cooper, Heron, & Heward, 2007). The following is a second example of a prompt hierarchy, but one that may be used to teach the spelling of a set of five words:

Prompt 1: The child is presented with the words to spell on a sheet of paper with the target word presented at the top. Below it, the target word is missing the last letter.

Prompt 2: After learning the discrimination at the initial level of prompting, the word is presented with two letters missing at the end. As the child continues to learn, progressively more letters of the word are removed one by one (see Figure 4.5).

A prompt hierarchy can be designed with the progression varying along one dimension, as illustrated in Figure 4.5, or prompt hierarchies may be arranged with the progression reflecting changes in a number of stimulus dimensions. Figure 4.6 shows an example of a prompt hierarchy for teaching a child who is already able to label pictures how to read individual words, in this case a picture of a dog. In the highest level of prompting, the word is presented below a picture of a dog. The child labels the combined picture and text stimulus as "dog." After the child achieves performance criteria for this level of prompting, the level of prompt is reduced by removing details (the first dimension) from the picture of the dog. In the subsequent prompt step, the picture is made smaller (the second dimension). The fourth prompt step consists of the removal of the picture altogether.

cattle

cattl_

catt_ _

cat_ _ _

ca_ _ _ _

c_ _ _ _ _

_ _ _ _ _ _

_____

Figure 4.5. Prompt-fading sequence for teaching the spelling of the word *cattle*.

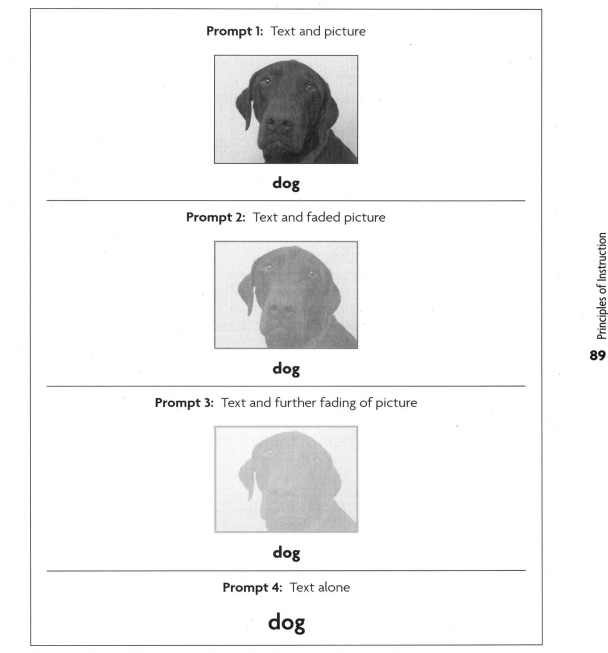

Figure 4.6. Prompt-fading sequence for teaching the reading of the word *dog*.

Most-to-Least and Least-to-Most Prompting

It is not always evident at what level in a prompt hierarchy to start teaching a particular skill to a child. One should start with the least intensive level of prompting that would be effective and then fade the degree of the prompt from that point on. There are two ways of determining this starting point, depending on how one wants to err.

A prompt hierarchy can be implemented starting at the highest level of prompting on the hierarchy and moving to lesser degrees of prompting as the child progresses. This strategy is referred to as **most-to-least prompting** and would be used when the child is not able to perform almost any aspects of the task being taught. As the child is successful, the intensity of the prompting is lessened, following the hierarchy that was developed.

In contrast, **least-to-most prompting** consists of starting at the lowest level of the prompt hierarchy and increasing the amount of prompts until the child is unsuccessful in responding correctly. Least-to-most prompting would be used when the child is able to perform some of the skill being taught.

Both least-to-most and most-to-least prompting are based on progressing along a prompt hierarchy. Least-to-most prompting starts in the low end of the continuum of intensity and moves to more intensive prompts as the child learns and follows the steps in the prompt hierarchy. Most-to-least prompting starts on the high end of the prompt hierarchy and moves to less intensive forms of prompts after successful responding of the child.

Time Delay Prompting

Another way of arranging the degree of prompting is by introducing a time delay in the delivery of the prompt. Two types of delayed prompting are (a) constant time delay and (b) progressive time delay (Ault, Gast, & Wolery, 1988). In both types of delay of prompting, the child is presented with a natural cue to which the child should be responding eventually without a prompt, such as, "What color?" when asking a child to label the color of indicated objects. Another example would be, "Touch the frog," in a task of receptive discrimination of pictures. In **constant time delay,** a fixed time interval (e.g., 3 seconds) is set between the natural cue and the prompt that initially controls the child's response. Here, is an example of a 3-second constant time delay:

> INSTRUCTOR: *What color is this? (Wait 3 seconds.) Blue.*
> CHILD: *Blue.*

It is expected that over time, the child would respond prior to the controlling prompt being delivered. Initially there would be a 0-second delay, with a cue and prompt presented at the same time. For example:

> INSTRUCTOR: *What color is this? Blue.*
> CHILD: *Blue.*

The child is expected to imitate the controlling prompt. Once the child makes a specific mastery criterion (e.g., three consecutive correct responses), the fixed delay in the delivery of the prompt would increase (e.g., to 3 seconds).

In **progressive time delay,** rather than have a fixed delay between the natural cue and the controlling prompt, the lag between the cue and the prompt progressively increases. In a stepwise progression, the interval is increased gradually between the natural cue and the controlling prompt (e.g., to 0.5 seconds, 1 second, 2 seconds, and so on). Progressive time delay was found to produce fewer errors than least-to-most prompting did in teaching four children with autism (Doyle, Wolery, Gast, & Ault, 1990). Moreover, the progressive time delay also was associated with lower rates of disruptive behavior.

The majority of research studies that have been completed on embedded instruction have used constant time delay procedures. For example, Riesen, MacDonald, Johnson, Polychronis, and Jameson (2003) used constant time delay to teach four children with moderate to severe disabilities to read a series of words. A paraprofessional presented each word on a flash card and immediately modeled the correct response

(0-second constant time delay). The student was expected to imitate the model provided by the paraprofessional and, if correct, was praised. If the student did not imitate the model or gave some other response, the paraprofessional labeled the error, repeated the prompt, and asked the child to imitate the model. The child was given feedback (e.g., "Good job") if he or she imitated the model. A 0-second delay was used until the student read all five words with the model on two consecutive presentations. Then, the paraprofessionals gave the natural cue ("Read this word"), waited 3 seconds, and then modeled the correct response. The child was reinforced for correct responding within the 3-second interval. If the child made an error, the same correction procedures as under the 0-second delay condition were used.

Prompt Fading

Prompts aid a child in correct responding to presented tasks. If they are not removed at some point, they can result in a child's being unable to respond correctly unless the prompt is in place, a situation referred to as "prompt dependency." Children with autism need to be able to complete learning activities with little or no prompting in order to function successfully in natural settings. Because of the goal of inclusion, prompts when introduced need to be faded once a child is responding correctly. Prompts can be faded along at least two or three dimensions: the amount of a prompt provided, the delay of presenting the prompt, and the location of the prompter.

In most instances, one can fade a prompt by systematically reducing the amount of prompt that is used. For example, in physical prompting of a child to print letters, one can move from a full physical prompt (e.g., hand-over-hand) to one level of partial physical prompting (e.g., hand-over-wrist) to a lesser level of a physical prompt (e.g., hand-over-forearm). Similarly, one can reduce a full verbal prompt to assist a child in learning to label the color red (e.g., saying "rrr" in a normal voice) to a partial verbal prompt (e.g., saying "rrr" in a whisper voice). The amount of prompt can be faded in similar ways for visual prompting, modeling, and other types of prompts as well.

In addition to fading prompts by reducing the amount of a prompt that is used, one can also fade prompts by increasing the delay between presenting the instructional stimulus (e.g., showing a flashcard of a word to read) and the delivery of a prompt (e.g., the instructor whispering the initial sound of the word). A time delay prompt was described in the use of embedded instruction.

If prompts to a child with autism are delivered by a person such as a paraprofessional who may be sitting beside the child with autism in a classroom, prompts can also be faded by increasing the distance between the paraprofessional and the child with autism. Initially, the paraprofessional may be located beside the child, but over time, move to be located right behind the child, then one meter behind, three meters behind, and then within 10 meters.

Prompts can be faded by a combination of amount, delay, and location of the prompter (if applicable) in a step-by-step sequence that is developed specifically for an individual child with autism in a particular situation. The criterion for fading prompts from one level to a lesser level of prompts should be based on the performance of the child. For instance, one may create a five-step prompt-fading sequence such as that shown in Table 4.1.

Figure 4.7 summarizes the types of prompts, prompt hierarchy, and prompt fading that were discussed in this section. Prompts and prompt fading are one of the most important behavior change procedures to help children with autism in a general education setting.

Table 4.1
Sample of a Prompt-Fading Sequence

	Prompt-fading dimensions		
Step	Amount of prompt	Delay of prompt	Location of prompter
1	Full verbal	0 sec	Beside
2	Full verbal	1 sec	Right behind
3	Partial verbal	1 sec	Right behind
4	Partial verbal	3 sec	1 m behind
5	Partial verbal	5 sec	3 m behind

Note. Potentially, different prompt-fading plans for a child with autism would need to be developed for each curriculum area in which the child is being prompted.

Reinforcers

Why should one expect a child with autism to perform academic work, to listen to a lesson being presented in class, or to line up quietly to go outside for recess? Pleasing the teacher, the paraprofessional, or other adults or gaining acceptance from peers may not be important motivators for a child with autism. Some children with autism engage in stereotypic behaviors (e.g., repetitive hand movements, humming, staring at lights) that compete with their ability to attend to information around them. For this reason, an important component of learning for a child with autism is the use of effective feedback following correct performance that tells the child exactly what he or she did correctly and motivates the child to use the correct response in the future. A reinforcer is an activity or object that is delivered after a behavior and increases the future occurrence of that behavior (Cooper et al., 2007). It is important to note that, by definition, an activity or object is not a reinforcer unless, in practice, it is effective in increasing the future occurrence of the behavior it follows. A reinforcer is defined by its effect on behavior. In other words, it is not sufficient to assume that giving a child access to his or her preferred toys will serve as a reinforcer unless the use of toys is shown to actually change behaviors.

Selecting Reinforcers

One of the challenges of treating children with autism is the difficulty in finding reinforcers that can be effective in helping the children to learn (Charlop-Christy & Haymes, 1998). Children with autism may not respond to stimuli that serve as reinforcers for other children, such as praise or stickers. For example, Charlop, Kurtz, and Casey (1990) showed that allowing a child with autism time to engage in self-stimulation contingent on correct responses was more effective than using edibles in increasing the child's correct performance. No adverse side effects (e.g., increasing the child's base rate of self-stimulation) were found to follow the use of access to self-stimulation as a reinforcer.

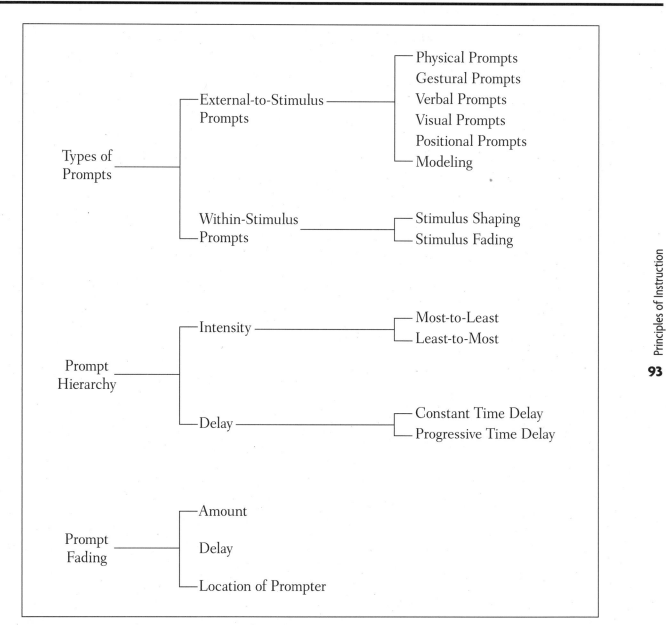

Figure 4.7. Summary of prompt types, prompt hierarchy, and prompt fading.

Care must be taken in selecting potential reinforcers. There are three basic methods of determining potential reinforcers for a child. The simplest method is **observation.** Simply observe what the child does and look for the types of objects or play activities the child selects. These items may be potential reinforcers.

A second method of identifying potential reinforcers is the use of a **questionnaire,** in which someone who knows the child rates the degree to which the child prefers a list of activities, edibles, objects, and so on. The survey can be completed by a number of individuals who know the child well. Reinforcer surveys are relatively easy to complete, but have the risk of potential inaccuracy of the rater (Green, Reid, White, Halford, Brittain, & Gardner, 1988).

The preferred way of identifying potential reinforcers is by conducting a **stimulus preference assessment.** There are a number of methods for conducting a stimulus preference assessment. All of them consist of presenting the child with a choice of presented stimuli (Roane, Vollmer, Ringdahl, & Marcus, 1998). The selection of potential reinforcers is determined by examining the child's pattern of choice (DeLeon & Iwata, 1996; Windsor, Piche, & Locke, 1994). This method is referred to as "stimulus preference" assessment because the assessment probes the child's preference for represented stimuli, which at the point of assessment have not been demonstrated to act as reinforcers (i.e., to increase the behavior they follow).

One method of stimulus preference assessment is a multiple-stimulus without replacement (MSWO) preference assessment (Carr, Nicolson, & Higbee, 2000), in which the child is given choices among a number of highly preferred presented stimuli. This method has been found to be relatively brief to conduct (less than 1 hour per child) and results in determining stimuli that later produce more behavior increases than lower preferred stimuli do for children with autism (Carr et al., 2000). The MSWO method of stimulus preference assessment is conducted as follows:

1. Potential reinforcers to be assessed are first nominated by the child's parents, teachers, or anyone else who knows the child well. A reinforcer survey may be given to nominators to aid in their identification of potential reinforcers. A maximum of eight potential reinforcers are selected.
2. In a room free from distraction, the eight stimuli are placed on a table in front of the child. There is a clear visual representation (e.g., an empty package of potato chips) behind the actual item (e.g., a plate with one potato chip). For activities (e.g., bouncing on a small trampoline), a picture to represent that item is used. Previously, it would have been shown that the child is able to associate the picture with the activity itself (i.e., a verbal child can label the picture and is able to verbally request the activity; a nonverbal child can exchange the picture for the activity).
3. The child is brought into the room and shown each of the potential reinforcers by labeling the item and giving the child a small sample.
4. The child is taken to a location approximately 5 feet from the table of potential reinforcers and is instructed to select one item.
5. The child is escorted as he or she selects a potential reinforcer to ensure that only one sample is selected. The child is allowed to consume the selected edible or to engage in the selected activity for 10 seconds. The child's selection is recorded and the item is removed from the table to determine the child's other preferences.
6. The child is returned to the starting point, and the procedure is continued until all items have been selected. This procedure is repeated two more times.
7. The number of times an item was selected is divided by the number of trials in which it was available, to derive a percent score. Items are then rank-ordered.
8. The stimulus preference assessment is repeated periodically to see if the child's preferences have changed.

Remember that the "acid test" of identifying potential reinforcers is whether the potential reinforcer actually changes behavior.

Not only is it important to select potential reinforcers that work, but it is also important to deliver reinforcers effectively. The principles of reinforcer delivery are as follows:

- *Make the reinforcement contingent*—The reinforcer should be delivered only after the child has exhibited the targeted behavior being reinforced.

- *Thin reinforcement*—Reinforce new behaviors often, and gradually thin the schedule of reinforcement as the child becomes more proficient.

- *Pair tangible reinforcement with descriptive praise*—Describe the behavior that is praiseworthy (e.g., "Wow! You came to sit when I asked"). Obviously, the form of praise needs to be geared to the situation and to the child.

- *Reinforce immediately*—Reinforcement has the greatest effect when delivered immediately following the target behavior. As the child learns the behavior, delay in the delivery of the reinforcement can be introduced.

- *Be enthusiastic*—Most children with autism, but not all, respond well to an animated and enthusiastic delivery of reinforcement.

- *Offer choices*—Have the child make choices from a few reinforcers.

Using Token Systems

With young children with autism, our team usually starts by using tangibles (e.g., edibles, activities) as reinforcers based on the results of a stimulus preference assessment. However, we move as quickly as we can to introduce tokens that the child earns and later exchanges for a selected backup reinforcer. Two significant advantages of the use of tokens are as follows:

- *Portability*—It is easy to carry tokens from place to place, whereas carrying edibles or toys can be much more cumbersome.

- *Ease of thinning out*—It is relatively easy to thin the schedule of reinforcement using tokens. We usually start with a token strip with five spaces for tokens. Later the child moves to a 10-space token strip. Because the backup reinforcer is not received immediately, tokens may help the child delay receiving a reinforcement and help in the gradual removal of tangibles.

Steps in Setting Up a Token System

The particular form of tokens is individualized for each child. Charlop-Christy and Haymes (1998) showed that using the object of an obsession of the child with autism (e.g., using a picture of a train) as tokens was more effective in reducing inappropriate behavior and in increasing correct performance than was using typical items as tokens (e.g., stars and happy faces). Our team usually selects pictures of objects or cartoon characters in which the child is interested to act as tokens. (If the child does not show a clear preference for a picture that can be used for tokens, we tend to use pennies because of their convenience.)

Behind each token is a piece of Velcro that allows the token to be secured to a token strip, as illustrated in Figure 4.8. The setup contains spaces for the tokens, in this case five, and at the end of the tokens, a picture of the selected backup reinforcer is placed to remind the child of what he or she is working for when the corresponding

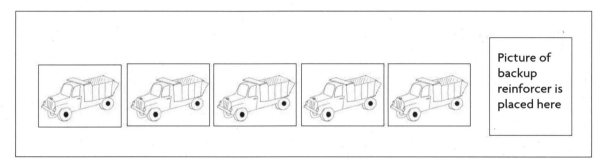

Figure 4.8. Example of a five-space token strip.

number of tokens are accumulated. The child then exchanges the picture of the object/activity for the sample of the real thing.

When beginning a token system for a child, we start with four of the five tokens already placed on the token strip. The child then only needs to earn one token, place the token on the remaining space on the token strip, take the picture of the backup reinforcer off the strip, and give it to the instructor to receive the backup reinforcer.

Disadvantages of a Token System

There are two major disadvantages of attempting to introduce a token system in a general education classroom for a child with autism. The first disadvantage is that time is needed to maintain the token system. Someone must conduct a stimulus preference assessment, select what form the tokens will take, create the tokens, create a token strip, arrange for backup reinforcers, and deliver the tokens. However, with so much evidence demonstrating the effectiveness of token systems in improving the academic performance (Eikeseth & Jahr, 2001) and appropriate behavior (Volkert, Lerman, & Vorndran, 2005) of children with autism, schools may be willing to accept these inconveniences if a paraprofessional or another individual is available to maintain the token system.

The second major disadvantage of the token system in a general education classroom is the potential reactivity of classmates to the child with autism receiving tokens and backup reinforcement that they are not receiving. Explaining to the class that the child with autism has special needs requiring special treatment may minimize some of this reactivity. Similarly, less reactivity would likely occur by having the child with autism exchange tokens for backup reinforcers only at the beginning of natural breaks in the day, such as at recess or at lunch. A third solution is to introduce a token system for the entire class. The token system described for the child with autism is one based on an individual contingency and individual payoff. That is, tokens are delivered based on the behavior of an individual child with autism, and the payoff of the backup reinforcer is given to the same child for tokens that were earned. It is possible to set up a classroom token system based on individual contingency and a group payoff or a group contingency and a group payoff. An individual contingency–group payoff token system consists of having tokens earned by individual children in the class based on their conduct or work. The earned tokens by the individuals are accumulated and exchanged for a reward that the entire class receives.

For example, I saw a wonderfully organized general education fourth-grade classroom in which the teacher created 1 in. by 6 in. strips of paper in red or green. On the red slips of paper were various praise statements about a student's schoolwork (e.g.,

"You are working hard" or "Great work"). The green slips of paper contained various praise statements about a child's conduct in the classroom (e.g., "I like the way you are behaving" or "Great paying attention"). The teacher would carry these slips of paper during the day and, without fanfare, give them to individual students when the teacher noticed good behavior and/or good working. Just before lunch break and just before home dismissal, each student who received one or more strips of paper from the teacher wrote his or her name on the paper strip and then glued it into a circle linking to a "chain" of other strips earned by students in the classroom. The students had previously selected a reward for the entire class (e.g., watching a videotape) that would be received when the chain of paper strips reached from the back of the classroom to the front. Tokens were delivered to individual students based on their individual performance, but the payoff of the backup reinforcer was delivered to the entire class.

Even easier to manage is a token system that involves giving tokens to the entire class contingent on the performance of the entire class (group contingency and group payoff). For example, the teacher may reward the entire class for lining up quietly to go outside for recess or for being actively engaged on task when a timer sounds set at random intervals. The class as a unit is given tokens (e.g., points) that are accumulated and later exchanged for a selected backup reinforcer (e.g., playing a class game, watching a video, having a pizza party). Both of these types of class token systems would make it easier for an individual token system to be used with a child who has autism.

Error-Correction Procedures

Reinforcement increases the likelihood of the behavior it follows. Therefore, it is important to use reinforcement to increase correct schoolwork and positive school conduct. One also needs to have a way of dealing with errors in the performance of children with autism so that the child learns from mistakes and is less likely to make the same error in the future. Error correction procedures are specifically designed for a particular child in a learning situation and may consist of the following:

- If possible, interrupt the error before it is fully completed (e.g., redirect a child's hand from touching an incorrect comparison stimulus).
- Do not deliver reinforcement following an error.
- Model the correct response.
- Re-administer the same item with an increased level of prompts, followed by a more moderate form of reinforcement (e.g., praise rather than praise plus a token) if a child responds correctly.

Suppose a child with autism is being taught to touch one of three pictures of animals when the corresponding name is stated (e.g., "dog"). Instead of touching the picture of a dog, the child touches the picture of an elephant or does not respond within 3 seconds. The instructor takes the child's hand and touches the dog picture while saying, "This is dog." The order of the three pictures is mixed, and, as part of the same correction procedure, the child with autism is again asked to touch the picture of a dog. If the child is correct, he or she is praised but does not receive a token. If the child still makes an error, more substantive revisions to the program would need to be made (e.g., increasing the level of prompts in the task). In this example, an increased level of prompting could look as follows:

INSTRUCTOR: *Ready?*

CHILD: *(Sits up straight and looks at the instructor.)*

INSTRUCTOR: *(Holds up a second picture of a dog for 1 second and then hides it.)*

INSTRUCTOR: *(Waits 3 seconds.) Dog.*

CHILD: *(Touches the picture of the dog.)*

The same components of error correction would be used in an assignment sheet or homework assignment. The error correction procedure would be introduced typically after the child has completed the entire assignment. For items with errors, the instructor would model the correct response and have the child repeat the item again. As in the previous example, if the child still makes errors, revisions to the program—and, in particular, increasing the level of prompting—would be examined.

Study Questions

1. What is a prompt?

2. Describe the following types of prompts: physical, gestural, verbal, visual, positional, modeling.

3. Why is the use of a positional prompt to teach a child to touch one of three named objects likely ineffective?

4. Describe stimulus fading and stimulus shaping.

5. Generate a prompt hierarchy for helping a child to form letters correctly.

6. What is the difference between most-to-least prompting and least-to-most prompting?

7. What is the difference between constant and progressive time delay?

8. What are three dimensions along which prompts may be able to be faded?

9. Describe the "multiple stimulus without replacement" method of stimulus preference assessment.

10. Describe how one can set up a token system for an entire class.

5 Facilitating the Communication of a Child With Autism in a General Education Setting

Chapter Topics

- Augmentative and alternative communication (sign language and the Picture Exchange Communication System)

- Communication interventions (mass-trial and incidental language instruction)

D eficits in communication skills is one of the cardinal diagnostic features of autism (DSM-IV; American Psychiatric Association, 2000). Children with autism not only have quantitative deficits in communication (i.e., they have delays in language development), but they also have qualitative impairments in their language development, including poor quality of voice production (i.e., prosody), weakness in the social use of language (i.e., pragmatics), among others. These deficits in language development are so profound that about half of children with autism never develop functional communication skills and the rest have significant language deficits (Charlop-Christy & Kelso, 2003). Deficits in language skills affect the development of children with autism in many other domains, such as play skills, preacademic skills, and prosocial behaviors (Taylor & Carr, 1992; Wetherby & Prizant, 1993). Also, children with deficits in communication ability tend to have a heightened risk for developing problem behaviors (Durand & Crimmons, 1988). With a weakness in expressing themselves, children with autism might learn to use problem behavior (e.g., hitting) to meet particular social needs (e.g., to escape from completing difficult schoolwork). This chapter will discuss issues about improving the communication of children with autism and describe ABA-based procedures for doing so in inclusive educational settings.

Augmentative and Alternative Communication

Because of the significant and often long-lasting problems in the communication abilities of children with autism, it may be suggested that the student use an alternative communication system to speech production. I have found that the AAC that a child with autism receives is typically selected by the time most children with autism reach kindergarten age. In my experience, communication systems are introduced at a clinic or in a special preschool setting. Although elementary schools may not be involved in initially setting up a communication system such as PECS, they are frequently involved in using it with individual children with autism (e.g., Johnston, McDonnell, & Magnavito, 2003).

There are several forms of augmentative and alternative communication (AAC), including picture-pointing systems and electronic voice output devices (Johnston et al., 2003). However, the two forms of AAC often considered for use with young children with autism are sign language and the Picture Exchange Communication System (PECS; Bondy & Frost, 1994). Teaching signing or PECS has two main goals (Tincani, 2004). One goal is that as a result of being taught a communication system, the child with autism would use the communication system to convey his or her wishes, thoughts, and feelings. The second goal of teaching signing or PECS is that in the process of learning an alternative way of communicating, there would be an improvement in the child's speech production.

Sign Language

There have been only a couple of studies that have attempted to directly compare the effectiveness of PECS and signs (Adkins & Axelrod, 2001; Tincani, 2004), and these have been limited by the small number of children participating in the comparison. Adkins and Axelrod found that PECS took fewer trials to learn than signs did and were used in more settings than were signs. Tincani found that of the two children who participated in the study, one learned PECS more quickly and the other learned signs more quickly (the child who showed faster acquisition with PECS had poor hand-motor development). Interestingly, both children showed more spontaneous spoken language with PECS than with signs. More comparison studies on PECS and signs are needed before firm conclusions can be drawn about which approach is superior or which factors (e.g., more fully developed imitation skills) can be identified that would predict which of the two communication methods an individual child with autism should use. Each of these forms of AAC is described in the sections that follow.

Sundberg and Parington (1998) have described a number of advantages of the use of signs as a form of communication for children with autism over the use of picture communication systems. The typical method of teaching signs is for a therapist to model a sign (e.g., a sign for cup) for the child to imitate as the child is shown an object (e.g., a cup) being labeled. A child's correct imitative response would be followed by the adult's delivery of a reinforcement. If the child does not respond or gives an incorrect or poorly formed sign, the adult would physically prompt the child to use the correctly formed sign. To learn signs in this way, a child needs to be able to attend to an adult when a model of a sign is presented and be proficient at manual imitation. The fact that some children with autism do not have well-developed attending or motor-imitative skills has been identified as one of the potential limitations of the use of signs as an AAC for children with autism (Tincani, 2004).

Another limitation that has been identified in the teaching of signs to children with autism is that since few people whom children with autism would encounter are proficient in signing, there would be a limited number of communicative partners available in natural environments (Bondy & Frost, 1994). On the other hand, Goldstein (2002) reviewed the literature on treatment intervention for children with autism and concluded that the evidence contraindicates the use of signs alone as an effective intervention strategy. He concluded that total communication (i.e., signs and speech) is a viable treatment strategy for children with autism who have a limited verbal communication repertoire. Total communication tends to increase children's production of both signs and speech. Yet, more promising may be the use of PECS, discussed below.

The Picture Exchange Communication System

The Picture Exchange Communication System consists of teaching children with autism to exchange pictures for desired objects or activities. The use of PECS has been described as not relying on preexisting skills for a child to learn before acquiring this communication approach (Bondy & Frost, 2001). This is in contrast to sign production, which requires the child to be able to attend to a presented model and imitate the target motoric response.

Bondy and Frost (2001) reported that 59% of children 5 years old and older who came into their program and used PECS for more than 1 year developed independent speech and no longer needed to use the picture cues to aid their communication. In recent years, there have been a few research studies evaluating the acquisition of PECS by children with autism. Schwartz, Garfinkle, and Bauer (1998) taught PECS to a group of 31 children with developmental disabilities within an average of 14 months. They followed a subsample of 18 children over 12 months and found that 44% of those children developed spontaneous oral communication without reliance on PECS. Studies by Ganz and Simpson (2004) and by Charlop-Christy, Carpenter, LeBlanc, and Kellet (2002) both found that all three children who were taught to communicate using PECS in their respective studies showed gains in spoken language and generalized the use of PECS to new situations.

The advantage of PECS being readily understood by a communicative partner may outweigh any potential superiority of signing to produce spoken language, particularly since it appears that nearly half of children with autism who learn PECS develop enough spoken language that they do not require the use of PECS any longer.

Bondy and Frost (2001) have produced a manual and a videotape on how to teach PECS. Anyone who would be involved in teaching PECS should be following that method under the supervision of an experienced clinician. The method is described in detail in the book and video. Below is a brief overview of the six phases of teaching PECS.

Before beginning PECS training, one should identify objects and activities that the child desires and therefore is likely to request to access. The method of identifying preferred stimuli (i.e., using a stimulus preference assessment) was described in Chapter 4. Once stimulus preferences for the child are identified, the child is trained in the PECS over six phases.

Phase I

The first phase of PECS training is to teach a child to exchange a picture for a desired object. Two trainers are needed: a communicative partner and a physical prompter. The communicative partner is the person with the desired object. The child will learn to release a picture into that person's open palm. The second trainer is positioned behind the child and serves as the physical prompter to facilitate the child's exchanging the picture for the desired object.

First, the communicative partner extends his or her hand, holding out the child's desired item (e.g., a toy). The child approaches the communicative partner and reaches for the desired item. As the child reaches, the communicative partner pulls back the object the child is reaching for and presents the picture of the item in the other hand. The physical prompter uses hand-over-hand prompting to help the child take the picture and place it in the then open palm of the communicative partner. When the child places the picture, the communicative partner labels the item (e.g., says "car") and then allows the child to have access to the item (e.g., allows the child to play with the toy car for a brief time). Over several trials, the physical prompter fades the amount of assistance given to the child until the child picks up the picture and places it in the communicative partner's hand without assistance.

Phase II

In the second phase of PECS training, the child is taught to be consistent at exchanging pictures even when the communicative partner is not looking at the child, or when the communicative partner is not immediately close. The child is also taught to retrieve the needed picture from across the room. A variety of contexts are used for the child to learn to persevere with the picture exchange with different people and under different routines.

Phase III

The child is taught to discriminate between a preferred item and a nonpreferred item when making requests. This ensures that the child is able to make a correspondence between a picture and a preferred item.

Phases IV, V, and VI

In the remaining three phases, the children learn to pick pictures to describe what they see or hear. Here, in addition to making requests, they also learn to answer direct questions, such as "What do you want?" and "What do you see?"

Communication Interventions in General Education Classrooms

Mass-Trial Language Instruction

The early approaches to interventions to improve the communication of children with autism consisted of teaching the children in a controlled environment (e.g., a separate room)—free of distraction—where the children practiced giving a specific language response to a therapist-presented cue (e.g., a model of the sound or a label of a presented object). The reinforcer used for correct responses in this training typically has an arbitrary connection to the child's response. For example, the child may correctly label a picture of a ball and then receive an edible reinforcer, rather than access to the ball. Koegel, Camarata, Koegel, Ben-Tall, and Smith (1998) indicted that mass-trial teaching of language tends to have three major difficulties: (a) gains are extremely slow; (b) speech gains are minimal; and (c) oftentimes, the participating child shows disruptive behaviors.

Carr (1983) identified additional problems associated with a mass-trial approach to teaching language. One was that gains that were observed in the controlled environment seldom generalized outside of that setting. Moreover, communicative responses learned by children were rarely used spontaneously. They tended to rely on an adult first asking a question (e.g., "What do you want?") or providing some other form of a prompt before the child employed the learned communicative response. In mass-trial language instruction, children's language response was brought under the stimulus control of highly specific stimuli, which hampered the generalization of learning responses across people, settings, and instructional tasks.

From this beginning, a more naturalistic approach to teaching language emerged, based on using the child's interest in desired items and creating learning opportunities to teach targeted communicative responses. These more naturalistic approaches were used in everyday environments, such as at home and in school (Woods & Goldstein, 2003).

Incidental Language Instruction

One of the earliest examples of a naturalistic approach to teaching language was the use of "incidental teaching of language" (Hart & Risley, 1968) to facilitate the communication of disadvantaged preschoolers. This incidental teaching of language has been modified for use with children with autism who are in classroom settings. Incidental language instruction consists of two components: (a) capitalizing on and creating situations in which the child with autism will request an object or activity (e.g., a child's desired toy is in sight, but it is out of reach, so the child attempts to reach for it) and

(b) a procedure for teaching a targeted language response to make the request. These two components reflect two goals of incidental teaching of language. The first is to increase the frequency of an unprompted initiation of a child's communicative response. Sometimes the child may be able to respond to a posed question (e.g., "What do you want?"), but when such a prompt is not available, the child will not use a learned communicative response. It is important for children with autism to imitate communication with prompting from adults.

A second goal of incidental teaching of language is to improve the quality of the child's communicative responses. For example, a child who makes requests using one word (e.g., "Cookie") may next be expected to request desired objects using a sentence (e.g., "I want cookie"). The particular targeted communicative response is individualized to the child and the situation.

The effectiveness of incidental teaching and discrete trial teaching was compared for two children with autism (Miranda-Linné & Melin, 1992). Children were taught to label eight desired food or toy items. Half the children were taught through discrete trial teaching, and the other half were taught using incidental teaching. The number of trials per day was the same under both conditions. The children learned to label items in half of the time under discrete trial teaching, but showed better generalization of learned responses with incidental teaching. Although it is not possible to draw firm conclusions with such a small sample size, this study does suggest that there is better generalization of learning to natural environments with incidental teaching of language versus using more traditional approaches. Koegel et al. (1998) found that both a traditional approach and a natural approach increased the speech intelligibility of five children with autism, but only the naturalistic approach resulted in correct production of the targeted sound during children's conversation.

Incidental teaching has been successfully used in classrooms with children with autism for such target behaviors as preposition use (McGee, Krantz, & McClannahan, 1985) and receptive discrimination of object labels (McGee, Krantz, Mason, & McClannahan, 1983).

Teaching Procedures

Step 1: Select an instructional target.

Since there may be a number of individuals using incidental teaching with the same child, it is important to ensure that everybody is working on strengthening the same type of communicative response for the child. It would be confusing to the child to have some people working to have the child request a desired object using one word that is clearly intelligible while others are expecting the child to use sentences and are not concerned about speech quality. The instructional target should be individualized to the child and consist of a response slightly more elaborate than what the child typically uses. When the child learns a more advanced communicative response, then the expectations for the child's communicative response would become more elaborate and be targeted by all those helping a child learn to communicate.

Figure 5.1 shows an example hierarchy of instructional targets for incidental teaching of language that begins with the child making a one-word request and progresses to the child making requests using full sentences, including the name of the person being addressed and a description of the desired object with an adjective (e.g., "Melissa, I want a red crayon."). As previously indicated, the instructional target needs to fit the needs of the child. For example, for a child who is not able to produce individual words, the initial instructional target may be for the child to make the initial sound of the name of the desired item or to exchange a picture for the desired item.

1. One-word request (e.g., "a crayon")

2. Carrier phrase (e.g., "I want") plus one word (e.g., "a crayon")

3. Name of person (e.g., "Melissa") plus carrier phrase (e.g., "I want"), plus one word (e.g., "a crayon")

4. Name of person (e.g., "Melissa") plus carrier phrase (e.g., "I want") plus adjective (e.g., "a red") plus one word (e.g., "crayon")

Figure 5.1. Example of a hierarchy of instructional targets for use in incidental teaching of language.

Step 2: Capitalize on or create opportunities for communication.

One of the critical aspects of incidental teaching is that the child with autism must show an initial interest in a desired item and initiate a form of communication to obtain the item. For example, a child may see a toy on a shelf with which he or she wants to play. Another child might want more juice poured in his or her cup. At another time, the child may need help to open a door to go outside to play. These initiations serve as possible opportunities for the child to make a request using the targeted communicative response. Leaf and McEachin (1999) referred to these communicative opportunities as "language temptations." Many communication opportunities occur naturally in the course of a school day that can be used to elicit a communicative response from a child with autism. It is also possible to create additional opportunities. Phil Strain and colleagues (Strain & Hoyson, 2000) have identified a number of specific strategies that can be used to create communication opportunities.

- *Forgetfulness*—Forgetfulness consists of providing a child with autism with a preferred activity but purposely omitting a necessary component. For example, a child may enjoy painting. The teacher provides the child with paper placed on an easel, and some paint, but omits a paintbrush. The teacher says to the child, "Go ahead, you can paint now."
- *Visible but Inaccessible*—A second strategy is to place desired items where they can be seen by the child with autism, but cannot be accessed. A favorite toy may be placed on a shelf. A snack may be placed in a difficult-to-open clear plastic container. To access these items, the child needs to make a request.
- *Sabotage*—In sabotage, the teacher deliberately hampers the child's ability to complete a task. For example, one of the child's outdoor shoes is hidden or a pencil given to the child is too small to write with, so the child needs to ask for assistance.
- *Piece by Piece*—The child may be engaged in an activity that involves the completion of a number of pieces, such as solving a jigsaw puzzle. Rather than having all of the pieces displayed at once, the pieces are given to the child one at a time after the child asks for one.

There should be a particular number of communicative opportunities targeted each day for the child to initiate the targeted communicative response. Figure 5.2 shows a morning routine for a child with autism in a kindergarten class and the strategies that the teacher will use to set up a communicative opportunity. In this example, the teacher has decided to attempt at least five communication opportunities during the morning.

Time	Activity	Strategies to create communication opportunities			
		Forgetfulness	Visible but inaccessible	Sabotage	Piece by piece
8:50	Bus arrives		Needs to ask to get juice		
9:00	Walk into school		Pencil in a clear container with a lid		
9:10	Opening exercises				
9:15	Language arts				
9:45	Math				
10:15	Recess				Raisin snack given one by one
10:30	Social science	Given a seatwork assignment, but no sheet			
11:00	Music			Given a recorder to play that does not have a mouthpiece	

Figure 5.2. Example of a schedule to plan the use of incidental language instruction for a child with autism.

Step 3: Wait.

It is critical that a child with autism learn to make a request in response to the natural cues in the environment, rather than to wait for someone to ask the child what he or she wants. For example, a child sees a favorite toy on a shelf, which cues the child to look at an adult and say, "Ball." If an adult does not wait for the child to initiate a communicative response and jumps in too quickly to ask the child what he or she wants, the child may likely wait for the adult's verbal prompt (i.e., the adult's question) before initiating a response in the future. Therefore, after the communication opportunity occurs, wait at least 5 seconds. If the child makes the targeted communicative response, give a confirmational statement (i.e., "Yes, you want the toy") followed immediately by allowing the child brief access to the toy. If the child fails to communicate after 5 seconds, or if the child's communicative response is not what is required for the target response, then the child is given up to three prompts, described below. The child needs to learn that his or her efforts will meet with success and therefore access to the desired items.

Step 4: Provide a nonverbal prompt.

If the child has not made the communicative response and is not looking at either the communicative partner or the desired item, the next step is to provide a nonverbal prompt that directs the child's focus. This prompt may consist of tapping the desired object or turning the child's face to look at the person with whom the child is communicating. If the Picture Exchange Communication System is being used, the nonverbal prompt may consist of pointing at a sentence strip.

If the child is not having difficulty with attending to the desired items or to the communicative partner, then the nonverbal prompt consists of the adult shrugging his or her shoulders in a gesture to indicate that the adult does not know what the child is trying to say. Following the delivery of a nonverbal prompt, wait for at least 5 seconds. If the child uses the target communicative response, then you would respond with the confirmational statement and reinforcer described in Step 3. If the child fails to give the target communicative response after the nonverbal prompt, proceed to Step 5.

Step 5: Ask.

Ask the child, "What do you want?" Wait for at least 5 seconds. If at this point the child gives the target communicative response, provide a confirmational statement as described in Step 3 and give the child access to the requested item. If the child still does not use the communicative response, then go to the next and final step.

Step 6: Say.

Provide a model of what the child is to say, and have the child imitate it. If the child imitates correctly, give a confirmational statement and provide access to the requested item. If the child does not imitate the modeled response, reinforce the child's attempt by giving access to the desired item. If the child still does not give a target response after wait, nonverbal prompt, and ask, the program needs to be revised since the child is not giving the target communicative response after three prompts. The first thing to look at is whether the provided "language temptations" are effective. Is the child motivated to access them? If not, make changes (e.g., use novel items) so that the child is more motivated to initiate the communicative response.

The second aspect of the program to examine is whether the target communicative response is too difficult. If so, substitute a targeted communicative response that would fall about halfway in difficulty between the target communicative response you are currently using and the response the child is capable of producing. For example, if a child is able to produce the initial sound of items, such as /c/ for "cookie" and /d/ for "drink," but cannot pronounce the target communicative response of the word (e.g., "drink," "cookie"), a revised communicative response would be to produce a more elaborative pronunciation of initial sound. For example, the child would be expected to say "dri" for "drink" and "coo" for "cookie." An example of an incidental language program for a 4-year-old girl attending an inclusive preschool program follows. In addition, a summary of the steps involved in incidental language instruction is shown in Figure 5.3.

Amy: Example of Incidental Language Program

Amy is a 4-year old girl with autism attending an inclusive preschool. She has a number of favorite toys that she enjoys placed on a shelf within sight, but not within reach. Amy is able to say some sounds of her favorite toys. She says "lee" for "dolly," "pa" for "puzzle," and "ba" for a toy that makes bubbles. These three toys are kept on a shelf in the play room of her preschool. Staff has decided that the target communicative response is for Amy to say the word of a favorite toy (e.g. "bubble," "dolly," "puzzle"). Periodically, Amy is taken to the playroom to play with her favorite toy. Staff

1. Select a clear communicative target.

2. Set up the environment to elicit the targeted communicative response. Capital-ize on or create opportunities for communication (via strategies such as forget-fulness, visible but inaccessible, sabotage, and piece by piece).

3. Wait at least 5 seconds for the child to initiate the targeted communicative response. If the child uses the targeted communicative response, give a confir-mational statement and then allow the child access to the requested item.

4. If the child does not start a communicative response within 5 seconds, give one of two types of prompts, depending on the situation. If the child is not attend-ing, provide an attentional prompt (e.g., turn the child's face to look where he or she should) or a gestural prompt (e.g., point at the picture symbols). If the problem is not a lack of attention, make a shrugging motion to indicate that you do not understand. Wait 5 seconds. If the child uses the targeted communica-tive response, give a confirmational statement and then allow the child access to the requested item.

5. If the child does not start a communicative response within 5 seconds, ask what the child wants. Wait at least 5 seconds.

6. If the child does not start a communicative response within 5 seconds, model (say) the target response. If the child uses the targeted communicative response, give a confirmational statement and then allow the child access to the requested item. If the child does not imitate the modeled response, give the child access to the desired item anyway to reinforce his or her attempt. Revise the program.

Figure 5.3. Summary of the steps in implementing incidental language instruction.

takes her so she can see the toys and then the staff waits. After about 2 seconds, Amy says "bab," which is not the target communicative response. Staff waits for 3 more seconds and then points to the bubble toy. Amy then says "bubbles." The teacher replies, "Yes, you want bubbles. Here is your bubble toy," and then hands the toy to Amy.

Data Collection

The progress of a child learning to make a communicative response through an inci-dental language approach should be monitored in order to make ongoing revisions to the child's individual program. If the program is successful, the target communicative responses need to become more ambitious. If data suggest the program is unsuccessful, the intervention needs to be revised.

Figure 5.4 illustrates a simple way of tracking a child's progress in incidental language instruction. It allows one to track whether the child is receiving the planned number of communicative opportunities (e.g., 10) and whether the child is acquiring the target communicative response. The recorder makes a vertical mark, indicating that a communication opportunity has occurred. If the child produces the target commu-nicative response without any prompts from adults, then the vertical line is converted into a plus mark. If one or more prompts are needed, then the vertical line is left as is.

Date	Nov. 2	Nov. 3	Nov. 4	Nov. 5
Record opportunities as | and the child's correct response to an opportunity as +	$\vert_2$ + + $\vert_2$ $\vert_1$ + + + $\vert_1$ $\vert_1$	+ $\vert_2$ + + + $\vert_3$ $\vert_1$ + + $\vert_1$ +	+ $\vert_1$ + + + + $\vert_1$ + + +	+ + + + + + $\vert_1$ + + $\vert_1$ +
A: Number of +s	5	7	8	9
B: Number of |s	5	4	2	2
A + B	10	11	10	11
Percent +	50.0%	63.6%	80.0%	81.8%

Figure 5.4. Example recording form for tracking the results of incidental language instruction.

The recorder then places a number between 1 and 3 beside the vertical line to indicate how many prompts were administered. For example, if the staff delivered an attentional prompt and then subsequently asked the child, "What do you want?" then a small number 2 would be entered below the vertical mark.

The data shown in Figure 5.4 suggest that the child is producing more target communicative responses. The child started with producing the target communicative response without any prompts on 50% of opportunities. The percentage of unprompted target communicative response increased to 63.6%, 80.0%, and then 81.8%. Moreover, staff managed to provide to the child the number of communication opportunities that they aimed for (i.e., at least 10) for each of the 3 days.

Although many innovative approaches other than incidental language have been evaluated to teach communicative responses to children with autism, few have been used in inclusive settings. Embedded instruction (described in Chapter 3) is another approach that has been used to improve the communication responses of children with autism in inclusive school settings (Williams, Johnson, & Sukhodolsky, 2005). As previously described, educators embed instruction into the routines of a school day. The main difference between embedded instruction and incidental language instruction is that the adult initiates the teaching episode, whereas in incidental teaching, the communication exchange is started by the child.

Study Questions

1. What are the communication problems associated with children with autism?

2. Why do you think there is a relationship between communication problems and problem behaviors for children with autism?

3. Describe the purpose of the first three phases in teaching PECS.

4. Describe the four methods of creating communication opportunities.

5. Describe the six steps of incidental language instruction.

6. Complete the following data sheet.

Date	Nov. 2
Record opportunities as | and the child's correct response to an opportunity as +	$\mid_2$ + | $\mid_2$ $\mid_1$
A: Number of +s	
B: Number of |s	
A + B	
Percent +	%

6 Promoting Peer Interaction in General Education Classrooms

Chapter Topics

- Using picture activity schedules to teach independent play

- Using picture activity schedules to teach interactive play

- Making environmental arrangements to promote peer interaction

- Using adult mediation to prompt peer interaction

- Directly teaching peer interaction (using social scripts training or a classwide approach)

The formation of meaningful social relationships is important for the healthy development of all children. In addition to other indications of social competence, making friends and gaining the acceptance of peers have been associated with the long-term positive social adjustment of children (Greenwood, Walker, & Utley, 2002; Guralnick, 1990). Impairment in the ability to form social relationships is one of the diagnostic features of children with autism (American Psychiatric Association, 2000).

In play situations, children with autism have been found to interact with peers less frequently (Kamps, Leonard, et al., 1992; Koegel, Koegel, Frea, & Fredeen, 2001), interact with adults more frequently (Hundert, Mahoney, Mundy, & Vernon, 1998), and show less mature forms of play when they do interact with children than typically developing children do (Anderson, Moore, Godfrey, & Fletcher-Flinn, 2004). Even compared to children with other forms of developmental disabilities, children with autism have been found to interact less often with peers. In one study, children with autism were found to play with peers at one third the level that children with mental retardation did (Hauck, Fein, Waterhouse, & Feinstein 1995).

The lower levels of peer interaction shown by children with autism cannot be explained by the reluctance of typically developing peers to approach children with autism. Sigman and Ruskin (1999) found that typically developing preschoolers extended play invitations to children with autism at about the same frequency as they extended invitations to their typically developing peers. The difference was that children with autism did not respond to these play invitations. Furthermore, children with autism appear to have as much opportunity to play with peers as their classmates do, but they do not prefer to interact with peers and do not know how to initiate and maintain social exchanges, even if they wished to interact with peers (Pierce-Jordan & Lifter, 2005).

The goal of teaching peer interaction to children with autism is for those children to be able to initiate and respond to reciprocal peer interaction under conditions of minimal adult involvement and to generalize that learning to interactions with other peers and to new situations. Obtaining gains in the interactive play of children with autism under conditions of minimal teacher involvement is ambitious. There are not many examples of interventions to increase the peer interaction of children with autism that have been conducted in a general education class with minimal teacher involvement. Many studies on increasing peer interaction in children with autism have been conducted in highly controlled environments, such as laboratory schools or play groups that were created specifically for a research study (Morrison, Kamps, Garcia, & Parker, 2001). Moreover, the interventions to promote peer interaction in classrooms are often implemented by the experimenter involved in the study or by university students of the experimenter (e.g., Zanolli, Daggett, & Adams, 1996). Under these conditions, it may be possible to apply interventions to increase peer interaction that require a high amount of adult involvement, which may not be able to be maintained by the general education teacher when the study has ended. In fact, peer interaction that requires high teacher involvement may be counterproductive (McGee, Almeida, Sulzer-Azaroff, & Feldman, 1992), not only because it is labor intensive, but also because interventions that are effective only with substantial adult presence may interfere with the evolution of child–child interactions. If peer interaction occurs with a child with autism mainly because of (a) teacher organization of the play, (b) teacher participation in the play, or (c) teacher praise, other children are unlikely to continue to interact with the child with autism when the teacher's involvement is lessened or removed.

Naturally occurring and sustained child–child interactions with children with autism may require the development of peer interactions that are mutually reinforcing to the children involved. That is, under natural conditions, one child will continue to play with another child because the positive reaction of the second child and/or the fun associated with the play activity encourages continued interaction by the first child and vice versa. The changed play behavior of the second child, in turn, is maintained by its effect on the actions of the first child. If the continued play interaction of children is dependent on the presence of an adult, that interaction will likely end as soon as the adult is no longer available. Adult facilitation of play cannot substitute for the creation of mutually reinforcing child–child interactions.

Using Picture Activity Schedules to Teach Independent Play

Some children with autism are not able to play with toys or engage in imaginative play by themselves, let alone interact with peers while engaging in these activities. It would be premature to attempt to teach these children to interact with peers. They should first be taught to engage in play activities by themselves that later may be of interest to other children. One approach to teach children with autism to play with toys is the use of a picture activity schedule (PAS; MacDuff, Krantz, & McClannahan, 1993). (A fuller description of picture activity schedules to help children with autism to follow routines independently in general education classrooms can be found in Chapter 7.) To teach a child to play with toys, a series of photographs would be taken of the play sequence being taught. For example, the sequence of photographs for teaching a child to play with a shape sorter may be as shown in Figure 6.1. Picture 1 in Figure 6.1 shows the activity on a shelf. The child gets the shape sorter from the shelf. Picture 2 depicts the shape sorter on the floor with the shapes located beside the shape sorter. Picture 3 shows the shapes being placed in the shape sorter. And Picture 4 shows the shape sorter being returned to the shelf. Each picture would be mounted on a separate page in a PAS booklet. Below each picture would be a token that the child would receive for performing the activity depicted in the picture above it. This setup of pictures and tokens is shown in Figure 6.2.

Using Picture Activity Schedules to Teach Interactive Play

If a child is able to play independently, then the next step is to prepare the materials for a PAS booklet to teach peer interaction. Select a play activity that is short in duration, that would be of interest to other children, and that has a clear beginning and end so that the child will know when the task is completed. Examples of possible play activities for a 5-year-old child would include Mr. Potato Head, a shape sorter, or a jigsaw puzzle. After a child with autism has learned to play one of these activities by him- or herself, modify the activity so that it involves turn taking and introduce a second child to play with the child with autism. For example, take photographs of the pieces to Mr. Potato Head and place them on one side of cards in a deck facedown. Teach the two children to pick a card, find the corresponding piece, and then place it in Mr. Potato Head.

How to arrange a picture activity schedule is described in detail in Chapter 7. Only a brief overview is presented here. The first step is to take a picture of materials

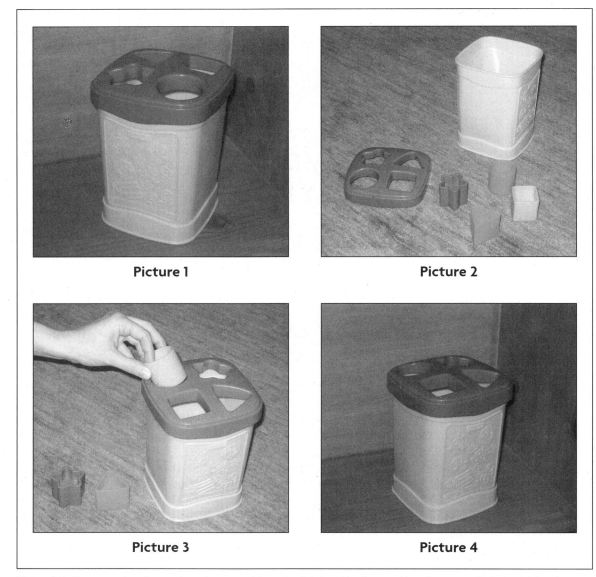

Picture 1

Picture 2

Picture 3

Picture 4

Figure 6.1. Pictures taken for use in a picture activity schedule booklet for teaching the steps of playing with a shape sorter.

associated with the play activity that you are about to teach. Objects that may be confusing or distracting would typically not be used. Each picture is mounted on a piece of construction paper and inserted into a plastic sleeve if displaying them in a binder or into the page slot if using a small photo album.

The next step is to identify possible reinforcers for the child to earn for successful completion of the activity being taught. A stimulus preference assessment (as described in Chapter 4) would be conducted to identify these potential reinforcements. The child may accumulate tokens (e.g., pictures of cartoon characters) to be exchanged for the backup reinforcer. As illustrated in Figure 6.2, the token is placed on the plastic sheet using adhesive Velcro. it can be given to the child after he or she completes the corresponding activity.

Once the PAS booklet is ready, the child is given an instruction such as "Go play with your toys" or "It's time to get busy." The PAS trainer moves behind the child and guides him or her to the PAS booklet. The child is prompted to open the PAS book-

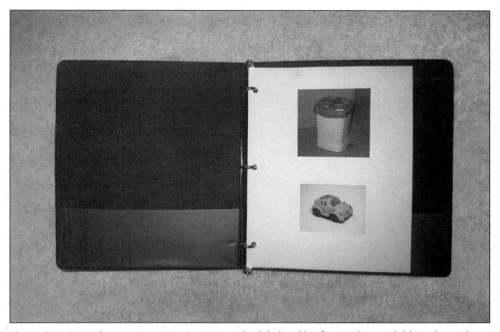

Figure 6.2. Example page in a picture activity schedule booklet for teaching a child to play with a shape sorter.

let, point to the first picture in the activity schedule, and complete the action depicted in the picture. Only the amount of guidance needed to prevent the child from making errors is provided. Once the activity is completed, the child is guided to pick up the materials and return them to their original location, again, using physical guidance as a form of prompting. Then the child is guided back to the schedule and prompted to turn the page, point to the next picture, and so on.

Early on in teaching schedule-following, the therapist delivers rewards frequently. Then gradually the rewards are given less often as the child learns the activity. The support person delivers the rewards from behind the child so that the child attends to the schedule rather than the person. Throughout this training, the amount of verbal dialogue with the child is kept to a minimum. Once a child is able to follow the PAS when presented with adult prompts, the prompts are faded.

There are a number of other evidence-based approaches to the promotion of peer interaction. Many originate from studies that were conducted in preschool settings, where play is typically a focus of the curriculum and opportunities to practice play are incorporated into the routines of the school day. The sections that follow describe other strategies to promote peer interaction.

Making Environmental Arrangements to Promote Peer Interaction

One strategy to promote peer interaction in children with autism is to plan physical and social environments that encourage increased play among groups of children that include children with autism. For example, the types of play activities available can determine how much children will interact with each other. Play activities that encourage child–child interactions, such as dress-up play or pick-up sticks, have been found to produce more interactive play than "isolated" play activities, such as arts-and-crafts or puzzles (Quilitch & Risley, 1973). Similarly, children will engage in more social interaction when they are involved with preferred rather than nonpreferred activities (Ferrara & Hill, 1980). Moreover, the novelty of play material will affect the amount of time children spend with that material (Rabinowitz, Moely, Finkel, & McClinton, 1975). Rotating play material will help to ensure novelty.

Another example of environmental arrangement is how children are grouped in play. Children with developmental disabilities have been found to show higher levels of play when playing with typically developing children than when playing with other children with developmental disabilities (Mundschenk & Sasso, 1995).

Although arranging the environment to enhance play is an important strategy, its use has been mainly explored in early childhood settings where indoor and outdoor play sessions are routinely conducted as part of the curriculum. The applicability of the same strategies to the play of children with autism in elementary school is less clear. In a review of interventions to increase the social interaction of young children with autism, McConnell (2002) concluded that environmental arrangements "produce weak to moderate effects on the social interaction of young children with autism" (p. 360). Although potentially beneficial, arranging the school environment to encourage play, by itself, is unlikely to have sufficient impact to produce substantial improvement on the quality or quantity of the play of children with autism.

Using Adult Mediation to Prompt Peer Interaction

Another strategy to increase the interactive play of children with autism consists of organizing adults to prompt children with autism to play with peers and then to reinforce those children once they begin to play. Figure 6.3 depicts this strategy of an adult prompting and reinforcing a child with autism to play with peers. The focus of the adult is on directly encouraging a child with autism to initiate and sustain play with his peers.

Figure 6.3. An adult-mediated approach to enhancing peer interaction in which the teacher prompts and praises the child with autism to play with typically developing peers.

An adult-mediated strategy has been shown to produce significant increases in the social play of children with disabilities (McConnell, 2002).

There are at least two significant limitations of an adult-mediated strategy to increase peer interaction. First, if the improved play behavior of a child with autism is dependent on teacher prompting and reinforcement, then that child's play behavior is unlikely to continue if the teacher supporting the behavior is absent or is no longer providing that support (Strain & Kohler, 1998). The second limitation of adult-mediated approaches is that they may be time-consuming for a general education teacher to implement under typical classroom conditions and, therefore, of questionable practicality.

Peer Mediation

A strategy that has been widely researched is that of training typically developing peers to elicit play from children with autism. In its simplest form, peers are selected from the class of the child with autism and trained in a set of skills (e.g., how to initiate play, how to organize play, how to compliment, how to encourage sharing) that would start and sustain play with children with autism. As illustrated in Figure 6.4, a peer-mediated strategy differs from an adult-mediated strategy to promote peer interaction in that the focus of the teacher is on training, prompting, and reinforcing peers, rather than the children with autism directly.

Peer-mediated training of peer intervention of children with autism has been found to increase child–child interactions, but it is associated with limitations similar to those of an adult-mediated approach (Morrison et al., 2001; Strain & Kohler, 1998). First, the amount of teacher time needed to start and maintain peer-mediated training is similar to that needed to conduct adult-mediated training. Time is needed to select and train peers; to monitor play situations; and to provide prompts, feedback, and reinforcement to peers. The difference is that the adult's focus is on the actions of typically developing children, rather than directly on children with autism.

Because the behaviors of the trained peers to elicit play with a child with autism are maintained by the actions of the adult, there may be little generalization of any increased play of children with autism to situations in which the adult prompting

Figure 6.4. A peer-mediated approach to enhancing peer interaction in which the teacher prompts and praises typically developing peers to play with a child with autism.

and reinforcement is not available (Odom & Brown, 1993). Moreover, because peers tend to be the ones initiating play exchanges in this approach, children with autism tend to learn how to respond to play invitations, but they do not learn how to initiate play themselves (McConnell, 2002). In both the adult-mediated and peer-mediated approaches, the interactive play of children with autism is unlikely to continue under minimal teacher involvement unless it can be maintained by naturally reinforcing social exchanges between the child with autism and his or her play partners.

Three examples of a peer-mediated approach are described in more detail below. One has been successfully implemented in a preschool setting, and the other two have been introduced in an elementary-school setting with minimal teacher involvement.

Peer Incidental Teaching

McGee et al. (1992) trained typically developing preschool peers to entice children with autism to interact. Prior to the start of the study, McGee et al. (1992) assessed the play preferences of the children with autism who were participating in the study. Three typically developing peers were selected to interact with each of the three children with autism. Each of the children with autism was paired with a trained peer during a free-play period in the preschool. Peers were trained over 8 to 23 five-minute sessions held once a day during regularly scheduled free-play periods. Training continued until peers each demonstrated in role play with adults that they could implement the training procedure correctly.

Training of peers consisted of adult modeling of the intervention, followed by child practice with feedback to the peers on their use of the trained procedures. The peers were taught to (a) hold onto the preferred toy of the target child, (b) wait for the target child to initiate some form of request for the preferred toy (e.g., reach for the toy), (c) ask the target child to ask for the preferred toy (e.g., "Say duck," if the preferred toy is a duck), (d) give the toy to the target child after the target child labels it, (e) praise the correct answer (e.g., "Yes, that is a duck. Nice asking"), and (f) prompt turn taking by asking if the peer could have a turn.

The trainer held a pictorial checklist of the components of peer incidental teaching and prompted the trained peers to use each component. If a trained peer used a component, the trainer placed a mark on the checklist and praised the peer. Once the trained peers were implementing the procedure accurately, the trainer began to fade her involvement by removing the use of the checklist, reducing the frequency of approval to the trained peer for the use of training components, and intervening only if a trained peer did not use any of the training components. The final step was that the external trainer withdrew and the program was maintained by the classroom teacher.

This procedure was able to produce an increase in the play initiation and responding of the target children with disabilities that was maintained by the general teacher with minimal involvement. The generalization of the targeted children's play to novel situations and to new peers was not assessed.

It would appear that by using preferred toys, the children with autism initiated the play exchange in order to engage in their preferred play activity and that the actions of the trained peers were able to be maintained with only periodic feedback from the general education teacher.

Recess Buddies

A second example of a peer-mediated approach is the use of peer buddies described by Laushey and Heflin (2000) and previously studied by English, Goldstein, Schafer, and Kaczmarck (1997). The Laushey and Heflin (2000) paper outlined a relatively simple intervention introduced for all children in each of two kindergarten classes, including two children with autism who attended these classes. Each child in the class was assigned a buddy daily, and a list of the pairing of children was posted in a manner similar to that depicted in Figure 6.5. The assignment of buddies was rotated daily. There was one child with autism in each of the two kindergarten classes, each of which contained approximately 20 to 25 children.

The entire class received training in the buddy system, which started with a buddy skill trainer addressing the class on the ways in which people can be the same and different. The training proceeded to explain the importance of staying with, playing with, and talking to each child's buddy. Each day for the first 4 weeks after the introduction of the buddy system, the names of the buddies who followed the buddy system rules were placed in a drawing for a small prize.

Laushey and Heflin (2000) conducted a study to examine the effect of the buddy system on the amount of peer interaction shown by the children with autism. They started by observing the level of interactive play of the children with autism under baseline conditions. After the buddy system was introduced, there was a large increase in the interactive play of children with autism. To demonstrate that the observed increase in the interactive play of children with autism was due to the buddy system, it was removed. Accordingly, there was a reduction in the interactive play of children with autism. This research design is referred to as a reversal or ABA design (Cooper, Heron, & Heward, 2007). Using this ABA design, Laushey and Heflin (2000) found a large increase in the amount of interactional play of children with autism after the introduction of the buddy system.

Although the buddy system is relatively easy to implement in a general education classroom, there seem to be at least two profound limitations to this study. First, in using a reversal design to demonstrate the effect of the buddy system, they also found that the heightened peer interaction did not continue when the buddy system was removed. A second limitation of the study was that the two children with autism who participated were described as being able to make requests in four- to six-word sentences, read kindergarten-level stories with comprehension, and perform many other kindergarten-level tasks. It is unclear whether the buddy system would be as effective for children with autism who are more limited in their skills than the two children with autism who participated in the Laushey and Heflin (2000) study.

Child	Mon.	Tues.	Wed.	Thurs.	Fri.
Abbey	Zack	William	Vanessa	Tom	Theresa
Ben	Abbey	Zack	William	Vanessa	Tom
Brian T.	Ben	Abbey	Zack	William	Vanessa
Brian S.	Brian T.	Ben	Abbey	Zack	William
Carly	Brian S.	Brian T.	Ben	Abbey	Zack
Carol	Carly	Brian S.	Brian T.	Ben	Abbey
Chris	Carol	Carly	Brian S.	Brian T.	Ben

Figure 6.5. Example of a daily planning sheet for pairing of children in the "recess buddies" program. Pairing is shown for only the first few children in the class.

Peer Networks

Peer networks have some features in common with recess buddies. They both involve (a) pairing typically developing children with children who have autism and (b) providing the peers with some training in how to interact to improve the adjustment of children with autism (Garrison-Harrell, Kamps, & Kravits, 1997; Kamps, Potucek, Gonzalez-Lopez, Kravits, & Kemmerer, 1997). Peer networks differ in that a group of between three and five same-grade peers are selected and rotated to interact with the child with autism at appointed times in the school day, individualized to each child with autism. Peers are selected to participate in peer networks based on teacher judgment, social status, parent consent, and the absence of a negative history with the particular child with autism. Peers from one network at a time were trained in intervention procedures to foster interaction during particular situations in the school day (e.g., academic tutoring, playing at recess, turn taking at games, interaction during lunch). For example, one child received support from his peer network during morning recess, learning centers, math, and lunch. Before interventions began, peers were trained over the course of eight 30-minute sessions using modeling, practice, and feedback. During peer network sessions that lasted between 10 and 20 minutes, a teacher or a paraprofessional provided supervision, feedback, and reinforcement to the peer. Kamps et al. (1997) found that the introduction of peer networks increased the social interaction of three children with autism (6–8 years old) in all intervention settings. For two of the children, there was also an increase in social interaction in a setting in which a peer network was not introduced. Teachers and paraprofessionals rated peer networks positively, but found the time required to prepare materials and manage the peer network challenging.

Directly Teaching Peer Interaction

Social Scripts Training

A number of years ago, I made arrangements to observe a boy with developmental disabilities in a general kindergarten class. I arrived in time to observe the class opening activities, which started with "calendar time." Each morning, the teacher invited a student to lead the rest of the class in the calendar time routine. On this particular morning, the teacher invited the young boy whom I was observing to lead the daily calendar time routine. The child, who was nonverbal, knew exactly what to do. He took the teacher's pointer and touched the area on the board that contained pictures depicting different weather conditions (e.g., sunny, cloudy, snowy). When the pointer touched the group of pictures, the class responded in unison, "Sunny." The boy took the corresponding picture and placed it on the appropriate location on the calendar. Next, the boy placed the pointer on the area of the board containing the names of the days of the week. Again, the class responded in unison with, "Wednesday." The boy placed the word *Wednesday* on the calendar and then sat down beaming, proud of his accomplishments. The boy I was observing and his classmates had learned a routinized way of interacting. Each knew their parts as if they were in a theatrical play. The class reacted to what the boy did, who in turn reacted to the class, following a learned series of steps until the series of exchanges ended.

Although this situation did not involve play, it did illustrate how a student with disabilities and typically developing peers can learn to interact by following a sequence of scripted exchanges. Goldstein and Cisar (1992) used social script training to increase the peer interaction of children with disabilities in general education preschool classrooms. Scripts were developed that described how to participate in particular play activities newly introduced to the classroom, such as how to engage in play about the ball/hoop game at carnivals. A script described the sequence of interactions among two to three participants involved in a play activity. A script described the play materials that were needed and the sequence of actions and comments that children should make to play the game. Scripts used by Goldstein and Cisar described modifications that would be made to the play exchanges to accommodate a child with minimal verbal ability and for a child with no verbal ability. For instance, the script for a ball/hoop game involved three participants: a booth attendant, a customer, and an assistant. The child playing the role of the booth attendant would start by holding up a ball and saying, "Come one, come all, play the ball/hoop game!" The customer would then say, "How much does it cost?" and so on. A child who lacked verbal skills would just hold up the balls. The script continued until the customer threw the balls at the hoops. Scripts would be modeled to children prior to their introduction in the classroom.

Goldstein and Cisar (1992) trained three preschoolers with "autistic characteristics" and six typically developing peers in each of three social scripts (pet shop, carnival, and magic show). Following the teaching of each of the social scripts, there was an increase in the social and communicative interactions between the children with autism and typically-developing peers.

Using a social script and script fading, Krantz and McClannahan (1998) taught children with autism who could already follow picture activity schedules for play activities to also say, "Watch me" and "Look" when engaged in play activities that resulted in an increase in interaction. Script fading has also been used to teach children with autism to engage in conversational exchanges (Sarokoff, Taylor, & Poulson, 2001).

Developing and Delivering Social Scripts Training

The first step in the development of a social script is to bring together people who know the child with autism and who will be implementing the intervention. This group typically consists of the child's teacher, the child's paraprofessional, the child's parents, and a consultant. The group develops a play script that draws on the interest of the child with autism and develops a sequence of play actions at the child's level of abilities in play and in communication. The group also attempts to incorporate use of the child's obsessions or high-preference play activities to ensure that the play script will be of interest to the child with autism. For example, if the child with autism has an interest in trains, the group might consider a play script that involves trains.

The prompts needed for the play are written out, along with the sequence of play steps. The play sequence must involve interdependent interactions between the child with autism and at least one peer. Each player is dependent on the other for the play script to progress. For example, if a play is designed about a train, one child may play the role of a conductor who moves the train around a track and another child plays the role of a station manager who loads items onto the train and uses a flashlight to signal the conductor when to make the train stop and go.

A member of the planning group writes out a script that describes the action and the type of commentary that should occur with each step. An example of a social script is shown in Appendix 6A. This script was used successfully to increase the peer interaction of a 7-year-old boy (Leo) at recess.

Once the script is completed and the play material is obtained, the play script should be modeled to the class so that peers are presented with the steps in the script and have an opportunity to practice it. Modeling may be live and/or achieved through the use of a videotape depicting two competent children following the steps of the script. Following the modeling, the teacher would ask for two children to volunteer to play the game with the child with autism (e.g., "Who would like to be a good friend with [name of child with autism] and play this game?"). One child volunteer is prompted on the social script with the child with autism as the second child volunteer is observing to learn the script and play with the child with autism when it is next practiced.

Typically, two adults are needed when the play script is first introduced—one to prompt and praise the child with autism and another to prompt and praise the peer in following the script. The adult prompters are situated behind the children and provide verbal and physical prompts for actions and verbal responses associated with each step of the script.

It is not critical that the children follow the script word for word or perform the scripted actions precisely. The children do need to be able to perform the steps of the script in general so that the play sequence flows as designed.

Once the child with autism and peers can follow the script sequence, the degree of prompting should be gradually faded by (a) reducing the amount of prompts delivered (e.g., from full to partial physical or verbal prompts), (b) delaying the delivery of the prompts, and (c) increasing the physical distance between the adult prompter and the child being prompted.

It is my experience that prompt fading can be started after approximately three sessions. At this point, the children are encouraged to vary the script so it is not always being played in the same way. Once the script is fully in place, it is available for either the child with autism or peers to request at recess (for elementary schools) or during free play (for preschools). A second play script can be introduced in the same manner.

Prior to the play period when the social script would be used, I encourage the teacher to hold a brief discussion with the class. The teacher reminds the class to find opportunities to play cooperatively and, depending on the age of the children, asks selected students (including the students with autism) to state with whom they intend to play, with what they will be playing, and how they will share during recess or at a free play period. Following the play session, the children report on what they did and are praised for accurately reporting incidents that involved sharing. This procedure of guiding children to state how they plan to act in a forthcoming play session and then subsequently delivering reinforcement based on their accurate report is adopted from "correspondence training" (Morrison et al., 2001).

The steps involved in a social script training are summarized in Table 6.1.

Video Modeling and Video Self-Modeling of Social Scripts

In more recent years, children with autism have been taught to increase their peer interaction through exposure to videos depicting a play interaction script. Video modeling consists of the demonstration of a desired behavior by using a video representation of that behavior. Video self-modeling (VSM) is a variation of video modeling in which demonstration of a desired behavior consists of an individual observing a video of him- or herself successfully performing the desired behavior. Recently, Bellini, Akullian, and Hopf (2007) conducted a literature review of the effectiveness of video modeling and VSM for children with autism. They concluded that both interventions were effective in improving the social functioning of the children with autism and satisfy the criteria to be considered evidence-based practices.

In video modeling, peers and/or adults are typically used as models of how to play, and the video of them is shown to a child with autism. The child with autism is then directed to perform one action shown on the video without any additional teaching.

Table 6.1
Summary of Steps Involved in Developing a Social Script

1. In collaboration with those implementing social script training, select a theme for the script that (a) is of interest to the child with autism, (b) is at the ability level of the child with autism, (c) is of interest to other children, and (d) involves interdependence between two play partners.

2. Write the script, including the needed play materials.

3. Model the script using video modeling (see explanation later in this chapter) or role playing.

4. Arrange for two children to participate each session, one as a play partner and one as an observer.

5. Prompt the children to follow the play script.

6. Fade prompts and encourage spontaneity in following the script.

7. Prompt and praise the use of the social script in natural play situations.

8. Repeat with a second script.

For example, MacDonald, Clark, Garrigan, and Vangala (2005) used video modeling to teach play scripts that contained 16 verbalizations and 14 actions. The play scripts all consisted of pretend play using figurines (e.g., pirates) and play materials (e.g., a ship, a treasure chest). Two preschool children with autism learned each of three play scripts and maintained their increased pretend play after scripted play training finished. Although the study indicated that the participating children acquired the scripted play, there was no generalization to unscripted play. Following video modeling, the children could follow a play-activity in the manner shown on the video, but they were not able to play in any new ways that were not specifically depicted in the video.

The MacDonald et al. (2005) study described the use of video modeling to increase the pretend play of children with autism when playing along. Nickopoulos and Keenan (2003) videoed simple scripts consisting of an adult or a peer initiating play with the experimenter. The model in the video spent a few seconds wandering around the room, took the experimenter's hand, and led him to a particular toy while saying, "Let's play." Each of seven children with autism, aged 9 to 15 years, who were attending a residential special education school were shown the video and then taken into a room with the experimenter. There was an increase in the social interaction for four of the seven children, which generalized across toys and settings and was maintained 1 and 2 months later. This study was not conducted with peers in a natural setting.

However, there have been a number of studies describing the use of VSM to improve the play behavior of children with autism in school settings. In one study, two children attending separate preschools watched 2-minute videos of themselves edited to show appropriate peer interaction with peers at the beginning of each school day (Bellini et al., 2007). Following the observation of the video, children were given an opportunity to play with their classmates, but they did not receive any prompting or reinforcing. During baseline, the children with autism were rarely interacting with peers. After the introduction of VSM, there was a large increase in the frequency of peer interaction that was maintained after the intervention was withdrawn.

Buggey (2005) developed a video of peer interaction for two boys with autism, aged 9 and 10, who attended a small, private inclusive school. The video followed a written script in which each of the boys individually approached a group of students outside of school and carried on a brief conversation. The boys observed the 3-minute video each day before classes began. As was found in the Bellini et al. (2007) study, there was a large increase in the frequency of the boys' social interactions with peers that was maintained after the removal of VSM.

Sherer et al. (2001) found that VSM was most effective for children with autism who seemed to already enjoy watching videos and had a preference for visual learning. They also found that "self" and "other" video modeling techniques were equally effective in enhancing the conversational skills of four children with autism.

Buggey (2007) described how to develop a self-modeling video. The first step is to select the audiovisual technology that will be used to develop and show the video. A camcorder can capture the scenes that then can be edited down to a 2- to 5-minute video. Bellini et al. (2007) started with a total of 1.5 hours of raw footage that was edited into 2-minute videos. The editing may be conducted by connecting a camcorder into a VCR and selecting relevant segments.

Even easier is the use of a camcorder that is able to export the video to a computer to be digitized. There are several easy-to-use programs for a Macintosh or PC computer to edit videos and export the final video to an mpeg clip that can be shown on a computer, a DVD player, or the camcorder itself.

The next step is to film the child with autism displaying the target behavior. One may set up situations in which adults and/or peers prompt the child to use the target behavior and later edit out the adult prompting. For children with less severe autism, a storyboard may be developed with the child to plan the sequence of scenes to be shown. For children with more severe autism, it may be necessary to continuously videotape the child until he or she demonstrates the target behavior a sufficient number of times to create a video segment. The next step is to have the child with autism observe the 2- to 5-minute video typically just before a time when the child can use the target behavior demonstrated on the videotape.

If one is developing a VSM in school, then one needs to be sensitive to issues of the confidentiality of other students who may be captured on the video. Parental consent would be necessary for parents who have agreed to have their child participate, and images of children whose parents have not consented need to be edited out of the video.

A Classwide Approach

A second example of a strategy to direct children with autism how to play with peers is to introduce social skills training for the entire class. A classwide approach to peer interaction is of interest to schools not only as a means to assist the inclusion of children with autism, but also as a way to deal with concerns about violence and aggression in school (Elliott, Hamburg, & Williams, 1998). With evidence that approximately 15% of all children 4 to 16 years of age have one or more behavior–emotional problems at clinically significant levels (Offord et al., 1987), there have been attempts to reduce aggression through the introduction of school-based social skills programs.

There are numerous potential advantages to teaching inclusive classes of children how to interact appropriately with one another. First, all children in the classroom can be taught the same skills at the same time for a brief period of time each day. This is considerably more efficient then attempting to teach interactive play to children one by one. Second, the format of teaching peer interaction to a class is similar to that of teaching any subject area. Therefore, it is typically judged by teachers as an acceptable intervention. A third potential advantage of teaching entire classes of children about peer interaction is that it may increase the responsiveness of typically developing children in the class toward their classmates with autism (Gresham, 1998). Finally, there is no stigma associated with a classwide approach since all children receive the intervention, rather than assistance being provided only to children with autism.

A classwide approach was used by Lefebvre and Strain (1989), who taught play skills to a preschool class over nine 10- to 15-minute sessions held during circle time. Using role-play modeling of skills by two adults, children were taught such play skills as giving a toy to your friend and asking a friend to wait. Play groups were formed consisting of one child with autism and two typically developing children. The teaching of social skills produced very little gain in the social interaction of the children with autism until a group reinforcement contingency was introduced. Children received tokens exchangeable for a daily group-selected backup reinforcer (e.g., a popcorn party, the opportunity to listen to music) for appropriate use of trained strategies of peer interaction. With the introduction of a group contingency, children increased their peer interaction. Subsequently, the group contingency was removed and was associated with a decline in children's peer interaction. This result suggests that teaching social skills will have little effect unless accompanied by a reinforcement contingency for children to use the trained social skills.

Kamps, Leonard, and colleagues (1992) implemented a similar intervention in a first-grade classroom that contained three children with autism. During 10-minute sessions conducted four times a week, the entire class received instruction on initiating an interaction, giving and accepting compliments, helping others, including others in activities, sharing, and taking turns. Following the completion of social skill training, social interactions of children were monitored each minute during free-play sessions, and those observed to be interacting received stars. Both the children with autism and their peers increased their engagement in social interaction during and following training, which continued when the frequency of monitoring was reduced to two 5-minute checks, and feedback was given to the entire group.

Classwide Social Skills Program (CSSP)

The Classwide Social Skills Program (CSSP) is a program to teach a series of social skills to entire elementary-school classes (Hundert, 1995; Hundert & Taylor, 1993). The CSSP has been found to produce improvement in the recess and social behavior of participating students, as well as in teacher rating of student adjustment. These gains were found for children identified as being at risk for behavioral–emotional problems. No increase in parent rating of child adjustment was found (Hundert et al., 1999).

There are three versions of CSSP: one for preschool and kindergarten children that targets five social skills (listening to others, joining in, sharing, helping others, and problem solving) and uses puppets to model target skills; one for Grades 1 to 4 that teaches 22 social skills; and one called the Classwide Problem Solving Program, which presents videotape-based vignettes for students in Grades 5 to 8.

Sample CCSP Lesson.

Step 1: Presenting the rationale—A new social skill is introduced during a session lasting approximately 10 minutes. Typically, two adults are needed to present a new role play depicting the social skill being introduced to the class. First, there is a brief rationale presented on the importance of the skill (e.g., "Today we are going to learn about sharing. When you are at recess, do you share with your friends?" [*Pause for response.*] "How do you feel when someone shares with you?" [*Pause for response*]).

Step 2: Modeling—The next step is to model the skill components of sharing. Accompanying each skill lesson is a sequence of three to five 8 in. by 10 in. cards, each with a line drawing and a brief textual label of the skill component.

The two adults model a brief (e.g., 1 minute) role-play model of the skill. In the case of sharing, one adult may pretend to be playing with toys when the second adult comes over and expresses interest in the play activity, at which point the first adult offers to share the toy. If a second adult is not available, a child volunteer may be substituted.

Step 3: Identifying the skill components—Immediately following the role play, the lead teacher helps the class to identify the components of the social skill they saw depicted in the role play (e.g., "What was the first thing that I did when I saw Mrs. Booth playing with the toys that I liked? Did I stay over here?" [*Wait for a response close to "Go over."*]). The teacher then shows the first cue card ("That is correct: I went over to Mrs. Booth"). This is repeated for each of the cue cards, which then are left on display. This would also be the time when the lead teacher asks the class to identify the impact of the skill on people's feelings (e.g., "How do you think I felt when Mrs. Booth shared the toy with me?").

Step 4: Child–adult practice—A child volunteer is solicited to practice the skill that was just modeled (e.g. "Who would like to come up and practice sharing, just like Mrs. Booth and I did?" [*Pause for response.*]. "Thank you, [name of child]. Let's remember the steps of sharing. What is the first step?" [*Point to the first cue card*].) This is repeated for all the cue cards. The child volunteer role-plays the same situation as depicted by the two adults. The teacher uses the child–adult role play on the social skills components (e.g., "Did I go over to [name of child]? Did [name of child] share fairly?"). The child is then praised (e.g., "Let's give [name of child] a hand for showing how to share").

Step 5: Presenting a nonexemplar of the social skill—To assist the class in identifying the social skills components, the next step is for the two adults to role-play but leave out one or more of the skill components (e.g., "Mrs. Booth and I are going to practice sharing again, but this time we are going to make mistakes. I want you to be good detectives and see if you can find which steps we left out"). The two adults role-play sharing, but the first adult does not ask to play and instead grabs the toys from the second adult. The second adult looks surprised and upset (e.g., "What step did I leave out? Did I go over?" [*Pause for a response.*] "Did I ask?" [*Pause for a response.*] "You are right. I did not share the toys. I just grabbed them. How do you think that this made Mrs. Booth feel?").

It is important not to have the children practice making the mistake. They should practice only the social skills being implemented correctly.

Step 6: Child–child practice—The class has a second opportunity to practice the target social skill. However, this time it is done with two children role-playing a different play situation. Two volunteers from the class are selected (e.g., "I need two volunteers to practice sharing. Who is interested?"). Before the role play, there is discussion with the two child volunteers about a different time when sharing can be done. This is an attempt to have the role play resemble more natural situations that the class would experience. (e.g., "I would like you to pretend to share in a different situation. When would you use sharing at school?"). The two child volunteers are reminded of the steps in performing the social skill. After the two children finish, there is discussion on how the children depicted the skill components. To ensure that the child volunteers are successful in their role play, the lead teacher helps the children if needed.

Step 7: Correspondence Training—At this point, the target social skill has been introduced and practiced. The next step is for the class to use the social skills in natural environments during the school day. The particular social skill may be the focus of class practice for 1 to 4 weeks, depending on the preference of the teacher and the needs of the students. If the CSSP is being introduced for an entire school or for particular grades in the school, it would be important to coordinate the progression through the skills so that there could be a school or grade division focus on the same skills. For example, the principal may be able to make announcements of the "skill of the week" and there may be postings of artwork depicting the social skills.

At this point, the teacher leads a discussion with the class immediately following the social skills "lesson." During each subsequent morning's exercises, the teacher discusses with the class the time in that school day in which the target social skills can be used (e.g., "When can we use sharing during recess, music class, or any other time today?").

At the end of the school day, the teacher leads a discussion about when the children used the target social skill during that school day. The teacher might comment on times when he or she observed children using the target social skills (e.g., "Jimmy, I saw you share your ball with Catherine at recess today. That was a great example of sharing").

Step 8: Reinforcement—Because in the bustle of the classroom it may be difficult for teachers to remember to praise children who display target social skills, a reinforcement system is introduced to strengthen the children's use of social skills, but also to remind teachers to catch the children practicing the targeted social skills. Each day, the teacher selects five children to wear a "sunshine" badge (or something similar). These badges may consist of small stick-on badges worn by students or laminated badges stuck onto the shirt of a child or worn around the neck. In the course of the school day, the teacher notices times when the children who are wearing badges employ a target social skill. The teacher places a yellow mark from a highlighter pen on the child's badge. These yellow strokes are referred to as "rays of sunshine." Teachers may also deliver "invisible rays of sunshine," which consist of a vertical-stroke motion of a finger on the child's shirt where a badge would be. Reinforcement of children when they are practicing social skills is a very important part of the Classwide Social Skills Program.

At the end of the school day, the children are asked to report how they received their rays of sunshine as part of the correspondence training described earlier. Each child wearing a badge reports how he or she received a ray of sunshine. The teacher tries hard to find times when each child wearing a badge demonstrates social skills during the day.

Children receiving "invisible" rays of sunshine also report on their event. Other children as well may volunteer a description of when they saw the target skill being used.

Children earning rays of sunshine are invited to add a token to a poster in the classroom that displays an accumulation of tokens. The poster may consist of a drawing of anything that the teacher feels would be suitable and may reflect general themes the teacher has introduced to the classroom. For example, in the autumn, the poster may consist of a line drawing of a tree and tokens are paper leaves that are placed at designed locations on the tree. This poster is illustrated in Figure 6.6. Once all the leaves are on the tree, a party or other special event is held for the entire class. Another example of a poster may be a picture of a bubble-gum machine with empty spaces for colored circles to represent bubble gum. The special celebrations that are given to the class are selected by the teacher and the class and could consist of such events as holding a pizza party, watching a special video, going on an outing, or any other event that would be fun for the children. In this system, the reinforcement is earned based on individual children, but the payoff of the reinforcement is delivered to the entire group.

Step 9: Home note—The CSSP uses home notes for each lesson to inform families of the social skills being targeted in the classroom. An example of a home note is shown in Figure 6.7. The home note also encourages parents to praise their child when he or she is found practicing the social skill at home or in other places in the community. Parents are asked to write a brief description of a time when the child practiced the target social skill on a tear-off section of the home note and return that

Figure 6.6. Example of a classroom poster on which children place earned tokens (i.e., paper leaves are placed at designated locations for reinforcement).

CLASSWIDE SOCIAL SKILLS PROGRAM—HOME SHEET

SKILL #1: LISTENING

Dear Parents:

Our class is learning some ways to be good friends and to work well in the classroom. Each week, we shall be learning a new skill and the students will try to practice that skill at school as well as at home.

This week, the class will be learning about being good listeners. The students know that to be a good listener, you must:

STOP what you
are doing

LOOK at the
person speaking

be QUIET until it is
your turn to talk

If you observe your child trying to listen at home, please fill out the form below and return it with your child. We shall discuss it in class.

- -

HAPPY NEWS

_____ did a good job listening when _____
(Name of student)

_____

_____
Signature of parent

Figure 6.7. Example of a home note in the Classwide Social Skills Program.

description to the school. The teacher reads these comments during the morning exercises, when there is discussion about the social skills being taught. For children whose parents do not return a description of the child using a social skill at home, the teacher can ask the child to describe times at home when he or she used the skill and then praise the child's efforts.

Assessment of CCSP.

There are 22 skills in the Grade 1 to 4 version of the Classwide Social Skills Program. Which particular social skills are taught and the order of teaching the skills is determined by the classroom teacher based on an initial rating of the class in each of the 22 skills. An example of a rating scale used by teachers is shown in Figure 6.8. With a child with autism in the class, it would be particularly important to select social skills that would complement areas that need to be targeted for that particular child with autism, including such skills as sharing or joining in.

The Classwide Social Skills Program is designed to improve the social skills within a general classroom setting. The program by itself is unlikely to be intensive enough to produce gains in the peer interaction of children with autism who lack many of the requisite skills for successful peer interaction. In fact, my team members and I collected data on the effect of the CSSP on the amount of peer interaction displayed by a 4-year-old child with autism attending a community day care. Baseline levels of peer interaction were taken prior to the introduction of the Classwide Social Skills Program. The child with autism showed near zero levels of peer interaction prior to any programming introduced in the classroom. As shown in Figure 6.9, there was little increase in the amount of peer interaction of the child with autism after the introduction of the CSSP. Although the rest of the class seemed to be profiting from the CSSP, this particular child still wandered during free play, engaged in stereotypic behavior, and never initiated or responded to peer interaction. It was not until social script training was introduced that the child with autism increased his rates of peer interaction. Not only was there an increase in the child's level of peer interaction, but there was a concomitant decrease in the amount of interaction that was occurring with the classroom teacher. These data need to be replicated in a more systematic study. However, they do suggest that more targeted interventions to promote peer interaction may be necessary for some children with autism in addition to the Classwide Social Skills Program.

Classwide Social Skills Program—Class Rating Form

Your Name: _____ Class: _____

School: _____ Date: _____

Rate the degree to which the class is proficient in the following social skills. Use this rating to determine which social skills you will be teaching in the *Classwide Social Skills Program*. To what extent does each of the following skills need to be taught to the class? Put a check mark in the column that best indicates your answer.

#	Social skill	Definitely	Somewhat	Not at all
	COMMUNICATION SKILLS			
1	Listening to others			
2	Following instructions			
3	Introducing myself			
	INTERPERSONAL SKILLS			
4	Staying out of fights			
5	Handling being corrected			
6	Joining in			
7	Sharing			
8	Complimenting			
9	Helping others			
	COPING SKILLS			
10	Relaxing			
11	Problem solving			
12	Expressing anger appropriately			
13	Apologizing			
14	Ignoring distractions			
15	Responding to teasing			
16	Negotiating/compromising			
	CLASSROOM SKILLS			
17	Bringing material to class			
18	Completing assignments			
19	Asking for help			
20	Making corrections			
21	Contributing to discussions			
22	Attending to task			

Figure 6.8. Rating scale used by teachers to identify social skills to be taught in the Classwide Social Skills Program.

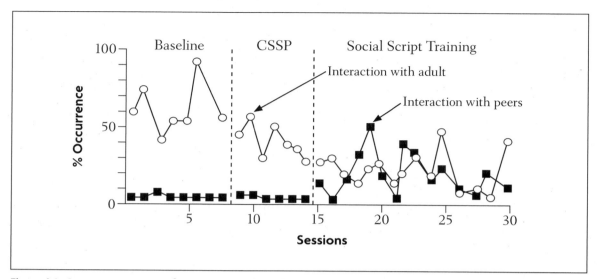

Figure 6.9. Percent occurrence of interaction with an adult and interactive play with peers by a child with autism during baseline, the Classwide Social Skills Program, and social scripts training.

Study Questions

1. What are the major areas of deficits in the peer interaction of children with autism?

2. Compare the approaches of a picture activity schedule and video modeling on the acquisition of play for children with autism.

3. What are some examples of arranging the classroom environment to promote peer interaction?

4. Compare adult-initiated and peer-initiated approaches to promoting peer interaction.

Social Script for the Ball and Pipe Game

Materials

- A soccer-size ball that has unique color (e.g., yellow) that is only used for this game
- Black plastic 2-in.-diameter PVP pipe cut into 2-foot lengths (total of four)

Rules of the Game

On a playground, Leo (child with autism) and a peer are positioned approximately 3 yards apart with one foot touching a marker (e.g., a beanbag) placed on the ground. The players face one another. Approximately 1 yard behind Leo, one pipe is placed upright into the ground. Behind the peer, three separate pipes are placed in a row 1 yard behind the peer and spread approximately 1 yard from one another. The one pipe behind Leo has a number 1 marked on it, and each of the three individual pipes behind the peer has a number 3 marked on it. A 2-in. paper coin is constructed, on one side of which the word *Leo* is written and on the other side of which the word *Friend* is written. The coin is flipped, and the person whose name is showing gets to go first.

The player who is starting places the ball anywhere within kicking range from his or her marker. The player kicks the ball, aiming at a pipe, keeping the nonkicking foot on the marker. The goal of the game is to knock down a pipe and earn the number of points marked on the pipe. Leo has three pipes to aim at, each worth 3 points. The peer has only one pipe to aim at, worth 1 point. (The game is set up in favor of Leo, who is likely to be less skilled than his peer is.)

When a shot is made, the opponent tries to block the shot but cannot move his or her foot from the marker. The peers take turns making shots until one accumulates 10 points and then becomes the winner.

Set Up

Before this game is initially played, class volunteers are asked by an adult to learn how to play the game. The explanation given is that this is Leo's game and that we are looking for volunteers to learn how to play this game with him. Leo then picks up to three children initially to play the game.

At the next recess, the four children (including Leo) go to the playground, and the game is explained by Leo's paraprofessional. The paraprofessional first describes the rules of the game and then models how the game is played. Next, one game is played between Leo and one peer, with the paraprofessional located beside Leo, providing physical and verbal prompts when necessary. The other two peers watch how the game is played. After the first round, a different peer is asked to play with Leo. Thereafter, Leo or a peer can initiate the ball and pipe game.

It is important to systematically fade out the presence of the paraprofessional over time. It is likely that the adult will need to be present as long as Leo needs help in following the rules of the game. If Leo does not follow a rule of the game (e.g., he does not keep his foot on the marker), the game is paused for correction and the ball is given to the peer for a free kick. The same correction method is used if a peer violates a rule.

The prompts should be faded out in five steps, with the progression of fading steps occurring when Leo completes one game with no rule violations:

1. The adult is located behind Leo, assisting him in playing the game.
2. The adult is located approximately 2 yards off to the side providing Leo with verbal instructions.
3. The adult is located 2 yards off to the side providing verbal instructions but periodically walking away for 30 seconds at a time.
4. The adult is located approximately 5 yards away and present only during the initial set up.
5. The adult sets up the game, but then walks away.

Data Collection

Prior to the introduction of the social script, the amount of interactive play that Leo exhibits is observed for three consecutive recesses. This continues for the first three recesses following the social script training and then gets reduced to twice-a-week observations.

PEER INTERACTION DATA SHEET

(SHORT FORM)

Child: _____   Observer: _____

Using an audiotape of prerecorded sound cues via an earphone, observe Leo in play for an instant every 30 seconds. Record whether or not Leo is engaged in interactive play based on the following definition.

Interactive Play (IP): The child is engaged in a play activity (e.g., pushing a toy truck, coloring) within 2 yards of at least one other child and is interacting verbally (e.g., talking about a play activity) or nonverbally (e.g., allowing another child to take turns playing with a toy, listening when another child is talking specifically to him/her) with another child.

Observe for 10 minutes (20 observations). In the first box corresponding with the date of the observation session, circle IP if at the instant of the observation, the child *was* engaged in interactive play or circle—if the child *was not* engaged in interactive play. Do this for each successive box.

Date												
Time												
1	IP —	IP —	IP —	IP —	IP —	IP —	IP —	IP —	IP —	IP —	IP —	IP —
2	IP —	IP —	IP —	IP —	IP —	IP —	IP —	IP —	IP —	IP —	IP —	IP —
3	IP —	IP —	IP —	IP —	IP —	IP —	IP —	IP —	IP —	IP —	IP —	IP —
4	IP —	IP —	IP —	IP —	IP —	IP —	IP —	IP —	IP —	IP —	IP —	IP —
5	IP —	IP —	IP —	IP —	IP —	IP —	IP —	IP —	IP —	IP —	IP —	IP —
6	IP —	IP —	IP —	IP —	IP —	IP —	IP —	IP —	IP —	IP —	IP —	IP —
7	IP —	IP —	IP —	IP —	IP —	IP —	IP —	IP —	IP —	IP —	IP —	IP —
8	IP —	IP —	IP —	IP —	IP —	IP —	IP —	IP —	IP —	IP —	IP —	IP —
9	IP —	IP —	IP —	IP —	IP —	IP —	IP —	IP —	IP —	IP —	IP —	IP —
10	IP —	IP —	IP —	IP —	IP —	IP —	IP —	IP —	IP —	IP —	IP —	IP —
11	IP —	IP —	IP —	IP —	IP —	IP —	IP —	IP —	IP —	IP —	IP —	IP —
12	IP —	IP —	IP —	IP —	IP —	IP —	IP —	IP —	IP —	IP —	IP —	IP —
13	IP —	IP —	IP —	IP —	IP —	IP —	IP —	IP —	IP —	IP —	IP —	IP —
14	IP —	IP —	IP —	IP —	IP —	IP —	IP —	IP —	IP —	IP —	IP —	IP —
15	IP —	IP —	IP —	IP —	IP —	IP —	IP —	IP —	IP —	IP —	IP —	IP —
16	IP —	IP —	IP —	IP —	IP —	IP —	IP —	IP —	IP —	IP —	IP —	IP —
17	IP —	IP —	IP —	IP —	IP —	IP —	IP —	IP —	IP —	IP —	IP —	IP —
18	IP —	IP —	IP —	IP —	IP —	IP —	IP —	IP —	IP —	IP —	IP —	IP —
19	IP —	IP —	IP —	IP —	IP —	IP —	IP —	IP —	IP —	IP —	IP —	IP —
20	IP —	IP —	IP —	IP —	IP —	IP —	IP —	IP —	IP —	IP —	IP —	IP —
#												
%												

7 Following School Routines Independently

Chapter Topics

- Use of visual schedules (including picture activity schedules and computer activity schedules)
- Participation in group lessons
- Completion of seatwork assignments

f students with autism are to function independently in general education classrooms, they need to learn to follow routines for much of the school day without assistance. These routines include knowing how to enter the school when the school bell rings, remove and hang up their coats/jackets, take out whatever books and notebooks are needed in class from their backpack, and sit down in an assigned desk. A similar routine is expected for students when going to the washroom, making a transition to the gym, participating during class lessons, completing a seatwork assignment, going to the playground for recess, having lunch, putting materials away, and leaving at the end of the school day, among many other examples.

Most typically developing children know how to complete these and other similar school routines with little or no assistance. However, many children with autism do not know what is expected in completing school routines, or if they do know, they do not initiate the desired actions without a considerable amount of adult verbal instruction, physical prompting, and/or modeling. Unfortunately, all too easily, children with autism become dependent on adult prompts, thus routine-following behavior would not occur without these prompts (Bryan & Gast, 2000; MacDuff, Krantz, & McClannahan, 1993). Over time, repeated adult prompting of the actions of a child with autism results in the child not initiating those actions without the discriminative stimulus of adult prompts.

Not only do children with autism have difficulty performing routines independent of direct adult prompting, but they also have difficulties making transitions from one activity to the next. Schmit, Alper, Raschke, and Ryndak (2000) estimated that preschool and primary-grade students spend 18% to 25% of their school day in transitions. Transitions are also a situation frequently associated with tantrums and other problem behaviors (Volkmar, 1996). Because of these difficulties, it is important for educators to develop strategies to increase the ability of children with autism to perform age-appropriate activities while reducing their dependence on adults. A few such strategies are discussed below.

Use of Visual Schedules

One routine-following strategy that has been extensively used is to present children with autism with visual cues that assist them in following routines. Visual stimuli may be presented as photographs (e.g., Schmit et al., 2000), line drawings (e.g., Dooley, Wilczenski, & Torem, 2001; Pierce & Schreibman, 1994), or text (e.g., Stromer, MacKay, McVay, & Fowler, 1998). For many years, the Treatment and Education of Autistic and related Communication-handicapped CHildren (TEACCH) program (Schopler & Mesibov, 1994) has used visual cues to teach children with autism to follow a schedule of activities. A schedule board is created that depicts the sequence of forthcoming activities in a child's routine at school by representing each activity as a separate line drawing with associated printed text, as depicted in Figure 7.1.

Each picture is secured to a schedule board with Velcro strips. When the child with autism first arrives in the classroom, the teacher or paraprofessional takes the child to his or her individualized schedule board and reviews the schedule for the day. The child is taught to take the picture of the next activity and match it with a container of material for that activity or to a corresponding picture at the entrance to a setting (e.g., washroom). The child with autism then engages in the designated activity (e.g., complete a sheet of math problems, use the washroom). Once the child has completed the activity, he or she deposits the picture for that activity in a container, indicating that the activity is finished.

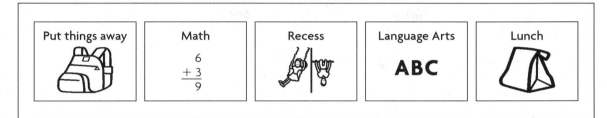

Figure 7.1. Example of a picture activity schedule to help a child with autism follow routine morning activities at school.

Dooley et al. (2001) used an activity schedule to teach a 3-year-old boy with autism to follow routines in a special education preschool class. The boy exhibited hitting and kicking toward staff and other children. He learned to take a picture from his schedule board, complete the activity, and deposit the card in a container, after which the boy received a pretzel. The teacher signaled the time for the boy to move to the next activity by presenting a verbal cue paired with turning the classroom lights off and on. After 6 days of this training, the teacher stopped using the pretzel reward. The results indicated that with the introduction of the schedule board and pretzel, there was a reduction in the boy's aggression and an increase in his on-schedule behavior. This improvement in the child's on-schedule behavior continued after the pretzel reward was removed. Unfortunately, this study did not use an experimental design that would allow one to assign the observed improvements in the boy's behavior to the intervention.

A similar use of pictures indicating scheduled activities was described by Schmit et al. (2000) for a 6-year-old boy with autism attending a special education classroom in a community school. Rather than line drawings, Schmit et al. used photographs paired with a textual label (e.g., "computer," "library") to indicate the activities in the boy's schedule. The photographic cueing of activities resulted in a reduction of the boy's problem behavior during transitions across different school settings.

Both the Schmit et al. (2000) and the Dooley et al. (2001) studies were straightforward illustrations of the use of visual schedules to cue the on-schedule behavior of children with autism exhibiting aggression during transitions. However, the children still needed adult prompting (turning off and on the light in the Dooley et al. [2001] study and verbal instructions in the Schmit et al. [2000] study) to follow schedules. Although there was an increase in the boys' schedule following and a reduction in their problem behaviors, there was no information on whether the boys were on task during the activities of the schedule.

Bryan and Gast (2000) examined whether the picture activity schedule (PAS) initially described by MacDuff et al. (1993) would produce an increase in both on-schedule and on-task behaviors for children with autism. In the study, children with autism between the ages of 7 years 4 months and 8 years 11 months attended general education classrooms with special education support for half of their school day, and the other half of the school day they attended a resource classroom located in the same school. The resource classroom was divided into four learning centers, each containing associated learning materials. For example, a reading center contained books on bookshelves, a few large pillows, and a beanbag chair. Each child had a photo album that contained four line-drawn pictures of academic activities, each presented on a separate page. Graduated guidance was used to teach a boy to follow his PAS. Learning center sessions were started by the resource classroom teacher gaining the attention of all children and signaling for them to start completing learning materials in a specified learning center. The teacher waited 10 seconds for the child to move to his PAS book. If the child did not initiate moving toward the book, the teacher physically prompted the child to do so. The child was required to complete the activity, put away any materials, return to his PAS book, and to move to the next activity. Manual prompting from behind was used with the degree of the prompt (e.g., hand-over-hand, touching the child's shoulder, light touch) decreasing over time in a most-to-least prompting sequence. Praise was delivered for on-task and on-schedule behavior on average once every 3 minutes. Students completed activities in the four learning centers over a 40-minute session, with 10 minutes devoted to each learning center.

The on-task and on-schedule behaviors of the four children with autism were recorded before any teaching was introduced. Next, children were taught to follow the PAS by teacher-delivered graduated guidance (i.e., the teacher physically guided them on what to do). Graduated guidance was then removed, and the children were expected to follow their PAS books without teacher prompts. The next condition consisted of a return to baseline when the PAS book was withdrawn. Finally, the children were tested on whether they could apply the picture activity schedule to novel academic material.

Children increased their on-schedule and on-task behavior after the introduction of graduated guidance and the PAS book. They were able to maintain that increased behavior when graduated guidance was removed, and they generalized their improved performance to novel academic activities. However, children's increased behaviors were not maintained when the PAS book was removed. This study suggests that children with autism can follow a schedule of activities using a picture activity schedule without added prompts and apply that learning to both trained and novel learning activities. However, even after becoming proficient in following the picture activity schedule, children did not maintain their on-schedule behavior when the PAS book was not available.

There are numerous descriptions of how to design and implement schedules for children with autism (McClannahan & Krantz, 1999; Mesibov, Browder, & Kirkland, 2002; Stromer, Kimball, Kinney, & Taylor, 2006). The following steps represent a synthesis of this information.

1. Determine if the child with autism has the prerequisite skills to complete a visual schedule successfully—McClannahan and Krantz (1999) postulated that there are a number of skills important for a child to be successful at learning a picture activity schedule. First, a child must be able to discriminate a picture from its background. This ability would be indicated when a child is able to point to a picture that is mounted on a solid color background sheet when asked. A child must be able to match a picture of an object to the identical object. The child must be able to accept manual guidance that is used in teaching the picture activity schedule.

2. Identify the purpose of the schedule—Schedules can be used to teach children to make transitions; to perform a series of activities within the repertoire of the children, but not done independently; or to teach new skills, such as how to initiate a play activity with a peer (Morrison, Sainato, Benchaaban, & Endo, 2002). It is recommended that the initial PAS be brief and contain activities the child is already familiar with (McClannahan & Krantz, 1999). Once children have learned to follow schedules of familiar activities, it may be possible to use picture activity schedules to teach new skills (Stromer et al., 2006).

3. Select the type of stimuli to cue schedule following—The stimuli used to teach schedule following can include line drawings (Krantz & McClannahan, 1998; Pierce & Schreibman, 1994), photographs (Schmit et al., 2000), text with photographs (Krantz & McClannahan, 1998), or even audio cards (Stevenson, Krantz, & McClannahan, 2000). Stevenson and colleagues (2000) taught four boys with autism, 10 to 15 years old, to initiate play interactions with peers. When their schedule indicated that it was time to initiate a social interaction, the boys took a prerecorded audio card that was in the schedule notebook, listened to a prerecorded script as to what to say to initiate play with a peer, approached a peer, and imitated the vocal model.

Mesibov et al. (2002) described that there are a number of symbols that can be used in creating an individualized schedule that range in difficulty from using actual objects (e.g., a towel to signal swimming), to a symbol of the objects associated with the activity (e.g., miniature towel to signal swimming), to a photograph of the activity, to a line drawing of the activity, to text describing the activity (e.g., "swimming"). When objects are used to cue activities, they should be arranged from top to bottom on a bookshelf or physically arranged in some way to show the temporal order of events. It is important to use types of cues for the schedule that the child can easily follow.

4. *Select a presentation format*—Pictures for individualized schedules can be presented in a sequence on a strip (e.g., Dooley et al., 2001), printed one at a time in a notebook or photo album (MacDuff et al., 1993), or presented on a computer (Stromer et al., 2006). McClannahan and Krantz (1999) have suggested that a picture of each activity be placed in a plastic sheet and mounted one to a page in a notebook or small photo album. The child attends to the picture of a scheduled activity, points to that picture, completes the activity, comes back to the PAS book, and turns the page to look at what activity is next.

Each activity should have a clear beginning and end so that the child will know when the activity is finished. For example, the activity may consist of the child completing all of the math problems on a worksheet. For activities that do not have a clear beginning or end, Stromer and colleagues (2006) suggested the use of a timer that cues the child when to end the activity. Decide on the type and number of activities to include in a child's schedule. McClannahan and Krantz (1999) suggested that at the beginning of teaching a PAS to a child, one should use no more than five or six activities and should also end with a preferred snack or game.

5. *Decide how to teach the schedule-following procedure*—McClannahan and Krantz (1999) described the use of graduated guidance to teach children with autism how to follow a picture activity schedule. Once all of the materials are arranged, the teacher gives an initial instruction such as "It's time to do your schedule" or "Go play." The teacher waits 10 seconds for the child to initiate the first activity before providing manual guidance. Obviously, when a PAS is first introduced, the child will not know how to follow the schedule and will need assistance from the teacher to learn the routine. The teacher is positioned behind the child and provides the least amount of manual guidance needed for the child to follow the presented schedule. The child is prompted to open the PAS book and point to the first picture. The child is then guided to complete the activity shown in the picture mounted on the page. Once the activity is completed, the teacher prompts the child to replace the material, return to the PAS book, and turn the page to progress to the next activity in the schedule.

McClannahan and Krantz (1999) suggested that on completion of the schedule, the child be reinforced for making correct responses and following the schedule. They suggested the use of a token system (see Chapter 4) in which the teacher delivers tokens while standing behind the child. The child learns to exchange tokens for a backup reward, as described earlier. Dooley et al. (2001) gave a child with autism a pretzel for each activity he completed in his individualized schedule. Picture activity schedules that our team has designed commonly have a token attached to the same page as the picture of the activity. Once the child completes the activity, he or she returns to the PAS book and removes the token from the page. As previously described, McClannahan and Krantz (1999) suggested that the final activity on a picture activity schedule consist of a highly preferred activity for the child.

6. *Fade the use of graduated guidance*—As a child becomes able to follow a PAS with adult manual guidance, the amount of manual guidance provided by the adult should be systematically reduced. The sequence of fading prompts was described in Chapter 4. It consists of changing the manual prompt from hand-over-hand; to a light hold on the child's forearm, then upper arm, then elbow; and then reducing it to a light touch on the child's shoulder. Next McClannahan and Krantz (1999) suggested the use of "shadowing," in which the teacher follows the child's hand movements with his or her hands, but does not touch the child. Finally, the teacher increases the physical distance between him- or herself and the child. If errors occur when the child is following the PAS, the teacher returns to the previous level of prompting provided.

7. *Shift from pictorial to textual cues*—Stromer et al. (2006) made the analogy between picture activity schedules and "to-do" lists that many people use to remember tasks that need to be done in a time period. If possible, it would be desirable to transition a child who is following a PAS to the use of textual cues. McClannahan and Krantz (1999) described how one can systematically introduce textual cues by first pairing words (e.g., "boots on") with a picture associated with a child putting boots on. Over time, the picture is slowly faded by removing parts of it and/or by making the picture fainter (this can be done with computer software). Eventually, the child is left with individual cards that contain words describing the next activity. It may be possible to teach a child with autism to follow a schedule such as the one illustrated in Figure 7.2, used to help a child to follow a routine at the end of a school day. The child would be asked to check off each activity as it is completed.

A summary of the steps in designing and conducting a visual schedule is shown in Figure 7.3.

Example Picture Activity Schedule

In Chapter 3, the use of picture activity schedules to teach a child how to complete a play activity independently was described. I shall use a different example of a PAS to illustrate teaching a young 5-year-old boy with autism to wash his hands. The PAS is used to teach completing the steps within the task of washing hands, rather than

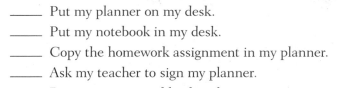

_____ Put my planner on my desk.

_____ Put my notebook in my desk.

_____ Copy the homework assignment in my planner.

_____ Ask my teacher to sign my planner.

_____ Put on my coat and backpack.

Figure 7.2. Example of a text schedule.

1. Determine if the child with autism has the prerequisite skills to be able to complete a visual schedule successfully.
2. Identify the purpose of the schedule.
3. Select the type of stimuli to cue schedule following.
4. Select a presentation format (e.g., picture strip, picture album, computer presentation).
5. Decide how to teach the schedule-following procedure.
6. Fade the use of graduated guidance.
7. Shift from pictorial to textual cues.

Figure 7.3. Summary of steps for designing and implementing visual schedules.

following the steps between one task and the next, as occurs when one is teaching on-schedule behavior.

The boy required an extensive amount of adult assistance to complete a hand-washing routine and never initiated any steps of the routine independently. The boy could make simple requests using a picture exchange communication system, match 2-D to 3-D objects, and accepted manual guidance. A picture schedule board was selected as the method to present the visual stimuli because the child could see the entire sequence at once. A notebook was not practical to use, because the child's hands would be wet through most of the hand-washing sequence. A six-step sequence of washing hands was taught with a line drawing of each step depicted on a 5 cm by 5 cm card, shown in Figure 7.4. The cards were laminated and placed (with Velcro) progressing from left to right on a strip of cardboard.

Beneath each picture was a token fastened by Velcro. A seventh card was used to depict the child's preferred reinforcer (a cookie) that would be received after hand washing was finished. A paraprofessional used manual guidance to teach the child to look at and touch the first card in the picture sequence. The paraprofessional waited 5 seconds for the child to initiate turning on the water. After the child completed the action, he was prompted to remove that picture, place it in a container, remove the corresponding token, and place it on a token strip. If the child did not perform the designated activity, the paraprofessional physically prompted the child to do so following a most-to-least prompting sequence.

The paraprofessional then prompted the child to perform the next action in the hand-washing routine in the same manner. After the child completed the six steps

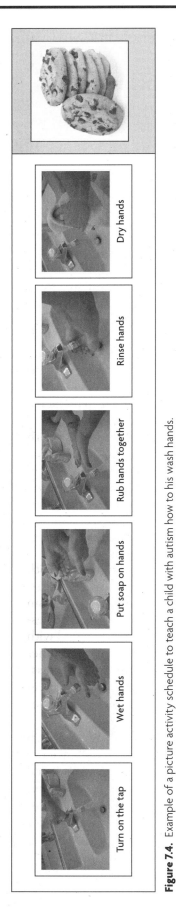

Figure 7.4. Example of a picture activity schedule to teach a child with autism how to his wash hands.

of the hand-washing routine, he was then allowed to have his preferred reinforcer (a cookie).

Over time, the amount of prompting was gradually reduced. Teaching sessions were held three times a day during naturally occurring times when the child was washing hands (e.g., before snacks and lunch).

Computer Activity Schedules

Stromer and colleagues (2006) extended the work of McClannahan and Krantz (1999) by using computers as the medium to present activity schedules to children with autism. One of the rationales for the use of computers to present activity schedules is that children with autism may prefer instruction presented by a computer over instructions presented by a teacher (Romanczyk, Weiner, Lockshin, & Ekdahl, 1999). In fact, children with autism may learn tasks faster using a computer than having the same content taught by a teacher (Moore & Calvert, 2000). Computer activity schedules follow the same steps as picture activity schedules except that the picture cues are presented on a computer rather than on paper. Computer schedules have the added benefit of being able to embed a video model of the desired activity in the computer presentation.

The steps involved in designing computer activity schedules have been described in Rehfeldt, Kinney, Root, and Stromer (2004). The first step is to collect digital photographs, sound files, and video clips that can be used to develop the activity schedule. The second step is to develop a Microsoft PowerPoint presentation in which the pictures, video, and sound files are embedded with text into slides. The first slide contains text (e.g., "Let's go to your activity schedule") to introduce the schedule, and the final slide contains a photograph of the preferred item or activity the child earns for completing the activity schedule.

Kimball, Kinney, Taylor, and Stromer (2004) used two slides for each activity in the activity schedule. The first slide consisted of a photograph of the activity, and the second slide displayed a brief (5-second) video of the activity being done. Each slide contained an action button. The child was taught to look at the slide and then click on the action button to advance to the next slide. When slides with embedded video were presented, the child clicked on the video to activate it. After watching the video, the child performed the demonstrated activity. When the child completed the activity, he or she returned to the computer and advanced the slide to view the next activity. If the activity did not have a clear beginning and end, the child performed the activity until a timer (built into the computer program) sounded.

Stromer et al. (2006) described two limitations to the use of computer activity schedules. First, the knowledge and time for preparing the computer-based slides is extensive and may be beyond the capabilities of many educators. Second, the expense and lack of portability of some computers may prove to be prohibitive. It is likely that both of these limitations can be overcome if the computer activity schedule seems beneficial for one or more children with autism in a school. Computer activity schedules have the advantage of being able to incorporate video models, as well as using cartoons or video games as possible reinforcers for a child's schedule (Rehfeldt et al., 2004). In all, computer activity schedules hold considerable promise as an advancement to picture activity schedules.

Participation in Group Lessons

One of the features of general education classrooms is that students typically receive much of their instruction through a lesson presented to the class by the teacher. There is a need for students to be able to attend to the teacher when he or she is talking and to attend to other students when they are answering questions. In addition, students need to learn to raise their hand when they want to answer a question.

There are at least a couple of significant challenges for a child with autism to be able to participate in a group lesson. The first is an issue discussed in Chapter 3: The content of the lesson needs to be adjusted so that it can accommodate the learning needs of the child with autism. Embedded instruction (Polychronis, McDonnell, Johnson, & Jameson, 2004) and individualized group instruction (Hoyson, Jamieson, Strain, & Smith, 1998) are examples of strategies to modify a group lesson format to include a child with autism in the class.

A second challenge is how to provide adult-delivered prompts to a child with autism so that he or she may participate in a group lesson without fostering dependence of the child on adult prompting. It is quite common for a child with disabilities to follow classroom routines when a paraprofessional is seated beside the child and delivering full manual or verbal prompts (Marks, Schrader, & Levine, 1999). In these situations, the child may learn to orient toward the paraprofessional, rather than focusing on the instructions of the classroom teacher. The child with autism may wait for the prompts from the paraprofessional before following the classroom routines.

There are a number of procedures that should be put into place for a child with autism to learn how to attend to a teacher's lesson and to answer posed questions. First, as much as possible, instructions, prompts, and reinforcement for a child with autism in a classroom should come from the classroom teacher rather than from a paraprofessional. During lessons, the paraprofessional should be positioned behind the child with autism so as not to distract the child from focusing on the classroom teacher or other students when they respond to teacher instruction. In the busy environment of a classroom, the general education teacher may not be able to deliver prompts or reinforcement to the child with autism at the frequency that the child may need. As a result, some prompting and reinforcement may need to originate from the paraprofessional.

The paraprofessional should use graduated guidance to deliver prompts in such a way that the child with autism continues to focus on the classroom teacher. Once the child with autism is participating well, the paraprofessional prompting can be faded along three dimensions that were described for prompt fading in Chapter 4: amount of prompt, delay in delivering a prompt, and location of the prompter. First, there can be a gradual reduction in the amount of a prompt the paraprofessional delivers. For example, paraprofessionals may initially prompt a child with autism to attend to the classroom teacher by briefly cupping his or her hands on either side of the child's face to direct the child's gaze to the classroom teacher. Later, this prompt may be reduced by having the paraprofessional place only one hand at the side of the child's face, and eventually may be reduced to simply using a light touch. The amount of prompting, as well as the reinforcement contingency and schedule provided to a child with autism in a group lesson, need to be specified and coordinated between a classroom teacher and paraprofessional.

An example of a completed planning form for specifying the levels of prompting and reinforcement to be used can be seen in Table 7.1. This table also shows an example of how the levels of prompting and reinforcement can be gradually reduced as the child continues to focus on the classroom teacher.

Completion of Seatwork Assignments

Following a class lesson, children in the classroom may be instructed to complete a specified seatwork assignment that was covered in the class lesson. The issues involved in assisting a child with autism to complete a seatwork assignment independently are similar to those described for helping a child with autism participate during class lessons. As with class lessons, it is critical that a child with autism be given work of a difficulty level that the child is able to complete.

Our educational team intersperses previously mastered content into new content that the child receives. In addition, we use within-stimulus prompts (as described in Chapter 3) so that the child with autism is able to answer at least 50% of presented work correctly on initial presentation. There should be clear expectations to the child as to how much work is to be completed. Only that amount of seatwork should be given at one time. At the end of the section of work that is to be completed, we place a drawing of an open hand that signals to the child to raise his or her hand to have the work checked. A visual timer (such as a clock) that depicts the passage of time by showing a diminishing pie shape on a clock face or the use of a countdown timer is set for the child. A model of how to complete the assigned task is given. The child with autism is then instructed what to do if he or she needs help (e.g., skip the question and continue with the other questions, raise his or her hand). As with class lessons, the type and amount of prompting and reinforcement needs to be specified and gradually reduced as the child's performance warrants.

Table 7.1
An Example of Reduction in the Delivery of Prompting and Reinforcement for a Child With Autism Participating in a Group Lesson.

Date	Amount of prompt	Delay of prompt	Position	Reinforcement contingency	Reinforcement schedule
Nov. 17	Both hands	0 sec	Behind	For on-task behavior	VI 1
Nov. 23	One hand	0 sec	Behind	For on-task behavior	VI 2
Nov. 24	One hand	1 sec	1 ft away	For on-task behavior	VI 2
Nov. 27	Light touch	1 sec	1 ft away	For on-task behavior	VI 2
Nov. 29	Light touch	2 sec	1 ft away	For on-task behavior	VI 3

Note. VI = variable interval schedule of reinforcement (e.g., VI 1 would indicate that, on average, reinforcement would be delivered for a correct response once a minute).

Study Questions

1. What are some of the routines with which children with autism would have difficulty in school?

2. Describe the steps in the formation of a visual schedule for a child with autism.

3. How does a computer activity schedule differ from a picture activity schedule?

4. What is the role of paraprofessionals in helping children with autism participate in group lessons?

5. How does one help children with autism complete seatwork assignments independently?

8 Teaching Thinking Skills

Chapter Topics

- Teaching self-regulation
- Teaching self-monitoring
- Teaching answering of inferential *why*-questions
- Teaching perspective taking

Almost all of the techniques described in this book to prepare children with autism for inclusive educational settings involve structuring a detailed learning environment around the child to produce desired child outcomes. For example, a picture activity schedule (MacDuff, Krantz, & McClannahan, 1993) may be used to help children with autism to independently complete an activity such as executing a bathroom routine or following opening exercises at school. Similarly, frequent adult-delivered prompts and reinforcement of desired behaviors are almost always components of applied behavior analysis programs for children with autism. However, unless at some point children with autism in general education classrooms demonstrate an ability to learn new skills under conditions similar to those experienced by their classmates and apply that learning to novel situations, they will always be dependent on intensive adult assistance for their continued learning. One possibility for reducing the amount of adult assistance needed for learning is to teach children with autism to regulate their own behavior so that they are able to learn with levels of adult supervision similar to those of their classmates in a general education class. Self-regulation is a much more complex skill to teach children with autism than those discussed so far in this book.

Eventually, if children with autism in inclusive classrooms are expected to participate in learning some of the same curriculum as their peers, they are likely to encounter questions that require them to draw inferences. For example, in second grade, students may read a story from a book and be questioned on why particular events occurred for which the answer was not explicitly stated in the book. Consider the following simple example that a second-grade class might read: "Michael ran home from school to play his favorite video game. When he got home, he had to wait on the porch for someone else in the family to come home." After reading this passage, the class might be asked, "Why did Michael not go into the house to play his video game?" Answering this type of inferential question would be more difficult than responding to factual recall questions such as "Who ran home?" "Where did Michael run?" or "What did Michael want to do when he got home?" For these factual questions, the child would simply need to comprehend the question and recall what was specifically stated in the reading passage. In answering inferential *why*-questions, a child would need to draw from his or her general knowledge and infer plausible answers, such as that the door may have been locked, so Michael needed to wait for a parent to return home to unlock it.

Children with autism have been described as having a weakness in their ability to view situations from someone else's perspective. An example of difficulties children with autism have in perspective taking is illustrated by the "Sally-Anne task," described by Baron-Cohen, Leslie, and Frith (1985) in their "Theory of Mind" study. Children observed one doll (Sally) placing a marble in a box and then leaving the room. While Sally is away, a second doll, Anne, transfers the marble from the box to a basket. The child who has been observing the series of actions is asked, "Where will Sally look for the marble?" Typically developing children and children with Down syndrome will tend to state that Sally will look in the box. Children with autism are much more likely to choose the basket. Baron-Cohen (1995) proposed that weakness in the ability to perceive a situation from someone else's perspective is a central cognitive-processing deficit that lies at the heart of autism. Criticism of that position has been described by Smukler (2005).

This chapter will describe interventions that have been used with children with autism in general education classrooms to teach self-regulation, self-monitoring, answering inferential *why*-questions, and perspective taking. Terms such as *thinking* and *inference making* are used for convenience of communication, and, to be consistent with a behavior analytic perspective, they must be operationally defined when used to describe the behavior of a particular child.

Teaching Self-Regulation

Deficits in self-regulation have been identified as a possible core problem for persons with developmental disabilities (Whitman, 1990b), as well as for persons with autism (Hill, 2004; Ozonoff, 1997; Whitman, 2004). Whitman (1990b) concluded that persons with developmental disabilities can be taught adaptive and cognitive skills. The difficulty, he argued, was that these individuals tend not to use what they have learned outside of training situations. Whitman (1990b) proposed that persons with developmental disabilities lacked an ability to regulate their actions. Commenting on the thesis proposed by Whitman (1990b), Baer (1990) stated that self-regulation is a behavior that can be learned, mediates other behaviors, and itself is under stimulus control. For example, Guevremont, Osnes, and Stokes (1986) prompted two preschoolers to verbalize that they will engage in particular target behaviors (e.g., raising their hand during group lessons, asking other children to play) later in the day. Children were reinforced for performing the target behaviors that they stated that they would do. Children were found not only to increase their target behavior during the preschool setting in which "correspondence training" was provided but also to increase the target behavior in other preschool settings and at home, in the absence of direct reinforcement contingencies. After children's target behaviors came under the control of their previous verbalizations about the target behaviors, there was an increase in children's target behaviors in other settings.

Figure 8.1 illustrates the role self-regulation plays in a behavior change process in contrast to an adult-mediated behavior change. In adult-mediated behavior change, the behavior of a child with autism is changed through environmental events such as prompts, reinforcement, presentation of learning material, and so on, arranged by an adult. In self-regulated behavior change, the child's self-regulatory behavior elicits the child's targeted behavior at a later time without the direct influence of an adult.

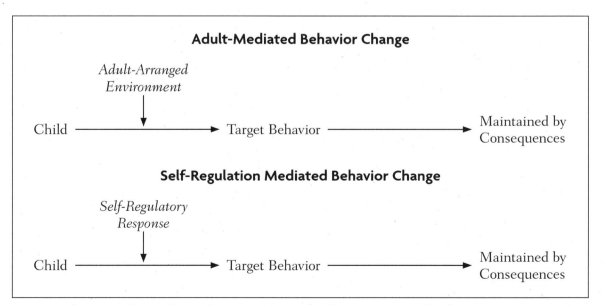

Figure 8.1. Illustration of the difference between adult-mediated behavior change and self-regulation mediated behavior change.

Whitman (1990a) suggested that self-regulation be viewed as a response chain that leads to an individual emitting a target response. An individual sets a goal for behavior change, monitors his or her behavior, compares the actual to the desired occurrence of behavior, and then adjusts his or her target behavior accordingly. If self-regulation is a response chain, it may be possible to teach a child with autism to self-regulate using "backward chaining" (Cooper, Heron, & Heward, 2007). Backward chaining consists of teaching a series of responses by starting at the last step in the sequence and teaching each step one at a time, moving backward in the response sequence. For example, if backward chaining is used in teaching a child to put on a sock, an adult would position the sock over the child's toe and pull it over the heel of the foot. The child is then taught to pull the sock over the ankle independently. Using graduated physical guidance, the child is taught to pull the sock over the heel of the foot, which then leads to (acts as a discriminative stimulus for) the previously learned response of the child pulling the sock over the ankle. The instruction progresses in this way backward through the response chain.

The same logic may be used for teaching a child with autism to self-regulate his or her on-task behavior in a classroom. An adult may execute all of the steps of a self-regulatory sequence of actions that would subsequently be transferred to a child, starting at the last step. The adult selects the goal of an increase in a child's on-task behavior and records the occurrence of the student's on-task behavior during a time period of interest (e.g., independent seatwork). The first step taught to the child may consist of the child learning to look at the adult's record of the number of times the target behavior occurred and then selecting a corresponding amount of reinforcement for the occurrence of the target behavior.

To record instances of target behaviors, the instructor may design a simple data sheet on which there are a series of boxes containing a check mark or an X, The instructor selects the standard that the child with autism needs to achieve (e.g., being on task at least 8 of 10 observations). A timer (e.g., the MotivAider from Tools for Wellness) is set to vibrate on average every 5 minutes. On that signal, the instructor judges whether or not the child with autism is on task (i.e., completing assigned work, looking at the teacher when talking, looking at another student when answering a question posed by the teacher, and so on). If the child is on task, the instructor circles a check mark on the data sheet (see Figure 8.2). If the child is not on task, the instructor circles an X. This evaluation continues for a set time period (e.g., 50 minutes). The instructor tallies the number of check marks and enters that number at the bottom of the data sheet. In this example, during the 50-minute observation, the child was on task on 8 of 10 occasions when the timer signaled.

As previously indicated, at this initial step, the instructor teaches the child to write down the corresponding number of points or to take the corresponding number of tokens corresponding to the check mark. This instruction continues until the child can accurately exchange the total number of check marks for tokens.

Following the same format, the next step may consist of the child self-monitoring whether or not he or she was on task at the signal of the timer, which is now placed in the child's pocket so that it can be felt by the child. To teach a child to be accurate in self-monitoring, the instructor provides 2 points if the child self-monitors that he or she was on task and the instructor's rating agrees with that self-evaluation. The child receives 1 point for self-recording that he or she was not on task when the instructor also makes the same evaluation. No points are given for child self-evaluations that do not agree with the evaluations made by the instructor. These accuracy checks by the instructor occur gradually less often as the child continues to be accurate with his or her self-rating. Once the child is accurately self-monitoring when the instructor is checking

On-Task = Looking at the teacher, looking at other students when they answer questions, writing, reading, and/or answering questions.

✓	X
✓	Ⓧ
✓	X
✓	X
✓	X
✓	X
✓	X
✓	X
✓	Ⓧ
✓	X
8	

GOAL = 8 checkmarks.

Then you will earn 10 minutes of:

Figure 8.2. Example of a simple data sheet used to monitor the on-task behavior of a child in a classroom.

accuracy only once per session at an unpredictable time, the child is moved to the third step of this response chaining of self-regulation.

At the third step, the child is taught to select a goal to work on from several presented options. For example, the child may be given a list of five possible goals, as shown in Figure 8.3. Please note that the child does not formulate the goal, but rather he or she picks a goal from the alternatives presented.

After the child is able to select one instructional goal at a time and complete the sequences of self-regulation responses that were previously taught (i.e., self-monitoring and self-reinforcement), the child may be expected to apply this learning to novel goals selected by the child. That is, the child selects a personal goal not previously selected by the instructor and then self-monitors its occurrence, as well as self-administers reinforcement, if the occurrence of the newly targeted behavior meets the selected goal.

Koegel, Openden, Fredeen, and Kern-Koegel (2006) suggested that it is possible to teach children with autism certain key responses that will result in collateral changes in untrained behaviors. They described this intervention approach as "pivotal response treatment" (PRT), a strategy that has been identified as a promising early intervention approach for young children with autism (National Research Council, 2001). Koegel and colleagues identified five areas for which pivotal response treatment has been studied: self-management, self-initiation, motivation, responsivity to multiple cues, and empathy.

Pick a Target

- I shall answer at least 16 of 20 math problems correctly.

- I shall pay attention at least 8 times out of 10 checks.

- I shall talk to my "neighbors" no more than once in 30 minutes.

- I shall complete my math assignment before I go home.

- I shall say, "Hello" to at least 5 people during the school day.

Figure 8.3. An example of potential goals from which a child could choose to target using self-regulation.

There are a number of differences between PRT and more traditional behavioral treatment approaches for children with autism. First, PRT is conducted in natural, rather than contrived, environments. Second, child attempts, not just correct responses, are reinforced. Reinforcers are used that have a natural, rather than an arbitrary, relationship with the response being taught (e.g., a child asks for an item and is reinforced by receiving the requested item) (Koegel, Koegel, Harrower, & Carter, 1999).

Teaching Self-Monitoring

Children with autism have been taught to self-monitor their daily-living skills (e.g., making lunch), their answering of social questions (Koegel, Koegel, Hurley, & Frea, 1992), and their stereotypic behaviors (Koegel & Koegel, 1990; Mancina, Tankersley, Kamps, Kravits, & Parrett, 2000). In addition, children with developmental disabilities have been taught to monitor following directions (Agran et al., 2005), carrying on a conversation (Hughes et al., 2002), and implementing "survival skills" (Gilbert, Agran, Hughes, & Wehmeyer, 2001).

Koegel, Koegel, and Parks (1992) have written a manual outlining in detail the steps of self-monitoring. The general procedures are also summarized in Koegel et al. (1999) and illustrated in Koegel and Koegel (1990), which consisted of a study to teach two children with severe disabilities to participate in a full-inclusion kindergarten class. The training steps for self-monitoring described in Koegel et al. (1999) are shown in Figure 8.4.

The first step is to operationally define the target behavior intended to be changed through self-monitoring. In the Koegel and Koegel (1990) study, the target behavior consisted of a reduction in the stereotypic behaviors of four children with autism who were referred to a clinic. The children ranged in age from 9 to 14 years and had mental ages less than half their chronological ages. Each also displayed a range of stereotypic behavior, including arm flapping, jumping, and loud humming.

The second step is to select reinforcers that the children can earn for accurate self-monitoring of a targeted behavior. Children in the Koegel and Koegel (1990) study received edibles or small prizes.

The third step is to choose a self-monitoring device (such as cue cards, a clock that emits a sound, or some other event) that cues the child when to self-monitor. Children with autism in the Koegel and Koegel (1990) study were given a wristwatch that

1. Operationally define the target to be self-monitored.

2. Select reinforcers for accurate self-monitoring.

3. Choose a self-monitoring device.

4. Teach the child how to use the self-monitoring device accurately.

5. Fade adult prompts.

6. Fade the self-monitoring device.

7. Promote generalization of self-monitoring in natural environments.

Figure 8.4. Summary of Koegel et al.'s (1999) training steps for teaching self-monitoring.

emitted an audio signal at the end of a time interval (e.g., 15 seconds) for a child to evaluate his or her behavior.

The fourth step is to teach the child how to use the self-monitoring device. Koegel and Koegel (1990) placed a check mark or sticker in a box marked on paper if the child did not display stereotypic behavior during that interval. Prior to the introduction of the wristwatch, the children were taught to discriminate whether their behavior at points in time was stereotypic or not. This instruction consisted of an adult modeling appropriate behavior and stereotypic behavior for the child to label as stereotypic (e.g., singing) or not (e.g., not singing).

Children earned two reinforcers for intervals in which the child displayed appropriate behavior and the support adult rated the child as displaying appropriate behavior. Children were given one reinforcer if they correctly marked that their behavior was inappropriate and there was agreement by the supporting adult. No reinforcement was earned for self-monitoring that did not agree with the support adult's rating.

The fifth step is to fade adult prompts. In Koegel and Koegel's (1990) study, adult prompts were systematically faded until the children independently put on their wristwatch, self-monitored, and requested a reinforcer.

The sixth step is to fade the use of the self-monitoring device so that at this point, the child is self-monitoring without the assistance of adult prompts or a timer. In the Koegel and Koegel (1990) study, the self-monitoring watch was able to be removed for one of the four children with autism. The support adult was present but did not interact with the child.

The seventh step is to determine if the child is using self-monitoring in natural environments. The results of the Koegel and Koegel (1990) study indicated that with self-monitoring, there was a marked drop in stereotypic behavior for all participating children. For one child, the occurrence of stereotypic behavior increased when self-monitoring was removed. The reintroduction of self-monitoring resulted in a return of stereotypic behaviors to low levels.

A second study was conducted with two of the participants of the Koegel and Koegel (1990) study to determine if children could be taught to use self-monitoring in a community setting to reduce stereotypic behavior. The frequency of adult prompts was systematically faded, with the supporting adult providing accuracy checks once a week. The Koegel and Koegel (1990) study suggested that children with autism could be taught to self-monitor their behavior—in this case, their stereotypic behavior—and do so independent of an adult.

Children did not spontaneously use self-monitoring in a community setting, and the beneficial effects of self-monitoring of the targeted behavior were reversed when self-monitoring was abruptly removed. However, children with autism were able to apply self-monitoring to a community setting when specifically taught to do so, and they maintained the positive effects of self-monitoring with very little adult involvement.

One limitation of the Koegel and Koegel (1990) study was that the intervention was not conducted in an inclusive setting. In the study by Koegel, Harrower, and Koegel (1999), children with developmental disabilities (not autism) were able to maintain the effects of self-monitoring when the support adult withdrew all prompts.

In that study, two children with cognitive disabilities attended full-inclusion kindergarten classrooms. The students were taught to self-monitor their appropriate behavior and completion of academic tasks in two phases. In the first phase, a support person (an undergraduate student) spent 10 minutes before school activities teaching a child to discriminate between desired and undesired behaviors for that child. The support person modeled both desired and undesired behaviors for each child to imitate and to label verbally. The children were reinforced for accurate discrimination of desired and undesired behaviors. The children were also taught to place a mark in a printed box on a sheet of paper after intervals of time during which they judged they had engaged in the desired behavior. Children were reinforced with small prizes for appropriate behavior and accurate recording. Over the course of this initial phase, prompts from the support person were gradually faded.

During the second phase, practice sessions were discontinued and the children self-monitored their school work performance using a wristwatch that emitted a sound, initially every 5 minutes then it progressed to every 20 minutes. The support person recorded each child's behaviors at the same time that the child was self-monitored to check self-monitoring accuracy. Over time, the children self-monitored for longer periods of time before receiving reinforcement. Similarly, the support person gradually faded physical proximity and interactions with the children. By the end of this phase, the children put on the watch and self-monitored the desired behavior until the end of the school day's academic activities. The children learned to take a small prize placed in a corner of the classroom for reinforcement.

During baseline, both children who participated in this study engaged in appropriate schoolwork performance between 20% and 35% of all observations, compared to 80% to 100% appropriate schoolwork performance exhibited by classmates. The baseline levels of disruptive behavior for one child with autism were considerably higher than those of his classmates. After the introduction of self-monitoring, the appropriate schoolwork performance of both children increased into the range shown by their typically developing classmates and their disruptive behavior reduced to the class range as well. These improvements in child-appropriate behaviors continued as the adult assistance for self-monitoring was faded and both the use of the signaling watch and the accuracy checks with the support adult were removed completely. This study illustrates the effectiveness of self-management, at least for two children with disabilities attending full-inclusion classrooms.

Self-monitoring of persons with developmental disabilities has been studied by Agran, Wehmeyer, Hughes, and colleagues to increase participation in general education classrooms (Agran et al., 2005; Gilbert, Agran, Hughes, Wehmeyer, 2001; Hughes et al., 2001). In a study by Hughes et al. (2002), four high school students with developmental disabilities, aged 16 to 19 years, were successfully taught to self-monitor a target behavior. In general education classrooms, individual targets were selected for each student and individualized ways to self-monitor were selected for each student.

Gilbert et al. (2001) extended training of students with developmental disabilities in self-monitoring one step further by arranging for 8th-grade typically developing peers to teach the self-monitoring protocol. Eighth-grade students received class credits for participating and were trained to instruct four students, 12 to 16 years old, to self-monitor. The four peer tutors taught students with developmental disabilities to self-monitor by modeling examples and nonexamples of the target behaviors, demonstrating how to place a check mark in a box if the student displayed appropriate behavior and how to praise the student's behavior. Subsequently, the peer tutors gradually withdrew their prompts and feedback.

It would appear that children with developmental disabilities can learn to monitor their own selected target behaviors and be accurate on their appraisal of their behavior (Koegel & Koegel, 1990). With reinforcement of accurate self-monitoring of appropriate behavior, children with developmental disabilities have been shown to change the target behavior in desired directions. These changes have occurred in situations of very little adult involvement.

There appears to be little, if any, generalization of changed behaviors to other settings until self-monitoring is introduced in those settings. In other words, children with autism have been shown to be able to follow a self-monitoring protocol with very little adult involvement, and as a result, there is a positive change in the behavior being monitored. There has not been substantial evidence that children with autism can apply self-monitoring skills to changing a different target behavior that was not selected by an adult. Nonetheless, self-monitoring is an important strategy to produce behavior change in children with autism under conditions of very little adult involvement.

Teaching Answering of Inferential *Why*-Questions

One of the most prominent features of children with autism is their difficulty with comprehension and production of language (Wetherby, 1986). About half of children with autism will never develop functional expressive communication (Lord & Rutter, 1994). Competence in answering questions is important for the development of conversation (Paul, 1985) and for the development of skills in asking questions (Bloom & Lahey, 1978). Brown (1968) indicated that typically developing children tend not to be able to *ask* wh-questions until they are able to *answer* those forms of questions.

Children with autism have been taught to answer simple questions that have a corresponding factual answer, such as "What did you eat for lunch?" or "What is your sister's name?" Studies by Krantz, Zalenski, Hall, Fenske, and McClannahan (1981) and by Secan, Egel, and Tilley (1989) used picture cues as a basis for teaching children with autism to answer questions that started with *what, how, or why*. Participants were shown pictures from magazines and books depicting situations that were relevant to children, such as a child having a birthday party. Individual children were asked to look at the picture and then were asked a *what*-question (e.g., "What is the child eating?"), a *why*-question (e.g., "Why is she crying?"), or a *how*-question (e.g., "How is this person helping his mother?"). Children were praised for correct answers. If a child made an error, the instructor modeled the correct response and then asked the same question again. Under these conditions, children with autism were able to answer questions that had a correct/incorrect factual base when presented with a picture cue. After training, the children with autism were able to answer novel questions of the same format, but they did not fully generalize answering questions when a picture reference was not available, particularly for *why*-questions (Secan et al., 1989).

Jahr (2001) taught children with autism to answer questions without the use of pictures. As with Krantz et al. (1981) and Secan et al. (1989), Jahr used *why*-questions that had a factual base (e.g., "Why do you eat?"). Errors were corrected by modeling the correct answer and re-administering the question. Children with autism learned each form of question (i.e., *what, where, who,* and *why*) after it was taught and could generalize the training to novel questions of the same type, but they did not generalize the training from one form of question to another. In other words, after being taught how to answer *what*-questions, the children with autism could answer novel *what*-questions but were not able to answer *who*-questions or any other question form until specifically trained in that question form.

Consider the following two types of *why*-questions. The first type of *why*-question requires the child to recall a fact that was previously stated: "Joshua did not go outside to play all day on Saturday, because he was excited to play his new computer game. Why did Joshua not go outside to play on Saturday?" To answer this question, a child with autism would need to know the meaning of the question and also would need to recall the answer that was specifically stated in the presented information (i.e., "Joshua was excited to play his new computer game"). Now consider the following *why*-question that does not contain the answer: "Joshua liked the new computer game he received for his birthday. He did not have a chance to play it before he went to school. After school, Joshua ran home. Why did Joshua run home?" In this latter question, the child would need to piece together a plausible answer based on the presented information and on his or her ability to comprehend events considering the motivational state of Joshua in the story. The child with autism would need to infer an answer from the partial information presented.

Inferential questions such as these are common in school curricula in which students are expected to comprehend presented information, such as questions about reading passages in language arts, responding to causal factors effecting events in history (e.g., "Why did the United States enter the Great War in 1917?"), as well as other school subjects. Inferential questions would also likely occur during conversations (e.g., "Why was your friend angry with you?").

High-functioning children with autism have been found to be weaker than their nondisabled peers in their ability to infer the mental states of others (Baron-Cohen, 1995), to answer inferential questions from stories (Norbury & Bishop, 2002), and to comprehend language (Minshew, Goldstein, & Siegel, 1995).

Unfortunately, there have been few studies published on teaching children with autism how to answer inferential *why*-questions. Hundert and van Delft (in press) completed a study in which three high-functioning children with autism were taught how to answer inferential questions using embedded instruction. Three types of inferential questions were taught. The first consisted of a three-card picture story (e.g., a picture of a pizza on a table, a picture of a woman eating a pizza, a picture of a woman lying down). The question presented was "Why was the woman lying on the couch?" A second type of inferential *why*-question consisted of a verbally presented story (e.g., "Alice went to the store to buy some milk. She went into the store but left with nothing. Why did Alice not buy the milk?") The third format was a general question (e.g., "Why should we wear seat belts while riding in a car?").

There were a number of differences between the teaching procedure employed by Hundert and van Delft (in press) and the method of instruction described by Secan et al. (1989) and Jahr (2001). First, in the Hundert and van Delft study, the acceptable response to the inferential *why*-question consisted of any plausible answer to the presented information. For example, to the verbal story of the woman lying on the couch, acceptable answers that link the presented events would include "the woman felt sick," "the woman felt tired," or "the woman ate too much pizza." Any answer that was plausible and logically connected the events was accepted. To the question of why we should wear seat belts, acceptable responses included "It was the law," "To make us safe," "To prevent injury," and so on. There was not one correct response being taught for each question.

Because there was not one correct answer for each presented inferential *why*-question, the second difference in teaching methods between the Hundert and van Delft (in press) study and previous studies was that if a child did not give a plausible answer or if the child answered incorrectly, the instructor provided a series of verbal prompts. First, the instructor asked the child to describe what occurred in the picture story (e.g., "Tell me what's happening in the story"), to describe the verbal story (e.g., "Tell me the main points of the story that I said"), or to describe what the child knows about the general question (e.g., "What would happen if people did not wear seat belts?"). Following this type of prompt, the original question was re-administered. If the child still did not give a plausible answer, the instructor gave one possible answer as an example (e.g., "One answer might be that . . .") and then asked the child to generate a different answer.

A third difference in methodology was that the Hundert and van Delft (in press) inferential questions were taught using embedded instruction (Polychronis, McDonnell, Johnson, & Jameson, 2004). The child and the instructor were engaged in a child-preferred activity (e.g., playing a game), and an inferential question was asked at intervals of approximately 90 seconds at natural breaks in the game.

Ten questions were selected for each form of inferential question. At random, half were taught and the other half were used to assess generalization to novel questions. A multiple-probe design was used to evaluate the effect of training across the forms of inferential *why*-questions. Following a pretraining (baseline) phase, one child was taught to answer inferential questions about picture stories, then about verbal stories, and finally about general questions. For the second child, the sequence of teaching three forms of inferential questions was reversed to control for possible order effects. Probes were conducted of each child's ability to answer both trained (training probes) and untrained (generalization probes) inferential *why*-questions of the three formats used (picture sequence, verbal story, and general questions). Probes consisted of asking each child to answer the presented question without feedback on the correctness of the child's responses. The results for Child 1 are shown in Figure 8.5.

The children learned the first form of inferential *why*-questions and correctly applied their learning to novel questions of the same type. There was some (but incomplete) generalization of learning to the other forms of inferential *why*-questions, and the children had to be taught each specific form of the inferential *why*-question. As shown in Figure 8.5, after being taught to answer inferential *why*-questions using a picture story sequence, there was an increase in Child 1's ability to answer not only the taught items, but also the untrained picture story items measured by generalization probes. Following training, each child was able to answer both trained and untrained inferential *why*-questions of the format in which he or she was provided practice; however, the children were not able to demonstrate criterion-level (4/5 items correct) performance in answering the two other inferential *why*-question formats until specifically taught each.

A similar pattern occurred for Child 2 (as shown in Figure 8.6) and for Child 3 (as shown in Figure 8.7), with the sequence of teaching the three *why*-inference questions reversed for Child 3. Although there appears to be some generalization after each form was taught, the criteria levels of generalization to different forms of inferential "why" questions did not occur until that form was specifically taught to Child 2 and Child 3.

These results suggest that children with autism can be taught to answer inferential *why*-questions and apply this learning to answer novel inferential *why*-questions of the same type. Children with autism were not able to reach criterion level

(*text continues on p. 167*)

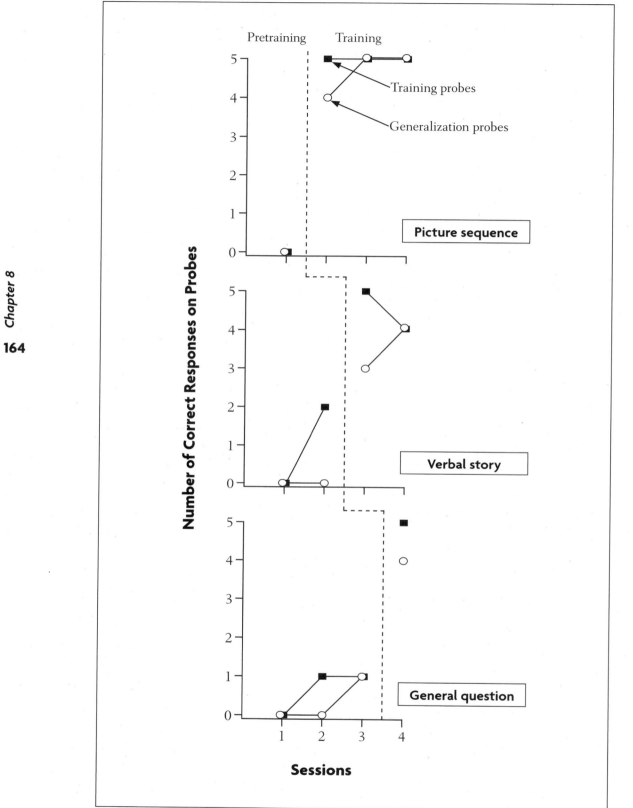

Figure 8.5. The results of Child 1 probes of correct responses to training and generalization probes before and after training in answering each type of inferential *why*-question. *Note.* From "Teaching Children With Autism to Answer Inferential 'Why'-questions," by J. Hundert and S. van Delft, in press, *Focus on Autism and Other Developmental Disabilities.* Copyright by PRO-ED, Inc. Reprinted with permission.

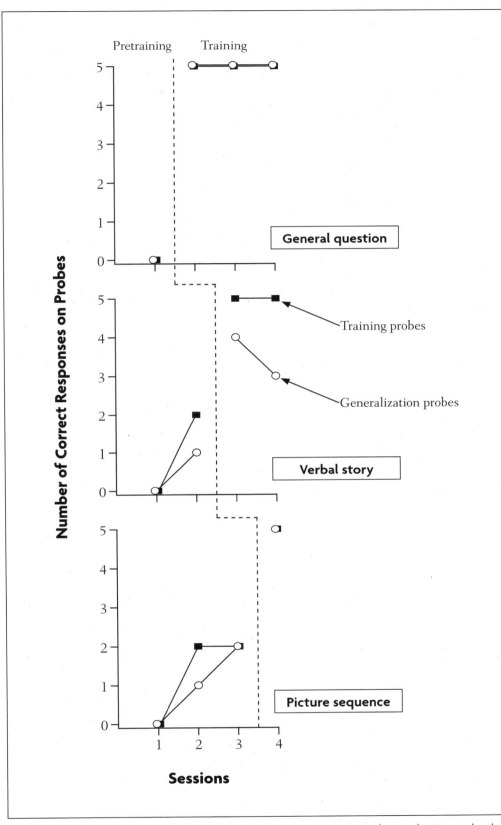

Figure 8.6. The results of Child 2 probes of correct responses to training and generalization probes before and after training in answering each type of inferential *why*-question. *Note.* From "Teaching Children With Autism to Answer Inferential 'Why'-questions," by J. Hundert and S. van Delft, in press, *Focus on Autism and Other Developmental Disabilities.* Copyright by PRO-ED, Inc. Reprinted with permission.

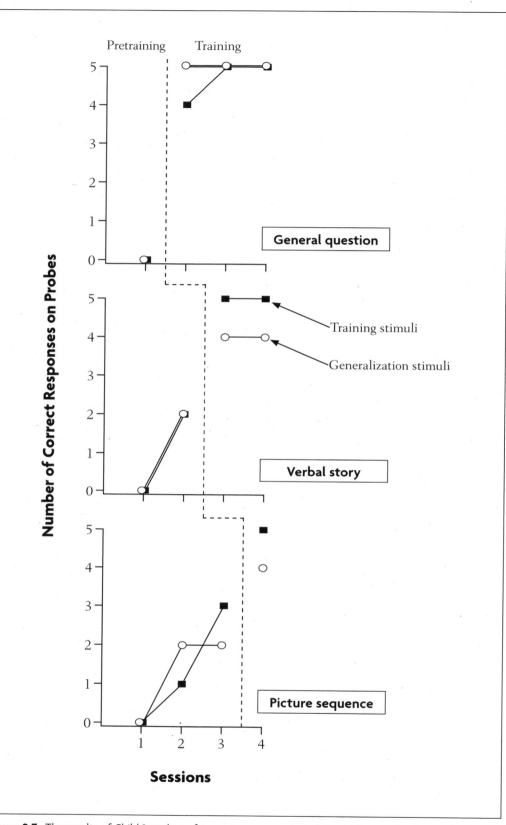

Figure 8.7. The results of Child 3 probes of correct responses to training and generalization probes before and after training in answering each type of inferential *why*-question. *Note*. From "Teaching Children With Autism to Answer Inferential 'Why'-questions," by J. Hundert and S. van Delft, in press, *Focus on Autism and Other Developmental Disabilities*. Copyright by PRO-ED, Inc. Reprinted with permission.

of generalization to other forms of inferential *why*-questions. This would suggest that children with autism need to be specifically trained in each form of inferential *why*-question.

It should be emphasized that the Hundert and van Delft (in press) study was not conducted in an inclusive classroom, although their use of embedded instruction would be conducive to doing so. Future studies should demonstrate that inferential *why*-questions can be taught in an inclusive setting and that children with autism would be able to apply the training to answer similar inferential *why*-questions posed to the entire class by the classroom teacher.

Teaching Perspective Taking

Perspective taking has been defined as the understanding that someone else's beliefs about events may not be based on fact, but they guide that person's future actions (Capps, Sigman, & Yirmiya, 1996). By age 3, most typically developing children understand that even when someone else's beliefs are false, that individual will act according to his or her beliefs (Dean & Siegler, 1986). However, children with autism often have difficulties completing "false-belief" tasks, such as Sally–Anne task described earlier (Baron-Cohen et al., 1985).

Given that children with autism show delays in the ability to see events from someone else's perspective and to use this knowledge to predict how someone will act, it is important to examine if children with autism can be taught to perspective take. There have been a number of studies indicating that children with autism can be successfully taught to complete false-belief tasks. In one of the earliest studies completed on this topic, Swettenham (1996) taught eight children with autism, who had a mean chronological age of 10 years 8 months, to answer a false-belief task similar to the Sally–Anne task but presented on a computer. When a participant responded correctly to where Sally thought that the ball should be, music sounded, a text message praising the child appeared, and there was a brief animation clip. When a child made an incorrect choice, a text message appeared on the screen next to Sally, indicating where Sally thought she had left the ball. The child was asked to try the task again. Training took place over 4 days. After training, children with autism were asked to respond to similar variations in the Sally–Anne false-belief task. Other studies have also found that children with autism can be taught to respond to training in completion of the false-belief task (Charlop-Christy & Daneshvar, 2003; Fisher & Happe, 2005; LeBlanc & Coates, 2003; Wellman et al., 2002).

Studies that have been completed on this topic have used a variety of approaches to training children with autism in perspective taking, including computer-based instruction (Swettenham, 1996), use of pictures to depict the thoughts of dolls (Charlop-Christy & Daneshvar, 2003; Fisher & Happe, 2005; LeBlanc & Coates, 2003; Wellman et al., 2002), use of a cartoon thought bubble (Wellman et al., 2002), training groups (Gevers, Clifford, Mager, & Boer, 2006), and video modeling (LeBlanc & Coates, 2003).

Although children with autism have been found to be able to learn a false-belief task and apply that training to similar variations of the same type of task, there are mixed results for whether children with autism are able to apply perspective-taking training to new forms of false-belief tasks. Swettenham (1996) found that none of the children with autism who participated in a task similar to the Sally–Anne task were able to apply the training to different formats of false-belief tasks, such as the M&M tasks, in which the candy in an M&M packet needed to be removed and replaced with a pencil. Children were asked to predict what another child would think would be in the packet. In contrast, a group of typically developing 3-year-olds and a second group of children with Down syndrome, who completed the same training as described in the Swettenham study, did generalize training in different formats of false-belief tasks.

LeBlanc and Coates (2003) taught three boys with autism either the M&M task or a hide-and-seek task in which a puppet hid a treasure in one location and then left footprints. The puppet then moved the treasure to a second location without leaving footprints. The child was asked to predict where a person who did not observe the puppet's actions would guess where the treasure would be. The training consisted of showing the children a videotape of correct solving of a task. Children were reinforced for quick responses. LeBlanc and Coates (2003) found that children were able to learn the false-belief task and apply the training to variations of that same task, but they did not correctly solve a second false-belief task until directly trained in that second task. In contrast, Charlop-Christy and Daneshvar (2003) trained children with autism in multiple exemplars of false-belief tasks and found that they were able to generalize the training both within the same type of task and to untrained types of false-belief tasks.

It would appear that with repeated practice in different types of perspective-taking tasks, children with autism may be able to correctly judge the perspective of someone else and apply that training to new types of perspective-taking tasks. Because of its relative ease of use, video modeling may be the most effective and efficient way of teaching children with autism perspective taking. It should be noted that only the LeBlanc and Coates (2003) study was conducted in a school setting; none of the other studies were run in a special education classroom.

Study Questions

1. What is the key difference between an adult-mediated approach to teaching and self-regulation?

2. What are the steps in teaching self-regulation?

3. What is Koegel and Koegel's (1990) procedure for teaching self-monitoring?

4. What are three differences in the methodology used by Hundert and van Delft (in press)?

5. Can children with autism be taught to take the perspective of someone else?

9 Preventing and Dealing With Problem Behaviors

Chapter Topics

- Functions of behavior

- Triggers of problem behavior

- Assessing problem behaviors (using indirect and direct methods and then developing a hypothesis)

- Indirect assessment of problem behaviors (ABC recording, functional assessment cards, scatter plot grid, Functional Assessment Observation Form, ecobehavioral analysis)

- Direct assessment of problem behaviors (functional assessment)

- Positive behavior support

- Making problem behavior irrelevant

- Making problem behavior inefficient

- Making problem behavior ineffective (including interventions for problem behaviors maintained by attention, access to desired activities or objects, sensory stimulation, or escape)

- Modified competing behavior model

Surveys of teachers' attitudes toward their job indicate that one of the biggest concerns teachers have about teaching is the challenge of dealing with problem behaviors of students in their class (Fimian & Santoro, 1983). Teachers reported that they feel ill-prepared to handle disruptive behavior in the class and that student problem behavior constitutes the greatest source of stress they experience on the job (Mantzicopoulos, 2005). Moreover, teachers have estimated that they spend a large amount of each school day responding to problem behaviors of students in their class and that the time taken to deal with the student problem behaviors detracts from their ability to teach the class curriculum (Boxer, Musher-Eizenman, Dubow, Danner, & Heretick, 2006).

These teacher surveys were of teachers in general education classrooms and refer to problem behavior exhibited by typically developing students in those classrooms. Teacher challenges for managing problem behavior become more complex when a child with autism is added to the class. Children with autism present more frequent and more severe problem behaviors than their typically developing peers do. The prevalence of problem behavior in children with autism is about two to three times that of nondisabled children (Sigafoos, Arthur, & O'Reilly, 2003). These problem behaviors include disruptive behavior (e.g., getting out of seat, flopping on floor, yelling, throwing objects), aggression (e.g., hitting, kicking), stereotypic behavior (e.g., rocking, hand flapping, jumping, humming), noncompliance (e.g., refusal to follow teacher instructions), and self-injury (e.g., self-hitting, self-biting, eye gouging). The frequency and severity of problem behaviors have a direct relationship with a child's delay in communication (Sigafoos, 2000), the severity of a child's symptoms of autism (Wolfe & Neisworth, 2005), and the early onset of problem behaviors (Lovaas, Litrownik, & Mann, 1971).

Although for some children it may appear that there are no patterns to the occurrence of problem behaviors, one of the assumptions of a behavioral analytic approach is that behaviors (not just problem behaviors) do not occur by chance (Cooper, Heron, & Heward, 2007). When and where a problem behavior occurs follow established natural laws of behavior, based on principles of learning. For instance, a child may flop to the floor because he or she has learned that flopping will result in delay, reduction, or removal of an undesired event, such as completion of assigned work. In this example, flopping would be a learned response that has been strengthened by the child successfully avoiding or escaping work that the child finds unpleasant. Problem behavior is maintained by the effects that it has on the child's environment (i.e., results in the lessening of the amount/difficulty of the task) and is triggered by events that signal the occurrence of problem situations (e.g., the teacher handing out worksheets). The idea that the behaviors follow principles of learning is important since an understanding of environmental events that trigger and maintain a problem behavior are more likely to lead to interventions that will reduce the problem behavior (Carr et al., 1999).

Functions of Behavior

O'Neill, Horner, Albin, Storey, and Sprague (1997) described seven major ways that a behavior acts on its environment. These "functions" of behavior are depicted in Figure 9.1. Behaviors serve either to obtain desired events (e.g., the attention of peers, if motivating) or to escape unpleasant events (e.g., being asked to come in from recess, if ending recess is unpleasant to the child). When behaviors serve to access desired

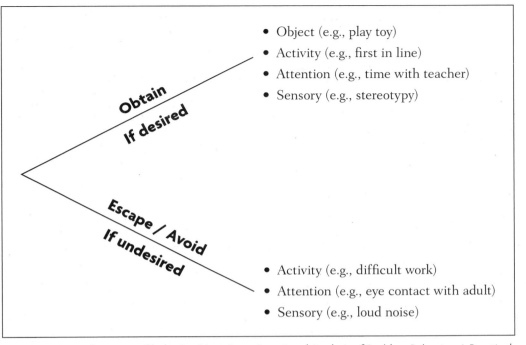

Object (e.g., play toy)
Activity (e.g., first in line)
Attention (e.g., time with teacher)
Sensory (e.g., stereotypy)

Obtain
If desired

Escape / Avoid
If undesired

Activity (e.g., difficult work)
Attention (e.g., eye contact with adult)
Sensory (e.g., loud noise)

Figure 9.1. Seven functions of behavior. *Note.* From *Functional Analysis of Problem Behavior: A Practical Assessment Guide* (p. 13), by R. E. O'Neill, R. H. Horner, R. W. Albin, K. Storey, and J. R. Sprague, 1997, Pacific Grove, CA: Brooks/Cole. Copyright 1997 by Cengage. Adapted with permission.

events, the problem behavior is maintained through the effect of positive reinforcement (the occurrence of a desired event following a behavior that increases the future occurrence of that behavior). The child may engage in stereotypic behavior (e.g., rocking, hand flapping, jumping) for the sensory stimulation that those actions provide. The child's grabbing of a preferred play toy from a peer at recess may be maintained by the positive reinforcement of obtaining the desired object. Similarly pushing in at the front of a line of children at a water fountain may be reinforced by the child gaining more immediate access to a drink of water.

Sometimes problem behaviors are maintained by escape or avoidance of undesired events. Problem behaviors that serve to escape undesired events are maintained through negative reinforcement (the offset of an undesired event that increases the future occurrence of the behavior that it follows). A child may cover his or her ears to block the sound of loud music—sensory stimulation that the child finds unpleasant. Covering his or her ears is reinforced by the muffling of the unpleasant sounds. Similarly, a child may scream and flop to the floor when given an undesired task, which may be reinforced by the child avoiding the task altogether or by someone removing the task because the child became upset.

The idea that problem behaviors occur because of the function they play for the child has been a major addition to the understanding and treatment of problem behaviors. It also has directly influenced how problem behaviors are assessed. It is important to assess not only the circumstances in which problem behaviors occur, but also the functions that maintain these behaviors. The form that a problem behavior takes (e.g., hitting, screaming, throwing) does not necessarily indicate its function. Different forms of problem behavior may serve the same function for a child. On some occasions, a child may flop to the floor to escape a seatwork assignment. On other occasions, the same child may scream to escape the work. Flopping and screaming are different forms of problem behavior, but both serve the same function—escape.

Just as it is possible for different forms of behavior to have the same function, it is also possible for the same form of behavior to serve different functions in different situations or at different times. A child may cry at home to avoid a parental instruction, such as going to bed. At school, crying may solicit adult attention and comforting.

Consider what might be the function of the problem behaviors in the following two examples.

> **Example 1:** Thomas is an 8-year-old boy with autism who has a one-to-one paraprofessional to help him in his third-grade class. Sometimes when Thomas is given seatwork to complete, his paraprofessional will leave Thomas's side to help other students in the room. When the paraprofessional leaves, Thomas will whine and eventually scream, even when the work given to him is quite easy for him. What would you guess the function of whining might be?

> **Example 2:** Nicholas is a 13-year-old nonverbal boy who hits his teacher and his paraprofessional. He attends a general education seventh-grade class but is working on his own curriculum. To prevent Nicholas from getting upset and possibly becoming aggressive, his paraprofessional responds immediately if Nicholas shows early signs of agitation (e.g., moaning, pushing the worksheet away). At this point, the paraprofessional removes the work and asks Nicholas what else he wants to do. What event would be maintaining Nicholas's moaning?

Example 1 appears to be a case in which Thomas' whining and screaming is attention maintained. That is, it is triggered by the paraprofessional moving away and is reinforced by the paraprofessional returning to confront him. In the second example, Nicholas has likely learned to moan to escape completing the assigned seatwork. When he begins to moan, his paraprofessional immediately removes the assigned work.

For intervention planning, it is critical to be able to understand the function(s) served by problem behavior for a child. Interventions based on a hypothesis of functional problem behavior are more likely to be effective than interventions derived in some other manner (Carr et al., 1999). For example, if a child's disruptive behavior in a classroom is escape motivated, then the use of removal of the child from the classroom may be counterproductive, and in fact, may inadvertently worsen the disruptive behavior. On the other hand, if disruptive behavior is attention motivated, removal of the child from the classroom may be an effective strategy, which could be confirmed by monitoring the actual change in the child's disruptive behavior once that intervention is tried.

Triggers of Problem Behavior

Horner, Vaughn, and Ard (1996) suggested that problem behaviors might have two types of triggers. "Antecedent stimuli" or "triggering antecedents" consist of environmental events (e.g., a child being instructed to end a preferred activity) that, after a number of pairings with an effective consequence, signal the occasion for the problem behavior. Horner et al. also suggested that there are events that occur much earlier in the time sequence to the problem behavior and perhaps in a different setting that predispose a child to be reactive to events that immediately trigger problem behavior.

Horner et al. (1996) referred to these slow triggers as "setting events" or what Michael (1988) termed "establishing operations." Establishing operations (EOs) are events that momentarily alter the value of consequences. For example, an earache may be an EO that could hamper the effectiveness of the reinforcement being used to strengthen a child's prosocial behavior. Horner et al. presented the hypothetical example of a fifth-grade boy, Eric, with severe disabilities and limited communications. On some, but not all, days at school, Eric is given work to complete and he immediately rips the work materials, screams, and runs around the classroom. Yet, on days during which Eric fights with another child at recess, he becomes disruptive when he returns to class and is given a worksheet assignment. The previously experienced event of a fight with a peer decreases the value of the reinforcers (teacher praise) that would be provided on Eric's completion of the task and increases the value of escaping the task. Eric could have asked the teacher for a break or for help in completing the assigned task, but both of these alternative responses would have involved a considerable amount of effort for Eric because of his communication deficits. It was more efficient for Eric to get his needs met through running away than it was for him to try to communicate. The teacher has other students to attend to, and Eric eventually settles down to being left alone, which he finds more enjoyable than completing the work assignment. If the teacher looks only at the immediate antecedent (i.e., work task), Eric's problem behavior appears to be unpredictable since sometimes he completes the assignment without difficulty, and other times, he is oppositional.

Eric's physical fight at recess was an EO for his destroying the worksheet and running around the room. Horner et al. (1996) depicted a conceptualization of Eric's problem behavior that is reproduced in Figure 9.2.

In a similar vein, Kennedy and Itkonen (1993) found that the number of problem behaviors (e.g., biting others, yelling, pulling hair) shown by a high school student with severe disabilities throughout the school day was directly related to the number of stops the car in which she was traveling made for traffic lights and stop signs as she was

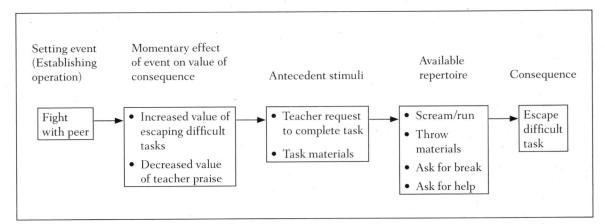

Figure 9.2. A five-term model of problem behavior. *Note.* From *Positive Behavior Support: Including People With Difficult Behavior in the Community* (p. 383), by L. K. Koegel, R. L. Koegel, and G. Dunlap (Eds.), 1996, Baltimore: Brookes. Copyright 1996 by Paul H. Brookes. Adapted with permission.

coming to school in the morning. On days that the driver took a highway route to school requiring only two stops, the girl showed about three problem behaviors, compared to an average of 16 problem behaviors on days that the driver took a city route requiring about 20 stops on the way to school.

Pain caused by such ailments as earaches or toothaches, fatigue caused by the lack of sleep, and other similar events have all been identified as potential EOs that may act as a slow trigger to a problem behavior in persons with developmental disabilities (Horner et al., 1996; Kennedy & Itkonen, 1993). Given that these events occur at an earlier time, and perhaps in a different setting from those associated with the occurrence of the problem behavior, it typically is difficult to detect if EOs are affecting a situation in which a child is displaying problem behaviors.

Typically, it would be easier to identify more immediate triggers ("triggering antecedents") to problem behaviors. These are the events that occur immediately before a problem behavior that result in the problem behavior. For example, an antecedent may be a child being told to wait his or her turn in a game. For another child, a trigger may be the proximity of a classmate who, when hit by the child with autism, will react and then yell at the offending child. The attention given by the peer reinforces the aggression.

A seminal study about functions of problem behavior and their triggers was conducted by Carr and Durand (1985). Four children, aged 7 to 14 years, who attended a school for children with developmental disabilities were given seatwork assignments to complete. In one condition, the task was structured to be easy (each child was previously assessed and determined to be able to answer each item correctly, such as pointing to named pictures). In another condition, the children received a difficult task (each child was previously assessed and could not correctly respond to all items of assigned tasks). A third condition consisted of adults providing attention to a child on 100% of time intervals. Finally, a fourth condition consisted of children receiving adult attention on only 33% of time intervals. Carr and Durand found that a higher rate of children's problem behavior was associated with either difficult work or low rates of adult attention. It appeared that the children's problem behavior functioned to escape difficult work in one situation and to solicit teacher attention in another situation.

This hypothesis was confirmed by results of a second study they conducted. Carr and Durand (1985) taught the children relevant communicative responses that matched the hypothesized function of the problem behavior each child displayed. Children were taught to say, "I do not understand" in the difficult work condition and "Am I doing good work?" in the low-attention condition. After this training, children showed reduced problem behavior in the same conditions that were previously associated with the heightened occurrence of problem behaviors. Once children had learned a communicative response that was equivalent in function to their problem behavior, they no longer needed to resort to using problem behavior to meet their needs. The use of functional equivalent responses will be described in more detail later in this chapter as an intervention called "functional communication training."

An understanding of factors that influence the occurrence of problem behavior includes not only the identification of triggers of those problem behaviors but also a consideration of the possible responses children have within their repertoires to deal with a situation without resorting to using problem behaviors. In the previous example, Eric, after being given the task to complete, could have asked his teacher for help with the assignment, but he was weak in his communication skills. As illustrated by the Carr and Durand (1985) study, having a child use a communicative response that has the same function as the problem behavior may reduce the need for the child to use the problem behavior. For this reason, it would be important to determine a child's repertoire of responses that could potentially be used as a functional equivalent to a presenting problem behavior.

Assessing Problem Behaviors

The development of an intervention to reduce the problem behaviors of a child with autism should be based on an understanding of the following factors:

- The topography (form) of the problem behavior
- The occurrence of the problem behavior (e.g., when, where, how often, and under what conditions it occurs and does not occur)
- The function(s) of the problem behavior
- The establishing operations (setting events), which may serve as "slow" triggers to the problem behavior
- The triggering antecedents that precipitate the problem behavior
- The child's repertoire of responses (e.g., communication, social behavior) that are functionally equivalent to the problem behavior

This section will describe indirect and direct approaches to assess these factors.

Iwata and Worsdell (2005) described three general approaches to functional assessment of behaviors: The use of indirect information, directly recording a child's behavior as it occurs naturally, and directly manipulating environmental events to observe the effect on target behavior.

Use Indirect or Anecdotal Information

The first approach to conducting a functional behavioral assessment is to use indirect or anecdotal information by interviewing key individuals (e.g., teachers, parents) who know the child (Iwata & Worsdell, 2005). *The Motivation Assessment Scales* (MAS; Durand & Crimmins, 1988) is one example of an indirect approach to collecting information about a child's problem behaviors. It consists of 16 questions, which are then used to develop a hypothesis about possible functions of problem behaviors.

My colleagues and I have developed a somewhat similar method of interviewing school staff about a child's problem behaviors soon after incidents have occurred. Copies of the *Problem Behavior Interview* (PBI) (preschool, elementary, and adolescent versions) are shown in Appendix 9A. The PBI differs from the MAS in that it interviews staff about a specific incident of problem behavior that has recently occurred. The interview form is used by a school behavioral consultant, psychologist, or someone in a similar position as an assessment tool to unravel possible factors contributing to the occurrence of a child's problem behaviors. The consultant directly interviews the staff who observed the incident or leaves the questionnaire for staff to complete on their own. Although interview information may be helpful for identifying possible triggers of, maintaining consequences for, and functions of problem behavior, it still only provides indirect information. The information is based on an individual's recall of a child's problem behavior and on factors that may be contributing to that problem behavior. As a result, indirect information may be prone to incomplete or selective accounts of what occurred because of the subjectivity of the reporter's views.

Direct Recording of Behaviors and Environmental Events (Descriptive Assessment)

A second approach to the assessment of problem behavior is to directly record a child's behavior and note environmental events that may be associated with its occurrence. Iwata and Worsdell (2005) referred to this general method of assessment as "descriptive" or "correlational" because the collected data provide information of events that are associated with, but not necessarily causing, a problem behavior. A demonstration of a causal link between a problem behavior and an observed event (e.g., difficult work) that may trigger or maintain problem behavior requires an experimental manipulation to show that changes in environments produce changes in the child's problem behavior. Five examples of descriptive assessments of problem behaviors are presented next.

ABC Recording

One of the simplest methods of assessing problem behaviors is an Antecedent–Behavior–Consequence (ABC) recording sheet. First, the problem behavior is operationally defined so that it is clear to anyone who is recording whether or not the behavior in question has occurred. To be quantified, each problem behavior would be defined in terms of what could be directly perceived by the senses, rather than defined in general or inferential terms. For example, it would be very difficult to reliably track a problem behavior that has been defined only in general terms, such as "aggression." To render an operational definition measurable, one must define the specific behaviors that are involved (e.g., "a hand making contact with another person with force"). A sheet is developed that has three columns with the headings Antecedent, Behavior, and Consequence. Recorders (consisting of individuals who have ongoing contact with the child) are asked to make an entry onto a data sheet when the target child displays a problem behavior. Under the heading Antecedent, the recorder notes the events that were occurring prior to the start of a problem behavior that may have been involved in triggering the problem behavior. Under the heading Behavior, the recorder describes the behavior that occurred. Under the heading Consequence the recorder describes the events that occurred after the problem behavior that might have served to maintain that behavior. A completed ABC recording may look as depicted in Figure 9.3. A reproducible ABC Recording Form can be found in Appendix 9A.

There are at least three significant limitations to ABC recordings. One limitation is the subjectivity and lack of precision of the entries that may be made to describe the antecedent, behavior, and consequence. From the number of possible events that preceded the problem behavior, the reporter may record an event that has little to do with the occurrence of the problem behavior or describe a triggering antecedent in such general terms that it is unclear what exactly occurred. A second limitation is that recordings on the ABC data sheet are only made when problem behavior has occurred. ABC recordings do not note antecedent or consequent events associated with times when problem behaviors do not occur. The identification of possible triggers and maintaining consequences is as much informed by events associated with the occurrence of problem behaviors as it is with events associated with the nonoccurrence of problem

ABC Recording Form

Child: __Erica__   Begin Time: __10:00 a.m.__

Observer: __Michael__   End Time: __12:35 p.m.__

A – Antecedents	B – Behavior	C – Consequences
Describe activities and events that preceded the problem behavior (e.g., outdoor play; child took a toy away)	Describe exactly what the child said and/or did (e.g., hit)	Describe activities and events that followed the problem behavior (e.g., recovered the toy; was reprimanded by teacher)
At story time, Erica was sitting beside Jason	Erica did not say anything. She started to lean against Jason while laughing	Jason started to push Erica
At snack time, the entire class was given instruction to come sit for snack	Erica begins to run around the room	Erica was asked again to come sit and was reprimanded for not listening
Lining up to go outside	Pushed child in front (Teddy) while giggling	Teddy told her to stop pushing him. Teacher reprimanded Erica

Figure 9.3. Example of a completed data sheet for ABC recordings.

behaviors. A third limitation of ABC recordings is that they do not provide direct information about possible functions of the problem behavior. It is left up to the person examining the ABC record to discern any themes that would suggest possible functions of the problem behavior.

Functional Assessment Cards

Carr et al. (1994) outlined a descriptive method of assessing problem behaviors which is in several ways similar to the ABC recording method but with two significant improvements. Functional assessment cards (FACs) consist of individual index cards with space for recording an antecedent, behavior, and consequence similar to ABC recording. However, each card also contains a space at the bottom (see Figure 9.4) in which the recorder indicates what presumed function was served by an observed problem behavior. Several FACs are given to each individual (e.g., recess supervisor, classroom teacher, paraprofessional) who is in a position to observe the problem behavior of the child. These people are asked to complete a card for each occurrence they observe of the problem behavior. The individuals complete the cards over a specified period of

---

Functional Assessment Card

Child's Name: Alex	Observer: KN	Date: Nov. 23, 2008	Time: 10:30 a.m.

General Context: Playground

ANTECEDENT:

Alex was running with his ball. Joe and Steven came over and asked if they could play with his ball.

PROBLEM BEHAVIOR:

Alex screamed and hit Joe.

CONSEQUENCE:

Joe and Steven left to tell the supervisor.

Complete this section later. Circle the function(s) demonstrated by this behavior:

(Escape/avoidance)   Get attention   Get desired object/activity   Self-stimulation

---

Figure 9.4. Example of a completed functional assessment card. *Note.* From *Communication-Based Intervention for Problem Behavior: A User's Guide for Producing Positive Change* (p. 36), by E. G. Carr, L. Levin, G. McConnachie, J. I. Carlson, D. C. Kemp, & C. E. Smith, 1994, Baltimore: Brookes. Copyright 1994 by Paul H. Brookes. Adapted with permission.

time (e.g., 2 weeks). An example of a completed FAC is shown in Figure 9.4. A blank, reproducible FAC can be found in Appendix 9A.

After a specified period of time, the individuals who have been tracking the child's problem behavior using FACs meet and sort their cards into groups based on the identified function of each problem behavior incident. The sorting of FACs by function helps identify the possible function(s) of a sample of the problem behavior.

The second advantage of functional assessment cards is that the assessment uses a collaborative process to derive information about the nature, occurrence, and functions of problem behavior. As with the ABC recording, FACs are still prone to subjectivity, recorder bias, and possible sampling bias.

Scatter Plot Grid

Touchette (1985) described a method of tracking a behavior that enables one to look for patterns between environmental events and a problem behavior to suggest possible factors that cause the problem behavior. A data sheet is developed in which the time period of interest (e.g., a school day) is divided into equal intervals (e.g., 15 or 30 minutes).

An observer tallies the number of times a problem occurs during that interval of time. The same recording is repeated over a number of days (e.g., a school week). To help summarize the data, each cell in the scatter plot grid is coded by one of three markings that represent the frequency of problem behavior during that interval of time: (A) If no problem behaviors occurred within the interval of time, then the cell is left blank. (B) A cell filled in black indicates that the problem behavior occurred at a relatively high rate. The definition of what a high rate is would be set after the data on the frequency of the problem behavior have been collected (e.g., four or more problem behaviors during that time interval). Because of this, a frequency count of the problem behavior should be completed before starting a scatter plot. (C) The third code indicates that the problem behavior occurred during the interval of time, but at a relatively lower rate. This is represented by a slash mark in the cell. Each column in the grid represents a different day. Results of a scatter plot may look like the example shown in Figure 9.5. A blank, reproducible copy of the scatter plot grid can be found in Appendix 9A.

Scatter Plot Grid

Child: __Josh__   School: __Main Street School__   Class: __Mrs. Mancini__

Starting Date: __Nov 15, 2008__   Target Behavior: __out of seat, running__

☐ 0   ◹ 1–3   ■ 4 or more

Time	Activity	M	T	W	TH	F
8:30–9:00	Gets off the bus and goes into school					
9:00–9:30	Opening exercises/discussion		◹			
9:30–10:00	Language arts	■	■		■	■
10:00–10:30	Language arts	■	◹		■	■
10:30–11:00	Recess					
11:00–11:30	Math (Mon–Thurs); Music (Fri)					■
11:30–12:00	Math (Mon–Thurs); Music (Fri)					■
12:00–12:30	Lunch					◹
12:30–1:00	Lunch					
1:00–1:30	Math (Mon–Thurs); Art (Fri)					◹
1:30–2:00	Phys. Ed. (Mon, Wed, Fri); History (Tues, Thurs)	■		■		■
2:00–2:30	Phys. Ed. (Mon, Wed, Fri); History (Tues, Thurs)	■		■		■
2:30–3:00	Science	◹				
3:00–3:30	Homework					

Successive Days

Figure 9.5. Example of a completed scatterplot grid. *Note.* From "A Scatter Plot for Identifying Stimulus Control of Problem Behavior," by P. E. Touchette, 1985, *Journal of Applied Behavior Analysis, 18,* p. 349. Copyright 1985 by the Society for the Experimental Analysis of Behavior. Adapted with permission.

As with all of the measures discussed in this section, it is important to collect information about a problem behavior before introducing an intervention. The collection of data on the occurrence of a problem behavior under unaltered conditions is referred to as *baseline data*. Baseline data serve a number of critical functions. They provide information about the occurrence of the problem behavior prior to an intervention, from which one can make comparisons to determine if there is an improvement in the problem behavior after the intervention is introduced. Baseline data also provide information about factors that may be involved in the triggering and maintenance of the problem behavior from which one formulates an intervention.

I use an additional column in my scatter plots to help with the interpretation of results. This additional column allows me to enter a description of activities that were occurring during the time intervals in which data were collected. An examination of scatter plot data may reveal trends that would suggest the possible triggers associated with occurrence of the problem behavior. What would be your interpretation of the scatter plot data shown in Figure 9.5?

The occurrence of the problem behavior is high on Friday. On Fridays, the child has classes of physical education, music, and art. High rates of problem behavior may occur during periods of transition from one class to another and/or during subject matter taught by a teacher other than the child's homeroom teacher.

The second theme that can be seen on the scatter plot shown in Figure 9.5 is that higher rates of problem behaviors occur each day between 9:30 and 10:30. This result corresponds to the time period in which the child received group instruction in language arts. There may be some difficulty with the match between the instruction provided and the skills of the child. Although a scatter plot does not definitively indicate the triggers to a child's problem behavior, it may suggest areas for further examination. As with the previous examples in this section, a scatter plot is a descriptive assessment and indicates events that may be associated with problem behaviors without clearly demonstrating a causal link.

Functional Assessment Observation Form

O'Neill et al. (1997) described a method of assessment of problem behavior that combines direct observation of the child's problem behavior with an interpretation of the functions of that behavior. The Functional Assessment Observation Form (FAOF) consists of a series of columns for recording problem behavior and its associated events. A blank, reproducible version of an FAOF can be found in Appendix 9A.

In the Behaviors column, one writes the name of the child's problem behavior(s) being tracked. In the Predictors columns, one writes the types of events that may precipitate (trigger) problem behavior, such as a request being made of the child (demand), a transition, and so on. In the Perceived Functions columns, one writes possible functions of the child's problem behaviors. Of these functions, the first set of triggers are items that involve positive reinforcements (e.g., getting attention, getting a desired object, getting a desired activity). In the second set of columns, one writes the descriptors of functions that involve the child escaping events (e.g., an undesired activity, such as eating a nonpreferred food).

For the rows of the FAOF, one divides the time interval into equal observation intervals (e.g., 15 or 30 minutes) based on the desired detail of analysis and frequency of the problem behavior. There is a column for writing a description of activities that occur during the time intervals, much the same as was done in the construction of a scatter plot (Touchette, 1985).

Once the FAOF is designed, the recorder follows the child and records each problem behavior by entering a number code depicting the occurrence of each problem behavior in sequence. For the first instance of the problem behavior, the recorder enters a numeral 1, and for the next problem behavior, he or she enters a 2, and so on, for each occurrence of the problem behavior. The recorder notes the triggering antecedent, the maintaining consequence, and the presumed function of that occurrence of the problem behavior. An example of a completed FAOF is shown in Figure 9.6.

In the example in Figure 9.6, numeral 1 is entered in five cells. The first occurrence of a problem behavior was whining which occurred between 9:00 and 9:30 A.M. during the mathematics period. The recorder judged that the incident of whining was a reaction to a demand situation, and the recorder interpreted that the function of whining was to escape the demand situation. The data for five problem behaviors are shown in Figure 9.6. As each numeral in sequence is used to code problem behaviors, it is crossed out at the bottom of the form. At the end of the observation period, the observer tallies each column to summarize what has occurred during the observation session.

The results shown in Figure 9.6 suggest that the child's problem behaviors are precipitated by situations in which the child is asked to engage in undesired activities. The child's initial reaction is whining, then screaming, and throwing objects. These behaviors, when escalated, result in adults' terminating or reducing the demands placed on the child. The Functional Assessment Observation Form is still a descriptive measure because problem behavior and events associated with the problem behavior are recorded as they unfold naturally, without any manipulation of the environmental events. Moreover, the records of predictors and functions of the behavior reflect the observer's interpretation of observed events, not the direct occurrence of environmental events. For example, the observer interpreted that a seatwork assignment (which is observable) given to the child constituted a demand made on the child (which is not observable). Nevertheless, the FAOF is a useful tool to track the occurrence of a child's problem behaviors and to contribute to the developmental hypothesis of the functions of those behaviors.

Ecobehavioral Analysis

Another descriptive method of assessing a child's problem behavior that has been extensively used in schools is ecobehavioral analysis, described by Charles Greenwood and colleagues (Greenwood, Carta, Kamps, Terry, & Delquadri, 1994). In an ecobehavioral analysis, one tracks the co-occurrences of contextual environmental events that may be related to the lowered or heightened probability of problem behaviors (e.g., a child's problem behavior is more likely to occur during times when the child's paraprofessional is located away from the child). Greenwood et al. (1994) have developed a series of three elaborate coding systems for tracking the relationship between a target behavior and specified school events (e.g., activities, interactions with the teacher, etc.) in preschools (ESCAPE; Carta, Greenwood, & Atwater, 1985), in elementary-school general education classrooms (MS-CISSAR; Carta, Greenwood, Schulte, Arreaga-Mayer, & Terry, 1987), and in elementary-school special education classrooms (CISSAR; Stanley & Greenwood, 1981). They also developed a computer-based system for coding these behavioral analyses and computing the results (EBASS: Greenwood, Carta, & Dawson, 2000).

An ecobehavioral analysis compares whether a behavior of interest is more or less likely to occur under particular environmental conditions compared to the base rate occurrence of that problem behavior. Most often, one would select what child

Functional Assessment Observation Form

Name: _Josh_

Starting Date: _November 15, 2007_   Ending Date: _November 15, 2007_

Activities	Time	Behaviors: Whining	Screaming	Throwing object	Predictors: Demand/Request	Difficult task	Transitions	Interruptions	Alone (no attention)						Get/Obtain: Attention	Desired item/activity	Self-stimulation	Escape/Avoid: Demand/request	Activity ( )	Person	Other/Don't know	Actual consequences: Asked what's wrong	Gave help
Math	9:00	1			1													1				1	
Math	9:30	2	3	3	2/3	3									3			2				2	3
Language Arts	10:00																						
Recess	10:30																						
Language Arts	11:00	4	5		4/5	5												4/5				4	5
Social Science	11:30																						
Lunch	12:00																						
Lunch	12:30																						
Totals		3	2	1	5	2									1			4				3	2
Events:	1 2 3 4 5	6	7 8	9 10	11 12	13 14	15	16	17	18	19	20	21	22	23	24	25	26	27	28 29	30		

Figure 9.6. Example of a completed Functional Assessment Observation Form. *Note.* From *Functional Analysis of Problem Behavior: A Practical Assessment Guide* (p. 38), by R. E. O'Neill, R. H. Horner, R. W. Albin, K. Storey, and J. R. Sprague, 1997, Pacific Grove, CA: Brooks/Cole. Copyright 1997 by Cengage. Adapted with permission.

behavior to use as the target behavior and what environmental events to measure that may covary with the target behavior. The steps in developing an ecobehavioral analysis are as follows:

1. Select a target behavior of interest. This may be a problem behavior or any other behavior of interest. In the example that will be presented, the target behavior consists of active engagement of an adolescent with autism.

2. Identify environmental events that co-occur with the target behavior that may be associated with heightened or lowered occurrence of the problem behavior. For example, my colleagues and I collected data on the active engagement of a 15-year-old boy with autism attending a general education high school with the assistance of a full-time paraprofessional. We selected the following general categories of codes to track alongside of measuring the occurrence of the adolescent's active engagement: location, position of teacher aide, focus of teacher aide, teacher aide prompt, teacher aide consequence, activity, teacher focus, teacher consequence.

3. Define the selected target behavior and environmental events. How to operationally define behaviors was discussed earlier in this chapter. The operational definitions of the codes used in the example are shown in Table 9.1.

4. The recorder is trained in the observation code definitions and the observation method used. The training consists of the recorder reading a written description of the behavior codes and observation method used and then practicing coding either a videotape of the target child or live sessions. Training continues until each observer passes a paper-and-pencil quiz of the behavior codes and observation procedures, achieving high (e.g., 90%) agreement with the trainer on the coding of the videotaped or live observation with the target child.

5. A recorder tracks the child's behavior and selected environmental events using a momentary time sampling (see Chapter 2). During each observation, the recorder notes whether the target behavior and particular environmental event has occurred. Only one code for each category of environmental events is recorded for each observation.

6. A predetermined length and number of observation sessions is selected to adequately sample the behaviors (e.g., 2 half-days). The results are summed across all observation sessions. The base rate of the target behavior is calculated based on the total number of times the target behavior occurred across all observations, divided by the total number of observations taken. The base rate occurrence of task engagement of the adolescent in the example presented was 0.25. In the example, 100 observations were taken, of which the child was engaged on 25 occasions.

7. To determine if the target behavior occurred any less or more often during particular classroom conditions than it did at its base rate level, one calculates conditional probabilities of the target behavior given each of the measured environmental events. The number of times the target behavior occurred at the same time as a particular environmental event is counted and divided by the total number of times the environmental event occurred across all observations. For example, suppose of 100 observations that were taken, the paraprofessional was situated beside the child 50 times. During those 50 occasions when the paraprofessional was beside the child, the target child was actively engaged 40 times. The

Table 9.1
A Sample of Codes Used in the Ecobehavioral Example

Code	Operational Definition
Active engagement	A motor or verbal behavior that correctly corresponds to the activity or teacher instruction at the time (e.g., writing, reading, answering a question)
Location of Teacher Aide	
Beside (B)	Directly beside the target child
1–3	Within 1 to 3 meters of the target child
>3	More than 3 meters away from the target child
Not present (NP)	Out of eyesight from the target child
Focus of Teacher Aide	
G+	Focus on a group including the target child
G–	Focus on a group that does not include the target child
I+	Focus on the target child
I–	Focus on a student other than the target child
OA	Focus on another adult
U	Unclear
Out	Out of the room
Teacher Aide Prompt Type	
Ve	Verbal (instructing what action to take, providing hints verbally of correct answers, directing the child what to do)
P	Physical (physically guiding in some fashion the actions of the child)
G	Gestural (pointing)
Vi	Visual (showing pictures of expectations)
N	None
Teacher Aide Consequence	
P	Praise (a statement of approval of the child's actions)
T	Tangible (e.g., token, edible)
R	Reprimand (a statement of disapproval of the child's actions)
N	No consequence
U	Unclear
Activity	
C	Classwork (the child is engaged in the same learning activity that the rest of the class is)
I	Individual curriculum (the child is engaged in a different activity than the rest of the class is),
T	Transition (in the process of moving from one activity to another)
S	Self-care (e.g., eating, washing)
U	Unclear

(continues)

Table 9.1 *Continued*

Code	Operational Definition
Focus of Teacher	
G+	Focus on a group including the target child
G−	Focus on a group that does not include the target
I+	Focus on the target child
I−	Focus on a student other than the target child
OA	Focus on another adult
U	Unclear
Out	Out of the room
Teacher Consequence	
P	Praise (a statement of approval of the child's actions)
T	Tangible (e.g., token, edible)
R	Reprimand (a statement of disapproval of the child's actions)
N	No consequence
U	Unclear

probability of the paraprofessional being beside the target child would be 0.5 (50 times in 100 observations). The conditional probability of active engagement given that the paraprofessional was beside the target child is 0.80 (40 occurrences of active engagement when the paraprofessional was beside the child divided by 50 occasions in which the paraprofessional was seated by the child).

8. Next, the results are displayed in a chart. The base rate probability of the target behavior is depicted as a horizontal line reflecting the mean occurrence of the target behavior, in this example, the child's active engagement. The results of the conditional probability of the target behavior occurring given each code are depicted as vertical bars deviating from the base rate of the target behavior. In this example, the base rate of active engagement was 0.25. The probability of the child being actively engaged on-task when the paraprofessional was beside the child was 3.2 times higher than the base rate occurrence of active engagement. The conditional probability of active engagement given the paraprofessional being 1 to 3 meters away or not present was lower than base rate occurrence of active engagement. The chart is shown in Figure 9.7.

9. One can calculate whether the difference between the conditional probability of the target behavior given a particular environmental event and the base rate occurrence of the target behaviors is statistically significant (unlikely due to chance). In the calculation, a z score takes into consideration the size of the difference between the conditional probability of the target behavior (e.g., active engagement) given a particular environmental event (e.g., the paraprofessional being located 1–3 meters

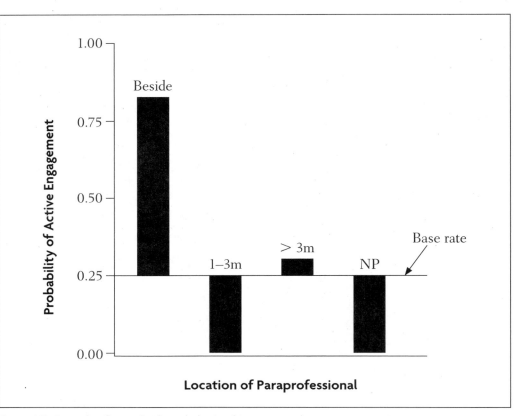

Figure 9.7. Example of a graph of eco-behavioral assessment data.

away) and the base rate occurrence of the target behavior. The calculation also takes into consideration the number of observations that occurred.

The formula for calculating a z score for the results of an ecobehavioral analysis is shown in Figure 9.8. A z score is a statistic that represents the size of an effect on a normal distribution into a standard score. A z score of 1.0 would mean that the probability of getting the obtained difference by chance is 0.16, which is insufficient to accept that the target behavior was more likely to occur under the examined environmental event. However, if the z score was 2.33, the likelihood of the obtained result occurring by chance would be .01, which meets the convention for concluding that the obtained result did *not* occur by chance. In most introductory statistics textbooks, tables are available showing the probabilities of a normal distribution from which one determines the degree of chance associated with a z score.

You will need to obtain the following numbers to calculate the statistical probability of a conditional probability exceeding base rate levels (Odom, Peterson, McConnell, & Ostrosky, 1990).

1. Count the total number of observations taken (mi). In the example presented, mi = 100

$$z = p(Ri/Ai) - p(Ri) / [p(Ri) (1/100 + 1/mo)]^{1/2}$$

$$z = p(Ri/Ai) - p(Ri) / [p(Ri) (1/mi + 1/mo)]^{1/2}$$

Figure 9.8. The formula for calculating a z-score.

2. Count the total number of times a particular environmental event occurred (mo). In the example presented, mo = 20.

$$z = p(Ri/Ai) - p(Ri) / [p(Ri) (1/100 + 1/20)]^{1/2}$$

3. The base rate probability of the target behavior, p(Ri), is determined by the total number of times the target behavior occurred, divided by the total number of observations taken. In the example, p(Ri) consisted of 25 occurrences of active engagement over 100 observations, or 0.25.

$$z = p(Ri/Ai) - 0.25 / [0.25 (1/100 + 1/20)]^{1/2}$$

4. Add 1/mi and 1/mo and multiply the sum by p(Ri).

$$z = p(Ri/Ai) - 0.25 / [0.02]^{1/2}$$

5. Calculate the square root of $[p(Ri) (1/100 + 1/mo)]^{1/2}$.

$$z = (p(Ri/Ai) - 0.25) / 0.12$$

The probability of the target behavior (Ri) given an environmental event (Ai) (p(Ri/Ai) is calculated by dividing the number of co-occurrence of the target behavior and a particular environmental event by the number of occurrences of the target behavior. In this example, the conditional probability of active engagement given the paraprofessional beside the target child is 0.80.

$$z = (0.80 - 0.25) / 0.12$$

6. Subtract p(Ri) from p(Ri/Ai).

$$z = 0.55 / 0.12$$

7. To calculate the z-score, divide the difference between p(Ri) from p(Ri/Ai) by $[p(Ri) (1/mi + 1/mo)]^{1/2}$.

$$z = 0.55 / 0.12$$

$$z = 4.58$$

A z-score of 2.33 would typically be used as a cut-off score to represent statistical significance. Statistical significance represents that the occurrence of the obtained results is greater than the bounds of results that would be expected by chance, in this case, 1/100. The probability of $Z = 4.58$ occurring by chance is less than .01.

Use Direct Experimental Manipulation of Environmental Events

The third type of assessment of behavior described by Iwata and Worsdell (2005) consists of direct determination of the function of a behavior through direct experimental manipulation of environmental events and observation of the impact of the manipulation on the target behavior. Iwata, Dorsey, Slifer, Bauman, and Richman (1982) described how to conduct a functional analysis to identify environmental variables affecting self-injurious behavior for eight individuals with developmental disabilities, aged 3 to 17 years. Participants were exposed to each of four environmental conditions (attention, demand, play, and alone), and data were collected on the occurrence of self-injurious behavior under each of those conditions. The four conditions were introduced in random order during separate 15-minute sessions.

Under the attention condition, the experimenter directed a participant to play with available toys and then occupied him- or herself with reading and writing. The experimenter gave attention (e.g., "Don't do that. You're going to hurt yourself") only when the participant engaged in self-injurious behavior.

Under the demand condition, the experimenter presented a participant with tasks that the participant never had completed independently (e.g., stringing beads, touching named body parts). If the participant showed self-injurious behavior, the experimenter terminated the request and turned away from the participant for 30 seconds. This condition was to test whether self-injury was maintained by escape.

Under the play condition, the participant was left to play with available toys with the experimenter present in the room. The experimenter maintained close proximity to the participant. No demands were placed on the participant, and self-injurious behavior was ignored. This condition served as a control for the presence of the experimenter.

Under the fourth condition, the child was placed in the room alone without toys with which to play. This condition served to test if self-injurious behavior was maintained by its sensory stimulation since there was no other stimulation in the room.

The results indicated that high levels of self-injurious behavior were consistently associated with one particular condition. Of the nine participants, self-injury was associated with the alone condition for four of the participants, suggesting that the self-injurious behavior was maintained by sensory stimulation. Two participants showed more self-injurious behavior when the escape from demand condition was in place. For one participant, injurious behavior was higher under the attention condition. For the remaining two participants, the results did not indicate any clear pattern.

By directly assessing how a target behavior changes under different environmental conditions that emulate potential maintaining conditions of the target behavior, one is able to experimentally pinpoint possible functions of a problem behavior. However, there are a number of limitations to conducting a functional assessment. One is that it tends to be time consuming. Fortunately, more time-efficient versions of conducting a functional analysis have been developed. In the Iwata et al. (1982) study, each participant spent an average of 8 days completing a functional assessment. Northup et al. (1991) developed a 90-minute version of a functional analysis that was conducted in an outpatient clinic. A similar brief functional assessment was conducted in a high school for four students with developmental disabilities (Cihak, Alberto, & Fredrick, 2007).

A second limitation is that there may be ethical and school policy issues that would arise from conducting a functional analysis in school, especially for problem behaviors that might involve the child hurting him- or herself or others. For these reasons, functional analysis would have a limited use in school settings.

Develop a Hypothesis

The final step of assessment is to put together the information that has been collected to generate a hypothesis of which factors may be contributing to the problem behavior. Assessment information about the occurrence of problem behavior would also serve as a baseline for future comparisons of the effectiveness of a subsequent intervention.

It may be helpful to develop a written hypothesis of events that contribute to problem behaviors. As shown in Figure 9.9, the significant areas to address are establishing operations, (slow triggers), triggering antecedents, and maintaining consequences. This hypothesis of events triggering and maintaining the problem behavior is a description of what is occurring currently before making plans for an intervention. The information shown in Figure 9.9 suggests that the problem behavior may be initiated by the child not completing routines at home, before leaving for school. This establishing operation makes it more difficult for the child to settle into routines when he later reaches the school. When presented with a nonpreferred task, the child hits the paraprofessional. The paraprofessional then does not persist with the request for the child to complete the task and allows the child with autism to select another activity to complete in place of the originally requested task. In this scenario, the child's hitting is likely maintained by negative reinforcement (the termination of a nonpreferred task) that occurs once the child displays the problem behavior.

Over many years, applied behavioral analysis has been used in schools to reduce problem behavior in children with autism and to build their prosocial skill alternatives. A synthesis of research in problem behavior intervention for children with autism (Horner, Carr, Strain, Todd, & Reed, 2002) drew a number of conclusions about the field. One conclusion was that, in general, interventions for problem behavior of children with autism have been effective. Two thirds of the studies that were conducted up until when the review was written reduced the problem behavior of children with autism by 80% or more. The authors also noted a shift in the type of interventions used to achieve these impressive gains. In recent years, studies have been more likely to use antecedent-based strategies than consequence-based strategies as the basis of interventions to reduce problem behaviors. Antecedent-based interventions are ones that manipulate factors prior to the occurrence of the problem behavior, including such

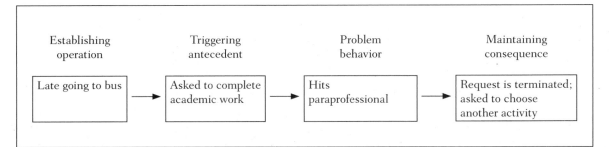

Figure 9.9. Example of a hypothesis for factors that trigger and maintain a problem behavior.

strategies as removing or reducing triggers, and teaching the child with autism prosocial skill alternatives. In previous years, however, more emphasis was placed on interventions that involved the use of consequences that followed the occurrence of problem behaviors, such as the use of reinforcement, the use of time out, and so on.

One of the most interesting conclusions of the Horner et al. (2002) paper was that there were no interventions that were effective only for children with autism. Interventions effective for problem behavior in children with autism have demonstrated to be effective for other populations as well.

Positive Behavior Support

Over the past 10 years, positive behavior support (PBS) has emerged as an area of practice of applied behavior analysis and has been extensively used in special education. In fact, the Individuals with Disabilities Education Act (IDEA; 1997) indicated that if a student with disabilities has problem behaviors that impede the student's learning or the learning of others, the Individualized Education Program (IEP) team should consider the use of "positive behavioral interventions, strategies and supports" (§ 1414 (d) (3) (B) (i)). In addition, IDEA indicated that IEP teams should conduct a functional behavioral assessment to understand the functions of the behavior.

PBS has applied behavior analysis (ABA) as its foundation and uses applied behavior analytical principles as the basis for its interventions. The main difference between PBS and ABA has to do more with the areas of emphasis than with substantial differences in conceptual models or interventions with substance. PBS emphasizes the need to have interventions that are comprehensive in structure and scope (Horner, 2000). Interventions need to be developed that apply across all appropriate contexts and time of day. The unit of intervention may need to be broadened from treating individuals one by one, to targeting entire classrooms (Lohrmann, Talerico, & Dunlap, 2004) or schools (Scott, 2001). Interventions need to fit the context in which they are being implemented (Horner, 2000), and they need to be consistent with the beliefs, values, skills, and available resources (e.g., time, knowledge, materials) of those implementing the interventions. PBS also avoids the use of punishment to obtain behavior change. Proponents of PBS describe that it should not only reduce problem behaviors but also beneficially affect how a person lives. After an intervention, a child with autism needs to be better off in general. Interventions should include life-quality improvements in such areas as activities in which the child engages, relationships with others, choices the child makes, and personal independence.

PBS has not been without controversy. Johnston, Foxx, Jacobson, Green, and Mulick (2006) have argued that PBS is not a separate science from applied behavior analysis or a new behavioral support technology. Nevertheless, positive behavior support has presented a palatable, easy-to-digest version of applied behavior analysis for educators.

Horner (2000) suggested that there are three general strategies for interventions to reduce problem behaviors. First, one needs to consider interventions that remove, reduce, buffer, or delay triggers of problem behaviors. For example, if a child is aggressive to escape difficult work, making the work less difficult and more enjoyable may eliminate the need for the child to become aggressive. The removal of triggers of problem behavior renders the problem behavior irrelevant. Strategies involving anticipating and preventing problem behavior will be described later in this chapter.

Horner (2000) suggested that problem behavior can become inefficient by teaching a child with autism how to respond to the problem situation with appropriate behavior that serves the same function(s) as the problem behavior does but that involves less effort. If these functionally equivalent replacement behaviors are effective in achieving the same outcomes as the problem behavior, there is no need for the child with autism to use problem behavior to get his or her needs met. There will be a description of functional communication training (Durand, 1990) later in this chapter in which a person is taught communicative responses that serve the same function(s) as the problem behavior.

The third strategy for dealing with problem behavior is to introduce interventions that stop the problem behavior from being effective in resulting in the maintaining consequence (Horner, 2000). That is, problem behaviors need to become less effective in resulting in the child escaping from a nonpreferred task if they are escape-motivated or getting attention if they are attention motivated, and so on.

Making Problem Behavior Irrelevant

If educators can identify and then reduce, delay, buffer, or remove triggers of problem behavior, there is no need for the child with autism to use problem behavior as a means to get his or her needs met. A number of procedures that can make a problem behavior irrelevant are discussed below.

- *Neutralizing routines*—Horner, Day, and Day (1997) found that aggression or self-injury of three adolescents with severe developmental disability occurred almost exclusively after each had experienced an establishing operation (e.g., poor sleep, cancellation of preferred activity) and later also experienced a trigger for problem behavior (e.g., waiting for a reinforcer). When the adolescents experienced a situation associated with the occurrence of problem behavior without an EO, the problem behaviors were unlikely to occur. Horner et al. then introduced what they referred to as "neutralizing routines." A neutralizing routine is "an establishing operation that reduces the value of reinforcers that are associated with problem behaviors" (Horner et al., p. 601). In other words, it serves as a calming activity. For the adolescent with sleep deprivation, the neutralizing routine consisted of allowing the child to take a nap. For the other two adolescents, the neutralizing routine consisted of engaging in highly preferred routines (e.g., drawing pictures, looking at pictures). After neutralizing routines were introduced, the problem behaviors of the adolescents were almost nonexistent, even though the EO and triggers of problem behaviors still occurred.

This study suggests that on days in which a child with autism has experienced an establishing operation for a problem behavior, it would be prudent to introduce a neutralizing routine immediately when that child comes to school or immediately following an establishing operation.

There are a number of strategies that can be used to reduce the impact of triggers of problem behavior when they are identified. For example, suppose a child's problem behaviors are triggered by difficult academic work. Some strategies for adapting the curriculum are identified in Chapter 3. One can make the task easier for the child. For example, our team presents learning materials to the child with autism so that the child is able to correctly answer at least 50% of items correctly, even on initial presentation. One can add prompts as aids to learning (see Chapter 3). Or, if a child prefers activities on a computer, one may be able to provide computer-based practicing in arithmetic computation facts rather than giving paper-and-pencil practice sheets.

• *High-probability (high-p) and interspersed requests*—Problem behavior may be associated with situations in which the child with autism is asked to perform a nonpreferred activity (e.g., cleaning up, coming in from recess, completing an academic task). One approach that has been shown to be effective in these situations is the use of high-probability requests (Davis, Brady, Williams, & Hamilton, 1992; Killu, Sainato, Davis, Ospelt, & Paul, 1998). The strategy here is to ask a child to perform actions that have a high probability of child compliance before asking the child a request that has a low likelihood of being followed. Prior to making a low-probability request, one gives the child a number of requests in rapid succession that have been established as resulting in a high probability of compliance (e.g., "Touch your nose," "High five," "Low five," "What's your name?"). Following these high-p requests, the child is more likely to follow low-probability requests. It is as if the child builds up momentum in complying to easy requests that carries through to compliance to more difficult requests.

Interspersed requests (Horner, Day, Sprague, & O'Brien, 1991) is a similar strategy used when presenting difficult or low-preferred tasks to a child with autism. One intersperses easy activities within the difficult or low-preferred task. For example, a child may already know how to answer single-digit addition problems to 10 and then is taught to answer single-digit subtraction problems. One might intersperse single-digit addition problems into practice sheets containing the newly taught subtraction problems.

• *Transitional warnings*—Ending one activity to move on to another activity is often a difficult situation for children with autism, especially when the child needs to make a transition from a high-preferred activity (e.g., a computer game) to a low-preferred activity (e.g., class lesson in language). A transitional warning consists of cues that are delivered before a transition that aid the child in making the transition without difficulty (Cote, Thompson, & McKerchar, 2005). A transitional warning may be verbally presented, such as giving the child a countdown to end an activity (e.g., "Toys all away in three, two, one. All done"), or it might consist of a visual cue, such as flicking overhead lights off to help a kindergarten class make a transition. Another example of visual cue is the use of a visual timer, such as the one depicted in Figure 9.10 (available from PRO-ED, Inc.). This timer shows the amount of time remaining from a set interval (e.g., 30 minutes) by a red, pie-shaped section on the timer that gets smaller as time passes. Such a device can be used to signal to children with autism how much time is left before an activity occurs (e.g., time remaining before the child needs to end a computer game).

• *Choice*—There is evidence that simply providing a choice as an intervention will reduce problem behaviors and increase task engagement of children (Kern et al., 1998). In fact, Kern, Montegna, Vorndran, Ballin, and Hilt (2001) speculated that choice making might inherently possess reinforcing properties because of the possibility that the individual

Figure 9.10. Countdown timer that can be used as a visual cue for transitional warnings.

may select a more preferred option than options selected by someone else. In an early study on the effectiveness of choice-making, Dyer, Dunlap, and Winterling (1990) assessed the effects of choice making with three students with autism and/or mental retardation between the ages of 5 and 11 years on such problem behavior as aggression, self-injury, and tantrums. Children were given the opportunity to choose from available tasks and reinforcers for task completion. In a no-choice condition, children were provided with the same task and reinforcement as in the choice condition, but on a schedule selected by a teacher, rather than the children. There were consistently lower levels of problem behaviors when children were given a choice over the task and reinforcer. In other studies (Kern et al., 2001; Moes, 1998), children were given a choice over the sequence in which tasks were presented, and a reduction of problem behavior and an increase in task engagement were found.

In these examples, children were not given a choice over whether or not to complete a task; rather, they could choose the order in which they completed tasks or which equivalent forms of tasks to complete. Our team provides choices to children with autism on the order of tasks to be completed. Three tasks are selected for the child to complete, and each is represented by a picture symbol on a 4.5 by 6 cm card. The cards are placed on a To Do/Done board using Velcro, as shown in Figure 9.11.

The three tasks to be completed are placed in a random order on the To Do side of the board. The child selects the task, removes the corresponding picture symbol for the activity to be completed, and places the picture symbol in the middle location at the bottom of the To Do/Done board. After the child completes the task, the child removes the symbol of the just-completed task and places it on an empty space on the Done side of the To Do/Done board. This sequence is repeated until the three tasks are completed.

Our team also provides children with autism with choices regarding the reinforcers they will work for. They are shown a number of pictures depicting the reinforcers that they can earn. They select a picture of the

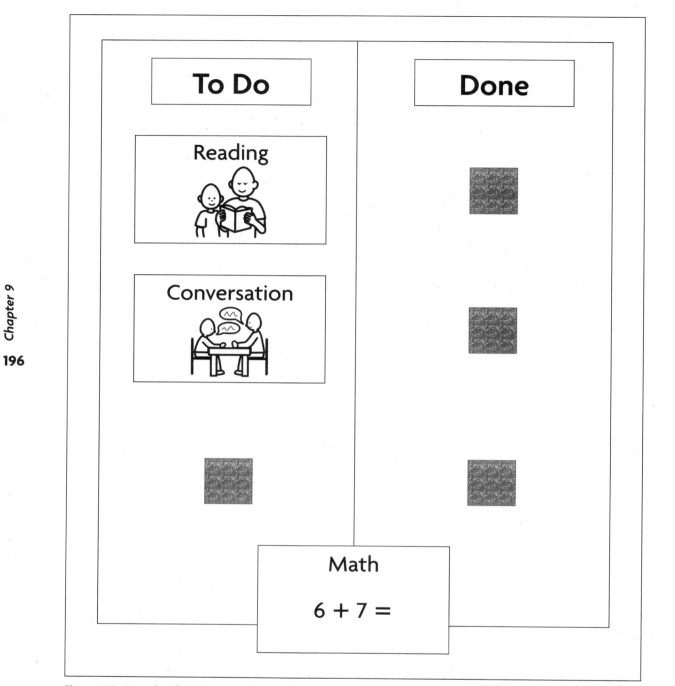

Figure 9.11. Example of a To Do/Done board.

reinforcer to be earned, which is then placed on a token strip to remind the children what they are working for (see description of reinforcement in Chapter 4).

• *Priming*—Priming consists of preexposing children to events with which they have difficulty so that the events become predictable and, as a result, children are more successful (Schreibman, Whalen, & Stahmer, 2001). One of the first uses of priming was to assist children with disabilities to participate successfully during class lessons. Wilde, Koegel, and Koegel (1992) arranged a communication note system between a classroom teacher and a home tutor that consisted of teacher description of the instruction that would later be covered in the class for a child with autism. Over the next couple of days, the parent or home tutor rehearsed learning material at home that the child was to later cover in class.

When priming, the material is presented in as similar a manner as possible as it will be presented in class. Preteaching material, especially material that will be new to a child with autism, is intended to prepare the child to be successful when encountering the material in class the next day. Although Wilde et al. (1992) described the use of priming between a classroom teacher and the home, there is no reason that academic priming cannot be arranged between a classroom teacher of a child with autism and other school personnel, such as a paraprofessional or a special education teacher.

Koegel, Koegel, Frea, and Green-Hopkins (2003) used priming for children with autism aged 5 and 15 years who were attending inclusive educational settings. For one child, priming was conducted by his parents each evening for about 1 hour in the areas of letter recognition, writing, and phonics. For the other child, priming was implemented by a special education staff member who worked with the child on grammar and written assignments in a room outside of a high school classroom. Both children showed much higher levels of appropriate behavior and academic responding during classroom periods associated with priming. The key to the effectiveness of this type of priming is coordination between the classroom teacher and individuals providing the priming.

- *Video Priming*—Schreibman et al. (2001) used video priming to reduce the problem behavior of three young children with autism who displayed problem behaviors in public settings. Each child, aged 4 to 6 years, exhibited extreme problem behaviors (e.g., screaming, kicking, hitting) when taken to a particular community setting, such as shopping with a child's mother at a local mall. Videotapes were recorded from a child's perspective of the community outing. These 1- or 2-minute videotapes (e.g., moving from one store to the next in the mall) would depict a preferred event at the end of the video, such as going into a child's favorite store in the mall. The video did not include any modeling of appropriate behavior, nor was the child given any specific instructions on how to act. Each child observed the video just before being taken to the community setting that was associated with the problem behavior for the child. Video priming produced a marked reduction in problem behaviors of the children.

Although video priming has been used by parents for preparing children with autism for community outings, a similar strategy may be effective for helping children with autism deal with a situation that would be encountered at school (e.g., transition from one program activity to the next, lining up). The effectiveness of video priming at school has yet to be demonstrated.

- *Social stories*—Social stories are a strategy developed by Carol Gray (1998, 2000) in which text and pictures are crafted into a brief storybook and read to a child with autism. The story depicts a problem situation for that particular child and describes how the situation can be managed with the role of the child written into the script. Social stories are described here under the general topic of priming because they involve preexposing children to problem situations typically just before the child experiences the situation. Social stories are consistent with the strategy of anticipating and preventing problem behaviors.

Social stories have been used for children with autism to deal with a wide range of problem behaviors, including social interaction (Delano & Snell, 2006; Scattone, Tingstrom, & Wilczynski, 2006), disruptive behavior (Crozier & Tincani, 2005), aggression (Swaggart et al., 1995), and social language (Thiemann & Goldstein, 2001). Delano and Snell (2006) estimated that half of outcome studies on the effectiveness of social skills for children with autism have consisted of studies that targeted improvement in children's problem behavior. Gray (2000) described five components of social stories (summarized in Figure 9.12).

The development of social stories is quite involved and prescribed. According to Gray (1998), the first step in the development of a social story is to target specific problem situations for intervention. The problem situation then becomes the focus of the social story. Through direct observation, one should identify salient features of the problem situation for the child, including the nature, duration, and triggers of problem behaviors. The information that is gathered is then used to generate a social story (Gray, 1998).

A social story is written for a child's level of comprehension and typically is phrased in the first person. Gray (2000) defined six types of sentences that may compose a social story (each is described in Figure 9.12). She indicated that there should be two to five descriptive, perspective,

---

1. Write the story in the first person, from the perspective of the child.
2. Use the following types of sentences:
   - *Descriptive*—Identify facts about the situation being described (e.g., "At our school, children go outside to play at recess").
   - *Perspective*—Describe a person's feelings (e.g., "Most children like going outside to play").
   - *Directive*—Suggest a response to a situation, usually phrased as what a person will try to do (e.g., "Carol will try to ask a friend to play with her").
   - *Affirmative*—Emphasize important points (e.g., "It is important to ask before trying to share someone else's toy").
   - *Control*—Point out strategies for using the information in the social story (e.g., "Carol will ask the teacher for help if she needs it").
   - *Cooperative*—Indicate how help will be delivered (e.g., "Ms. Lopes will help Carol remember what to say").
3. Use two to five descriptive, perspective, affirmative, or cooperative sentences for every directive or control sentence.
4. Deliver the story through reading, audio equipment, video equipment, computer, and so forth.
5. Assess the child's comprehension of the social story.

Figure 9.12. Gray's (2000) five components of writing social stories.

affirmative, or cooperative sentences for each directive or control sentence in the story. This ratio ensures that the majority of the content of social stories does not consist of directions to the child on how to act.

The sentences are composed into a booklet with pictures (if they do not distract the child or limit the child's ability to attend to the content of the social story). Social stories may be read to a child or presented with audio or video equipment or with a computer. After presentation, it is necessary to assess the child's comprehension of the social story with such strategies as having the child answer questions about the story or role-play what he or she would do in the story. The social stories may be presented immediately before the child experiences the problem situation (e.g., recess at school).

It should be noted that there has been no examination of whether social stories developed following the format described by Gray (1998) are more effective than any other configuration of developing and delivering social stories (Sansosti, Powell-Smith, & Kincaid, 2004). In fact, Crozier and Tincani (2005) used a 3:5 ratio of directive to perspective and descriptive sentences, rather than the 1:2.5 ratio recommended by Gray (2000), and still found a positive effect from social stories. Social stories have been used in speech and language therapy sessions (Ivey, Heflin, & Alberto, 2004), in homes of children with autism (Knoch & Mirenda, 2003), in special education classes (Crozier & Tincani, 2005), and in general education classes (Delano & Snell, 2006; Scattone et al., 2006).

A review of social story interventions for children with autism suggests that the effectiveness of this intervention has not been extensively evaluated (Sansosti et al., 2004). Many of the studies that have been completed have found social stories to be effective in changing the target behaviors of children with autism, but have not been conducted in ways to show clearly that the social stories were solely responsible for the observed effects. It is recommended that until further research is completed, social stories be used only in conjunction with behavior change procedures that are known to be effective, such as prompting and reinforcing.

There have been a handful of studies describing the use of social stories to reduce problem behavior for children with autism in schools. Crozier and Tincani (2005) used a modified version of social stories to reduce the verbal disruptive behavior of an 8-year-old boy with autism who was attending school for children with disabilities and challenging behaviors. Agosta, Graetz, Mastropieri, and Scruggs (2004) targeted the reduction of yelling, screaming, humming, and other distracting behaviors of a 6-year-old boy with autism in a self-contained special education class. The classroom teacher was taught how to implement the social stories, and there was a reduction of the child's problem behaviors.

Scattone, Wilczynski, Edwards, and Rabian (2002) completed a similar intervention for three students with autism between 7 and 15 years of age, each of whom was enrolled in a self-contained special education class in either an elementary or secondary school. Social stories targeted reduction in children's disruptive behavior (e.g., shouting). The teacher or teacher's aide read the developed social story to the child individually just before the situation that was associated with the occurrence of the child's problem behavior and proceeded to test the student's comprehension by asking a set of five questions about the content of the social story.

Following a baseline phase, the introduction of social stories resulted in a reduction in the disruptive behavior of each student.

There have been few, if any, demonstrations on the use of social stories for children with autism who are attending a general education class, although there would be no reason to expect it not to be effective. In my experience, social stories are widely utilized for children with autism who attend general education classrooms. Implementation of social stories in general education classrooms would require someone to develop social stories following the guidelines of Gray (1998, 2000). It would also require one or more individuals with the time and knowledge to implement social skills during the school day.

- *Noncontingent reinforcement and noncontingent escape*— Recall that this section describes interventions to reduce problem behavior in children with autism by reducing, delaying, removing, or buffering triggers of the problem behavior. Another way of making a problem behavior irrelevant is to provide the consequences that maintain the problem behavior on a time basis, not connected to the child's problem behavior that typically would result in that maintaining consequence. For example, a functional assessment may reveal that a child's aggression is maintained by escape from task. If so, one may be able to render the child's aggression irrelevant by providing the child with breaks from tasks on a time interval, rather than when demanded by the child's problem behavior. The child does not need to become aggressive to escape the task. Breaks are given on a time basis regardless of how the child acts. If the strategy of noncontingent escape is to be used, it would still be important to also modify the task from which the child is attempting to escape.

Similarly, if a child's problem behavior is maintained by teacher attention, the delivery of teacher attention on a time schedule, not contingent on the child's problem behavior, may reduce the occurrence of the problem behavior. For example, Hagopian, Fisher, and Legacy (1994) first established that the aggression of 5-year-old quadruplet girls with Pervasive Developmental Disorders (PDD) was maintained by social attention. Next, adult attention (gentle touching, praise) was delivered to each of the girls almost on a continuous basis, which resulted in a marked reduction in their aggression. Over time, the frequency of noncontingent aggression was gradually reduced.

In the same vein, if a problem behavior is maintained by sensory stimulation, then the noncontingent reinforcement would consist of access to a sensory object on a time interval. The use of noncontingent access to mouthing objects was effective in reducing the amount of object mouthing by an 8-year-old girl with multiple disabilities (Luiselli, 1994). Vollmer, Marcus, and Ringdahl (1995) reduced the self-injurious behavior of an 18-year-old young man with profound mental retardation and a 4-year-old boy with multiple disabilities by providing noncontingent escape. Twenty- to 30-second breaks from a task were provided once every 10 minutes for the older child and once every 2.5 minutes for the younger child.

One of the limitations of noncontingent reinforcement and noncontingent escape is that the intervention does not teach the child a more appropriate behavioral alternative for the problem behavior. As a result, noncontingent reinforcement should be paired with reinforcement of alternative behaviors (Iwata & Worsdell, 2005) or functional communication training (Doughty & Anderson, 2006).

Making Problem Behavior Inefficient

Altering the environment to remove triggers of problem behavior, preexposing children with autism to problem situations to reduce their reactivity, or using consequences to suppress problem behavior when it occurs will not equip a child with autism with appropriate behavior for handling the situation. Horner (2000) suggested that a general strategy for dealing with problem behavior is to teach positive behaviors that serve the same function as the problem behaviors. If the effort required to use these replacement behaviors is less than the effort required to engage in the problem behaviors, and the replacement behaviors result in at least the same level of effectiveness in soliciting the maintaining consequence, then there is no need for the child with autism to use problem behaviors to get his or her needs met (Durand & Merges, 2001).

In functional communication training, the acceptable behavior that is taught to replace problem behavior is a communicative response. For functional communication training to be effective, the communicative response must be one that is easy for the child with autism to use (Horner & Day, 1991). The communicative response may not necessarily be a spoken phrase. Durand (1999) taught five children with severe disabilities, including severe limitations in communication, to use assisted communication devices in school to request activities and objects that were assessed to maintain the problem behaviors. Some of the children were taught to request "I need help" when experiencing difficult tasks. Others were taught to request "I want more, please" when they wanted additional objects or activities. After the introduction of functional communication training, there was an increase in children's unprompted use of their assistive device and a reduction in their problem behaviors. Children also learned to use their assistive devices in community settings, such as a store or a library.

Durand (1990) described the steps in implementing functional communication training. The first step is to undertake a functional assessment of a child's behavior from which one hypothesizes the function(s) of the problem behavior and selects an appropriate communicative response to replace that problem behavior. The second step is to select the response modality for the child's communication (e.g., a voice output device, picture communication system, signs, oral communication) that would be most appropriate for the individual.

Next, one selects a communicative response that the child can learn rapidly and that involves low effort. The replacement communicative response should evoke the same consequences as the problem behavior being replaced. It should also involve less effort than the problem behavior. Horner and Day (1991) demonstrated that aggressive behavior of a 12-year-old boy with developmental disabilities did not decline when he was required to make a high-effort response to sign his request ("I want to go, please") in a complete sentence. Once the requirement for the communicative response was changed to a low-effort response (i.e., signing "break"), there was a decrease in the occurrence of the child's problem behaviors.

Our team often teaches children with autism to show a red card with the word "break" as the communicative response in functional communication training even when the children have the ability to pronounce individual words. The use of a "break" card is to ensure a low-effort communicative response. In addition, it is easier to prompt the use of a "break" card during initial training than it is to prompt the child's speech production.

The use of communicative responses to replace problem behavior is taught during naturally occurring opportunities associated with the child's problem behavior. The particular communicative response to use would be selected based on the function of the problem behavior. In situations in which the problem behavior is escape-motivated, one would present the task (with any modifications). After a brief period (e.g., 10 to 15 seconds), the work is pulled back. The child is verbally and/or physically prompted to use a communicative response (e.g., "Use your words") and/or prompted to use a break card. Immediately upon using the communicative response, the child is given the activity (e.g., break, attention, object) that he or she requested. If the child was prompted to request a break from task, then the child is given a break. If the child requested help or attention (e.g., "How am I doing?"), then attention is provided to the child.

The next step is to reduce the amount of physical prompt used (e.g., move from hand-over-hand prompting to just touching the child's hand). The step after that may be to remove the physical prompt altogether and then introduce a 3-second time delay between pulling the work back and issuing a verbal prompt. Next, the verbal prompt is removed altogether.

The steps in prompt fading would be based on the child's performance. After the child is able to consistently use an acceptable response to triggers previously associated with the problem behavior, one then moves to prompting generalization of the child's replacement communicative response to a natural environment outside of the training situation.

There may be a concern that a child will "abuse" the taught communicative response by using it too much to escape or request a desired object or activity. It may be wise to initially tolerate higher rates of the child asking for breaks or desired objects so that the child learns that the communicative response will be effective. The length of breaks and access to desired objects can be kept brief (e.g., 30 seconds). If someone on my team is concerned about a child's requesting too many breaks, we present three break cards on the child's desk to reflect the maximum number of breaks the child is able to request within a period of time. Once a child makes a request, one of the break cards is removed, leaving the remainder to be used. Once all three break cards are removed, no further breaks are given to the child for that designated period of time.

The child is given a verbal prompt such as "touch break" if a break card is used or "sign break" if signs are used. Immediately, the trainer physically prompts the child to use the communicative response and the child is given a brief break from the task. This instructional sequence is shown in Figure 9.13.

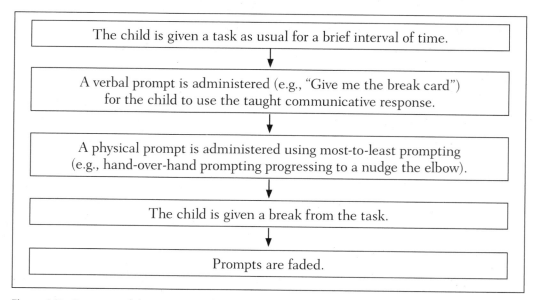

Figure 9.13. Summary of the steps in implementing functional communication training.

Teaching a child to make requests for tangibles or attention will progress in a similar fashion. Training would occur during activities associated with the occurrence of the problem behavior that is maintained by these events. The nature of the request is based on the assessed function of the problem behavior. For requests for tangibles, the communicative response is to name the desired object. For requests for attention, the child is taught questions such as "How am I doing?" or a request for an activity (e.g., "Tickle, please").

Functional communication training is a systematic approach to replace problem behavior with a communicative response that serves the same function as the problem behavior. It is based on initial functional assessment, followed by specific training to replace the problem behavior with a communicative response. There also is evidence that simply teaching the picture exchange communication system (PECS) to children with autism can reduce problem behavior (Frea, Arnold, & Vittiberga, 2001). There appears to be value both as an aid to communication and as an intervention for problem behavior to teach children with autism an approach to communicate their needs.

Making Problem Behavior Ineffective

Horner's (2000) third general strategy for dealing with problem behavior is to arrange environments so that a child's problem behavior will be less effective in eliciting the consequences that have been associated with maintaining the problem behavior. This strategy involves having individuals use an intervention for dealing with the problem behavior when it occurs.

As with interventions to anticipate and prevent problem behavior and to teach the child an acceptable replacement of behavior, interventions to deal effectively with problem behaviors when they occur first need to be based on assessment of the function(s) of the problem behavior. The intervention that is later developed needs to match the function of the problem behavior.

Interventions for Problem Behavior Maintained by Attention

Interventions for problem behaviors maintained by attention need to make the problem behaviors less effective in getting that attention. Three behavioral techniques will be presented: extinction/planned ignoring, differential reinforcement, and clear requests.

Extinction/Planned Ignoring

Extinction or "planned ignoring" of attention-maintained problem behavior consists of the removal of reinforcement from a previously reinforced behavior, resulting in a decrease in the occurrence of that behavior (Cooper et al., 2007). First, one needs to determine whose attention (e.g., teacher, other student) is maintaining the problem. For problem behaviors maintained by the attention of adults and/or peers, one would use planned ignoring. Planned ignoring can only be used for relatively benign problem behaviors (e.g., whining) that that do not result in property damage, harm to the child, or harm to others. Therefore, the first question to be answered in considering the use of planned ignoring is whether the problem behavior can be ignored. Self-injurious behavior, aggression, throwing of objects, and other activities that may be harmful to individuals or the environment cannot be ignored. Strategies other than planned ignoring would need to be used for these types of problem behaviors.

Planned ignoring consists of not altering what one says or does when the child's problem behavior occurs. For example, if the child's whining is maintained by the teacher asking the child with autism what he or she needs, then planned ignoring would consist of the teacher carrying on as if the child were not whining. Planned ignoring does not consist of walking away from the child or the teacher announcing that he or she is not going to pay attention to the child. Altering one's actions when the problem behavior occurs could actually be providing attention to the child. It is important to note that extinction (planned ignoring of attention-maintained behavior) will not work immediately. It is likely to take several experiences before one would see a decline in the child's problem behavior. In fact there is likely to be an "extinction burst" when planned ignoring is first introduced. The child is likely to increase the rate and/or amplitude of the problem behavior (e.g., whine more often, louder, or for longer periods of time) when one begins to ignore what was previously attended to. Consistency and persistence are critical when using planned ignoring.

Similarly, if a child's problem behavior is maintained by the reaction it gets from peers in the classroom, then an intervention may be needed to result in peers ignoring that child's problem behavior and attending to his or her appropriate behavior. Soloman and Wahler (1973) found that almost all of the problem behaviors shown by five sixth-grade boys were attended to by peers. They subsequently trained peers to ignore the problem behavior and to respond positively to the appropriate behavior of these five boys. This intervention resulted in a reduction in the occurrence of the problem behaviors of the five boys by half.

Differential Reinforcement

Another intervention for attention-maintained problem behavior is to reinforce the occurrence of behaviors other than the problem behavior. For example, if a child with autism talks out of turn in class to get the teacher's attention, the teacher may decide to praise the child when the child is quiet or when raising his/her hand without being disruptive. There are a number of ways in which differential reinforcement may be used. One way is differential reinforcement of other behavior (DRO), in which reinforcement is delivered contingent on a time lapse during which the problem behavior does not occur. For example, Newman, Tuntigian, Ryan, and Reinecke (1997) coupled DRO and self-management for three students with autism who showed high rates of disruptive behavior. A kitchen timer was set every minute. Initially, the experimenter delivered a token exchangeable for a preferred object or activity for each time interval in which the child was not out of his or her seat. Later, students earned a token for not being out of their seats for progressively longer periods of time.

Differential reinforcement of incompatible behavior (DRI) consists of reinforcing a child with autism for behaviors that are incompatible with the problem behavior. For example, a child's out-of-seat behavior may be reduced by reinforcing a child when he or she is seated. There are other forms of differential reinforcements—such as differential reinforcement of low rates of behavior (DRL) and differential reinforcement of alternative behavior (DRA)—that are consistent in principle with the differential methods discussed so far. To appropriately deliver differential reinforcement, one should use the following steps:

1. Ensure that the object (e.g., stickers) or activity (e.g., praise) used in differential reinforcement is motivating for the child. As discussed in

Chapter 4, one needs to directly assess the effectiveness of potential reinforcers with a particular child. Just because most children in the class will respond to teacher praise does not mean that praise will be effective for use with a child with autism.

2. A tangible (e.g., token) reinforcer should be paired with descriptive praise (e.g., "I like the way you are sitting in your seat"). Pairing a tangible reinforcer with praise informs the child (assuming the child has sufficiently developed receptive language skills) about what behavior is being reinforced. Also, over time, it may be possible to remove the tangible reinforcer, and praise alone may be effective as a reinforcer through its pairing with tangibles (Cooper et al., 2007).

Brown and Mirenda (2006) used a three-picture sequence that they referred to as "contingency mapping" to explain the reinforcement contingency in place for a 13-year-old boy with autism. The child was reinforced in class for completing his assigned work and for taking the completed assignment to his educational assistant. A separate set of three pictures indicated what would occur if the independent routine did not happen. The educational assistant pointed to each picture card in the two card sequences while verbally explaining the contingencies. Contingency mapping was implemented in the boy's Grade 6/7 general education class. During baseline, the boy never independently initiated the work completion. There was no improvement in the boy's completion routine after the educational assistant explained the contingencies verbally without visual mapping. With the introduction of contingency mapping, the boy completed his work assignment and immediately brought it to be checked by his educational assistant.

3. Deliver the reinforcer immediately following the occurrence of the behavior being reinforced. If a child lines up to enter school without difficulty in the morning, but does not receive reinforcement for that behavior until morning recess, there is unlikely to be much of an effect of that reinforcement on the child's behavior. Reinforcement needs to be temporally paired with the behavior being reinforced.

4. When new behavior is being taught, reinforce frequently, such as each time it occurs. As the child's desired behavior increases, the schedule for delivering reinforcement can be made less frequent and less predictable.

Clear Requests

A common problem behavior in children with autism is noncompliance to adults' requests. The rate of noncompliance to parent requests tends to be higher in children with autism than in children with other forms of developmental disability or in typically developing children (Sigafoos, 2000). In teaching a child to follow requests such as "put your work away," "line up for recess," or "stop throwing the pencil," one starts with instruction of the desired action for the child to do and then reinforces the child for compliance to that request.

Ducharme and DiAdamo (2005) have developed an "errorless" strategy to teach compliance to children with developmental disabilities in a special education setting. Their first step was to assess children's likelihood of following specific types of requests. Based on that assessment, requests were sorted into four levels based on the probability of child compliance. As much as possible, the children were asked only requests with a high probability of compliance (76%–100% compliance) and lower probability requests were avoided. After the children's compliance level to requests reached 75% or higher, lower probability requests (those which the children during assessment followed less than 75% of the time) were introduced. The two 5-year-old girls in their study learned to follow requests that previously were associated with low-probability compliance. Unfortunately, there has not been demonstration that errorless compliance training can be implemented for children with autism in a general education setting and conducted by staff in those settings.

The way in which requests are given to children with autism makes a difference in the likelihood that the children will follow those requests (Green, 2001). The following are tips on how to give effective requests to children with autism.

1. Get the child's attention before giving a request. This is particularly important for children who may be engaged in stereotypic behavior and frequently not attending to any event around them. Strategies to gain the attention of a child with autism can range from a verbal prompt (e.g., "Anthony, look at me") to a physical prompt (e.g., cupping one's hands under either side of the child's face) to taking a visual object that would get the child's attention (e.g., a trinket that flashes) and then moving it slowly above his or her eyes as the child tracks the object.

2. Verbal requests should be given only to children who are capable of understanding verbally presented information. The request should be phrased as simply and briefly as possible and may need accompanying visual aids (e.g., photographs or line drawings)

3. If possible, the request should describe what you would like the child with autism to do (e.g., "Please hold this book with two hands"), rather than the action you want the child *not* to do (e.g., "Stop stimming").

4. Give one request at a time. It is easy for a child with autism to lose track of what you are asking him or her to do if you give a request that contains two or more actions. Give just one request and then give the next request when the child completes the first.

5. Do not repeat your request. It is important for the child to learn to follow a request the first time it is made. If not, you are teaching the child to wait until you escalate your request before the child has to comply.

Interventions for Problem Behavior Maintained by Access to Desired Activities or Objects

Some problem behaviors in children with autism are maintained by access to desired activities (e.g., pushing ahead of other students waiting to get a drink of water from a water fountain, hitting another child to get off a swing so that the child can get on the swing). Interventions are needed so that these problem behaviors become less effective in obtaining the desired activities in the future.

One approach for dealing with this situation is the use of a response cost that is naturally connected to the problem behavior. Using a response cost consists of the delay or removal of a reinforcer following the occurrence of a problem behavior that results in a reduction of the likelihood of the problem behavior (Pelios, MacDuff, & Axelrod, 2003). The reinforcer being removed would be the activity or object that is the target of the child's problem behavior. In the case of a child pushing in line at the water fountain, the child who did the pushing would be placed at the end of the lineup for the water fountain or denied the drink altogether. For hitting of the child to get off the swing, the response cost would be the loss of the aggressor's use of the swing for that day and the following day. As with all other strategies, the intervention is selected based on assessment of the function of the problem behavior. For example, if either of the two examples of problem behavior were maintained by attention, rather than access to a desired object or activity, the adult attention to deliver the response cost may inadvertently reinforce the problem behavior.

Interventions for Problem Behavior Maintained by Sensory Stimulation

Problem behaviors maintained by sensory stimulation would primarily consist of repetitive, stereotypic behaviors (e.g., hand flapping, finger flicking, object twirling, humming, rocking). As previously stated, when children with autism are engaged in stereotypic behavior, they are less attentive to their learning environment and, as a result, the stereotypic behavior interferes with their learning (Lovaas, Koegel, & Schreibman, 1979). Again, one would need to assess the function of stereotypic behavior to determine if it is maintained by sensory stimulation (i.e., if the child engages in the behavior simply because it feels good [automatic reinforcement]). Sometimes, problem behaviors that appear to be maintained by sensory stimulation (e.g., repetitive vocalization) are, in fact, maintained by attention (Iwata et al., 1982).

There have been several approaches used to reduce stereotypic behavior of children with autism, but very few have been applied in general education settings (Conroy, Asmus, Sellers, & Ladwig, 2005). One general strategy for dealing with stereotypic behavior that is suitable to be used in an inclusive educational setting is response interruption and redirection (Ahearn, Clark, MacDonald, & Chung, 2007). It may not be possible to reduce stereotypic behavior in all situations, but it is important to target stereotypic behavior that interferes with learning, such as when the child needs to complete seatwork, attend to instructions, or make a transition. Stereotypic behavior should be interrupted by some intervention such as physical touch (e.g., touching the child's hand if the child is engaged in hand flapping) or asking the child to perform some other response (e.g., look at the requester). Next, the child is redirected to engage in a functional activity that is incompatible with a child's stereotypic behavior. For example, a child who is engaged in hand flapping may be asked to hold a book with both hands when walking from one location to the next or to place his or her hands in pockets. For vocal stereotypy (e.g., humming, noncontextural vocalizations), this intervention would consist of asking the child to answer simple questions (e.g., "What is your name?"), to initiate verbal sound, or to perform some other vocal response. A number of children with autism that our team serves begin an escalating sequence of stereotypic behavior with hand flapping or with finger flicking. The strategy that we have successfully used is to provide a vest with pockets in the front for the child to wear and redirect the child to place his or her hands in the pockets during transition times.

The child is reinforced for engaging in an incompatible behavior (e.g., holding on to a book). For example, Taylor, Hoch, and Weissman (2005) reduced the vocal stereotypy (humming, echolalia) of a 4-year-old girl with autism by reinforcing the child playing for 1 minute without vocal stereotypy to gain access to a music toy. The child would be allowed to play with less preferred toys and, after 1 minute free of the vocal stereotypy, was allowed to play with a highly preferred toy that made music. Over time, the girl earned access to the music toy for progressively longer periods of time free of vocal stereotypy. This resulted in a decrease in the girl's vocal stereotypy to near zero. There was no reduction in the vocal stereotypy when the girl received access to the music toy based on time, rather than the absence of vocal stereotypy. This result would indicate that the decrease in the girl's vocal stereotypy was due to the differential reinforcement of the alternative behavior, rather than to simply being exposed to periods of the music toy.

As previously indicated, it is unlikely that one can suppress stereotypic behavior in children with autism all of the time, but it may be critical to reduce stereotypy during particular times that effect children's learning. Children will learn when they can engage in stereotypic behavior and when they cannot. Conroy and colleagues (2005) introduced a visual cue (a 3-in. white card with a red circle) to signal times when it was acceptable for an 8-year-old boy with autism to engage in hand flapping, such as during free time in the classroom. A different visual cue (3" white card with red circle and line through circle) signaled times when it was unacceptable for the child to engage in hand flapping. Through practice and feedback, the boy learned to reduce stereotypic behavior during unacceptable times.

Interventions for Problem Behavior Maintained by Escape

Likely, the most difficult problem behaviors to deal with effectively are problem behaviors maintained to escape undesired situations. A child with autism may fall to the floor when asked to complete a worksheet. Another child may scream, hit, and throw objects to escape being asked to eat a fruit at lunch provided by his or her parents. If the problem behavior is maintained by escape, then the intervention to make the problem behavior less effective should consist of strategies to prevent the child from escaping. The difficulty is that extinction of escape-motivated problem behavior should consist of continuing with the expectations placed on the child even when a child is exhibiting problem behaviors (Iwata, Pace, Kalsher, Cowdery, & Cataldo, 1990). Physically guiding a child to return to a nonpreferred task may easily result in an escalation of the child's behaviors and the need to engage in more intensive physical guidance or even physical restraint. Physical restraints may potentially injure the child, school staff, and/ or other children (Ryan & Peterson, 2004). For this reason, interventions to deal with escape-motivated behavior should be considered only under the following conditions:

- *As part of a larger behavior support plan for the child that includes strategies to anticipate and prevent problem behaviors and strategies to teach an acceptable alternative behavior*—Physical guidance should only be considered if less intrusive interventions are not effective.
- *Under the supervision of a credentialed behavior consultant*—The Autism Special Interest Group of the Association of Behavior Analysis (2007) recommends that ABA consultants for children with autism possess board certification. Information about appropriate qualifications of ABA professionals can be found in Shook and Neisworth (2005).
- *After being reviewed by a team consisting of educators, consultants, and parents who have given informed consent*—The team should ensure the following: (i) the problem behavior is of sufficient concern to warrant a potentially restrictive intervention such as physical guidance; (ii) there is no less intrusive alternative; (iii) implementers of

strategies are adequately trained and supervised; (iv) ongoing observations are taken of the behavior; and (v) there are periodic evaluations and reviews of the plan.

Even with these safeguards, one needs to be extremely cautious when contemplating the use of physical guidance (Maag & Katsiyannis, 2006). Physical guidance has not been an uncommon intervention in special education. Ruhl and Hughes (1985) reported that 70% of special education teachers surveyed reported that they have used physical restraint with students who have behavior disorders.

Modified Competing Behavior Model

There has been discussion of the need to understand the topography, occurrence, and functions of problem behaviors as a basis for developing a hypothesis about factors that trigger and maintain problem behavior. Establishing operations (slow triggers) may contribute to the child's responsivity to reinforcement. There may be triggering antecedents that elicit problem behaviors, which then are maintained by the effect that they have on the environment (e.g., escape, get activities or objects, get sensory stimulation). The intervention should be based on the understanding of the functions of the problem behavior and should consist of three general strategies: (a) anticipating and preventing problem behavior, (b) teaching a replacement behavior, and (c) dealing with the problem behavior when it does occur to lessen its effectiveness.

Only part of the competing behavior model (O'Neill et al., 1997) has been discussed so far. The complete competing behavior model with a modification is shown in Figure 9.14. This figure shows additional components to consider that are built on the understanding of factors attributing to the maintenance of the problem behaviors. The shaded boxes reflect the areas for intervention of the three general strategies de-

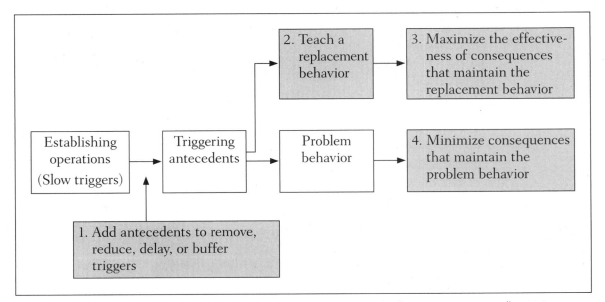

Figure 9.14. A modified competing behavior model. *Note.* Based on R. E. O'Neill, R. H. Horner, R. W. Albin, K. Storey, and J. R. Sprague, *Functional Analysis of Problem Behavior: A Practical Assessment Guide,* 1997, Pacific Grove, CA: Brooks/Cole, 9780534260224.

scribed by Horner (2000). One would use this model to first identify a hypothesis of what is occurring with the problem behavior and then to suggest strategies to modify the problem behavior. The shaded Box 1 is the location to describe what interventions can be introduced to reduce, delay, remove, or buffer the triggers (both the establishing operation and the triggering antecedent). The shaded Box 2 is the location where one would enter a description of replacement behaviors that could serve the same function as the problem behavior. Box 3 would consist of a plan of strategies to maximize the effects of consequences to maintain the replacement behaviors. Finally, Box 4 would be the description of interventions to render the maintaining consequences less effective.

The following is a case example used to illustrate how the modified competing behavior model would be used to suggest possible hypotheses for the problem behavior and areas for intervention.

Matt: Example Modified Competing Behavior Model

Matt is an 8-year-old boy with a moderate level of autism who attends a third-grade general education class with 23 classmates and the full-time support of a paraprofessional, Jennifer. Matt is able to understand most of what is said to him, as long as the language is not too complex. However, he does have difficulty expressing himself. Matt tends to speak in simple sentences. Although Matt attends a third-grade class, his academic skills are approximately at a kindergarten level. Matt spends about half of his time in a resource room receiving an individualized curriculum prepared and delivered by Jennifer.

Matt can be aggressive at times, both to himself and to others. He will bang his head against a desk, hit Jennifer (his paraprofessional), and throw objects perhaps once or twice each day. These episodes of self-injurious behavior and aggression almost always occur when Matt is in the third-grade classroom. An initial assessment was completed consisting of a scatter plot, a problem behavior debriefing, and a Functional Assessment Observation Form. The results of that assessment indicated that Matt's aggression was triggered by difficult work and maintained by attention received from Jennifer after he is aggressive. The establishing operation that was identified as contributing to the occurrence of aggression was that of the high noise level in the class.

The elements to the behavior support plan for Matt consisted of strategies to anticipate the problem behavior, teach functional equivalents, and minimize the attention maintaining the self-injurious behavior and aggression. First, to buffer the effects of the ambient noise, Matt was allowed to listen to soothing music while he completed his seatwork. He would choose the music he wanted to listen to, as well as the order of work to be completed. The work was also simplified to use visual prompting to assist in getting the correct answer to questions. In addition, worksheets were structured so that at least 50% of items were a review of previously mastered items.

As a replacement behavior, Matt was taught to give a break card when he gets upset. When Matt touched the break card, he was immediately given a 30-second break.

If, despite these measures, Matt still became aggressive, then Jennifer would not talk to or look at Matt, until he calmed down. The ignoring strategy would be used only if there was evidence that the aggression was attention-maintained and that Matt would calm down when there was no attention paid to him. The ignoring strategy would not be used if it would result in an escalation of Matt's aggression and place him and others at risk.

The plan would be written out and evaluated. Data would be collected on the frequency at which Matt was aggressing and on the amount of seatwork he completed before and after this behavior support plan was put into place. This plan is shown in Figure 9.15.

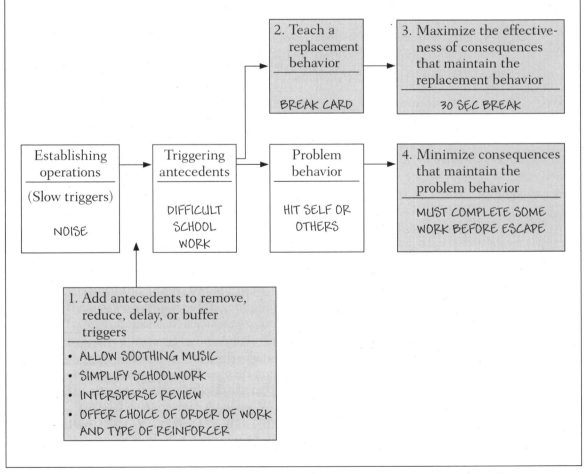

Figure 9.15. Example of a completed modified competing behavior model. *Note.* Based on R. E. O'Neill, R. H. Horner, R. W. Albin, K. Storey, and J. R. Sprague, *Functional Analysis of Problem Behavior: A Practical Assessment Guide,* 1997, Pacific Grove, CA: Brooks/Cole, 9780534260224

Study Questions

1. Jason engages in jumping whenever he has a chance. It happens when he is in transition, at recess, or when left alone. What do you think is the function of Jason's jumping?

2. In the following example, what is the establishing operation and what is the triggering antecedent? Sarah has not had a good night's sleep in 3 days. With the lack of sleep, Sarah starts screaming as soon as her paraprofessional sits down beside her.

3. What would you do to reduce the impact of the establishing operation in the example in Study Question 2?

4. Compare and contrast ABC recording, functional assessment cards, scatter plot, Functional Assessment Observation Form, and ecobehavioral analysis.

5. What were the three general types of assessment approaches described by Iwata and Worsdell (2005)?

6. Do you think that a functional analysis can be conducted in a school? If so, how would you overcome the obstacles that were discussed? If not, why not?

7. What are the major differences between PBS and ABA?

8. Give two examples of strategies to anticipate and prevent problem behavior.

9. Describe how you would use priming with the child's home to have the child practice future class content.

10. Describe the steps in implementing functional communication training.

11. Complete a modified competing behavior model based on the following information:

    Eddie takes a long bus ride each day to school. When he arrives, there are only about 5 minutes before the school bell rings for students to enter the school in the morning. Eddie is met by his paraprofessional, who escorts him through the crowds and noise to his classroom. Eddie almost always screams and hits his paraprofessional as he is being escorted. A functional assessment indicated that Eddie's screaming and hitting is escape motivated.

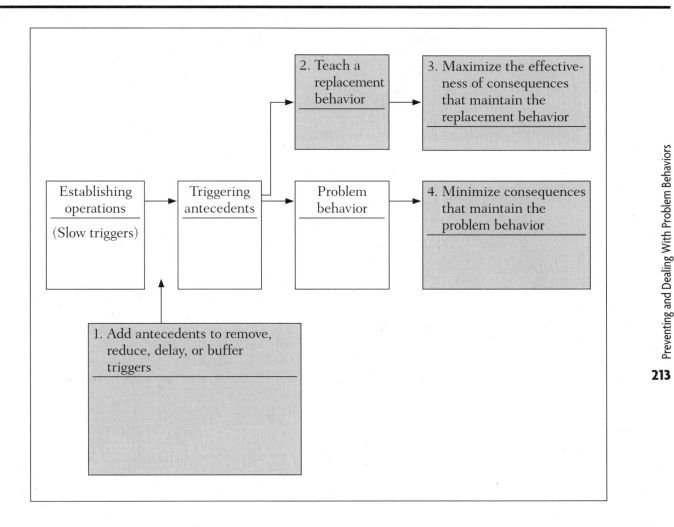

Data Collection Forms for Assessing Problem Behaviors

Problem Behavior Interview: Preschool Version   216

Problem Behavior Interview: Elementary School Version   220

Problem Behavior Interview: Adolescent Version   225

ABC Recording Form   230

Functional Assessment Card   231

Scatter Plot Grid   232

Functional Assessment Observation Form   233

Problem Behavior Interview

Preschool Version

Child: _____ Interviewee: _____ Date: _____

Interviewer: _____ Relationship to Child: _____

1. Describe the problem behavior (What does the child do?): _____

   _____

2. Did the problem behavior result in injury? If so, what type and to whom? _____

   _____

3. Time and duration of the problem behavior. Start time: _____ End time: _____

4. Where did the behavior occur?

   ☐ Classroom   ☐ Washroom

   ☐ Hallway   ☐ Playground

   ☐ Lunchroom   ☐ Bus

                        ☐ Other: _____

5. Which staff were present? _____

   _____

6. If the problem behavior was directed toward staff or children, name who:

   Staff: _____

   Child(ren): _____

7. Could other children easily see or hear the event?

   ☐ No

   ☐ Yes, see what happened. About how many? _____

   ☐ Yes, hear what happened. About how many? _____

8. What type of programming (if any) was the child receiving just prior to the event?

   ☐ None   ☐ Music   ☐ After-school program

   ☐ Circle time   ☐ Sleep time   ☐ Indoor play

   ☐ Transitions   ☐ Snack or lunchtime ☐ Before-school program

   ☐ Outdoor play   ☐ Table tasks   ☐ Other: _____

9. Did the child make any type of complaint within the hour before the problem behavior occurred?

☐ N/A

☐ No

☐ Yes _____

10. Did another child do or say something that might have set off the event?

☐ N/A

☐ No

☐ Yes _____

11. Had the child received a consequence (e.g., loss of points, corrective feedback, time-out) for some other problem within a few minutes of the event?

☐ N/A

☐ No

☐ Yes _____

12. Was the child interrupted from doing/completing a preferred activity?

☐ N/A

☐ No

☐ Yes _____

13. Was a request made to the child to STOP doing something just before the event?

☐ N/A

☐ No

☐ Yes _____

14. Was a request made to the child to START to do something just before the event?

☐ N/A

☐ No

☐ Yes _____

15. What consequence was used for the problem behavior? If more than one was used, indicate the sequence by placing a number in each relevant box in the order that things took place.

☐ Ignored child

☐ Had calm, neutral discussion with child

☐ Interrupted/redirected child

☐ Sent child to office

☐ Called child's parent

☐ Sent child home

☐ Took away privilege from child

☐ Wrote child's name on board

☐ Sent child to another classroom

☐ Sent child to back of classroom

☐ Put child on time-out chair

☐ Other: _____

16. Do you think the child's problem behavior resulted in a payoff?

   ☐ Received attention   ☐ Received help

   ☐ Avoided work or tasks   ☐ Obtained desired object/activity

   ☐ Self-stimulation   ☐ Other: _____

17. Please comment on anything else that you think is relevant to the problem:

_____

_____

_____

_____

18. **Situational Variables**

   ☐ Is there any circumstance under which the problem behavior NEVER occurs?

     If so, describe: _____

   ☐ Is there any circumstance under which the problem behavior ALWAYS occurs?

     If so, describe: _____

   ☐ Does the problem behavior occur at certain times of the day?

     If so, at what times and situations? _____

     _____

   ☐ Does the problem behavior occur only with certain people? If so, who?

     _____

19. **Operant Variables**

   ☐ Does the child engage in the problem behavior to gain attention?

     If so, is the attention from peers or a teacher? _____

   ☐ Does the child engage in the problem behavior to obtain a desired activity or object?

     If so, what? _____

   ☐ Does the child engage in the problem behavior to escape a situation?

     If so, what situation? _____

   ☐ Does the child engage in the problem behavior when there is nothing else to do or there is a lack of challenging activities or materials?

   ☐ Does the problem behavior occur antecedent to or collateral with any other behavior?

   ☐ Could the problem behavior be related to any social or academic skills deficit?

20. Physiological Variables

☐ Does the problem behavior occur during certain seasons of the year? If so, which ones?

_____

☐ Does the problem behavior occur when the child has any of the following:

  ☐ Earache

  ☐ Gastrointestinal problems

  ☐ Sleep deprivation

  ☐ Cold or flu

☐ Could the child be signaling some emotional problem? If so, what?

_____

☐ Could the behavior be related to a side effect of medication (e.g., tired, unsteady, upset stomach, headache)?

☐ Does the child engage in the behavior as a self-stimulation activity?

21. Skill Variables

☐ Does the child show delays in communication skills that might be related to the occurrence of the problem behavior?

☐ Does the child show delays in self-help skills that might be related to the occurrence of the problem behavior?

☐ Does the child show delays in self-regulation that might be related to the occurrence of the problem behavior?

☐ Does the child show delays in academic skills that might be related to the occurrence of the problem behavior?

☐ Does the child show delays in social skills that might be related to the occurrence of the problem behavior?

COMMENTS:

_____

_____

_____

_____

_____

_____

_____

_____

Problem Behavior Interview

| Elementary School Version |

Child: _____ Interviewee: _____ Date: _____

Interviewer: _____ Relationship to Child: _____

1. Describe the problem behavior (What does the child do?): _____

   _____

2. Did the problem behavior result in injury? If so, what type and to whom? _____

   _____

3. Time and duration of the problem behavior. Start time: _____ End time: _____

4. Where did the behavior occur?

   ☐ Classroom   ☐ Washroom
   ☐ Gym   ☐ Playground
   ☐ Hallway   ☐ Bus
   ☐ Lunchroom   ☐ Other: _____

5. Which staff were present? _____

   _____

6. If the problem behavior was directed toward staff or children, name who:

   Staff: _____

   Child(ren): _____

7. Could other children easily see or hear the event?

   ☐ No
   ☐ Yes, see what happened. About how many? _____
   ☐ Yes, hear what happened. About how many? _____

8. What type of instruction (if any) was the student receiving just prior to the event?

   ☐ None   ☐ Small-group instruction
   ☐ 1:1 instruction   ☐ Small-group project
   ☐ Seatwork   ☐ Test/quiz
   ☐ Class lesson   ☐ Other: _____

9. What type of instruction or seatwork was occurring at the time of the event?

- ☐ Math
- ☐ Physical education
- ☐ Social studies
- ☐ Language arts
- ☐ Science
- ☐ History
- ☐ Reading
- ☐ Music
- ☐ Art
- ☐ Free time
- ☐ Lunch or snack
- ☐ Transition
- ☐ Other: _____

10. Did the student make any type of complaint within the hour before the problem behavior occurred?

- ☐ N/A
- ☐ No
- ☐ Yes _____

11. Did another student do or say something that might have set off the event?

- ☐ N/A
- ☐ No
- ☐ Yes _____

12. Did the student have any extra assignments or responsibility to meet on this day?

- ☐ N/A
- ☐ No
- ☐ Yes _____

13. Had the student received a consequence (e.g., loss of points, corrective feedback, name on the board) for some other problem within a few minutes of the event?

- ☐ N/A
- ☐ No
- ☐ Yes _____

14. Was the student interrupted from doing/completing another activity?

- ☐ N/A
- ☐ No
- ☐ Yes _____

15. Was a request made to the student to STOP doing something just before the event?

- ☐ N/A
- ☐ No
- ☐ Yes _____

16. Was a request made to the student to START to do something just before the event?

☐ N/A

☐ No

☐ Yes _____

17. What consequence was used for the problem behavior? If more than one was used, indicate the sequence by placing a number in each relevant box in the order that things took place.

☐ Ignored student   ☐ Took away privilege from student

☐ Had calm, neutral discussion with student   ☐ Wrote student's name on board

☐ Interrupted/redirected student   ☐ Sent student to another classroom

☐ Sent student to office   ☐ Sent child to back of classroom

☐ Called student's parent   ☐ Put student on time-out chair

☐ Sent student home   ☐ Other: _____

18. Do you think the student's problem behavior resulted in a payoff?

☐ Received attention   ☐ Received help

☐ Avoided work or tasks   ☐ Obtained desired object/activity

☐ Self-stimulation   ☐ Other: _____

19. Please comment on anything else that you think is relevant to the problem:

_____

_____

_____

_____

20. **Situational Variables**

☐ Is there any circumstance under which the problem behavior NEVER occurs?

If so, describe: _____

☐ Is there any circumstance under which the problem behavior ALWAYS occurs?

If so, describe: _____

☐ Does the problem behavior occur at certain times of the day?

If so, at what times and situations? _____

_____

☐ Does the problem behavior occur only with certain people? If so, who?

_____

21. **Operant Variables**

☐ Does the student engage in the problem behavior to gain attention?

If so, is the attention from peers or a teacher? _____

☐ Does the student engage in the problem behavior to obtain a desired activity or object?

If so, what? _____

☐ Does the student engage in the problem behavior to escape a situation?

If so, what situation? _____

☐ Does the student engage in the problem behavior when there is nothing else to do or there is a lack of challenging activities or materials?

☐ Does the problem behavior occur antecedent to or collateral with any other behavior?

☐ Could the problem behavior be related to any social or academic skills deficit?

22. **Physiological Variables**

☐ Does the problem behavior occur during certain seasons of the year? If so, which ones?

_____

☐ Does the problem behavior occur when the child has any of the following:

☐ Earache

☐ Gastrointestinal problems

☐ Sleep deprivation

☐ Cold or flu

☐ Could the student be signaling some emotional problem? If so, what?

_____

☐ Could the behavior be related to a side effect of medication (e.g., tired, unsteady, upset stomach, headache)?

☐ Does the student engage in the behavior as a self-stimulation activity?

23. **Skill Variables**

☐ Does the student show delays in communication skills that might be related to the occurrence of the problem behavior?

☐ Does the student show delays in self-help skills that might be related to the occurrence of the problem behavior?

☐ Does the student show delays in self-regulation that might be related to the occurrence of the problem behavior?

☐ Does the student show delays in academic skills that might be related to the occurrence of the problem behavior?

☐ Does the student show delays in social skills that might be related to the occurrence of the problem behavior?

COMMENTS:

_____

_____

_____

_____

_____

_____

_____

_____

224

Problem Behavior Interview

Adolescent Version

Youth: _____ Interviewee: _____ Date: _____

Interviewer: _____ Relationship to Child: _____

1. Describe the problem behavior (What does the youth do?): _____

   _____

2. Did the problem behavior result in injury? If so, what type and to whom? _____

   _____

3. Time and duration of the problem behavior. Start time: _____ End time: _____

4. Where did the behavior occur?

   ☐ Classroom   ☐ Washroom

   ☐ Gym   ☐ Office

   ☐ Hallway   ☐ Bus

   ☐ Cafeteria   ☐ Other: _____

5. Which staff were present? _____

   _____

6. If the problem behavior was directed toward staff or students, name who:

   Staff: _____

   Other student(s): _____

7. Could other students easily see or hear the event?

   ☐ No

   ☐ Yes, see what happened. About how many? _____

   ☐ Yes, hear what happened. About how many? _____

8. What type of programming (if any) was the youth receiving just prior to the event?

   ☐ None   ☐ Small-group instruction

   ☐ 1:1 instruction   ☐ Small-group project

   ☐ Seatwork   ☐ Test/quiz

   ☐ Class lesson   ☐ Other: _____

9. What type of activity was occurring at the time of the event?

☐ Math   ☐ Other language

☐ Physical education   ☐ Music

☐ Technology education   ☐ Art

☐ English   ☐ Geography

☐ Science   ☐ Lunch

☐ History   ☐ Transition

                          ☐ Other: _____

10. Did the youth make any type of complaint within the hour before the problem behavior occurred?

☐ N/A

☐ No

☐ Yes _____

11. Did another youth do or say something that might have set off the event?

☐ N/A

☐ No

☐ Yes _____

12. Did the youth have any extra assignments or responsibility to meet on this day?

☐ N/A

☐ No

☐ Yes _____

13. Had the youth received a consequence (e.g., loss of points, corrective feedback, detention) for some other problem within a few minutes of the event?

☐ N/A

☐ No

☐ Yes _____

14. Was the youth interrupted from doing/completing another activity?

☐ N/A

☐ No

☐ Yes _____

15. Was a request made to the youth to STOP doing something just before the event?

☐ N/A

☐ No

☐ Yes _____

16. Was a request made to the youth to START to do something just before the event?

☐ N/A

☐ No

☐ Yes _____

17. What consequence was used for the problem behavior? If more than one was used, indicate the sequence by placing a number in each relevant box in the order that things took place.

☐ Ignored youth   ☐ Took away privilege from youth

☐ Had calm, neutral discussion with youth   ☐ Wrote youth's name on board

☐ Interrupted/redirected youth   ☐ Sent youth to another classroom

☐ Sent youth to office   ☐ Gave youth detention

☐ Called youth's parent   ☐ Gave youth time-out

☐ Sent youth home   ☐ Other: _____

18. Do you think the youth's problem behavior resulted in a payoff?

☐ Received attention   ☐ Received help

☐ Avoided work or tasks   ☐ Obtained desired object/activity

☐ Self-stimulation   ☐ Other: _____

19. Please comment on anything else that you think is relevant to the problem:

_____

_____

_____

_____

20. **Situational Variables**

☐ Is there any circumstance under which the problem behavior NEVER occurs?

If so, describe: _____

☐ Is there any circumstance under which the problem behavior ALWAYS occurs?

If so, describe: _____

☐ Does the problem behavior occur at certain times of the day?

If so, at what times and situations? _____

_____

☐ Does the problem behavior occur only with certain people? If so, who?

_____

21. **Operant Variables**

☐ Does the youth engage in the problem behavior to gain attention?

If so, is the attention from peers or a teacher? _____

☐ Does the youth engage in the problem behavior to obtain a desired activity or object?

If so, what? _____

☐ Does the youth engage in the problem behavior to escape a situation?

If so, what situation? _____

☐ Does the youth engage in the problem behavior when there is nothing else to do or there is a lack of challenging activities or materials?

☐ Does the problem behavior occur antecedent to or collateral with any other behavior?

☐ Could the problem behavior be related to any social or academic skills deficit?

22. **Physiological Variables**

☐ Does the problem behavior occur during certain seasons of the year? If so, which ones?

_____

☐ Does the problem behavior occur when the youth has any of the following:

☐ Earache

☐ Gastrointestinal problems

☐ Sleep deprivation

☐ Cold or flu

☐ Could the client be signaling some emotional problem? If so, what?

_____

☐ Could the behavior be related to a side effect of medication (e.g., tired, unsteady, upset stomach, headache)?

☐ Does the youth engage in the behavior as a self-stimulation activity?

23. **Skill Variables**

☐ Does the youth show delays in communication that might be related to the occurrence of the problem behavior?

☐ Does the youth show delays in self-help skills that might be related to the occurrence of the problem behavior?

☐ Does the youth show delays in self-regulation that might be related to the occurrence of the problem behavior?

☐ Does the youth show delays in academic skills that might be related to the occurrence of the problem behavior?

☐ Does the youth show delays in social skills that might be related to the occurrence of the problem behavior?

COMMENTS:

_____

_____

_____

_____

_____

_____

_____

_____

ABC Recording Form

For each occurrence of problem behavior, write a description of the problem behavior (Behavior column), what occurred before the behavior that you think may have triggered the problem behavior (Antecedents column), and what occurred after the behavior that you think may help to maintain the problem behavior (Consequences column).

Child: _____   Begin Time: _____

Observer: _____   End Time: _____

A – Antecedents	B – Behavior	C – Consequences
Describe activities and events that preceded the problem behavior (e.g., outdoor play; child took a toy away)	Describe exactly what the child said and/or did (e.g., hit)	Describe activities and events that followed the problem behavior (e.g., recovered the toy; was reprimanded by teacher)

Functional Assessment Card

Each person who may witness the child displaying a problem behavior is given a number (e.g., five) of functional assessment cards. For each instance of a problem behavior, the observer notes a description of the problem behavior, what events may have triggered the behavior (antecedent), and what events may act to maintain the behavior (consequence). Circle what function(s) you think the problem behavior served.

Child's Name: Observer: Date: Time:

General Context:

ANTECEDENT:

PROBLEM BEHAVIOR:

CONSEQUENCE:

Complete this section later. Circle the function(s) demonstrated by this behavior:

Escape/avoidance   Get attention   Get desired object/activity   Self-stimulation

Scatter Plot Grid

Child: _____ School: _____ Class: _____

Starting Date:: _____ Target Behavior: _____

☐ 0   ◫ 1–3   ■ 4 or more

Time	Activity	M	T	W	TH	F
8:30–9:00						
9:00–9:30						
9:30–10:00						
10:00–10:30						
10:30–11:00						
11:00–11:30						
11:30–12:00						
12:00–12:30						
12:30–1:00						
1:00–1:30						
1:30–2:00						
2:00–2:30						
2:30–3:00						
3:00–3:30						

Successive Days

Functional Assessment Observation Form

Name: _____ Starting Date: _____ Ending Date: _____

Activities	Time	Behaviors	Predictors											Get/Obtain			Escape/Avoid				Actual consequences
			Demand/Request	Difficult task	Transitions	Interruptions	Alone (no attention)						Attention	Desired item/Activity	Self-stimulation	Demand/Request	Activity ( )	Person	Other/Don't know	

Events: 1 2 3 4 5 6 7 8 9 10 11 12 13 14 15 16 17 18 19 20 21 22 23 24 25 26 27 28 29 30

Totals

INSTRUCTIONS: Observe a child for a series of 15–30 intervals. For each, mark the time the interval started and the activity that best characterizes what the child was doing during the interval. Enter the names of problem behaviors the child is likely to display under the Behaviors heading. When a problem behavior does occur, enter a number to denote that behavior, starting with 1, then 2, etc., to denote the next problem behavior. Enter that same numeral in one or more columns under the headings Predictors, Get/Obtain, and Escape/Avoid in the rows that correspond with the triggers (under Predictors) and maintaining consequences (under Get/ Obtain and Escape/Avoid). Under the heading Actual Consequences, write in what actual consequence was delivered for the problem behavior. Place a line through the corresponding number at the bottom of the page to track what numeral you are coding.

233   Preventing and Dealing With Problem Behaviors

10 Working Collaboratively With Families

Chapter Topics

- Legislation
- Parent/professional relationships
- Stress and parents of children with autism
- Person-centered planning
- Training parents to implement interventions
- Trans-situational intervention

Successful inclusion depends not only on how well a school has prepared for children with autism to participate in general education classrooms, but also on the positive working relationships between the school and a child's family. There is a broad body of literature indicating that the quality of the parent/professional relationship influences educational outcomes for children with and without disabilities (Turnbull & Turnbull, 2001). Unfortunately, parent/professional relationships are not always co-equal, collaborative, or positive. One of the factors that may contribute to a lack of an equal relationship between professionals and parents is faulty assumptions that parents hold about educators, as well as faulty assumptions educators hold about parents. Wehmeyer (2002) described some of the faulty assumptions schools may hold of parents, including that parents of children with disabilities are needy clients themselves who should receive help. Such a view may lead schools to adopt a patronizing stance in dealing with parents and may contribute to an unequal relationship between professionals and parents. In addition, educators may see parents as partially responsible for the child's difficulties or as too emotionally enmeshed with a child to be objective. With such a view, the school may be less likely to pursue a collaborative relationship with parents in planning for the child with autism.

In addition to the attitudinal factors that influence how schools deal with parents of a child with autism, there may be systemic barriers to schools' collaboration with parents. For example, there may not be enough time in the work week for teachers to meet with parents to plan as frequently as they would like (Wehmeyer, 2002); there may be long waiting lists for special services from the school district; or personnel may not be well trained in how to educate children with autism.

Not only may school personnel have expectations of the parents that may hamper collaborative relationships, but parents may have faulty expectations of educators. For example, parents may view educators as general experts in the field of autism and have too high of expectations of what educators know. Parents also may have the faulty assumption that educators are totally objective when commenting on a child with autism. Just like anyone else, teachers' views on programming for a child are affected by many factors, including school policy or the potential impact of the child with autism on the rest of the class and on the teacher. Like anyone else, teachers' views about the needs of the child with autism may be somewhat subjective. Such barriers may contribute to estrangement in the relationship between professionals and parents (Scott, Clark, & Brady, 2000). In fact, Harry, Rueda, and Kalyanpur (1999) speculated that the legalistic framework of special education may place parents and educators in adversarial positions.

Legislation

In 1975, the U.S. federal government passed the Education for All Handicapped Children Act (P.L. 94-142), which called for appropriate and free education for children with disabilities in the least restrictive educational settings. This legislation was subsequently amended in 1990 and reauthorized in 1997 under the Individuals With Disabilities Education Act (IDEA; P.L. 105-17) and most recently has been reauthorized and revised as the Individuals With Disabilities Education Improvement Act (IDEIA; P.L. 108-446). One of the fastest growing areas of litigation in special education involves parents taking school districts to court to provide or to fund early intensive behavioral intervention (Yell & Drasgow, 2000). Between 1993 and 1998, there were 45 published hearings in which families sued school districts for not providing the appropriate education for their child with autism. Of these 45 cases, parents were the prevailing party 34 times (77.7%). There were five reasons why parents prevailed: (a) Schools did not follow appropriate procedures (e.g., lack of notice to parents about school decisions); (b) schools failed to properly evaluate the child with autism; (c) inadequate Individualized Education Programs (IEPs) were developed; (d) there were procedural errors involving placement decisions; and (e) there was a lack of qualified school staff (Yell & Drasgow, 2000).

In part, special education legislation has come about because of the advocacy efforts of parents of children with disabilities. Advocacy to ensure services for their child is one of the important roles provided by parents. Under IDEA, parents need to agree that free and appropriate education is being provided for their child (Yell, Drasgow, & Lowrey, 2005). In partnership with educators, they need to ensure that the appropriate supports are supplied for the child in an inclusive setting and that any applied behavior analysis (ABA) interventions are appropriately in place. Figure 10.1 contains suggestions or factors for parents to look at when considering the adequacy of an ABA-based supported inclusion program for a child with autism.

Parent–Professional Relationships

The relationship between professionals and parents of children with autism can become adversarial and even combative. Lucyshyn, Blumberg, and Kayser (2000) recommended three activities to improve the quality of supports for families: (a) Implement family-centered positive support service, (b) expand interventions to focus on family routines, and (c) teach professionals to build collaborative partnerships with families. It is the third recommendation that may be most important. Traditional models of working with families have positioned the professionals as experts (Rao & Kalyanpur, 2002). In the professional-as-expert model, professionals are assumed to have the capacity to understand and solve the child's problems and to design and implement effective interventions to deal with the child's problems. Within this model, professionals are seen as the sole authority for how to deal with a child who presents problems and teachers are viewed as naïve and ill-informed (Rao & Kalyanpur). Unfortunately, in the professional-as-expert model, parents' opinions about their child's problems tend to be dismissed and interventions at home are viewed as unacceptable or impractical to implement (Rao & Kalyanpur).

A number of authors have described an empowerment model for working with families of children with disabilities. (Brookman-Frazee, 2004; Jones, Garlow, Turnbull, & Barber, 1996; Trivette, Dunst, Hamby, & LaPointe, 1996). This model represents a shift from having professionals as experts, single-handedly solving problems pertaining to children with autism, to professionals partnering with families in the process of planning for the child. This shift in the parent–professional relationship is depicted in Figure 10.2. The top diagram depicts a situation in which the parents are attempting to address their child's needs with almost no professional involvement, perhaps because of a lack of trust with professionals. In these situations, parents are not likely capitalizing on supports that are available for their child and themselves. Too much of the responsibility to ensure the development of the child with autism is resting with the parents.

The middle diagram also shows a parent–professional relationship that is out of balance, because it has professionals acting as the sole authority for interventions for the child with autism. Parents would have minor involvement in planning for the child, as the bulk of the responsibility for interventions rests with the professional.

- The school district has a consultant with acceptable education and experience in applied behavior analysis (ABA). The Autism Special Interest Group of the Association for Behavior Analysis (www.autismsig.org) recommended that ABA consultants for children with autism be Board Certified Behavior Analysts. The necessary qualifications of a person to become a Board Certified Behavior Analyst can be found on the Web site for the Behavior Analysis Certification Board (www.bacb.com).
- Staff members receive ongoing supervision by a qualified behavior analyst who provides them with feedback on skills for the implementation of ABA programs in general education classrooms.
- The supervision is frequent, direct, and specific.
- Longer term (e.g., 3-month or 6-month) goals are set to describe key child outcomes to be achieved.
- Longer term goals for the child are set with parent input and reflect relevant functional areas of adjustment for the child.
- Skill-building and behavior-changing programs for the child with autism are designed, based on direct assessment of the child's skills and ongoing reassessment.
- Programs provide functional learning activities that have measurable child outcomes (objectives) that move the child's skills toward the established longer term goals for the child.
- Details of how to implement programs are written out and involve directly teaching skills and/or behaviors in which the child has deficits, rather than trying to teach presumed underlying mentalistic constructs (e.g., information processing, frustration) to those deficits.
- The majority of the child's school day is involved in programmed learning activities.
- Programs are based on systematic teaching procedures based on principles of applied behavior analysis and tested ABA interventions.
- There are means in place to ensure consistency across staff who are working with the child.
- There are strategies in place to probe for generalization of skills over time and across settings, people, and stimuli.
- Direct and frequent data are directly collected on the child's progress and used to make program revision decisions.
- Regular team meetings are held to review the child's progress and to make revisions.
- There is an adequate amount of child learning that takes place in general education settings with the rest of the child's class.

Figure 10.1. Suggested elements of what parents of children with autism should look for in ABA-based supported inclusion.

The third diagram depicts more of what would be considered a balanced parent–professional relationship, with the responsibility for helping the child with autism shared between parents and professionals. Parents are further ahead because of the involvement of the professionals, but they do not abandon their role in advocating for their child, no matter how capable or well intentioned the professional is.

Brookman-Frazee (2004) suggested that the essential components of an effective parent–professional partnership are as follows:

(a) Setting mutually agreed upon goals
(b) Sharing expertise toward solutions

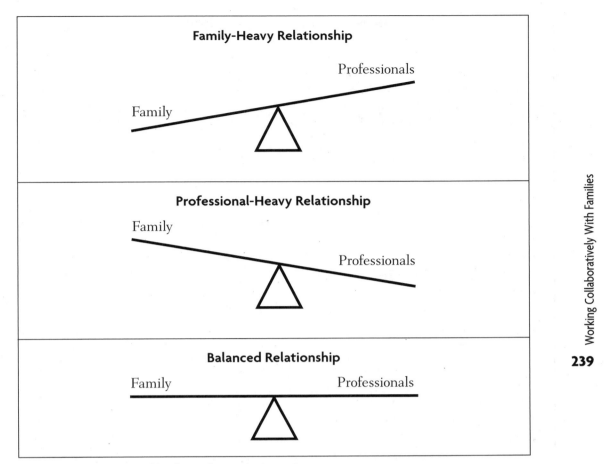

Figure 10.2. Three types of family–professional relationships.

(c) Sharing responsibility for the intervention plan
(d) Ensuring that there is a contextual fit of "social intervention" to the setting in which the individual will be introduced
(e) Problem solving collaboratively
(f) Emphasizing building the child's strengths, as well as addressing the child's needs

The effect of a partnership approach to educating children with autism was compared to a clinician-directed approach (Brookman-Frazee, 2004). Parents of three children with autism, aged 2 to 3 years, received parent education in pivotal response training (Koegel et al., 1989) at their home or clinic on how to increase verbal communication and appropriate interaction with their child. For some of the sessions, the clinician collaborated with the parents on the development of interventions for problem situations that had arisen between the parent and the child. For other sessions, the clinician chose intervention targets and suggested intervention procedures without parents' input. Sessions during which the professional and parent collaborated on an intervention were associated with higher observational ratings of parents' confidence, lower observational ratings of parental stress, higher appropriate child engagement and child response rate, and an observational rating of positive affect.

As pointed out by Scott and colleagues (2000), no section of IDEA specifies that educators must partner with parents in the planning for their child. However, the importance of adopting a partnership model between educator and parents is compelling.

Stress and Parents of Children With Autism

In addition to parents' role as collaborators with educators in planning for their child with autism, parents are also consumers of services. Not surprisingly, parents of children with autism, especially mothers, experience higher degrees of stress than parents of typically developing children (Wolf, Noh, Fisman, & Speechley, 1989). Moreover, symptoms of stress and depression have been found to be higher for parents of children with autism than for parents of children with cystic fibrosis (Bouma & Schweitzer, 1990; Wolf et al., 1989) or parents of children with Down syndrome (Wolf et al., 1989). High levels of parent stress have been associated with poor outcomes in early intervention (Boyd, 2002). In a 7-year longitudinal study of parent's stress in children with developmental disabilities, higher levels of parent stress have been associated with child problem behaviors. Hauser-Cram, Warfield, Shonkoff, and Krauss (2001) found that higher levels of parent stress occurred for families with children with developmental disabilities who were also presenting pronounced problem behaviors. Moreover, having a well-established social network was associated with lower levels of stress for mothers, but not for fathers (Hauser-Cram et al., 2001).

In general, there have been two types of services provided to parents of children with autism. One service has been to train parents how to help their children with autism to reduce their problem behaviors and increase their appropriate skills. The second strategy is the provision of general family support.

Person-Centered Planning

In the 1980s and 1990s, person-centered planning began to immerge in the field of developmental disabilities. At the time, planning for children and adults with developmental disabilities tended to be completed primarily by service providers (e.g., residential care providers, respite care providers, supported employment providers) in isolation from other service providers and in exclusion of family members or the person with developmental disabilities him- or herself. Finally, it also tended to focus on the person's problems, which then resulted in a referral to existing services.

Person-centered planning was derived from the community-inclusion movement to assist individuals with developmental disabilities to live in normalized settings. It brought a dramatic shift in the assumptions for planning for persons with developmental disabilities. First, person-centered planning brings together key people in the life of the individual with developmental disabilities—professionals as well as family and friends. Second, the planning process starts with the family and the person with developmental disabilities, if possible, expressing their dreams, hopes, and desires for the future. Participants then identify the person's strengths, upon which a future plan can be built. Plans to achieve identified goals attempt to consider the person's needs first and how those needs could be met in an individualized way.

A person-centered plan can take a number of different forms, such as the McGill Action Planning System (MAPS; Vandercook, York, & Forest, 1989), wrap-around (VanDenBerg & Grealish, 1996), or group action planning (Blue-Banning, Turnbull, & Pereira, 2000; Turnbull & Turnbull, 1996).

MAPS was used to plan the inclusion of an elementary-aged girl with severe disabilities (York & Vandercook, 1990). An initial meeting was held at the school with the parents, school faculty, and other professionals who knew the student well. One facilitator led the discussion and recorded responses on chart paper. The lead facilitator proposed a series of seven questions, first to the family, but then others also contributed:

1. What is the student's history?
2. What are your hopes and dreams for the student over the next year and into the future?
3. What are your fears or nightmares for the student's inclusion and future?
4. Who is the student (personality, characteristics, likes and dislikes)?
5. What are the student's unique gifts and talents?
6. What are the student's support needs for successful participation?
7. What would an ideal day look like?

This initial meeting took approximately 1.5 hours, and a summary of discussions was provided to all participants. A second meeting was held to review the MAPS and the student's IEP and to derive an initial plan on how the child needed to be supported.

Unfortunately, an empirical evaluation of the impact of person-centered planning has been limited to mainly case studies and anecdotal reports (Blue-Banning et al., 2000; Robertson et al., 2006). A survey of educators' and parents' views of advantages and disadvantages of person-centered planning was conducted after they attended a workshop on group action planning (Blue-Banning et al., 2000). Parents' view of group action planning seemed to be more positive than that of professionals'. Parents cited the advantages of person-centered planning as sharing responsibility for the child and having flexibility in the planning process. For disadvantages, professionals indicated that person-centered planning was an add-on to already too full work schedules and planning methods already in place.

Person-centered planning has also been embedded in positive behavioral supports (PBS) for families with young children with disabilities. IDEA (1997) specifies that local education agencies (LEA) use PBS to reduce problem behaviors by students. Kennedy et al. (2001) described the use of person-centered planning embedded in PBS to support two children with problem behaviors in an elementary school.

In Kansas, a statewide training program has been introduced to train developmental disabilities professionals how to implement PBS embedded with person-centered planning (Freeman et al., 2005). The West Virginia Autism Training Center is a statewide agency that provides training to educators and families of children with autism. Families, educators, and professionals form teams to plan for a child with autism. A lecture series was provided to all team members, including how to teach replacement skills, positive behavior supports, and person-centered planning.

Dunlap, Fox, and colleagues (Fox, Benito, & Dunlap, 2002; Fox, Dunlap, & Philbrick, 1997) used a combination of PBS intervention and person-centered planning to form the foundation of the "Individualized Support Project," a federally funded initiative to support young children with autism and their families. The first phase of helping these families was to conduct a family guided assessment, which included a functional behavioral assessment of the problem behaviors of the child with autism. Next, person-centered planning was used to bring together individuals central in the child's life to develop a support plan. The support plan included a focused intervention to introduce strategies to teach the child replacement behaviors to problem behaviors.

A sample form that our team has used in person-centered planning to organize the transition of a child with autism from a special education setting (in this case, the Behaviour Institute) to a general education classroom is shown in Appendix 10A. A very similar process could be followed for any of the other stated transitions.

1. **Make the invitation**—The sending school and parents decide whom to invite to the initial person-centered planning meeting. It is important to invite all of those people who can substantially help or hinder the development and implementation of a support plan for the child with autism. At a minimum, those invited would typically consist of:

The child with autism (if possible)
The parents or guardians
An administrator from the receiving school
The general education teacher from the receiving school
The special education teacher from the sending school
Any consultants who may be involved
Others (as determined by the school and parents)

2. **Solicit parent-prepared background information**—In preparation for the first collaborative planning meeting, the parents are asked to complete a brief background questionnaire about the child, including the child's interests, likes, dislikes, and the service the child is currently receiving. An example of a completed form is shown in Appendix 10A.

3. **Prepare for and conduct the first meeting: Visioning**—Before the initial meeting, the receiving general education teacher should arrange a time to observe the child with autism in the special education setting. A person-centered planning facilitator runs the meeting and keeps notes on chart paper. The facilitator leads the discussion on a series of questions (like those used in MAPS), with each question written on a separate piece of chart paper. Each question is posed initially to the parents and others to make contributions to the plan. Our team tends to start with a question dealing with the child's characteristics, likes, dislikes, and so forth. A copy of the parent-prepared background information is distributed at this point. Also, copies of the child's IEP are distributed. As each question is posed, the facilitator writes notes on the chart paper about the discussion. After the discussion, the facilitator summarizes the wishes, dreams, and long-term goals for the child with autism. This information will reflect priorities for planning for that child.

The second part of this initial meeting consists of a presentation by the special education teacher of the child's IEP. The teacher and/or consultant from the receiving school is asked to take the discussion about the child's strengths, needs, and existing special education IEP and look at how the IEPs can be adapted to fit the expectations of the receiving general education setting.

4. **Prepare for and conduct the second meeting: Support plan development**—Prior to a second meeting of the team, the facilitator should send out a copy of the summary of the first meeting. The

purpose of the second meeting is to create or review the child's IEP to be consistent with the general direction set in the first meeting. The review examines if the most appropriate objectives were set and if the plans to achieve each of those objectives are suitable. From that discussion comes a determination of what actions need to occur to support the implementation of the IEP. The support plan identifies the direction to be taken, by whom, and by what time period. Following the meeting, a copy of the support plan is sent to all participants.

5. *Prepare for and conduct the third meeting: Follow-up and review*—The third and final collaborative meeting between the special education and general education staff occurs 1 to 2 months later and consists of a review of the support plan and the child's adjustment in the receiving general education setting. Prior to this third collaborative meeting, the special education teacher and/or consultant should observe the child in the new setting. There would be discussion of how well the support plan is working and any additional revisions needed to the plan. If all parties are in agreement, additional follow-up meetings can be scheduled.

As indicated by the survey results reported by Blue-Banning and colleagues (2000), it is unlikely that educators will adopt a person-centered planning process if it is viewed as an "add-on" to already existing expectations for planning with parents. The adoption of person-centered planning would require it to be embedded in the existing IEP planning process.

Person-centered planning might be most applicable during times of transition of the child with autism, such as transition from an early childhood setting to elementary school, from a treatment setting into elementary school, from an elementary to a secondary school or from a special education class to a general education class. These situations all constitute the need for sending staff, parents, and receiving staff to develop a common plan for the child's needs.

Training Parents to Implement Interventions

Up until the 1980s, the prevailing understanding of autism was that it was caused by the psychopathology of the children's mother, what Bettelheim (1967) referred to as "refrigerator mothers." Viewing parents as responsible for their child's autism substantially hampered the willingness of the professionals to embrace parents as co-therapists for their child with autism. Not only is there no such evidence of heightened psychopathology in parents of children with autism (Koegel, Schreibman, O'Neill, & Burke, 1983), but there is a substantial body of research indicating that autism spectrum disorder is a neurodevelopmental disorder, not a disorder produced by poor parenting (Gillberg, 1999).

With the success of early intensive behavior intervention (EIBI), clinicians began to consider parents as therapists for the child with autism. In fact, now the involvement of parents in EIBI is viewed as a critical component of the approach (Dawson & Osterling, 1997; Lord & McGee, 2001). The interest in training parents as therapists was further fueled by a study by Lovaas, Koegel, Simmons, and Long (1973) in which the effects of clinical treatment for children with autism was maintained after they were discharged from the clinic only if their parents were also trained to carry on the intervention.

There have been many demonstrations that parents can be successfully trained to implement behavioral approaches with their child with autism (e.g., Harris, 1989; Ingersoll & Dvortcsak, 2006). This body of research suggests the following:

- Parents of children with autism can be successfully taught such behavioral techniques as prompting, reinforcement, error correction, imitation training, and functional communication training.
- Parents have been taught to acquire these skills using written manuals (Ingersoll & Dvortcsak, 2006; Koegel, Koegel, Kellegrew, & Mullen, 1996), modeling (Harris, 1989), and practice and feedback (Symon, 2005).
- Parents can successfully teach their children with autism new self-help skills (Koegel, Glahn, & Nieminen 1978), communication skills (Ingersoll & Dvortcsak, 2006), and reduction of problem behavior (Fox et al., 1997), among other targets.
- Parent training has been provided to parents individually (Fox et al., 1997), in small groups (Harris, 1989), or a combination of both targets (Fox et al., 1997).
- Parents have had difficulty continuing to implement behavior change strategies after the training has ended (Lovaas et al., 1973).

There are a number of significant challenges to delivering parent training. One is that the parent training that has been described in the research literature tends to involve a considerable amount of time to deliver. For example, the training of parents of children with autism described by Koegel, Schreibman, Johnson, O'Neill, and Dunlap (1984) took a total of between 25 and 50 hours to deliver. Stahmer and Gist (2001) described a clinic-based, 12-hour training of parents of children with newly diagnosed autism.

Another challenge to parent training of children with autism is that traditionally it has been offered by clinics or private schools, but rarely by publicly funded schools. One exception was an attempt by early childhood educators to train parents of children with autism who attended an early childhood program (Ingersoll & Dvortcsak, 2006). Early childhood educators spent about 50 hours implementing a parent workshop. Of this time, 18 to 20 hours were conducted outside of their regular workday. Even if parent training was effective, it is unclear how it can be added to a teacher's already busy schedule. One option is for schools to partner with local developmental services or children's mental health agencies to provide parent training in the schools during the evenings or on weekends (e.g., Cowen et al., 1996).

Even if training for parents of children with autism is offered in schools, one is faced with the difficulty of recruiting parents to attend. Baker (1996) reviewed studies that reported the recruitment rates of parents for parent training and found that only between 11% and 54% of parents invited to training actually attended. In a study by Ingersoll and Dvortcsak (2006), parent training was offered by early childhood special educators. Of the 12 children with autism who attended the early childhood setting, 9 (75%) of the parents chose to participate in the training.

Many parents who elect to attend training subsequently drop out. Forehand, Middlebrook, Rogers, and Steffe (1983) found that the average attrition rate of parent training was 22%. Of the nine families that began training in the Ingersoll and Dvortcsak (2006) program, two (22%) dropped out before the completion of training.

There are parents who complete training but still have not acquired sufficient skills to be able to change child behavior or to effectively teach their child new skills. Baker, Heifetz, and Murphy (1980) found that on completion of training, 24% of parents failed to apply the training to their children up to 14 months following the training. Based on these recruitment and attrition estimates, it would appear that out of a hypothetical 100 families of children with autism, 75 parents would accept the invitation for parent training. Of these 75 parents, 59 would complete the training. Out of the 59 families completing training, 45 would acquire sufficient skills to be successful in helping their child with autism.

Another challenge to training parents that may contribute to the described recruitment and attrition issues is the importance of ensuring that the content of training is practical for and a contextual fit to families. If the interventions taught to parents are not compatible with the practices and routines of the family, then those interventions are unlikely to be maintained once the training is finished. Holmes, Hemsley, Rickett, and Likierman (1982) reported that many of the parents trained in home-based behavior intervention for children with autism reported that they found the training intervention too difficult to continue to implement after the training ended.

Moes and Frea (2000) described the training that was provided to parents of a 3-year-old boy with autism who tended to hit, push, scream, throw, and drop to the ground when given a parent request. The initial approach to parent training was called "prescriptive treatment planning" and consisted of the experimenters selecting an intervention plan for the parents to implement. Parents had no input into the plan, nor was the plan based on an assessment of the family's routines or preferences. Prescriptive treatment planning provided little improvement in the child's problem behavior. Next, the authors assessed the family's routine, and efforts were made to fit an intervention into the routines that typically occurred. In addition, parents collaborated on the design of the intervention. This "contextualized treatment planning" resulted in a reduction in child problem behavior that generalized to a second setting and lasted after parent training ended. This study suggested that parent training needs to be designed collaboratively with parents and to fit the family routines and the context in which families will be implementing the intervention.

Trans-Situational Intervention

Schindler and Horner (2005) described a "trans-situational" intervention for young children with autism that was introduced in a one-to-one setting in preschools. Three children with autism, aged 4 and 5 years, who presented with aggression or tantrum behaviors participated in the study. Each attended preschool (the study did not specify if the school was an inclusive setting). Initially, a functional behavior assessment was completed for each child. Next, each child's problem behaviors were measured in four settings: (a) one-to-one training in preschool, (b) at snack time in the preschool, (c) during explore time in the preschool, and (d) in a selected setting in the child's home. In the home setting and in the two less structured settings in the preschool, parents, teachers, and teaching assistants were asked to implement a prescribed intervention derived from the functional behavior assessment results that involved low effort for the implementers (i.e., took little time to set up, used existing implementer skills, involved minimal change in routine) and that was based on functional communication training. The child problem behaviors remained elevated in all settings.

Next, in these settings for each of the three children, educators and parents were asked to discontinue the low-effort intervention and to deal with the child's problem behaviors as they did under baseline conditions. At this point, there was no improvement in the children's problem behavior. Meanwhile, functional communication training was introduced for each of the three children in their preschool one-to-one setting. Consistent with previous research, there was a reduction in the child's problem behavior in those settings, but there was no improvement in the problem behaviors in the three secondary settings. At this point, the experimenters asked the parents and educators to reintroduce the low-effort intervention. There was a reduction in children's problem behaviors at home and in the secondary preschool settings. In addition, the trans-situational intervention was rated both by teacher assistants and by parents as practical to implement and as having a good contextual fit.

Trans-situational intervention raises the possibility of reducing problem behavior in children with autism at home and other school settings after introducing a high-effort intervention in one setting and a low-effort intervention with the same intervention strategy at school or at home. It is unclear if the effect reported by Schindler and Horner (2005) can be replicated for problem behaviors that are maintained by functions other than escape or for interventions other than functional communication training. The study does suggest, however, that for children with autism who present problem behaviors across settings, one strategy is to introduce a needed intervention in a highly structured setting and train teachers and parents in a similar, but less effort, intervention in secondary settings.

In all, there are a number of significant barriers to the provision of parent training, with the most significant appearing to be its feasibility for schools to train parents of children with autism who are in attendance. It may be more feasible for schools to partner with clinics and agencies to deliver parent training in schools after school hours or a high-effort intervention in the clinic setting compatible with low-effect intervention that can be implemented at school.

Study Questions

1. How collaborative would you describe parent–professional relationships that you have seen?

2. What are the barriers to providing parent training, and what can be done to overcome each?

3. What were the suggested steps in providing person-centered planning for the transition of a child with autism from a special education to a general education setting?

4. Describe how a clinic could set up a trans-situational intervention in a 1:1 setting with the intent of producing generalization of behavior change to school and home settings.

A Person-Centered Approach to Supported Inclusion

1. Make the invitation—With parent input, decide on who would be invited as part of the person-centered planning process. Include all those who can help develop a support plan and/or are critical for its implementation. The core team would consist of the parents, child (if capable), principal or delegate, general education teacher, special education teacher, principal or administrator from the sending school or agency, general education teacher, and principal and consultants from the receiving general education class.

Send out an invitation such as the one shown below:

> You are invited to a future planning meeting
> for Noah at the Behavior Institute
> on November 13 from 1:30 to 3:00.
> The purpose of this meeting is
> to develop a collaborative
> vision of Noah's future,
> upon which a more immediate
> support plan would be based.
> Please respond indicating your attendance
> to Jane at 416-251-9277.

2. Parent Prepared Background Information—Prior to the initial meeting, ask the parents to complete the following background information about the child with autism. You may need to help the parents complete the forms. Please note that this information is phrased in the first person as if it is written by the child.

Child Profile

a. My name is Noah Griffin, and the following are the important people in my life:

[put photo here]

- Amanda, my younger sister, always bothers me but I like being with her.
- My mother, Terry, and my father, Vern
- My Grandpa Terry, Grandma Shirley, and Grandma Helen
- My behavior therapists, Nadine and Courtney

b. Here are the things I really like:
- Playing games on the computer
- Watching TV
- Playing soccer
- Bouncing on the trampoline

c. Here are the things I really do not like:
- Homework
- Chores
- Going to bed
- Eating vegetables

d. Here are my talents and strengths:
- I like talking with adults. I understand almost everything that is said to me.
- I like to follow a visual schedule of things to do.
- I can solve sheets of math problems as well as others in my class.

e. Here are the situations that upset me:
- Needing to wait for something I want
- Being asked to do a chore
- Being given schoolwork that I do not know how to do

f. When I get upset, I:
- Cry, yell, throw stuff, and sometimes hit people

3. *Prepare for and conduct the first meeting: Visioning*—Meet in a room free from distraction at either the sending or receiving school or setting. Bring chart paper, markers, and tape. Form an agenda such as the following:

A. Introduction
B. Purpose of the meeting
C. Develop a vision of Noah's future
D. Develop an overview of Noah's current programming
E. Create an action plan

Make copies of the agenda, of the parent-prepared background information, and of the summary of the child's IEP. Write the following questions (one per sheet) on chart paper:

- Who is Noah? (hand out parents' prepared background information)
- What is Noah's history?
- What are your hopes and dreams for Noah?
- What are your fears for Noah's future and inclusion at the school?
- What are Noah's unique gifts and talents?
- What are the supports needed for successful participation in school?
- What would an ideal day look like for Noah?

At the meeting, be sure to do the following:

- Distribute copies of the agenda, the parent-prepared background information, and the summary of the child's IEP.
- Pose each question on the chart paper to the parents and encourage any comments from any participants.
- Make notes on the chart paper about the discussion for each question.
- Ask the special education teacher to describe the child's IEP.
- Set the next meeting for about 4 weeks time, and suggest that the general education teacher and/or the consultant come with a plan of how the IEP can be adapted to fit the expectation of the general education setting.
- Give staff of the general education setting a form (such as the one that appears below) to prepare their thoughts.

	IEP		To meet the IEP, we need:		
	Seems OK as is	Needs adjustment	To accommodate the curriculum	Additional staffing	Additional instruction
Noah will raise his hand to answer questions in class.					
Noah will complete seatwork assignments with no assistance.					

	IEP		To meet the IEP, we need:		
	Seems OK as is	Needs adjustment	To accommodate the curriculum	Additional staffing	Additional instruction
Noah will be on task during group lessons at least 90% of the time.					
Noah will initiate and sustain reciprocal peer interaction at recess.					
Action					
By Whom			By When		

- Make copies of receiving class initial plan, and distribute this document in advance of the second meeting.

4. Prepare for and conduct the second meeting: Support plan development—For the second meeting (support plan), you will need to do the following:

- Bring chart paper, markers, and copies of the IEP changes.
- Lead discussions on the proposed adaptation of the child's IEP for the receiving class.
- At the end of the meeting, indicate what action needs to occur, by whom, and by what proposed date. At the bottom of the chart, summarize the action, who needs to be involved, and the target date for completion of that action.

5. Prepare for and conduct the third meeting: Follow-up and review—For the third meeting (follow-up and review), you will need to do the following:

- Call a meeting between the special education and general education staff 1 to 2 months later.
- Invite the special education teachers and/or consultant to observe the child.
- Discuss what, if any, additional revisions to the support plan need to be made.
- If needed, arrange for future meetings.

11 Preparing Staff for ABA-Based Supported Inclusion

Chapter Topics

- Difficulties with paraprofessional support of children with autism
- Factors affecting teacher adoption of interventions
- Intervention implementation fidelity
- Educator performance feedback
- Training teachers to implement ABA interventions
- Training teachers to develop ABA interventions
- How to develop teacher training in ABA procedures
- Systemic changes

Almost all of the applied behavior analytic procedures described in this book were ones that were developed by an experimenter or consultant and then taught to classroom staff to implement in their classrooms in hopes of helping children with autism in those settings. However, the impact of any intervention is determined not only by its effectiveness under optimal conditions, but also by the likelihood of the intervention's being implemented under natural conditions (McConnell, McEvoy, & Odom, 1992). In other words, an intervention demonstrated to be effective in research studies will not help children unless it is used by educators. Witt (1986) indicated that the *Program for Academic Survival Skills* (PASS; Greenwood et al., 1979) met the standards of best practice in the field at the time, but because it required a large amount of teacher time to implement, the PASS was unlikely to be adopted by many teachers. An intervention that could be effective for children may have little impact on children's adjustment because it does not become implemented or, if implemented, it is not executed in the correct manner. A colleague of mine would say, "Implementation is the Bermuda Triangle of good ideas." Therefore, one of the most challenging issues to the use of applied behavior analysis (ABA) to support children with autism in general education classrooms is the training of and consultation to staff who implement interventions.

Teachers and their support staff typically have little systematic training or experience in implementing best practices for children with autism in a general education setting (Causton-Theoharis & Malmgren, 2005; Lerman, Vorndran, Addison, & Kuhn, 2004; Schepis, Reid, Ownbey, & Parsons, 2001). Because of the typical lack of preservice preparation of educators for dealing with students diagnosed with autism, general education teachers are likely to need on-the-job training and consultation on strategies to accommodate a child with autism in their general education class. Not only would training and consultation typically be needed for general education teachers to implement ABA techniques for children with autism in their class, but it is likely also needed for paraprofessionals who would be involved in the support of children with autism in general education classrooms (Causton-Theoharis & Malmgren). In fact, the most common strategy of school districts for supporting children with severe disabilities in general education classrooms is the assignment of paraprofessionals (Causton-Theoharis & Malmgren). Without the involvement of a paraprofessional, many children with autism would be placed in segregated special education classrooms, rather than in general education classrooms.

Difficulties With Paraprofessional Support of Children With Autism

A number of concerns about the use of paraprofessionals to support children with autism have been expressed (Giangreco & Broer, 2005). These concerns include the possibility that without careful supervision and role clarification, paraprofessionals may inadvertently provide too much assistance to children with disabilities, to the point that (a) children may become unnecessarily dependent on the paraprofessionals, (b) the general education teacher forms a diminished sense of responsibility for the education of the child with disabilities supported by paraprofessionals, and (c) the close proximity of the paraprofessional to the child with disabilities interferes with peer interaction (Giangreco & Broer, 2005). In fact, in one study, paraprofessionals who were supporting children with a range of disabilities in general education classrooms indicated that 86% of their time during the school day was spent within 3 feet of their assigned child with disabilities. Most of paraprofessionals' time is spent hovering near the child they support. In another study (Marks, Schrader, & Levine, 1999), paraprofessionals indicated that they perceived that their main role was to ensure that the children with disabilities whom they were supporting were not disruptive to the general education teacher or to the rest of the class.

Preparation of educators for children with autism in general education classrooms must address the training needs of the general education teacher and the paraprofessional. It also must address what administrative supports and other systematic factors are needed to sustain educators' adoption of interventions over time. This chapter will discuss research literature on factors that are associated with teacher adoption of interventions, factors associated with teacher implementation of interventions with fidelity, and teacher continuation with interventions over time.

In general, there are three ways in which teachers' implementation of ABA interventions may fail. First, an intervention may be developed to support a child with autism in a general education class, but for several possible reasons, educators may never adopt it once the consultation is finished. The intervention never gets tried. A second way in which an intervention implementation may fail is that educators may use the intervention, but not in the way that it was designed. As a result of a lack of implementation fidelity, the intervention is not effective. Here, the intervention is tried, but not correctly. Finally, educators may adopt an intervention, implement it with fidelity, but abandon the intervention before it has had a chance to have its intended impact. This error is analogous to a patient with a bacterial infection not completing the entire regimen of prescribed antibiotics. Some interventions for children with autism need to be implemented over a period of time to have the intended impact. Abandoning an intervention after a few days, or (for some interventions) after a few weeks, does not allow enough time for the intervention to have the intended effect.

Factors Affecting Teacher Adoption of Interventions

The likelihood of teacher adoption of an intervention is determined by the goodness of fit between the intervention and contextual variables of the setting in which it is being implemented. First, to be adopted, the intervention needs to be perceived by teachers as addressing an important need that warrants an investment of their time and energy. The intervention needs to be seen as consistent with the beliefs and values of those implementing the intervention (Stein & Wang, 1988). This finding would suggest that to get a commitment from teachers to try an intervention, it would be important for teachers to understand the student need that the intervention would meet, the philosophical underpinnings of the intervention, and the possible negative consequences of intervening, as well as of not intervening (Lipsitz, Kallmey, Ferguson, & Abas, 1989).

Teachers also need to perceive the intervention as being able to be implemented with the time and knowledge that they have available. Teachers prefer interventions that are not time consuming (Elliot, Witt, & Kratochwill, 1991). As previously mentioned, the PASS is an intervention to reduce problem behaviors that was consistent with best practices in the field at the time, but was too time consuming to be practical for teachers to implement. Another example of an intervention that would be too difficult for a teacher to implement within their available time is a class token system described by Ringer (1973). A token system was introduced for all 37 students in a fourth-grade class. An experimenter moved around the class to see if each student was behaving appropriately and, if so, placed a mark on that student's token card. Once a student had all 20 squares on his or her token card filled, he or she was able to visit the school principal, who stamped the completed token card. Students' appropriate behavior improved with the introduction of the token system. Subsequently, the experimenter withdrew and management of the token system was transferred to the classroom teacher. When the teacher was in charge of the token system, there was a deterioration in student appropriate behavior. It may have been that the token system was too time consuming for the teacher to maintain in addition to her teaching.

A second major factor associated with teacher adoption of intervention is the visible and active endorsement for the intervention by school administrators, particularly the principal. There are many competing demands on teachers to implement school district policies and programs, such as a new emphasis on literacy or safe schools. In this context of competing demands on teacher time and priorities, interventions may not get sufficient teacher attention unless they are also actively supported by the school principal. The principal's support may be important for staff scheduling and any incidental expenses that would be associated with the intervention. Graden, Casey, and Bonstrom (1985) remarked that the reason some schools in school districts adopted a prereferral system for dealing with student problem behaviors was that those schools were ones in which the school principals were actively involved in endorsing an intervention.

Intervention Implementation Fidelity

As previously mentioned, a second type of implementation error that can occur is for teachers to implement an intervention for a child with autism, but not in the way it was designed. The extent to which an individual implements an intervention as defined is referred to as *treatment implementation fidelity*. Interventions that are implemented with fidelity have greater impact on changing a child's behavior than interventions that are not correctly implemented (Noell et al., 2005). For example, Greenwood et al. (1984) introduced classwide peer tutoring in elementary school to improve the spelling of the students in the class. The classroom teacher received a written description of the intervention, had the intervention procedures modeled, and received the direct assistance of a consultant in introducing the intervention in the classroom. However, soon after the consultant left, there was "drift" in the teacher implementation of the classwide peer-tutoring program. Accompanying the teacher drift was a decline in student correct performance.

In the absence of structured feedback, there is a tendency for rapid deterioration in teacher implementation fidelity (Noell et al., 2005). Witt, Noell, LaFleur, and Mortenson (1997) trained each of four elementary general education teachers to implement an intervention to improve student academic performance in the classroom. With the assistance of a consultant for each teacher, teacher implementation adherence to components of the intervention was 100% for all teachers. However, when the consultant left the classroom, the percentage of intervention components implemented correctly by teachers declined to between 20% and 60% within a few days.

Workshops in which intervention procedures are described have not been found to improve teacher implementation fidelity (Lerman et al., 2004). Similarly, Noell et al. (2000) trained five elementary-school teachers to implement a peer-tutoring intervention for students referred because of poor reading performance. Teachers were provided with all of the necessary material for the peer-tutoring program, received a written outline of the program, and a consultant directly assisted teachers in the implementation of the intervention. After the consultant was no longer helping teachers implement the interventions, teacher implementation fidelity declined for all teachers. At this point, the teacher's consultant introduced daily 5-minute follow-up meetings with each teacher to discuss how the intervention was going and to answer the teacher's questions. These follow-up meetings had no effect on the implementation fidelity for three of the five teachers and had modest effect for the other two. Next, Noell et al. (2000) arranged for the consultants to meet with teachers for 3 to 5 minutes daily to present a graph depicting student correct performance on daily assignments and a graph showing teacher correct implementation of intervention components. Teacher performance feedback produced an improvement in intervention implementation fidelity for four of the five teachers. For one teacher, the improvement in implementation fidelity did not occur until there was a discussion with the teacher that a follow-up meeting with the principal and the child's parents would need to be held.

Noell et al. (2005) replicated the Noell et al. (2000) study using random assignments of one of three conditions across 45 general education teachers who taught kindergarten through fifth grade. Participating teachers referred a child because of academic and/or behavior difficulties. Teachers received weekly brief follow-up meetings during which a consultant asked about how well a provided intervention was going and encouraged teachers to ask questions. Other teachers received the follow-up meetings combined with a social influence procedure designed to increase teacher commitment to implementing the interventions. A second group of teachers received performance feedback as described by Noell et al. (2000). The greatest treatment fidelity was found to occur with the group of teachers who received performance feedback. Follow-up meetings, talking about how things were going, or attempts to directly increase teacher commitment through providing information were not enough to ensure correct implementation of provided interventions.

Noell et al. (2005) asked teachers in all three conditions to rate the acceptability of the particular form of consultation that they had received. Recall that each of the three groups of teachers received a different form of consultation. Teachers perceived each of the three different forms of consultation very positively, with no difference found across the conditions.

There are two implications from these findings about acceptability of forms of consultation. One implication is that performance feedback was viewed just as positively as the other forms of consultation. A second implication is that the acceptability of a consultation does not predict its effectiveness in ensuring intervention implementation fidelity.

Educator Performance Feedback

It would appear that regardless of how teachers are taught aspects of ABA initially, the continued and accurate implementation of those procedures depends on feedback being provided to teachers on their performance. In fact, workshops and in-service training without performance feedback are likely to have little, if any, impact on the day-to-day performance of staff (Crow & Snyder, 1998).

In the studies discussed, teacher performance feedback was provided by someone who was not part of the school supervisory structure for the teachers. Although having a nonsupervisor provide performance feedback to teachers following training may have the advantage of being of low threat to teachers, there are a number of reasons to enlist teachers' immediate supervisors in providing performance feedback and perhaps even in delivering teacher training. A supervisor would be in an advantageous position to obtain added supports if a teacher is not implementing intervention as designed. Moreover, the observation of teacher performance would be able to be incorporated into teacher performance evaluations. Supervisors have been involved in teaching and training teachers in the implementation of interventions for children with disabilities with positive effects (Hundert, 2007; Schepis et al., 2001).

The extent to which teachers implement interventions as designed is certainly one aspect of staff training that would determine its effect on children. Another aspect of staff training is whether the training results in teachers being able to apply the training of the interventions to a range of situations that they will later encounter on the job. Teachers may need to adapt the interventions for different children, in different settings, and perhaps for different instructional targets than those used during staff training.

There have not been many examples of studies in which teachers were trained in ABA procedures and generalization to new situations was evaluated. Wallace, Doney, Mintz-Resudek, and Tarbox (2004) trained three educators to implement functional analysis as part of a workshop delivered to 35 attendees. Three participants practiced implementing the training procedure in role-play situations. For one of the participants, the trainee could apply the training procedures in her classroom 4 weeks after the workshop ended. Lerman et al. (2004) trained five teachers to implement behavioral interventions for children with autism who attended a university-based early intervention program for children with autism. Following training, teachers were assessed on whether they could apply the training to children with whom they did not practice and in settings different than that used in their training. Teachers showed a high degree of accuracy of implementation of the training procedures with different children in different settings than those used initially in their training.

Ducharme and Feldman (1992) directly manipulated the format used to train residential staff in self-care routines for adult clients with developmental disabilities and tested for generalization of the training to new situations. In one condition, staff were trained using role-playing only on the programs of one client. In a second condition, staff were trained on only one program, but practiced directly with the client. In the third condition, staff were trained using a number of clients and client programs selected to represent the range of programs that the staff would likely encounter. Training in a range of exemplars to reflect the range of situations the training would encounter is known as "general case training" (Horner, Sprague, & Wilcox, 1982). Only after general case training was used did staff demonstrate full generalization of training skills. Koegel, Russo, and Rincover (1977) described one of the few examples of training teachers of children with autism in a number of instructional targets across a number of children with autism. Teachers demonstrated their skills to correctly apply their training with new children and for new instructional targets.

Training Teachers to Implement ABA Interventions

Much of the training of educators in applied behavior analysis has focused on introducing special education teachers to specific interventions for children with special needs in those classrooms. For example, Petscher and Bailey (2006) taught three instructional assistants how to implement a token system for children with severe behavior problems. Sarokoff and Sturmey (2004) taught three special education teachers to implement discrete trial teaching for a 3-year-old child with autism who was receiving home-based ABA services. In addition, there has been demonstration that general education teachers and paraprofessionals can be taught to implement interventions for children with autism who are in general education classes. Kohler, Anthony, Steighner, and Hoyson (2001) taught two teachers and two teacher aides how to increase the peer interaction of four preschoolers with disabilities who were attending an inclusive preschool. Trainees were taught seven tactics of naturalistic teaching (e.g., use novel material, use incidental strategies, invite interaction with peers). The techniques were first introduced in a 40-minute meeting with the preschool director. Subsequently, trainers were provided with daily feedback and coaching on the implementation of the naturalistic tactics. After the introduction of daily feedback and coaching, there was an increase in the interaction of the four preschoolers with disabilities attending the preschool.

Schepis et al. (2001) taught five support staff how to teach children with disabilities who were enrolled in inclusive preschools. The support staff were trained to teach children with disabilities using the teaching-skills training program, which was originally designed to teach adults with disabilities in residential settings. Support staff were taught to teach skills to children with disabilities during the initial routines of the preschool using prompting, reinforcement, error correction, and task analysis procedures derived from discrete trial teaching. Two support staff were trained at a time, starting with 4 hours of classroom-based training, during which the experimenter demonstrated each teaching skill.

Participants then practiced the teaching skills using role-playing and received feedback on how well they implemented the procedures. At the end of the classroom-based staff training, the supervising teacher observed staff implementation of taught procedures with children with disabilities in the classroom and provided feedback on their performance. Following this training, there was an increase in the accuracy of staff implementation of trained procedures. Data were recorded on improvement in the skills of children in areas taught by the staff. These data were collected for only two of the five participating teachers. They found improvement in children's skills in areas that were the targets of teacher training, but not in areas that were not included in teacher training.

Johnson and McDonnell (2004) taught two general education teachers to embed instruction on Individualized Education Program (IEP) objectives for three children with developmental disabilities. Training consisted of a written script on how to conduct embedded instruction, as well as the provision of modeling, practice procedures, and role-play in situations set up with the experimenter. Training with individual teachers continued until each could demonstrate 100% accuracy in the implementation of each procedure. They modeled how to implement embedded instruction with the target student in the class. The classroom teacher practiced using embedded instruction and received performance feedback. Training continued until each teacher could implement the embedded instruction procedure with no errors. The results indicated that the teachers were able to implement embedded instruction with fidelity and that two thirds of students learned the target skill.

It is interesting to note that in both the Kohler et al. (2001) and Schepis et al. (2001) studies, the staff supervisor who was involved in the training also provided feedback to staff. Typically, training of teachers in ABA interventions has been conducted by an experimenter or consultant, rather than by a line supervisor. There may be a number of advantages to the use of line supervisors as trainers rather than outside consultants. It also should be noted that in none of these studies was teacher training restricted to teachers who taught children with autism.

Table 11.1 is a summary of the research studies that have been described. It shows who provided the training, a description of the type of training, the target children involved, and how the training was delivered. Most of the studies used a combination of training procedures that included instruction, modeling, practice, and feedback. Sometimes the practice consisted of role-playing, and other times practice consisted of direct rehearsal with the child with autism.

Training Teachers to Develop ABA Interventions

Almost all of the efforts to train teachers in applied behavior analysis have consisted of instruction in how to implement interventions designed by a consultant or experimenter, and continue with the intervention after the consultant or experimenter withdrawals (e.g., Kamps, Walker, Maher, & Rotholz, 1992; Kohler et al., 2001). There are few examples of training teachers how to develop their own interventions to enhance the skills and/or manage the problem behaviors of children with autism in a general education classroom. There are a number of potential advantages to teachers being able to design their own ABA interventions. By designing their own programs, teachers may be able to customize an intervention to fit the needs of individual children with autism, as well as the needs of the rest of the class, with the routines of the classroom. Teachers are unlikely to implement interventions that require more time than they have available (Phillips & McCullough, 1990) or that are judged to be inconsistent with school policy or the teacher's own philosophical beliefs (Stein & Wang, 1988). Without adaptation of interventions to fit individual classrooms, teachers may use externally developed interventions. For this reason, it is important to involve teachers who are implementing an intervention in the development of the intervention.

A second and associated advantage of training teachers to design their own interventions is that individuals are more committed to implementing an intervention if they have input into its design (York & Vandercook, 1990). An intervention may fail because it was not implemented at all, implemented incorrectly, or abandoned prematurely. For example, Witt et al. (1997) trained four general education teachers in an intervention designed to improve the academic performance of elementary-school students. During training, teachers implemented the intervention with 100% fidelity. However, following teacher training, there was a steady decrease in teachers' adherence to components of the intervention. It was not until teachers received feedback on their performance of the intervention that their implementation fidelity improved.

A third advantage of having teachers develop their own interventions is that, if successful, it is a more efficient way of delivering services than having a consultant develop the intervention and train teachers in its implementation, particularly if teachers can be trained in groups. Additional efficiency may occur if teachers would be able to apply the training to the development of interventions for programming targets not specifically covered in training. In other words, it may be possible for teachers to acquire a generalized ability to develop interventions that they employ for other areas of need in the classroom.

There are only a few examples of teachers being taught to develop their own ABA interventions for children with disabilities. Hundert (1982) taught teachers of children with hearing impairments in the principles of behavior programming and found

Table 11.1
Summary of Selected Training Variables Used in Recent Studies of Preparing Educators to Use ABA Interventions

Authors	Trainer	Trainees	Students	Target settings	Training targets	Training methods	Training location	Training time
Schepis, Ownbey, Parsons, & Reid (2000)	Staff supervisor, program director, & experimenter	6 support staff	5 children with disabilities, 3–5 yrs	Inclusive preschool classrooms	Basic skills for discrete trial teaching	F M P R V W	"Classroom training" followed by on-the-job feedback	4 hrs of "classroom training"
Petscher & Bailey (2006)	Experimenter	3 instructional assistants	11 children with severe behavior problems, 10–14 yrs	Self-contained special education classroom	Implementation of a token system	F M V Remote tactile prompting, self-monitoring	Small office, on-the-job	30 min
Schepis, Reid, Ownbey, & Parsons (2001)	Staff supervisor & program director	4 support staff	5 children with disabilities, 3–5 yrs	Inclusive child-care program	Teaching skills embedded into routine	F M P R V W	"Classroom training" followed by on-the-job feedback	1 session of 60–90 min of "classroom training" & 2–4 20-min on-the-job sessions
Wallace, Doney, Mintz-Resudek, & Tarbox (2004)	Experimenter	1 special education teacher, 1 general education teacher, & 1 psychologist	NA	Self-contained classroom for 1 participant	Implement functional analyses	R V	Conference room	3 hrs
Moore et al. (2002)	Experimenter	1 special education teacher & 2 general education teachers	1 student from each classroom taught by the 3 teachers	Teachers' classrooms	Implement functional analysis conditions	F P R V W	Each teacher's classroom	?

(continues)

Table 11.1 *Continued*

Authors	Trainer	Trainees	Students	Target settings	Training targets	Training methods	Training location	Training time
Koegel, Russo, & Rincover (1977)	Experimenter	11 special education teachers	12 children with autism, 5–13 yrs	?	Teaching skills (e.g., prompting, reinforcement, giving instruction)	F M P V	?	Less than 25 hrs
Sarokoff & Sturmey (2004)	Experimenter	3 special education teachers	1 child with autism, 3 yrs	?	Discrete trial teaching	F M P V W	Small room in child's home	?
Lerman, Vorndran, Addison, & Kuhn (2004)	Experimenter & university graduate students	4 special education teachers of children with autism	6 children with autism, 3–6 yrs, enrolled in a summer program	Classroom	Preference assessment, direct teaching, & incidental teaching	F P R V W	Summer workshop followed by children's classrooms	Daily 3.5 hrs for 5 days (total of 17.5 hrs)
Kohler, Anthony, Steighner, & Hoyson (2001)	Experimenter & director	2 teachers & 2 aides	4 preschoolers with disabilities and typically developing peers, 4 yrs	Inclusive preschool	Naturalistic teaching approach to increase peer interaction	F V	Classrooms	?
Causton-Theoharis & Malmgren (2005)	Experimenter	4 paraprofessionals	4 students with severe disabilities attending general education setting, 6–11 yrs	Classroom	How to facilitate peer interaction	M V	Classrooms	4 hrs

Note. F = feedback on performance; M = modeling; P = practice; R = role-play; V = videotape; W = written outline; NA = not applicable; ? = not specified.

that following training, teachers successfully developed a behavior-change program for one child's target behavior on which they received specific assistance during trainings, but also a second child target behavior for which no specific assistance was given.

In Henderson, Gardner, Kaiser, and Riley (1993), a consultant provided feedback to day care teachers on their teaching approach and made suggestions for areas of improvement. Following this feedback, teachers set goals for improving their teaching approach. This coaching resulted in increased use of effective teaching procedures and a corresponding increase in the social interaction of children with disabilities.

Hundert (2007) trained general and special education teachers in pairs how to develop an intervention to increase the peer interaction of preschoolers in a class that included children with disabilities. Prior to training, the general education teachers developed class plans and the special education teachers developed the specific plans for individual children with autism. General and special education pairs were taught how to adapt the overall class plan to promote peer interaction for all children. Preschool supervisors gave teacher pairs a six-page manual describing best practices in areas of (a) physical arrangement of the class to promote peer interaction (e.g., specific play areas), (b) curriculum and activities (e.g., the type and novelty of play materials), and (c) instructional procedures (e.g., teacher prompting and reinforcement). Teacher pairs were asked to make adaptations to a class plan that would increase the peer interaction of all children in the class. They were asked to consider each of 15 interventions to incorporate into the specific intervention. They then described the adaptation that they wished to make. One example of the changes made by a teacher pair in the Hundert (2007) study is shown in Figure 11.1. A blank copy can be found in Appendix 11A.

Hundert (2007) found that training teachers to develop interventions to promote peer interaction also resulted in teachers being able to develop successful interventions to improve the on-task behavior of disabled and nondisabled children. Teachers were given a general format for making adaptations to their class plan for increased peer interaction that they were able to apply to another problem in the class that was not specifically discussed in training. The successful training impact of any intervention for children with autism in inclusive settings may depend on the input of participating teachers for the intervention design.

How to Develop Teacher Training in ABA Procedures

There are two general strategies for the provision of training educators on ABA intervention for children with autism in general education classrooms. The simplest way to provide teacher training is when a teacher refers a child with autism for special education assistance, as used by Petschier and Bailey (2006). General education teachers in essence would request training when they seek assistance in educating a child with autism in their class. A second and more proactive approach to teacher training is for school districts to deliver training workshops to some or all of the general education teachers in the school district who have a child with autism in their class. A workshop to train a large number of educators would be designed and delivered to teachers without waiting for a referral. A large-scale training program such as this would need to gain support from school district administration and from participating schools.

ADAPTIVE CLASSWIDE PLAN

Class: _3B_   Date: _Nov 23/06_   Classroom Teacher: _Carol Mendez_

Resource Teacher: _Lois Lee_   Supervisor: _Benita Kozak_

Areas of Intervention: _Peer Interaction_

Measurable Objective of Intervention: _There will be at least a 30% increase in the amount of time that children with autism spend in peer interaction during free play._

I agree to the plan.   Classroom Teacher: _CM_   Resource Teacher: _LL_

Level of intervention	Keep as is?	Adaptations/changes/additions?	Who is to do what?
I. Organizational			
Sequence of activities	X	• Assign staff to play areas	• BK to draft a schedule and discuss at staff meeting
Location of activities	X		
Groupings of children	X		
Adult/child ratio	X		
Staff assignment			
II. Activities			
Type of play activities		• Get more "social" toys	• LL to get more social toys
Number of child spaces for each activity		• Use badges for number of spaces	• CM to create badges
Access to play activities		• Restrict access to play areas	• CM to have clear entry spots for play areas
Novelty & variety		• Rotate toys once a week	• CM to select toys for rotation each week
III. Teacher Behavior			
Positioning	X		
Using play starters		• Use play starters with target children	• CM & LL to role-play using play starters and to praise inclusive groups
Prompting target child	X		
Prompting other children	X		
Reinforcing target child		• Praise inclusive groups of children who are playing	• CM & LL to implement
Reinforcing other children			

Figure 11.1. Example of an adaptive classwide plan used in the Hundert (2007) study.

The following is a suggested sequence of steps in providing teacher training in applied behavior analysis for children with autism in general education classes.

1. Gain administrative support—Any proposal that would be submitted to school district administration would need to give a rationale for the training; a description of what needs and priorities of the school district would be met by the initiative; and a description of how the training would be done, including the content of training, recipients of training, training methods, logistics, and proposed budget. In fact, most of the areas covered in the description would likely need to be included in a proposal to school district administrators.

Not only is it important to gain support for a proposed training by the school district administrator, but it is also important to gain support of the participating schools. There are a number of advantages to starting a large-scale training with one school that then serves as a pilot site for teacher training. Starting with one school allows one to work out the bugs in the training procedures before it is more broadly disseminated.

A few schools (1–3) within a school district could be recruited to serve as a pilot site, and the initial step is to design the set of ABA procedures to be introduced in the demonstration school.

2. Determine the training content—The intervention to be taught should be one that could be readily used for children with autism in general education classrooms. The following is a list of suggested content:

- Adapting the curriculum
- Embedded instruction
- Incidental teaching of language
- How to prompt and reinforce participating in class lessons and seatwork and following routines
- Social script training
- Functional assessment and functional communication training
- Assessment of children's behaviors and skills
- The amount of training content is governed by the time set aside for training staff.

3. Develop the training material—As previously mentioned, many of the studies on staff training provided participants with written instructions, such as a manual of procedures. One should write out instructions on how to deliver each of the procedures being taught. Information about procedures can come in the form of a written manual, checklist of components, handouts from a computer-based presentation, or a combination of the above. In its minimal form, the written instructions should include a step-by-step checklist of how to implement a procedure in sufficient detail to guide the actions of the implementer.

Other materials to be developed could include videotaped examples of the procedures being taught. Sometimes both positive exemplars of the procedure (correct examples) and negative exemplars (incorrect examples) are presented (e.g., Koegel et al., 1977) to aid the learner to discriminate between the two. Video clips can easily be digitized and embedded into the presentation.

The most likely trainer of general education teachers in how to teach children with autism in a school-district-wide training would be special education consultants from the school district. Trainers would consist of those who work with children with autism themselves and demonstrate proficiencies in the interventions being taught. Before these individuals would be able to train others, they must complete a training intervention themselves.

4. Determine the method of training—Effective staff training typically uses a number of training components in combination. For example, instruction to learners could be presented both verbally and in written form. There should be specific performance criteria used to determine when an educator has achieved an adequate level of competence in the interventions being taught. Typically, these criteria rely on direct observation of an educator's performance implementing training procedures in the classroom. Coaching and feedback should continue with individual teachers until the mastery criterion is achieved.

The final component in staff training would be the provision of periodic follow-up evaluations and feedback to ensure maintenance of teachers' skills over time. The trainers would visit teachers in their respective classrooms to provide this coaching and feedback. Figure 11.2 shows an example of feedback sheets that could be used to train and evaluate staff. The sheet contains a list of components of correct implementation of incidental teaching of language. The trainer should observe staff using incidental teaching and, for each of three opportunities, check off whether each of the components was demonstrated. Following the completion of this checklist, the teacher should provide feedback to staff being trained.

5. Select staff to be trained—The question that would need to be addressed in the delivery of staff training is who should receive this training. Clearly, participants should include those who would typically be implementing interventions: general education teachers and paraprofessionals supporting children with autism in general education classrooms. School administrators and consultants would not need to undergo the intensive training in intervention implementation, but should understand its content and how it would fit into the existing process of supporting children with autism in the school.

One would need to determine if all the staff who meet the criteria for being trained in the school district should be trained at the same time (difficult to do), or in some staggered fashion (more practical). How long would a training workshop be (e.g., 1 week)? Based on that answer, when would the training take place? Lerman et al. (2004) provided training to five teachers for 1 week during the summer using children with autism attending early intervention programming. The participants practiced the interventions being taught with children to a mastery criterion and then received follow-up feedback of trained procedures in their respective classrooms.

Our institute has provided similar training in a 5-day summer workshop with 10 paraprofessionals supporting 10 children with autism in a school district. For the first and last days of the workshop, general education teachers, paraprofessionals, administrators of each school, and parents participated. Delivering training in such an intensive fashion raises the question of how many staff should be trained. To accommodate a large number of staff in a school district during a summer session, there would

Staff: _____ Child: _____

Length of Observation: _____ Live: _____ Video: _____

Date: _____ Evaluator: _____

Instructions: The purposes of this evaluation are to (a) provide feedback to staff on their skills associated with incidental language instruction and (b) monitor changes in the skill level of staff. Observe the staff implementing incidental language instruction on three occasions, and then rate the staff in the following areas. Circle ✓ if the skill was implemented without error; circle X if one or more errors occurred; circle NA if not applicable.

	1			2			3			Comments
Selected Appropriate Instructional Target										
• Defined in measurable terms	✓	X	NA	✓	X	NA	✓	X	NA	
• At the next level of difficulty	✓	X	NA	✓	X	NA	✓	X	NA	
• Appropriate for child	✓	X	NA	✓	X	NA	✓	X	NA	
Created Communication Opportunity										
• Used naturally occurring situations	✓	X	NA	✓	X	NA	✓	X	NA	
• Used techniques of "forgetfulness," visible but unreachable," "sabotage," or "piece by piece"	✓	X	NA	✓	X	NA	✓	X	NA	
Elicited Communication Target										
• Waited (3 sec)	✓	X	NA	✓	X	NA	✓	X	NA	
• Used nonverbal attentional prompt (e.g., point at PEC, get eye contact)	✓	X	NA	✓	X	NA	✓	X	NA	
• Waited (3 sec)	✓	X	NA	✓	X	NA	✓	X	NA	
• Asked	✓	X	NA	✓	X	NA	✓	X	NA	
• Waited (3 sec)	✓	X	NA	✓	X	NA	✓	X	NA	
• Said (modeled)	✓	X	NA	✓	X	NA	✓	X	NA	
Gave Confirmational Response										
• Gave a confirmational response (e.g., "Oh, you want candy")	✓	X	NA	✓	X	NA	✓	X	NA	
Collected Data										
• Each opportunity and child response was recorded	✓	X	NA	✓	X	NA	✓	X	NA	
Sum										
% ✓ (# ✓ / (#✓ + # X))										

Overall mean correct _____

Figure 11.2. Blank evaluation form for staff implementation of incidental language instruction.

need to be several workshops presented simultaneously. There are other options (e.g., deliver workshops over the weekend or during professional development days), all with associated logistical challenges. Depending on the number of staff to be trained, it would be preferable to train staff school by school.

An associated issue is what to do about staff attrition year by year. Trainers would need to provide training to teachers new to supporting children with autism in general education classrooms. An undertaking to train teachers in a school district in ABA procedures to support children with autism in general education classrooms should be seen as a multiyear undertaking.

6. Evaluate the staff training—Staff training should be evaluated by a number of indicators of success. One indicator includes process measures that describe what happened as participants completed training. Such indicators as the number of staff trained, the number of children with autism affected by training, the average length of training, and so on, would be examples of such process measures.

Another indication of training success are measures of staff performance, such as mean pre-/post-change in correct implementation of trained interventions. These types of outcome data could be used to determine the consultation needs of staff undergoing training. In a previously described large-scale training project, over 2,000 early interventionists were trained during 2-week workshops. Therapists learned techniques of discrete trial teaching through video modeling, a manual, role-playing, and subsequently on-the-job feedback. Learners completed pencil-and-paper quizzes for each of 14 written units of the manual that they read and needed to achieve at least 80% correct on a written test of content at the end of training. Moreover, each participant needed to demonstrate at least 70% correct implementation of discrete trial teaching procedures during a direct observation when interacting with a child with autism. Staff who did not achieve these standards had a development plan formulated with their immediate supervisor on the areas for improvement and later were reassessed.

The third type of data to be collected to indicate the success of staff training are the improvement and adjustment of children with autism who received the interventions on which the staff were trained. Improvement in child participation during class lessons or accuracy on seatwork assignments or increase in communication, initiations, or peer interactions would all be examples of child outcomes that may reveal the effect of staff training on children.

Because, to a great extent, the important outcomes to achieve differ from child to child, a means of evaluating gains across children needs to be determined. One possibility is the use of Goal Attainment Scaling (Kiresuk & Sherman, 1968). This evaluation strategy has been used to monitor the success of individuals in community mental health (Kiresuk & Lund, 1978), services for persons with developmental disability (Moriarity, 1974), children with mental health issues (Ricks & Weinstein, 1977), and other uses. A Goal Attainment Scale consists of selecting a number of instructional goals for a child based on the areas of need for that individual. For children with autism in general education settings, the goals would be likely derived from the child's IEP. For each of the goals, a scale is created that represents outcomes that would be expected to be achieved. One specifies what would constitute the expected outcomes to be achieved, as well as what represents more than expected and less than expected. Kiresuk and Sherman indicated that there should be a 5-point scale with *best outcome, more than expected success, expected success, less than expected success,* and *most unfavorable outcome*. To simplify the Goal Attainment Scale, my colleagues and I use a 3-point scale: 1 = *more than expected;* 0 = *expected;* and −1 = *less than expected*. We set measurable targets that we expect the child to be able to achieve within 6 months and define the scale that would be achieved during that time interval.

For each of the objectives, staff members specify what child performance outcomes are expected. The outcome strategy statement is phrased in measurable terms. Next, staff specify what child performance outcomes are expected if a gain was more than expected and what constitutes a less than expected outcome. This exercise is repeated for each of the goals for each child with autism.

At the specified period of time (e.g., 6 months), one examines what the child is able to do in comparison to the stated outcomes. A score of 1 is given for each objective in which the child outcome was more than expected, a 0 is given for each outcome that was expected, and a −1 is given for each outcome that was less than expected. Using a Goal Attainment Scale, the effect of staff training can be evaluated by the mean goal attainment score per child with autism who received interventions by staff in training.

A hypothetical example of a Goal Attainment Scale for one goal for a child with autism can be seen in Figure 11.3

Systemic Changes

Dunlap et al. (2000) described essential elements of a national in-service training model to train professional teams in positive behavior supports for individuals with

---

Area: <u>Communication</u>   Date: <u>November 14, 2008</u>

Objective: <u>Jay will increase the mean number of communicative attempts during the</u>

<u>school day.</u>

Time Frame: <u>6 months (June 14, 2009)</u>

Current Performance: <u>Average of 2.3 attempts per hour</u>

Expected Child Performance (0): <u>5–7 attempts per hour</u>

More Than Expected Child Performance (1): <u>More than 7 attempts per hour</u>

Less Than Expected Child Performance (−1): <u>Less than 5 attempts per hour</u>

Actual Outcome (To be completed in 6 months)

Expected (0) _____ More Than Expected (1) _____ Less Than Expected (−1) _____

Figure 11.3. Example of a Goal Attainment Scale form.

1. Establishing a collective vision and goals for intervention.

2. Collaborating and building teams among families and professionals.

3. Conducting functional assessments (i.e., gathering information and identifying behavior–environment relations).

4. Designing hypothesis-driven, multicomponent support plans.

5. Implementing intervention strategies that include environmental adjustments and lifestyle enhancements.

6. Monitoring and evaluating intervention outcomes.

7. Infusing positive behavior supports into broader systems.

Figure 11.4. Essential elements of positive behavior supports in a national training program, based on Dunlap et al. (2000).

disabilities and problem behaviors. They described seven features that are essential parts of this training. These elements are shown in Figure 11.4.

It is interesting to note that the fifth essential element of training does not pertain to the content or the delivery of training, but pertains to systemic issues before, during, and after training that are essential for the general acceptance and longevity of the training.

The systematic issue can easily be applied to how to gain acceptance and ensure the longevity of teacher training in interventions for children with autism in general education classrooms. They include the importance of soliciting administrative support, upon developing collaborative relationships, ensuring ongoing communications, and overcoming systemic barriers.

Study Questions

1. How does implementation fidelity affect the effectiveness of the intervention?

2. What are some of the potential difficulties of paraprofessional support of children with autism in general education classrooms?

3. What are the three ways in which implementation of an intervention may fail?

4. Describe the factors that affect teacher adoption of interventions.

5. What is the effect of performance feedback on teacher implementation fidelity?

6. Describe how teachers have been trained to implement ABA interventions.

7. Describe how teachers have been trained to develop ABA interventions.

8. Describe the steps in developing teacher training in ABA procedures.

Adaptive
Classwide Plan

ADAPTIVE CLASSWIDE PLAN

Class: _____ Date: _____ Classroom Teacher: _____

Resource Teacher: _____ Supervisor: _____

Areas of Intervention: _____

Measurable Objective of Intervention: _____

_____

_____

I agree to the plan. Classroom Teacher: _____ Resource Teacher: _____

Level of intervention	Keep as is?	Adaptations/changes/additions?	Who is to do what?
I. Organizational			
Sequence of activities			
Location of activities			
Groupings of children			
Adult/child ratio			
Staff assignment			
II. Activities			
Type of play activities			
Number of child spaces for each activity			
Access to play activities			
Novelty & variety			
III. Teacher Behavior			
Positioning			
Using play starters			
Prompting target child			
Prompting other children			
Reinforcing target child			
Reinforcing other children			

References

Adkins, T., & Axelrod, S. (2001). Topography-based versus selection-based responding: Comparison of mand acquisitions in each modality. *The Behavior Analyst Today, 2,* 259.

Agosta, E., Graetz, J. E., Mastropieri, M. A., & Scruggs, T. E. (2004). Teacher-research partnership to improve social behavior through social stories. *Intervention in School and Clinic, 39,* 276–287.

Agran, M., Sinclair, T., Alper, S., Covin, M., Wehmeyer, M., & Hughes, C. (2005). Using self-monitoring to increase following direction skills of students in the moderate to severe disabilities in general education. *Education and Training in Developmental Disabilities, 40,* 3–13.

Ahearn, W. H., Clark, K. M., MacDonald, R. P., & Chung, B. I. (2007). Assessing and treating vocal stereotyping in children with autism. *Journal of Applied Behavior Analysis, 40,* 263–275.

American Psychiatric Association. (2000). *Diagnostic and statistical manual of mental disorders* (4th ed., text rev.). Washington, DC: Author.

Anderson, A., Moore, W. D., Godfrey, R., & Fletcher-Flinn, M. C. (2004). Social skills assessment of children with autism in free-play situations. *Autism, 8,* 369–385.

Anderson, S., Jablonski, A., & Knapp, V. (2003, May). *Successful strategies for transitioning children from early intensive behavioral programs into kindergarten.* Paper presented at the convention of the Association for Behavior Analysis, San Francisco.

Autism Special Interest Group, Association of Behavior Analysis. (2007). Consumer guidelines for identifying, selecting, and evaluating behavior analysts working with individuals with autism spectrum disorders. Retrieved July 13, 2008, from http://www.abainternational.org/Special_Interest/autism-guidelines.asp

Ault, M. J., Gast, D. L., & Wolery, M. (1988). Comparison of progressive and constant time-delay procedures in teaching community-sign word readings. *American Journal on Mental Retardation, 93,* 44–56.

Baer, D. M. (1990). Why choose self-regulation as the focal analysis of retardation? *American Journal on Mental Retardation, 94,* 363–364.

Baer, D. M., Wolf, M. M., & Risley, T. D. (1968). Some current dimensions of applied behavior analysis. *Journal of Applied Behavior Analysis, 1,* 91–97.

Bailey, A., Le Couteur, A., Gottesman, I., & Bolton, P. (1995). Autism as a strongly genetic disorder: Evidence from a British twin study. *Psychological Medicine, 25,* 63–77.

Bailey, D. B., & Wolery, M. (1992). *Teaching infants and preschoolers with handicaps.* Columbus, OH: Merrill.

Baker, B. L. (1996). Parent training. In J. W. Jacobson & J. A. Mulick (Eds.), *Manual of diagnosis and professional practice in mental retardation* (pp. 289–299). Washington, DC: American Psychological Association.

Baker, K. L., Heifetz, L. J., & Murphy, D. M. (1980). Behavioral training for parents of mentally retarded children: One-year follow-up. *American Journal of Mental Deficiency, 85,* 31–38.

Baron-Cohen, S. (1995). *Mindblindess: An essay on autism and theory of mind.* Cambridge, MA: MIT Press.

Baron-Cohen, S., Leslie, A. M., & Frith, V. (1985). Does the autistic child have a "theory of mind"? *Cognition, 21,* 37–46.

Bellini, S., Akullian, J., & Hopf, A. (2007). Increasing social engagement in young children with autism spectrum disorders using video self-modeling. *School Psychology Review, 36,* 80–90.

Bettelheim, B. (1967). *The empty fortress: Infantile autism and the birth of the self.* New York: Free Press.

Billstedt, E., Gillberg, C., & Gillberg, C. (2005). Autism after adolescence: Population-based 13- to 22-year follow-up study of 120 individuals with autism diagnosed in childhood. *Journal of Autism and Developmental Disabilities, 35,* 351–360.

Bloom, L., & Lahey, M. (1978). *Language development and language disorders.* New York: Wiley.

Blue-Banning, M. J., Turnbull, A. P., & Pereira, L. (2000). Group action planning as a support strategy for Hispanic families: Parent and professional perspectives. *Mental Retardation, 38,* 262–275.

Bondy, A., & Frost L. (1994). The Picture Exchange Communication System. *Focus on Autistic Behavior, 9,* 1-19.

Bondy, A., & Frost L. (2001). *The Picture Exchange Communication System (PECS): Application with young children with autism.* Cherry Hill, NJ: Pyramid Educational Consultants.

Bouma, R., & Schweitzer, R. (1990). The impact of chronic childhood illness on family stress: A comparison between autism and cystic fibrosis. *Journal of Clinical Psychology, 46,* 722–730.

Boxer, P., Musher-Eizenman, D., Dubow, E. F., Danner, S., & Heretick, D. M. L. (2006). Assessing teachers' perceptions for school-based aggression prevention programs: Applying a cognitive-ecological framework. *Psychology in the Schools, 43,* 331–344.

Boyd, B. A. (2002). Examining the relationship between stress and lack of social support in mothers of children with autism. *Focus on Autism and Other Developmental Disabilities, 17,* 208–215.

Brookman-Frazee, L. (2004). Using parent/clinician partnerships in parent education programs for children with autism. *Journal of Positive Behavior Interventions, 6,* 195–213.

Brown, K. E., & Mirenda, P. (2006). Contingency mapping: Use of a novel visual support strategy as an adjunct to functional equivalence training. *Journal of Positive Behavior Interventions, 8,* 155–164.

Brown, R. (1968). The development of *wh*-questions in child speech. *Journal of Verbal Learning and Verbal Behavior, 7,* 279–299.

Bryan, L. C., & Gast, D. L. (2000). Teaching on-task and on-schedule behaviors to high-functioning children with autism via picture activity schedules. *Journal of Autism and Developmental Disorders, 30,* 553–567.

Buggey, T. (2005). Video self-modeling applications with student with autism spectrum disorder in a small private school setting. *Focus on Autism and Other Developmental Disabilities, 20,* 52–63.

Buggey, T. (2007). A picture is worth . . . Video self-modeling applications at school and home. *Journal of Positive Behavior Interventions, 9,* 151–158.

Buysse, V., & Bailey, D. B. (1993). Behavioral and developmental outcomes in young children with disabilities in integrated and segregated settings: A review of comparative studies. *The Journal of Special Education, 26,* 434–461

Byrd, M. R., & Rous, B. S. (1990). *Helpful entry level skills checklist* (Rev. ed.). Lexington, KY: Child Development Centers of Bluegrass.

Capps, L., Sigman, M., & Yirmiya, N. (1996). Self-competence and emotional understanding in high-functioning children with autism. *Annual Progress in Child Psychiatry & Child Development, 7,* 260–279.

Carnine, D. W., Silbert, J., Kameenui, E. J., Tarver, S. G., & Jong, K. (2006). *Teaching struggling and at-risk readers: A direct instruction approach.* Saddle River, NJ: Prentice-Hall.

Carr, E. G. (1983). Behavioral approaches to language and communication. In E. Schopler & G. Mesibov (Eds.), *Current issues in autism, Volume III: Communication problems in autism* (pp. 37–57). New York: Plenum.

Carr, E. G., & Durand, V. M. (1985). Reducing problem behavior through functional communication training. *Journal of Applied Behavior Analysis, 25,* 777–794.

Carr, E. G., Levin, L., McConnachie, G., Carlson, J. I., Kemp, D. C., & Smith, C. E. (1994). *Communication-based intervention for problem behavior: A user's guide for producing positive change.* Baltimore: Brookes.

Carr, E. G., Levin, L., McConnachie, G., Carlson J., Kemp, D. C., Smith, C. E., et al. (1999). Comprehensive multi-situational intervention for problem behavior in the community: Long-term maintenance and social validation. *Journal of Positive Behavior Interventions, 1,* 5–25.

Carr, J. E., Nicolson, A. C., & Higbee, T. S. (2000). Evaluation of a brief multiple-stimulus preference assessment in a natural context. *Journal of Applied Behavior Analysis, 33,* 353–357.

Carta, J. J., Greenwood, C. R., & Atwater, J. (1985). *Ecobehavioral System for Complex Assessments of Preschool Environments: (ESCAPE).* Kansas City: Juniper Gardens Children's Project, Bureau of Child Research, University of Kansas.

Carta, J. J., Greenwood, C. R., Schulte, D., Arreaga-Mayer, C., & Terry, B. (1987). *The Mainstream Code for Instructional Structure and Student Academic Response (MS-CISSAR): Observer training manual.* Kansas City: Juniper Gardens Children's Project, Bureau of Child Research, University of Kansas.

Causton-Theoharis, J. N., & Malmgren, K. W. (2005). Increasing peer interactions for students with severe disabilities via paraprofessional training. *Exceptional Children, 71,* 431–444.

Chandler, L. K. (1992). Promoting children's social/survival skills as a strategy for transition to mainstreamed kindergarten programs. In S. L. Odom, S. R. McConnell, & M. McEvoy (Eds.), *Social competence of young children with disabilities* (pp. 245–276). Baltimore: Brookes.

Charlop, M. H., Kurtz, P. E., & Casey, F. G. (1990). Using aberrant behaviors as reinforcers for autistic children. *Journal of Applied Behavior Analysis, 23,* 163–181.

Charlop-Christy, M. H., Carpenter, M., LeBlanc, L. A., & Kellet, K. (2002). Using the Picture Exchange Communication System (PECS) with children with autism: Assessment of PECS acquisition, speech, social-communication behavior and problem behavior. *Journal of Applied Behavior Analysis, 25,* 213–231.

Charlop-Christy, M. H., & Daneshvar, S. (2003). Using video modeling to teach perspective taking to children with autism. *Journal of Positive Behavior Interventions, 5,* 12–21.

Charlop-Christy, M. H., & Haymes, L. K. (1998). Using objects of obsession as token reinforcers for children with autism. *Journal of Autism and Developmental Disorders, 28,* 189–197.

Charlop-Christy, M. H., & Kelso, S. E. (2003). Teaching children with autism conversational speech using a cue card/written script program. *Education and Treatment of Children, 26,* 103–127.

Cihak, D., Alberto, P. A., & Fredrick, L. D. (2007). Use of brief functional analysis and intervention evaluation in public settings. *Journal of Positive Behavior Interventions, 9,* 80–93.

Cohen, H., Amerine-Dickens, M., & Smith, T. (2006). Early intensive behavioral treatment: Replication of the UCLA model in a community setting. *Journal of Developmental and Behavioral Pediatrics, 27,* 145–155.

Conroy, M. A., Asmus, J. M., Sellers, J. A., & Ladwig, C. N. (2005). The use of an antecedent-based intervention to decrease stereotypic behavior in a general education classroom: A case study. *Focus on Autism and Other Developmental Disabilities, 20,* 223–230.

Cooper, J. O., Heron, T. E., & Heward, W. L. (2007). *Applied behavior analysis* (2nd ed.). Upper Saddle River, NJ: Prentice-Hall.

Cote, C. A., Thompson, R. H., & McKerchar, P. M. (2005). The effects of antecedent interventions and extinction on toddler's compliance during transitions. *Journal of Applied Behavior Analysis, 38,* 235–238.

Cowen, E. L., Hightower, A. D., Pedro-Carroll, J. L., Work, W. C., Wyman, P. A., & Haffey, W. G. (1996). The primary mental health project: Roots and wellsprings. In E. L. Cowen, A. D. Hightower, J. L. Pedro-Carroll, W. C. Work, P. A. Wyman, & W. G. Haffey (Eds.), *School-based prevention for children at risk: The primary mental health project* (pp. 1–14). Washington, DC: American Psychological Association.

Crow, R., & Snyder, P. (1998). Organizational behavior management in early intervention: Status and implications for research and development. *Journal of Organizational Behavior Management, 18,* 131–156.

Crozier, S., & Tincani, M. J. (2005). Using a modified social story to decrease disruptive behavior of a child with autism. *Focus on Autism and Other Developmental Disabilities, 20,* 150–157.

Davis, C. A., Brady, M. P., Williams, R. E., & Hamilton, R. (1992). The effects of high-probability requests on the acquisition and generalization of responses to requests in young children with behavior disorders. *Journal of Applied Behavior Analysis, 25,* 905–916.

Dawson, G., & Osterling, J. (1997). Early intervention in autism. In M. J. Guralnick (Ed.), *The effectiveness of early intervention* (pp. 307–326). Baltimore: Brookes.

Dean, R. D., & Siegler, R. S. (1986). Children's understanding of the attributes of life. *Journal of Experimental Child Psychology, 42,* 1–22.

Delano, M., & Snell, M. E. (2006). The effects of social stories on the social engagement of children with autism. *Journal of Positive Behavior Interventions, 8,* 29–42.

DeLeon, I. G., & Iwata, B. A. (1996). Evaluation of a multiple-stimulus presentation format for assessing reinforcers preferences. *Journal of Applied Behavior Analysis, 29,* 519–533.

Deno, S. L., (1985). Curriculum-based measurement: The emerging alternative. *Exceptional Children, 52,* 219–232.

Dooley, P., Wilczenski, F. L., & Torem, C. (2001). Using an activity schedule to smooth school transitions. *Journal of Positive Behavior Interventions, 3,* 57–61.

Doughty, S., & Anderson, C. (2006). Effects of noncontingent reinforcement and functional communication training on problem behavior and mands. *Education and Treatment of Children, 29,* 23–50.

Doyle, P. M., Wolery, M., Gast, D. L., & Ault, M. J. (1990). Use of constant time delay in small group instruction: A study of observational and incidental learning. *Journal of Special Education, 23,* 369–385.

Ducharme, J. M., & DiAdamo, C. (2005). An errorless approach to management of child noncompliance in a special education setting. *School Psychology Review, 34,* 107–115.

Ducharme, J. M., & Feldman, M. A. (1992). Comparison of staff training strategies to promote generalized teaching skills. *Journal of Applied Behavior Analysis, 25,* 165–170.

Dunlap, G., Dyer, K., & Koegel, R. L. (1983). Autistic self-stimulation and intertrial interval duration. *American Journal of Mental Deficiency, 88,* 194–202.

Dunlap, G., Hieneman, M., Knoster, T., Fox, L., Anderson, J., & Albin, R. W. (2000). Essential elements of in-service training in positive behavior support. *Journal of Positive Behavior Interventions, 2,* 22–32.

Dunn, L. M. (1968). Special education for the mildly retarded: Is much of it justified? *Exceptional Children, 35,* 5–22.

Durand, V. M. (1990). *Severe behavior problems: A functional communication training approach; Treatment manuals for practitioners.* New York: Guildford Press.

Durand, V. M. (1999). Functional communication training using assistive devices: Recruiting natural communities of reinforcement. *Journal of Applied Behavior Analysis, 32,* 247–267.

Durand, V. M., & Crimmins, D. B. (1988). Identifying the variables maintaining self-injurious behavior. *Journal of Autism and Developmental Disorders, 18,* 99–117.

Durand, V. M., & Crimmins, D. (1988). *Motivation assessment scale.* Topeka, KS: Monaco.

Durand, V. M., & Merges, E. (2001). Functional communication training: A contemporary behavior analytic intervention for problem behaviors. *Focus on Autism and Other Developmental Disabilities, 16,* 110–119.

Dworet, D., & Bennett, S. (2002). The view from the North: Special education in Canada. *Teaching Exceptional Children, 34,* 22–27.

Dyer, K., Dunlap, G., & Winterling, V. (1990). Effects of choice making on the serious problem behaviors of students with severe handicaps. *Journal of Applied Behavior Analysis, 23,* 515–524.

Education for All Handicapped Children Act of 1975, 20 U.S.C. § 1400 *et seq.* (1975)

Eikeseth, S., & Jahr, E. (2001). The UCLA reading and writing program: An evaluation of the beginning stages. *Research in Developmental Disabilities, 22,* 289–307.

Eikeseth, S., Smith, T., Jahr, E., & Eldevik, S. (2002). Intensive behavioral treatment at school for 4- to 7-year-old children with autism. *Behavior Modification, 26,* 49-68.

Eikeseth, S., Smith, T., Jahr, E., & Eldevik, S. (2007). Outcome for children with autism who began intensive behavioral treatment between ages 4 and 7: A comparison controlled study. *Behavior Modification, 31,* 264–278.

Elliott, D. S., Hamburg, B. A., & Williams, K. R. (1998). *Violence in American schools.* England: Cambridge.

Elliott, S. N., Witt, J. C., & Kratochwill, T. R. (1991). Selecting, implementing, and evaluating classroom interventions. In G. Stoner, M. R. Shinn, & H. M. Walker (Eds.), *Interventions for achievement and behavior problems* (pp. 99–135). Silver Spring, MD: National Association of School Psychologists.

English, K., Goldstein, H., Shafer, K., & Kaczmarck, L. (1997). Promoting interactions among preschoolers with and without disabilities: Effects of a buddy system skill training program. *Exceptional Children, 63,* 229–243.

Ferrara, C., & Hill, S. D. (1980). The responsiveness of autistic children to the predictability of social and nonsocial toys. *Journal of Autism and Developmental Disorders, 10,* 51–57.

Fimian, M. J., & Santoro, T. M. (1983). Sources and manifestations of occupational stress as reported by full-time special education teachers. *Exceptional Children, 49,* 540–543.

Fisher, N., & Happe, F. (2005). A training study of theory of mind and executive function in children with autistic spectrum disorders. *Journal of Autism and Developmental Disorders, 35,* 757–771.

Fombonne, E. (2003). Epidemiological surveys of autism and other pervasive developmental disorders: An update. *Journal of Autism and Developmental Disorders, 33,* 265–284.

Forehand, R., Middlebrook, J., Rogers, T., & Steffe, M. (1983). Dropping out of parent training. *Behaviour Research and Therapy, 21,* 663–668.

Fox, L., Benito, N., & Dunlap, G. (2002). Early intervention with families of young children with autism and behavior problems. In J. M. Lucyshyn, G. Dunlap, & R. W. Albin (Eds.), *Families and positive behavior support: Addressing problem behavior in family contexts* (pp. 251–269). Baltimore: Brookes.

Fox, L., Dunlap, G., & Philbrick, L. A. (1997). Providing individualized supports to young children with autism and their families. *Journal of Early Intervention, 21,* 1–14.

Frea, W. D., Arnold, C. L., & Vittiberga, G. L. (2001). A demonstration of the effects of augmentative communication on the extreme aggressive behavior of a child with autism within an integrated preschool setting. *Journal of Positive Behavior Interventions, 3,* 194–198.

Freeman, R., Smith, C., Zarcone, J., Kimbrough, P., Tieghi-Benet, M., Wickham, D., et al. (2005). Building a statewide plan for embedding positive behavior support in human service organizations. *Journal of Positive Behavior Interventions, 7,* 109–119.

Freeman, S. F. N., & Alkin, M. C. (2000). Academic and social attainment of children with mental retardation in general and special education settings. *Remedial and Special Education, 21*, 2–18.

Ganz, J. B., & Simpson, R. L. (2004). Effects on communicative requesting and speech development of the Picture Exchange Communication System in children with characteristics of autism. *Journal of Autism and Developmental Disorders, 34*, 395–409.

Garrison-Harrell, L., Kamps, D., & Kravits, T. (1997). The effects of peer network on social-communicative behaviors of students with autism. *Focus on Autism and Other Developmental Disabilities, 12*, 241–257.

Gevers, C., Clifford, P., Mager, M., & Boer, F. (2006). Brief Report: A theory-of-mind-based social-cognitive training program for school-aged children with pervasive developmental disorders: An open study of its effectiveness. *Journal of Autism and Developmental Disorders, 36*, 567–571.

Giangreco, M. F., & Broer, S. M. (2005). Questionable utilization of paraprofessionals in inclusive schools: Are we addressing symptoms or causes? *Focus on Autism and Other Developmental Disabilities, 20*, 10–26.

Gilbert, G. H., Agran, M., Hughes, C., & Wehmeyer, M. (2001). The effect of peer delivered self-monitoring strategies on the participation of students with severe disabilities in general education classrooms. *Journal for the Association for Persons with Severe Handicaps, 26*, 25–36.

Gillberg, C. (1999). Neurodevelopmental processes and psychological functioning in autism. *Development and Psychopathology, 11*, 567–587.

Goldstein, H. (2002). Communication interventions for individuals with autism: A review of treatment efficiency. *Journal of Autism and Developmental Disorders, 32*, 373–396.

Goldstein, H., & Cisar, C. L. (1992). Promoting interaction during social play: Teaching scripts to typical preschoolers and classmates with disabilities. *Journal of Applied Behavior Analysis, 25*, 265–280.

Graden, J. L., Casey, A., & Bonstrom, O. (1985). Implementing a prereferral intervention system: Part II. The data. *Exceptional Children, 41*, 487–496.

Gray, C. A. (1998). Social stories and comic strip conversations with students with Asperger syndrome and high-functioning autism. In E. Schopler, G. B. Mesibov, & L. J. Kunce (Eds.), *Asperger syndrome or high-functioning autism?* (pp. 167–198). New York: Plenum.

Gray, C. A. (2000). *Writing social stories with Carol Gray.* Arlington, TX: Future Horizons.

Green, C. W., Reid, D. H., White, C. K., Halford, R. C., Brittain, D. P., & Gardner, S. M. (1988). Identifying reinforcers for persons with profound handicaps: Staff opinion versus systematic assessment of preferences. *Journal of Applied Behavior Analysis, 21*, 31–43.

Green, G. (2001). Behavior analytic instruction for learners with autism: Advances in stimulus control technology. *Focus on Autism and Other Developmental Disabilities, 16*, 72–85.

Greenwood, C. R., Carta, J. J., & Dawson, H. (2000). Ecobehavioral assessment systems software (EBASS): A system for observation in education settings. In T. Thompson, D. Felce, & F. J. Symons (Eds.), *Behavioral observation: Technology and applications in developmental disabilities* (pp. 229–252). Baltimore: Brookes.

Greenwood, C. R., Carta, J. J., Kamps, D., & Arreaga-Mayer, C. (1990). Ecobehavioral analysis of classroom instruction. In S. R. Schroeder (Ed.), *Ecobehavioral analysis and developmental disabilities: The twenty-first century* (pp. 33–63). New York: Springer-Verlag.

Greenwood, C. R., Carta, J. J., Kamps, D., Terry, B., & Delquadri, J. (1994). Development and validation of standard classroom observation systems for school practitioners: Ecobehavioral assessment systems software (EBASS). *Exceptional Children, 61*, 197–210.

Greenwood, C. R., Dinwiddie, G., Terry, B., Wade, L., Stanley, S. O., Thibadeau, S., & Delquadri, J. (1984). Teacher- versus peer-mediated instruction: An ecobehavioral analysis of achievement outcomes. *Journal of Applied Behavior Analysis, 17*, 521–538.

Greenwood, C. R., Hops, H., Walker, H. M., Guild, J. J., Stokes, J., Young, K. R., et al. (1979). Standardized classroom management program: Social validation and replication studies in Utah and Oregon. *Journal of Applied Behavior Analysis, 12,* 235–253.

Greenwood, C. R., Walker, D., & Utley, C. A. (2002). Relationships between social-communicative skills and life achievements. In H. Goldstein, L. A. Kaczmarek, & K. M. English (Eds.), *Promoting social communication: Children with developmental disabilities from birth to adolescence* (pp. 345–370). Baltimore: Brookes.

Gresham, F. M. (1998). Social skills training with children: Social learning and applied behavioral analytic approaches. In T. S. Watson & F. M. Gresham (Eds.), *Handbook of child behavior therapy: Issues in clinical child psychology* (pp. 475–497). New York: Plenum.

Guevremont, D. C., Osnes, P. G., & Stokes, T. F. (1986). Preparation for effective self-regulation: The development of generalized verbal control. *Journal of Applied Behavior Analysis, 19,* 99–104.

Guralnick, M. (1990). Social competence and early intervention. *Journal of Early Intervention, 14,* 3–14.

Guralnick, M. J. (2001). Framework for change in early childhood inclusion. In M. J. Guralnick (Ed.), *The effectiveness of early intervention* (pp. 1–35). Baltimore: Brookes.

Hagopian, L. P., Fisher, W. W., & Legacy, S. M. (1994). Schedule effects of noncontingent reinforcement on attention-maintained destructive behavior in identical quadruplets. *Journal of Applied Behavior Analysis, 27,* 317–325.

Hall, R. V., Lund, D., & Jackson, D. (1968). Effects of teacher attention on study behavior. *Journal of Applied Behavior Analysis, 1,* 1–12.

Harris, S. L. (1989). Training parents of children with autism: An update on models. *The Behavior Therapist, 12,* 219–221.

Harris, S. L., Handleman, J. S., Kristoff, B., Bass, L., & Gordon, R. (1990). Changes in language development among autistic and peer children in segregated and integrated preschool settings. *Journal of Autism and Developmental Disorders, 20,* 23–31.

Harrower, J. K., & Dunlap, G. (2001). Including children with autism in general education classrooms: A review of effective strategies. *Behavior Modification, 25,* 762–784.

Harry, B., Rueda, R., & Kalyanpur, M. (1999). Cultural reciprocity in sociocultural perspective: Adapting the normalization principle for family collaboration. *Exceptional Children, 66,* 123–136.

Hart, B., & Risley, T. R. (1968). Establishing the use of descriptive adjectives in the spontaneous speech of disadvantaged preschool children. *Journal of Applied Behavior Analysis, 1,* 109–120.

Hauck, M., Fein, D., Waterhouse, L., & Feinstein, C. (1995). Social initiations by children with autism to adults and other children. *Journal of Autism and Developmental Disorders, 25,* 579–595.

Hauser-Cram, P., Warfield, M. E., Shonkoff, J. P., & Krauss, M. W. (2001). Children with disabilities: A longitudinal study of child development and parent well-being. *Monographs of the Society for Research in Child Development, 66,* 1–131.

Hawkins, R. P., & Dobes, V. A. (1975). Reliability scores that delude: An Alice in Wonderland trip through the misleading characteristics of inter-observer agreement scores in interval recording. In E. Ramp & G. Semb (Eds.), *Behavior analysis: Areas of research and application* (pp. 359–376). Englewood Cliffs, NJ: Prentice-Hall.

Henderson, J. M., Gardner, N., Kaiser, A., & Riley, A. (1993). Evaluation of a social interaction coaching program in an integrated day-care setting. *Journal of Applied Behavior Analysis, 26,* 213–225.

Hill, E. L. (2004). Evaluating the theory of executive dysfunction in autism. *Developmental Review, 24,* 189–233.

Hollingsworth, L. S. (1923). *The psychology of subnormal children.* New York: Macmillan.

Holmes, N., Hemsley, R., Rickett, J., & Likierman, H. (1982). Parents as cotherapists: Their perceptions of a home-based behavioral treatment for autistic children. *Journal of Autism and Developmental Disorders, 12,* 331–342.

Horner, R. H. (2000). Positive behavior supports. *Focus on Autism and Other Developmental Disabilities, 15,* 97–105.

Horner, R. H., Carr, E. G., Strain, P. S., Todd, A. W., & Reed, H. K. (2002). Problem behavior interventions for young children with autism: A research synthesis. *Journal of Autism and Developmental Disorders, 32,* 423–446.

Horner, R. H., & Day, H. M. (1991). The effects of response efficiency on functionally equivalent competing behaviors. *Journal of Applied Behavior Analysis, 24,* 719–732.

Horner, R. H., Day, H. M., & Day, J. B. (1997). *Using neutralizing routines to reduce problem behaviors. Journal of Applied Behavior Analysis, 30,* 601–614.

Horner, R. H., Day, H. M., Sprague, J. R., & O'Brien, M. (1991). Interspersed requests: A nonaversive procedure for reducing self-injury during instruction. *Journal of Applied Behavior Analysis, 24,* 265–278.

Horner, R. H., Sprague, J., & Wilcox, B. (1982). Constructing general case programs for community activities. In B. Wilcox & G. T. Bellamy (Eds.), *Design of high school programs for severely handicapped students* (pp. 61–98). Baltimore: Brookes.

Horner, R. H., Vaughn, B. J., & Ard, W. R. J. (1996). The relationship between setting events and problem behavior In L. K. Koegel, R. L. Koegel, & G. Dunlap (Eds.), *Positive behavior support: Including people with difficult behavior in the community* (pp. 381–402). Baltimore: Brookes.

Howard, J. S., Sparkman, C. R., Cohen, H. G., Green, G. F., & Stanislaw, H. (2005). A comparison of internal behavior analytic and eclectic treatment of young children with autism. *Research in Developmental Disabilities, 26,* 359–385.

Howlin, P., Goode, S., Hutton, J., & Rutter, M. (2004). Adult outcome for children with autism. *Journal of Child Psychology and Psychiatry, 45,* 212–229.

Hoyson, M., Jamieson, B. V., Strain, P. S., & Smith, B. J. (1998). Duck, duck–colors and words: Early childhood inclusion. *Teaching Exceptional Children, 2,* 66–71.

Hughes, C., Copeland, S. R., Agran, M., Wehmeyer, M. L., Rodi, M. S., & Presley, J. A. (2002). Using self-monitoring to improve performance in general education high school classes. *Education and Training in Mental Retardation and Developmental Disabilities, 37*(3), 262–272.

Hundert, J. (1982). Training teachers in generalized writing of behavior modification programs for multihandicapped deaf children. *Journal of Applied Behavior Analysis, 15,* 111–122.

Hundert, J. (1995). *Enhancing social competence in young students: School-based approaches.* Austin, TX: PRO-ED.

Hundert, J. (2007). Training classroom and resource preschool teachers to develop inclusive class interventions for children with disabilities: Generalization to a new intervention target. *Journal of Positive Behavioral Interventions, 9,* 157–173.

Hundert, J., Boyle, M., Cunningham, C., Duku, E. C., Heale, J., McDonald, J., et al. (1999). Helping children adjust: A tri-ministry study II. Program effects. *Journal of Child Psychology and Psychiatry, 40,* 1061–1073.

Hundert, J., & Hopkins, B. (1992). Training supervisors in a collaborative team approach to promote peer interaction of children with disabilities in integrated preschools. *Journal of Applied Behavior Analysis, 25,* 385–400.

Hundert, J., Mahoney, B., & Hopkins, B. (1993). The relationship between resource teacher and classroom teacher behaviors and the peer interaction of children with disabilities in integrated preschool. *Topics in Early Childhood Special Education, 13,* 328–343.

Hundert, J., Mahoney, B., Mundy, F., & Vernon, M. L. (1998). A descriptive analysis of developmental and social gains of children with severe disabilities in segregated and integrated preschools in Southern Ontario. *Early Childhood Research Quarterly, 13,* 49–65.

Hundert, J., & Taylor, L. (1993). Classwide promotion of social competence in young students. *Exceptionality Education Canada, 3,* 79–10l.

Hundert, J., & van Delft, S. (in press). Teaching children with autism to answer inferential "why"-questions. *Focus on Autism and Other Developmental Disabilities.*

Individuals With Disabilities Education Act of 1990, 20 U.S.C. § 1400 *et seq.* (1990)

Individuals With Disabilities Education Act of 1990, 20 U.S.C. § 1400 *et seq.* (1990) (amended 1997)

Individuals With Disabilities Education Improvement Act of 2004, 20 U.S.C. § 1400 *et seq.* (2004)

Ingersoll, B., & Dvortcsak, A. (2006). Including parent training in the early childhood special education curriculum for children with autism spectrum disorders. *Journal of Positive Behavior Interventions, 8,* 79–87.

Ivey, M. I., Heflin, & Alberto, P. (2004). The use of social stories to promote independent behaviors in novel events for children with PDD-NOS. *Focus on Autism and Other Developmental Disabilities, 19,* 164–176.

Iwata, B. A., Dorsey, M. F., Slifer, K. J., Bauman, K. E., & Richman, G. S., (1982). Toward a functional analysis of self-injury. *Analysis and Intervention in Developmental Disabilities, 2,* 3–20.

Iwata, B. A., Pace, G. M., Kalsher, M. J., Cowdery, G. E., & Cataldo, M. F. (1990). Experimental analysis and extinction of self-injurious escape behavior. *Journal of Applied Behavior Analysis, 32,* 11–27.

Iwata, B. A., & Worsdell, A. S. (2005). Implications of functional analysis methodology for the design of intervention programs. *Exceptionality, 13,* 25–34.

Jacobson, J. W. (2000). Early intervention behavioral intervention: Emergence of a consumer-driven service model. *The Behavior Analyst, 23,* 149–171.

Jahr, E. (2001). Teaching children with autism to answer novel *wh*-questions by utilizing a multiple exemplar strategy. *Research in Developmental Disabilities, 22,* 407–423.

Johnson, J., McDonnell, J., Holzwarth, V. N., & Hunter, K. (2004). The efficacy of embedded instruction for students with developmental disabilities enrolled in general education classes. *Journal of Positive Behavior Interventions, 6,* 214–227.

Johnson, J. W., & McDonnell, J. (2004). An exploratory study of the implementation of embedded instruction by general educators with students with developmental disabilities. *Education and Treatment of Children, 27,* 46-63.

Johnson, S. C., Meyer, L., & Taylor, B. A. (1996). Supported inclusion. In C. Maurice, G. Green, & S. C. Luce (Eds.), *Behavioral intervention for young children with autism* (pp. 331–342). Austin, TX: PRO-ED.

Johnston, J. M., Foxx, R. M., Jacobson, J. W., Green, G., and Mulick, J. A. (2006). Positive behavior support and applied behavior analysis. *The Behavior Analyst, 29,* 51–74.

Johnston, S. S., McDonnell, A. P., & Magnavito, C. N. (2003). Teaching functional communication skills using augmentative and assistive communication in inclusive settings. *Journal of Early Intervention, 25,* 263–280.

Jones, T. M., Garlow, J. A., Turnbull, H. R., & Barber, P. A. (1996). Family empowerment in a family support program. In G. H. S. Singer, L. E. Powers, & A. L. Olson (Eds.), *Redefining family support: Innovations in public-private partnerships* (pp. 87–112). Baltimore: Brookes.

Kamps, D. M., Leonard, B. R., Vernon, S., Dugan, E. P., Delquadri, J. C., Gershan, B., et al. (1992). Teaching social skills to students with autism to increase peer interactions in an integrated first-grade classroom. *Journal of Applied Behavior Analysis, 25,* 281–288.

Kamps, D. M., Potucek, J., Gonzalez-Lopez, A. G., Kravits, T., & Kemmerer, K. (1997). The use of peer networks across multiple settings to improve social interaction for students with autism. *The Journal of Behavioral Education, 7,* 335–357.

Kamps, D., Walker, D., Maher, J., & Rotholz, J. (1992). Academic and environmental effects of small group arrangements in classrooms for students with autism and other developmental disabilities. *Journal of Autism and Developmental Disorders, 22,* 277–293.

Kasari, C. (2002). Assessing changes in early intervention programs for children with autism. *Journal of Autism and Developmental Disabilities, 72,* 447–461.

Kemp, C., & Carter, M. (2005). Identifying skills for promoting successful inclusion in kindergarten. *Journal of Intellectual and Developmental Disabilities, 30,* 31–44.

Kennedy, C. H., & Itkonen, T. (1993). Effect of setting events on the problem behavior of students with severe disabilities. *Journal of Applied Behavior Analysis, 26,* 321–328.

Kennedy, C. H., Long, T., Jolivette, K., Cox, J., Tang, J. C., & Thompson, T. (2001). Facilitating general education participation for students with behavior problems by linking positive behavior supports and person-centered planning. *Journal of Emotional and Behavioral Disorders, 9,* 161–171.

Kern, L., & Dunlap, G. (1998). Curriculum modifications to promote desirable classroom behavior. In J. K. Luiselli & M. J. Cameron (Eds.), *Antecedent control* (pp. 289–308). Baltimore: Brookes.

Kern, L., Mantegna, M. E., Vorndran, C. M., Bailin, D., & Hilt, A. (2001). Choice of task sequence to reduce problem behaviors. *Journal of Positive Behavior Interventions, 3,* 3–10.

Kern, L., Vordran, C. M., Hilt, A., Ringdahl, J. E., Adelman, B. E., & Dunlap, G. (1998). Choice as an intervention to improve behavior: A review of the literature. *Journal of Behavioral Education, 8,* 151–158.

Killu, K., Sainato, D. M., Davis, C. A., Ospelt, H., & Paul, J. N. (1998). The effects of high-probability requests sequences on preschoolers' compliance and disruptive behavior. *Journal of Behavioral Education, 8,* 347–368.

Kimball, J. W., Kinney, E. M., Taylor, B. A., & Stromer, R. (2004). Video enhanced activity schedules for teaching social skills. *Education and Treatment of Children, 27,* 280–898.

Kiresuk, T., & Lund, S. (1978). Goal attainment scaling. In C. C. Attkisson, W. A. Hargreaves, M. J. Horowitz, & J. Sorensen (Eds.), *Evaluation of human service programs* (pp. 123–153). New York: Academic Press.

Kiresuk, T., & Sherman, R. (1968). Goal attainment scaling: A general method of evaluating comprehensive community mental health programs. *Community Mental Health Journal, 4,* 443–453.

Kluth, P. (2003). *You're going to love this kid!* Baltimore: Brookes.

Knoch, H., & Mirenda, P. (2003). Social story interventions for young children with autism spectrum disorders. *Focus on Autism and Other Developmental Disorders, 18,* 219–227.

Koegel, L. K., Harrower, J. K., & Koegel, R. L. (1999). Support for children with developmental disabilities in full inclusion classrooms through self-management. *Journal of Positive Behavior Interventions, 1,* 26–34.

Koegel, L. K., Koegel, R. L., Frea, W. D., & Fredeen, R. M. (2001). Identifying early intervention targets for children with autism in inclusive classroom settings. *Behavior Modification, 25,* 745–761.

Koegel, L. K., Koegel, R. L., Frea, W., & Green-Hopkins, I. (2003). Priming as a method of coordinating educational services for students with autism. *Language, Speech, and Hearing Services in School, 34,* 228–235.

Koegel, L. K., Koegel, R. L., Harrower, J. K., & Carter, C. M. (1999). Pivotal response intervention I: Overview of approach. *Journal of the Association for Persons With Severe Handicaps, 24,* 174–185.

Koegel, L. K., Koegel, R. L., Hurley, C., & Frea, W. D. (1992). Improving social skills and disruptive behavior in children with autism through self-management. *Journal of Applied Behavior Analysis, 25,* 341–353.

Koegel, L. K., Koegel, R. L., Kellegrew, D., & Mullen, K. (1996). Parent education for prevention and reduction of severe problem behaviors. In L. K. Koegel, R. L. Koegel, & G. Dunlap (Eds.), *Positive behavioral support: Including people with difficult behavior in the community* (pp. 3–30). Baltimore: Brookes.

Koegel, L. K., Koegel, R. L., & Parks, D. R. (1992). *How to teach self-management to people with severe disabilities: A training manual.* Santa Barbara: University of California.

Koegel, R.L., Camarata, S., Koegel, L. K., Ben-Tall, A., & Smith, A. E. (1998). Increasing speech intelligibility in children with autism. *Journal of Autism and Developmental Disabilities, 28*, 241–251.

Koegel, R. L., Glahn, T. J., & Nieminen, G. S. (1978). Generalization of parent-training results. *Journal of Applied Behavior Analysis, 11*, 95–109.

Koegel, R. L., & Koegel, L. K. (1990). Extended reductions in stereotypic behavior of students with autism through a self-management treatment package. *Journal of Applied Behavior Analysis, 23*, 119–127.

Koegel, R. L., Openden, D., Fredeen, R., & Kern-Koegel, L. (2006). The basic pivotal response treatment. In R. L. Koegel & L. K. Koegel (Eds.), *Pivotal response treatments for autism* (pp. 3–30). Baltimore: Brookes.

Koegel, R. L., Russo, D. C., & Rincover, A. (1977). Assessing and training teachers in the generalized use of behavior modification with autistic children. *Journal of Applied Behavior Analysis, 10*, 197–205.

Koegel, R. L., Schreibman, L., Good, A., Cerniglia, L., Murphy, C., & Koegel, L. K. (1989). *How to teach pivotal behaviors to children with autism: A training manual.* Santa Barbara: University of California.

Koegel, R. L., Schreibman, L. E., Johnson, J., O'Neill, R. E., & Dunlap, G. (1984). Collateral effects of parent training on families with autistic children. In R. F. Dangel & R. A. Polster (Eds.), *Parent training: Foundations of research and practice* (pp. 358–378). New York: Guilford.

Koegel, R. L., Schreibman, L., O'Neill, R. E., & Burke, J. C. (1983). The personality and family-interaction characteristics of parents of autistic children. *Journal of Consulting and Clinical Psychology, 51*, 683–692.

Kohler, F., Anthony, L., Steighner, S. A., & Hoyson, M. (2001). Teaching social interaction skills in the integrated preschool: An examination of naturalistic tactics. *Topics in Early Childhood Special Education, 21*, 93–103.

Krantz, P. J., & McClannahan, L. E. (1998). Social interaction skills for children with autism: A script-fading procedure for beginning readers. *Journal of Applied Behavior Analysis, 31*, 191–202.

Krantz, P., Zalenski, S., Hall, L., Fenske, E., & McClannahan, L. (1981). *Teaching complex language to autistic children. Analysis and Interventions in Developmental Disabilities, 1*, 259–297.

Laushey, K. M., & Heflin, L. J. (2000). Enhancing social skills of kindergarten children with autism through the training of multiple peers as tutors. *Journal of Autism and Developmental Disorders, 30*, 183–193.

Leaf, R., & McEachin, J. (1999). *A work in progress: Behavior management strategies and a curriculum for intensive behavioral treatment of autism.* New York: DLR Books.

LeBlanc, L. A., & Coates, A. M. (2003). Using video modeling and reinforcement to teach perspective-taking skills to children with autism. *Journal of Applied Behavior Analysis, 36*, 253–257.

Lefebvre, D., & Strain, P. (1989). Effects of a group contingency on the frequency of social interactions among autistic and nonhandicapped preschool children: Making LRE efficacious. *Journal of Early Intervention, 13*, 329–341.

Lerman, D. C., Vorndran, C. M., Addison, L., & Kuhn, S. C. (2004). Preparing teachers in evidence-based practices for young children with autism. *School Psychology Review, 33*, 415–526.

Lipsitz, A., Kallmey, K., Ferguson, M., & Abas, A. (1989). The effects of observational feedback on treatment integrity in school-based behavioral consultation. *School Psychology Quarterly, 12*, 316–326.

Lohrmann, S., Talerico, J., & Dunlap, G. (2004). Anchor the boat: A classwide intervention to reduce problem behavior. *Journal of Positive Behavior Interventions, 6*, 113–120.

Lord, C., & McGee, J. P. (Eds.). (2001). *Educating children with autism*. Washington, DC: National Research Council.

Lord, C., & Rutter, M. (1994). Autism and pervasive development disorders. In M. Rutter, E. Taylor, & L. Herso (Eds.), *Child and adolescent psychiatry: Modern approaches* (3rd ed., pp. 569–593). Oxford: Blackwell.

Lovaas, O. I. (1987). Behavioral treatment and normal educational and intellectual functioning in young autistic children. *Journal of Consulting and Clinical Psychology, 55,* 3–9.

Lovaas, O. I. (2003). *Teaching individuals with developmental delays: Basic intervention techniques.* Austin, TX: PRO-ED.

Lovaas, O. I., Koegel, R. L., & Schreibman, L. (1979). Stimulus overselectivity in autism: A review of literature. *Psychological Bulletin, 86,* 1236–1254.

Lovaas, O. I., Koegel. R., Simmons, J. Q., & Long, J. S. (1973). Some generalization and follow-up measures on autistic children in behavior therapy. *Journal of Applied Behavior Analysis, 6,* 131–166.

Lovaas, O. I., Litrownik, A., & Mann, R. (1971). Response latencies to auditory stimuli in autistic children engaged in self-stimulatory behavior. *Behaviour Research and Therapy, 9,* 39–49.

Lucyshyn, E., Blumberg, R., & Kayser, A. T. (2000). Improving the quality of support to families of children with severe behavior problems in the first decade of the new millennium. *Journal of Positive Behavior Interventions, 2,* 133–115.

Luiselli, J. K. (1994). Effects of noncontingent sensory reinforcement on stereotypic behaviors in a child with posttraumatic neurological impairment. *Journal of Behaviour Therapy and Experimental Psychiatry, 25,* 325–330.

Maag, J. W., & Katsiyannis, A. (2006). Behavioral intervention plans: Legal and practical considerations for students with emotional and behavioral disorders. *Behavioral Disorders, 31,* 384–362.

MacDonald, R., Clark, M., Garrigan, E., & Vangala, M. (2005). Using video modeling to teach pretend play to children with autism. *Behavioral Interventions, 20,* 225–238.

MacDuff, G. S., Krantz, P. J., & McClannahan, L. E. (1993). Teaching children with autism to use photographic activity schedule: Maintenance and generalization of complex response chains. *Journal of Applied Behavior Analysis, 26,* 89–97.

Maloney, M., Brearley, L., & Preece, J. (2001). *Teach your children to read well.* Belleville, ON: QLC Educational Services.

Mancina, C., Tankersley, M., Kamps, D., Kravits, T., & Parrett, J. (2000). Brief report: Reduction of inappropriate vocalization for a child with autism using a self-management treatment program. *Journal of Autism and Developmental Disabilities, 30,* 599–606.

Mantzicopoulos, P. (2005). Conflictual relationships between kindergarten children and their teachers: Associations with child and classroom context variables. *Journal of School Psychology, 43,* 425–442.

Marks, S. U., Schrader, C., & Levine, M. (1999). Paraeducator experiences in inclusive settings: Helping, hovering, or holding their own? *Exceptional Children, 65,* 315–328.

Maurice, C. (1994). *Let me hear your voice: A family's triumph over autism.* New York: Knopf.

Maurice, C., Green, G., & Luce, S. (Eds.). (1996). *Behavioral intervention for young children with autism.* Austin, TX: PRO-ED.

McClannahan, L. E., & Krantz, P. J. (1999). *Activity schedules for children with autism: Teaching independent behavior.* Bethesda, MD: Woodbine.

McConnell, S. R. (2002). Interventions to facilitate social interaction for young children with autism: Review of available research and recommendations for educational intervention and future research. *Journal of Autism and Developmental Disorders, 32,* 351–372.

McConnell, S. R., McEvoy, M. A., & Odom, S. L. (1992). Implementation of social competence interventions in early special education classes. In S. L. Odom, S. R. McConnell, & M. A. McEvoy (Eds.), *Social competence of young children with disabilities: Issues and strategies for intervention* (pp. 277–306). Baltimore: Brookes.

McEachin, J. J., Smith, T., & Lovaas, O. I. (1993). Long-term outcome for children with autism who received early intensive behavioral treatment. *American Journal of Mental Retardation, 97,* 359–372.

McGee, G. G., Almeida, M. C., Sulzer-Azaroff, B., & Feldman, R. S. (1992). Promoting reciprocal interactions via peer incidental teaching. *Journal of Applied Behavior Analysis, 25,* 117–126.

McGee, G. G., Krantz, P. J., Mason, D., & McClannahan, L. E. (1983). A modified incidental teaching procedure for autistic youth: Acquisition and generalization of receptive object labels. *Journal of Applied Behavior Analysis, 16,* 329–338.

McGee, G. G., Krantz, P. J., & McClannahan, L. E. (1985). The facilitative effects of incidental teaching on preposition use by autistic children. *Journal of Applied Behavior Analysis, 18,* 17–31.

McGee, G. G., Morrier, M. J., & Daly, T. (1999). An incidental teaching approach to early intervention for toddlers with autism. *Journal of the Association for Persons with Severe Handicaps, 24,* 133–146.

McLaughlin, M. J., Dyson, A., Nagle, K., Thurlow, M., Rouse, M., Hardman, M., et al. (2006). Cross-cultural perspectives on the classification of children with disabilities: Part II. Implementing classification systems in schools. *The Journal of Special Education, 40,* 46–58.

Mesibov, G. B., Browder, D. M., & Kirkland, C. (2002). Using individualized schedules as a component of positive behavioral support for students with developmental disabilities. *Journal of Positive Behavior Intervention, 4,* 73–79.

Michael, J. (1988). Establishing operations and the mand. *Analysis of Verbal Behavior, 6,* 3–9.

Mills, P. E., Cole, K. N., Jenkins, J. R., & Dale, P. S. (1998). Effects of differing levels of inclusion on preschoolers with disabilities. *Exceptional Children, 65,* 79–90.

Minshew, N. J., Goldstein, G., & Siegel, D. J. (1995). Speech and language in high-functioning autistic individuals. *Neuropsychology, 9,* 255–261.

Miranda-Linné, F., & Melin, L. (1992). Acquisition, generalization and spontaneous use of color adjectives: A comparison of incidental teaching and traditional discrete-trial procedures for children with autism. *Research in Developmental Disabilities, 13,* 191–210.

Moes, D. R. (1998). Integrating choice-making opportunities within teacher-assigned academic tasks to facilitate the performance of children with autism. *The Journal of the Association for Persons with Severe Handicaps, 23,* 319–328.

Moes, D. R., & Frea, W. D. (2000). Using family context to inform intervention planning for the treatment of a child with autism. *Journal of Positive Behavior Interventions, 2,* 40–46.

Moore, M., & Calvert, S. (2000). Brief report: Vocabulary acquisition for children with autism; Teacher or computer instruction. *Journal of Autism and Developmental Disorders, 30,* 359–362.

Moore, J. W., Edwards, R. P., Sterling-Turner, H. E., Riley, J., DuBard, M., & McGeorge, A. (2002). Teacher acquisition of functional analysis methodology. *Journal of Applied Behavior Analysis, 35,* 73–77.

Moriarty, B. (1974). Successful goal planning with the mentally disabled. *Social and Rehabilitation Record, 1,* 29–31.

Morrison, L., Kamps, D., Garcia, J., & Parker D. (2001). Peer mediation and monitoring strategies to improve interactions and social skills for students with autism. *Journal of Positive Interventions, 3,* 237–250.

Morrison, R. S., Sainato, D. M., Benchaaban, D., & Endo, S. (2002). Increasing play skills of children with autism using activity schedules and correspondence training. *Journal of Early Intervention, 25,* 58–72.

Mundschenk, N. A., & Sasso, G. M. (1995). Assessing sufficient exemplars for students with autism. *Behavioral Disorders, 21,* 62–78.

National Research Council. Committee on Education and Interventions for Children with Autism. Division of Behavioral and Social Sciences and Education. (2001). *Educating children with autism.* Washington, DC: National Academy Press.

Neef, N. A., Iwata, B. A., & Page, T. J. (1977). The effects of known-item interspersal on acquisition and retention of spelling and sight reading words. *Journal of Applied Behavior Analysis, 10,* 738.

New York State Department of Health, Early Intervention Program. (1999). *Clinical practice guideline: Guideline technical report; Autism/pervasive development disorders, assessment and intervention for young children* (ages 0–3 years) (Tech. Rep. No. 4217). Albany: Author.

Newman, B., Tuntigian, L., Ryan, C. S., & Reinecke, D. R. (1997). Self-management of a DRO procedure by three students with autism. *Behavioral Interventions, 12,* 149–156.

Nickopoulos, C. K., & Keenan, M. (2003). Promoting social initiation in children with autism using video modeling. *Behavioral Interventions, 18,* 86–108.

Noell, G. H., Witt, J. C., LaFleur, L. H., Mortenson, B. P., Ranier, D. D., & LeVelle, J. (2000). Increasing intervention implementation in general education following consultation: A comparison of two follow-up strategies. *Journal of Applied Behavior Analysis, 33,* 271–284.

Noell, G. H., Witt, J. C., Slider, N. J., Connell, J. E., Gatti, S. L., Williams, K. L., et al. (2005). Treatment implementation following behavioral consultation in schools: A comparison of three follow-up strategies. *School Psychology Review, 34,* 87–106.

Norbury, C., & Bishop, D. (2002). Inferential processing and strong recall in children with communication problems: A comparison of specific language impairment, pragmatic language impairment and high-functioning autism. *International Journal of Language and Communication Disorders, 37,* 227–251.

Northup, J., Wacker, D., Sasso, G., Steege, M., Cigrand, K., Cook, J., et al. (1991). A brief functional analysis of aggressive and alternative behavior in an outclinic setting. *Journal of Applied Behavior Analysis, 24,* 499–508.

O'Neill, R. E., Horner, R. H., Albin, R. W., Storey, K., & Sprague, J. R. (1997). *Functional analysis of problem behavior: A practical assessment guide.* Pacific Grove, CA: Brooks/Cole.

Odom, S. L., & Brown, W. H. (1993). Social interaction skills interventions for young children with disabilities in integrated settings. In C. A. Peck, S. L. Odom, & D. D. Bricker (Eds.), *Integrating young children with disabilities into community programs* (pp. 39–64). Baltimore: Brookes.

Odom, S. L., Peterson, C., McConnell, S., & Ostrosky, M. (1990). Ecobehavioral analysis of early education/specialized classroom settings and peer social interaction. *Education and Treatment of Children, 13,* 316–330.

Offord, D. R., Boyle, M. H., Szatmari, P., Rae-Grant, N. I., Links, P. S., Cadman, D. T. et al. (1987). Ontario Child Health Study: II. Six-month prevalence of disorder and rates of service utilization. *Archives of General Psychiatry, 44,* 832–836.

Ozonoff, S. (1997). Components of executive function in autism and other disorders. In J. Russell (Ed.), *Autism is an executive disorder* (pp. 179–211). Oxford: Oxford University Press.

Paul, L. (1985). Programming peer support for functional language. In S. F. Warren & A. K. Rogers-Warren (Eds.), *Teaching functional language: Generalization and maintenance of language skills* (pp. 289–307). Baltimore: University Park Press.

Pelios, L. V., MacDuff, G. S., & Axelrod, S. (2003). The effects of a treatment package in establishing independent academic work skills in children with autism. *Education and Treatment of Children, 26,* 1–21.

Petscher, E. S., & Bailey, J. S. (2006). Effects of training, prompting, and self-monitoring on staff behavior in a classroom for students with disabilities. *Journal of Applied Behavior Analysis, 39,* 215–226.

Phillips V., & McCullough, L. (1990). Consultation-based programming: Instituting the collaborative ethic in schools. *Exceptional Children, 56,* 291–303.

Pierce, K. L., & Schreibman, L. (1994). Teaching daily living skills to children with autism in unsupervised settings through pictorial self-management. *Journal of Applied Behavior Analysis, 27,* 471–481.

Pierce-Jordan, S., & Lifter, K. (2005). Interaction of social and play behaviors in preschoolers with and without Pervasive Developmental Disorder. *Topics in Early Childhood Special Education, 25,* 34–47.

Polychronis, S. C., McDonnell, J., Johnson, J. W., & Jameson, M. (2004). A comparison of two-trial distribution schedules in embedded instruction. *Focus on Autism and Other Developmental Disabilities, 190,* 140–151.

Quilitch, H. R., & Risley, T. R. (1973). The effects of play materials on social play. *Journal of Applied Behavior Analysis, 6,* 573–578.

Rabinowitz, F. M., Moely, B. E., Finkel, N., & McClinton, S. (1975). The effects of toy novelty and social interaction on the exploratory behavior of preschool children. *Child Development, 46,* 286–289.

Ramey, C. T., & Ramey, S. L. (1998). Early intervention and early experience. *American Psychologist, 53,* 109–120.

Rao, S., & Kalyanpur, M. (2002). Promoting home-school collaboration in positive behavior support. In J. M. Lucyshyn, G. Dunlap, & R. W. Albin (Eds.), *Families and positive behavior support: Addressing problem behavior in family contexts* (pp. 219–239). Baltimore: Brookes.

Reed, P., Osborne, L. A., & Corness, M. (2007). Brief report: Relative effectiveness of different home-based behavioral approaches to early teaching interventions. *Journal of Autism and Other Developmental Disorders, 37,* 1815–1821.

Rehfeldt, R. A., Kinney, E. M., Root, S., & Stromer, R. (2004). Creating activity schedules using Microsoft Power Point. *Journal of Applied Behavior Analysis, 37,* 115–128.

Richarz, S. (1993). Innovations in early childhood education: Models that support the integration of children with varied developmental levels. In C. A. Peck, S. L. Odom, & D. D. Bricker (Eds.), *Integrating young children with disabilities into community programs* (pp. 83–108). Baltimore: Brookes.

Ricks, F., & Weinstein, M. (1977). Goal attainment scaling: Planning and outcome. *Canadian Journal of Behavioural Sciences, 9,* 1–11.

Riesen, B., MacDonald, J., Johnson, J., Polychronis, S., & Jameson, M. (2003). A comparison of constant time delay and simultaneous prompting within embedded instruction in general education classes with students with moderate to severe disabilities. *Journal of Behavioral Education, 12,* 241–259.

Ringer, V. M. J. (1973). The use of a "token helper" in the management of classroom behavior and in teacher training. *Journal of Applied Behavior Analysis, 6,* 671–177.

Roane, H. S., Vollmer, T. R., Ringdahl, J. E., & Marcus, B. A. (1998). Evaluation of a brief stimulus preference assessment. *Journal of Applied Behavior Analysis, 31,* 605–620.

Robertson, J., Emerson, E., Hatton, C., Elliott, J., McIntosh, B., Swift, P., et al. (2006). Longitudinal analysis of the impact and cost of person-centered planning for people with intellectual disabilities in England. *American Journal of Mental Retardation, 111,* 400–416.

Romanczyk, R. G., Weiner, T., Lockshin, S., & Ekdahl, M. (1999). Research in autism: Myths, controversies, and perspectives. In D. B. Zager (Ed.), *Autism: Identification, education, and treatment* (2nd ed., pp. 23–61), Mahwah, NJ: Erlbaum.

Ruhl, K. L., & Hughes, C. A, (1985). The nature and extent of aggression in special education settings serving behaviorally disordered students. *Behavioral Disorders, 10,* 95–104.

Ryan, J. B., & Peterson, R. L. (2004). Physical restraint in school. *Behavioral Disorders, 29,* 154–168.

Sallows, G. O., & Graupner, T. D. (2005). Intensive behavioral treatment for children with autism: Four-year outcome and predictors. *American Journal on Mental Retardation, 110,* 417–438.

Sands, D. J., Kozleski, E., & French, N. (2000). *Inclusion education for the twenty-first century.* Belmont, CT: Wadsworth/West.

Sansosti, F. J., Powell-Smith, K. A., & Kincaid, D. (2004). A research synthesis of social story interventions for children with autism spectrum disorders. *Focus on Autism and Other Developmental Disabilities, 19,* 194–204.

Sarokoff, R. A., & Sturmey, P. (2004). The effects of behavioral skills training on staff implementation of discrete-trial teaching. *Journal of Applied Behavior Analysis, 37,* 535–538.

Sarokoff, R. A., Taylor, B., & Poulson, C. L. (2001). Teaching children with autism to engage in conversational exchanges: Script fading with embedded textual stimuli. *Journal of Applied Behavior Analysis, 34,* 81–84.

Scattone, D., Tingstrom, D. H., & Wilczynski, S. M. (2006). Increasing appropriate social interactions of children with autism spectrum disorders using social stories. *Focus on Autism and Other Developmental Disabilities, 21,* 211–222.

Scattone, D., Wilczynski, S., Edwards, R., & Rabian, B. (2002). Decreasing disruptive behavior of children with autism using social stories. *Journal of Autism and Developmental Disorders, 12,* 535–543.

Schepis, M. M., Ownbey, J. B., Parsons, M. B., & Reid, D. H. (2000). Training support staff for teaching young children with disabilities in an inclusive preschool setting. *Journal of Positive Behavior Interventions, 2,* 170–178.

Schepis, M. M., Reid, D. H., Ownbey, J., & Parsons, M. B. (2001). Training support staff to embed teaching within natural routines of young children with disabilities in an inclusive preschool. *Journal of Applied Behavior Analysis, 34,* 313–327.

Schindler, H. R., & Horner, R. H. (2005). Generalized reduction of problem behavior of young children with autism: Building trans-situational interventions. *American Journal on Mental Retardation, 110,* 36–47.

Schmit, J., Alper, S., Raschke, D., & Ryndak, D. (2000). Effects of using a photographic cueing package during routine school transitions with a child who has autism. *Mental Retardation, 38,* 131–137.

Schopler, E., & Mesibov, G. B. (1994). *Behavioral issues in autism.* New York: Plenum Press.

Schreibman, L. (1975). Effects of within-stimulus and extra-stimulus prompting on discrimination learning in autistic children. *Journal of Applied Behavior Analysis, 8,* 91–112.

Schreibman, L., Whalen, C., & Stahmer, A. C. (2001). The use of video priming to reduce descriptive behavior in children with autism. *Journal of Positive Behavior Intervention, 2,* 3–11.

Schuster, J. W., Hemmeter, M. L., & Ault, M. J. (2001). Instruction of students with moderate and severe disabilities in elementary classrooms. *Early Childhood Research Quarterly, 16,* 329–341.

Schwartz, I. S., Garfinkle, A. N., & Bauer, J. (1998). The Picture Exchange Communication System: Communication outcomes for young children with disabilities. *Topics in Early Childhood Education, 18,* 144–159.

Scott, J., Clark, C., & Brady, M. P. (2000). *Students with autism: Characteristics and instructional programming for special educators.* San Diego, CA: Singular.

Scott, T. M. (2001). A schoolwide example of positive behavioral support. *Journal of Positive Behavior Interventions, 3,* 88–94.

Secan, K. E., Egel, A. L., & Tilley, C. S. (1989). Acquisition, generalization, and maintenance of question-answering skills in autistic children. *Journal of Applied Behavior Analysis, 22,* 181–196.

Sheinkopf, S. J., & Siegel, B. (1998). Home-based behavioral treatment of young children with autism. *Journal of Autism and Developmental Disorders, 28,* 15–23.

Shook, G. L., & Neisworth, J. T. (2005). Ensuring appropriate qualification for applied behavior analyst professionals: The Behaviour Analyst Certification Board. *Exceptionality, 13,* 3–10.

Sigafoos, J. (2000). Communication development and aberrant behavior in children with developmental disabilities. *Education and Training in Mental Retardation and Developmental Disabilities, 35,* 168–176.

Sigafoos, J., Arthur, M., & O'Reilly, M. (2003). *Challenging behavior & developmental disability.* London: Whurr.

Sigman, M., & Ruskin, E. (1999). Continuity and change in the social competence of children with autism, Down syndrome, and developmental delays. *Monographs of the Society for Research in Child Development, 64,* 1–114.

Singer, G. H., Goldberg-Hamblin, S. E., Peckham-Hardin, K. D., Barry, L., & Santarelli, G. E. (2002). Toward a synthesis of family support practices and positive behavior support. In J. M. Lucyshyn, G. Dunlap, & R. W. Albin (Eds.), *Families and positive behavior support: Addressing problem behaviors in family contexts* (pp. 155–184). Baltimore: Brookes.

Skinner, B. F. (1938). *The behavior of organisms: An experimental analysis.* New York: Appleton-Century.

Smith T., Groen, A. D., & Wynn, J. W. (2000). Randomized trial of intensive early intervention for children with pervasive developmental disorder. *American Journal on Mental Retardation, 15,* 269–285.

Smukler, D. (2005). Unauthorized minds: How "Theory of Mind" theory misrepresents autism. *Mental Retardation, 43,* 11–24.

Soloman, R. W., & Wahler, R. G. (1973). Peer reinforcement control of classroom problem behavior. *Journal of Applied Behavior Analysis, 6,* 49–56.

Stahmer, A. C., & Gist, K. (2001). The effects of accelerated parent education program on technique mastery and child outcome. *Journal of Positive Behavior Interventions, 3,* 75–82.

Stahmer, A. C., & Ingersoll, B. (2004). Inclusive programming for toddlers with autism spectrum disorders: Outcomes from the Children's Toddler School. *Journal of Positive Behavior Interventions, 6,* 67–82.

Stanley, S. O., & Greenwood, C. R. (1981). Assessing opportunity to respond in classroom environments through direct observation: How much opportunity to respond does the minority, disadvantaged student receive in school? *Exceptional Children, 49,* 370–373.

Stein, M. K., & Wang, M. C. (1988). *Teacher development and school improvement: The process of teacher change; Social skills in the classroom.* Odessa, FL: Psychological Assessment Resources.

Stein, M. K., & Wang, M. C. (1988). Teacher development and school improvement: The process of teacher change. *Training and Teacher Education, 4,* 171–187.

Stevenson, C. L., Krantz, P. J., & McClannahan, L. E. (2000). Social interaction skills for children with autism: A script-fading procedure for nonreaders. *Behavioral Interventions, 15,* 1–20.

Strain, P. S., & Cordisco, A. (1994). The LEAP program. In S. L. Harris & J. S. Handleman (Eds.), *Preschool education programs for children with autism* (pp. 115–126). Austin, TX: PRO-ED.

Strain, P. S., & Hoyson, M. (2000). The need for longitudinal, intensive social skill intervention: LEAP follow-up outcomes for children with autism. *Topics in Early Childhood Special Education, 20,* 116–122.

Strain, P. S., & Kohler, F. (1998). Peer-mediated intervention for young children with autism. *Seminars in Speech and Language, 19,* 391–404.

Strain, P. S., McGee, G. G., & Kohler, F. W. (2001). Inclusion of children with autism in early intervention environments. In M. J. Guralanick (Ed.), *Early childhood inclusion* (pp. 338–363). Baltimore: Brookes.

Stromer, R., Kimball, J. W., Kinney, E. M., & Taylor, B. A. (2006). Activity schedules, computer technology, and teaching children with autism spectrum disorders. *Focus on Autism and Other Developmental Disabilities, 21,* 14–24.

Stromer, R., MacKay, H. A., McVay, A. A., & Fowler, T. (1998). Written lists as mediating stimuli in the matching-to-sample performances of individuals with mental retardation. *Journal of Applied Behavior Analysis, 31,* 1–19.

Sundberg, M. L., & Parington, J. W. (1998). *The assessment of basic language and learning skills: An assessment, curriculum guide, and teaching system for children with autism and other developmental disabilities.* Danville, CA: Behavior Analyst.

Swaggart, B. L., Gagnon, E., Bock, S. J., Earles, T. L., Quinn, C., Myles, B. S., et al. (1995). Using social stories to teach social and behavioral skills to children with autism. *Focus on Autistic Behavior, 10,* 1–15.

Swettenham, J. (1996). Can children with autism be taught to understand false belief using computers? *Journal of Child Psychology and Psychiatry and Allied Disciplines, 37,* 157–165.

Symon, J. B. (2005). Expanding interventions for children with autism: Parents as trainers. *Journal of Positive Behavior Interventions, 7,* 159–173.

Taylor, B. A., Hoch, H., & Weissman, M. (2005). The analysis and treatment of vocal stereotypy in a child with autism. *Behavioral Interventions, 20,* 239–253.

Taylor, J. C., & Carr, E. G. (1992). Severe problem behaviors related to social interaction: I; Attention seeking and social avoidance. *Behavior Modification, 16,* 305–335.

Theiman, K. S., & Goldstein, H. (2001). Social stories, written text cues, and video feedback: Effects on social communication of children with autism. *Journal of Applied Behavior Analysis, 34,* 425–446.

Tincani, M. (2004). Comparing the Picture Exchange Communication System and sign language training for children with autism. *Focus on Autism and Other Developmental Disabilities, 19,* 152–163.

Touchette, P. E. (1985). A scatter plot for identifying stimulus control of problem behavior. *Journal of Applied Behavior Analysis, 18,* 343–351.

Trivette, C. M., Dunst, C. J., Hamby, D. W., & LaPointe, N. J. (1996). Key elements of empowerment and their implications for early intervention. *Infant-Toddler Intervention, 6,* 59–73.

Turnbull, A. P., & Turnbull, H. R. (1996). Group action planning as a strategy for providing comprehensive family support. In L. K. Koegel, R. L. Koegel, & G. Dunlap (Eds.), *Positive behavioral support: Including people with difficult behavior in the community* (pp. 99–114). Baltimore: Brookes.

Turnbull, A. P., & Turnbull, H. R. (2001). *Families, professionals and exceptionality: Collaborating for empowerment* (4th ed.). Upper Saddle River, NJ: Prentice-Hall.

VanDenBerg, J. E., & Grealish, E. M. (1996). Individualized services and supports through the wraparound process: Philosophy and procedures. *Journal of Child and Family Studies, 5,* 7–21.

Vandercook, T., & York, J. (1990). A team approach to program development and support. In W. Stainback & S. Stainback (Eds.), *Support networks for inclusive schooling* (pp. 95–122). Baltimore: Brookes.

Vandercook, T., York, J., & Forest, M. (1989). The McGill action planning system (MAPS): A strategy for building the vision. *Journal of the Association for Persons with Severe Handicaps, 14,* 205–215.

Volkert, V. M., Lerman, D. C., & Vorndran, C. (2005). The effects of reinforcement magnitude on functional analysis outcomes. *Journal of Applied Behavior Analysis, 38,* 147–162.

Volkmar, F. R. (1996). Diagnostic issues in autism: Results of the DSM-IV field trial. *Journal of Autism and Developmental Disorders, 26,* 155–157.

Vollmer, T. R., Marcus, B. A., & Ringdahl, J. E. (1995). Noncontingent escape as treatment for self-injurious behavior maintained by negative reinforcement. *Journal of Applied Behavior Analysis, 28,* 15–26.

Watson, J. B. (1913). Psychology as the behaviorist views it. *Psychological Review, 20,* 158–177.

Wallace, M. D., Doney, J. K., Mintz-Resudek, C. M., & Tarbox, R. S. F. (2004). Training educators to implement functional analyses. *Journal of Applied Behavior Analysis, 37,* 89–92.

Weeks, M., & Gaylord-Ross, R. (1981). Task difficulty and aberrant behavior in severely handicapped students. *Journal of Applied Behavior Analysis, 14,* 449–463.

Wehmeyer, M. L. (2002). *Teaching students with mental retardation: Providing access to the general curriculum.* Baltimore: Brookes.

Wellman, H. M., Baron-Cohen, S., Caswell, R., Gomez, J.C., Swettenham, J., Toye, E., et al. (2002). Thought-bubbles help children with autism acquire an alternative to a theory of mind. *Autism, 6,* 343–363.

Wert, B. Y., & Neisworth, J. T. (2003). Effects of video self-modeling on spontaneous requesting in children with autism. *Journal of Positive Behavioral Intervention, 5,* 30–34.

Wetherby, A. M. (1986). Ontogeny of communication functions in autism. *Journal of Autism and Developmental Disorders, 16,* 295–316.

Wetherby, A. M., & Prizant, B. M. (1993). Profiling communication and symbolic activities in young children. *Journal of Childhood Communication Disorders, 15,* 23-32.

Whitman, T. L. (1990a). Development of self-regulation in persons with mental retardation. *American Journal on Mental Retardation, 94,* 373–374.

Whitman, T. L. (1990b). Self-regulation and mental retardation. *American Journal of Mental Retardation, 94,* 347–362.

Whitman, T. L. (2004). *The development of autism: A self-regulatory perspective.* London: Jessica Kingsley.

Wilde, L. D., Koegel, L. K., & Koegel, R. L. (1992). *Increasing success in school through priming: A training manual.* Santa Barbara: Robert Koegel.

Williams, S. K., Johnson, C., & Sukhodolsky, D. G. (2005). The role of the school psychologist in the inclusive education of school-age children with autism spectrum disorders. *Journal of School Psychology, 43,* 117–136.

Williamson, P., McLeskey, J., Hoppey, D., & Rentz, T. (2006). Educating students with mental retardation in general education classrooms. *Exceptional Children, 72,* 347–361.

Windsor, J., Piche, L. M., & Locke, P. A. (1994). Preference testing: A comparison of two presentation methods. *Research in Developmental Disabilities, 15,* 439–455.

Wing, L. (1988). The continuum of autistic disorders. In E. Schopler & G. M. Mesibor (Eds.), *Diagnosis and assessment in autism* (pp. 91–110). New York: Plenum Press.

Witt, J. C. (1986). Teachers' resistance to the use of school-based interventions. *Journal of School Psychology, 24,* 37–44.

Witt, J. C., Noell, G. H., LaFleur, L. H., & Mortenson, B. P. (1997). Teacher use of interventions for general education settings: Measurement and analysis of the independent variable. *Journal of Behavior Analysis, 30,* 693–696.

Wolery, M., Anthony, L., Caldwell, N. K., Snyder, E. D., & Morgante, J. D. (2002). Embedding and distributing constant time delay in circle time and transitions. *Topics in Early Childhood Special Education, 22,* 14–25.

Wolery, M., Anthony, L., & Heckathorn, J. (1998). Transition-based teaching: Effects on transitions, teachers' behavior, and children's learning. *Journal of Early Intervention, 21,* 117–131.

Wolf, L. C., Noh, S., Fisman, S. N., & Speechley, M. (1989). Brief report: Psychological effects of parenting stress on parents of autistic children. *Journal of Autism and Developmental Disorders, 19,* 157–166.

Wolfe, P., & Neisworth, J. T. (Eds.). (2005). Autism and applied behavior analysis. *Exceptionality, 13,* 1–2.

Woods, J., & Goldstein, H. (2003). When the toddler takes over: Changing challenging routines into conduits for communication. *Focus on Autism and Other Developmental Disabilities, 18,* 176–181.

Yeargin-Allsopp, M., Rice, C., Karapurkar, T., Doernberg, N., Boyle, C., & Murphy, C. (2003). Prevalency of autism in a U.S. metropolitan area. *Journal of the American Medical Association, 289,* 49–55.

Yell, M. L., & Drasgow, E. (2000). Litigating a free appropriate public education: The Lovaas hearings and cases. *Journal of Special Education, 33,* 205–214.

Yell, M., Drasgow, E., & Lowrey, A. (2005). No child left behind and students with autism spectrum disorders. *Focus on Autism and Other Developmental Disabilities, 20,* 130–139.

York, J., & Vandercook, T. (1990). Strategies for achieving an integrated education for middle school students with severe disabilities. *Remedial and Special Education, 11,* 6–16.

Zachor, D. A., Ben-Itzchak, E., Rabinovich, A., & Lahat, E. (2007). Change in autism core symptoms with intervention. *Research in Autism Spectrum Disorders, 1,* 304–317.

Zanolli, K., Daggett, J., & Adams, T. (1996). Teaching preschool age autistic children to make spontaneous initiations to peers using training. *Journal of Autism and Developmental Disabilities, 26,* 407–421.

About the Author

Dr. Joel Hundert is a psychologist and a director of Behaviour Institute, a private agency providing applied behavior analysis (ABA) for children with autism. In this capacity, he supervises the implementation of ABA programs for children in their homes and in both general and special education settings. He is an associate clinical professor in the Department of Psychiatry and Behavioural Neurosciences and an associate member of the Psychology Department, McMaster University, Hamilton, Ontario. Joel is a Board Certified Behavior Analyst and sits on the Board of Directors of the Behavior Analysis Certification Board. Joel has published numerous research articles in scholarly journals and is on the editorial board of several professional journals. His previous book was titled *Enhancing Social Competence in Young Students: School-Based Approaches,* also published by PRO-ED. In addition to published books and articles, he has written several staff-training manuals on the implementation of ABA procedures.

Index

AAC (augmentative and alternative communication), 102–105

ABA. *See* Applied behavior analysis (ABA)

ABC (Antecedent–Behavior–Consequence) recording, 178–179, 230

Access to desired activities or objects, and problem behavior, 206–207

Adaptation of curriculum. *See* Curriculum

Adaptive Classwide Plan, 274

Adolescent Version of Problem Behavior Interview, 225–229

Alternative curriculum, 66. *See also* Curriculum

Antecedent–Behavior–Consequence (ABC) recording, 178–179, 230

Applied behavior analysis (ABA). *See also* Assessment; Classroom skills; Early intensive behavioral intervention (EIBI); Inclusion; Instruction
    critical features of, 12
    history of, 9–11
    research on generally, 54, 56
    staff preparation and training for, 254–270

Arithmetic
    assessment of, 26, 28
    curriculum on, 77
    modifications to general education class curriculum on, 69–71

ASDs (Autism Spectrum Disorders), 2, 243

Asperger's Syndrome, 2

Assessment
    ABC (Antecedent–Behavior–Consequence) recording, 178–179, 230
    of arithmetic, 26, 28
    of Classwide Social Skills Program (CSSP), 132–134
    criterion-referenced assessment, 25–28
    curriculum-based measurement (CBM), 25–28
    data collection forms, 46–51, 139, 216–233
    data summary, 40, 41
    descriptive assessment, 178–190
    direct experimental manipulation of environmental events, 190–191
    direct recording of behaviors and environmental events, 178–190
    ecobehavioral analysis, 183, 185–190
    functional assessment cards (FACs), 179–180, 231

Functional Assessment Observation Form (FAOF), 182–184, 233
Goal Attainment Scale, 268–269
hypothesis development and, 191–192
hypothetical developmental trajectory and, 22–24
of incidental language instruction, 110–111
of inclusive classroom skills, 29–38
of independent seatwork, 36–37, 50
indirect or anecdotal information for, 177–178
inter-observer reliability, 38, 40
multiple-stimulus without replacement (MSWO) preference assessment, 94
norm-referenced assessment, 22–24
of on-task behavior, 29–32, 36–37, 46
of peer interaction, 30, 33, 34, 47
of problem behavior, 38, 39, 51, 177–192
of reading, 26, 27
of responding to questions during lessons, 33, 35–36, 48–49
scatter plot grid, 180–182, 232
stimulus preference assessment, 93–94
Association of Behavior Analysts, 208
Attention-maintained problem behavior, 203–206
Augmentative and alternative communication (AAC), 102–105
Autism Spectrum Disorders (ASDs), 2, 243. *See also* Children with autism

Backward chaining, 70–71
Ball and Pipe Game, 137–139
Behavior. *See also* Problem behavior
functions of, 172–174
history of research on, 9–10
modified competing behavior model, 209–211
positive behavior support (PBS), 192–193, 241–243, 270
Behavior analysis, 9–10, 55. *See also* Applied behavior analysis (ABA)
Behavior problems. *See* Problem behavior
Behavioral intervention. *See* Applied behavior analysis (ABA); Early intensive behavioral intervention; Families; Problem behavior; Teachers
Behavioral interventions. *See* Reinforcers

Canada, 13
CBM (curriculum-based measurement), 25–28
Child Profile, 250
Children with autism. *See also* Assessment; Classroom skills; Communication; Families; Instruction; Peer interaction
growth trajectory of, 22–24
outcome for, 2
statistics on, 2
symptoms of, 2–3, 102, 154
Choice, 194–196
CISSAR, 183
Classroom skills. *See also* Instruction
assessment of, 29–38
participation in group lessons, 149–150
peer interaction, 18, 30, 33, 34, 47, 114–139
responding to questions during lessons, 18, 33, 35–36, 48–49

seatwork assignments, 18, 36–37, 50, 150
visual schedules, 142–149
Classwide Social Skills Program (CSSP), 127–134
Clear requests, 205–206
Cluster inclusion, 11–12. *See also* Inclusion
Commercially available curricula. *See* Curriculum
Communication. *See also* Peer interaction
augmentative and alternative communication, 102–105
functional communication training, 201–203
general education classroom interventions, 105–111
incidental language instruction, 105–111, 267
as instructional target in supported inclusion, 18
mass-trial teaching of language, 105
Picture Exchange Communication Systems (PECS), 102, 103–105
sign language, 102–103
Computer activity schedules, 148–149
Constant time delay, 90, 93
Criterion-referenced assessment, 25–28. *See also* Assessment
CSSP (Classwide Social Skills Program), 127–134
Curriculum. *See also* Instruction; Teachers
adaptation of commercial curricula, 71–73, 76–80
alternative curriculum, 66
commercially available curricula, 71–73, 76–80
definition of, 82
example modifications to general education class curriculum, 69–71
form for Curriculum Adaptation Plan, 67
general education class curriculum adaptation, 65–71
selection criteria for commercially available curricula, 72–73
simplified curriculum, 66
strategies for adaptation of general curriculum, 67–69
supplementary curriculum, 66
Curriculum-based measurement (CBM), 25–28
Curriculum Adaptation Plan, 67

Data collection. *See also* Assessment
ABC Recording Form, 230
forms, 46–51, 139, 216–233
functional assessment cards (FACs), 231
Functional Assessment Observation Form (FAOF), 233
incidental language instruction, 110–111
on-task behavior, 46
peer interaction, 47, 138–139
problem behavior, 51, 216–233
Problem Behavior Interview: Adolescent Version, 225–229
Problem Behavior Interview: Elementary School Version, 220–224
Problem Behavior Interview: Preschool Version, 216–219
responding to questions, 48–49
scatter plot grid, 232
seatwork assignments, 50
Data summary, 40, 41. *See also* Assessment
Descriptive assessment, 178–190. *See also* Assessment
Developmental trajectory of children, 22–24
Diagnostic and Statistical Manual of Mental Disorders (DSM), 2

Differential reinforcement of alternative behavior (DRA), 204

Differential reinforcement of incompatible behavior (DRI), 204

Differential reinforcement of low rates of behavior (DRL), 204

Differential reinforcement of other behavior (DRO), 204

DRA (differential reinforcement of alternative behavior), 204

DRI (differential reinforcement of incompatible behavior), 204

DRL (differential reinforcement of low rates of behavior), 204

DRO (differential reinforcement of other behavior), 204

DSM, 2

Early intensive behavioral intervention (EIBI). *See also* Applied behavior analysis (ABA)
    description of, 4
    IQ gains associated with, 3–8
    outcome studies of, 3–8
    parents' involvement in, 243–244

EBASS, 183

Ecobehavioral analysis, 183, 185–190

Education for All Handicapped Children Act (P.L. 94-142), 13, 236

Educators. *See* Teachers

EIBI. *See* Early intensive behavioral intervention (EIBI)

Elementary School Version of Problem Behavior Interview, 220–224

Embedded instruction
    design recommendations for, 58
    examples of, 56–57, 60–61
    increase in number of embedded instruction trials, 58
    index cards for, 59–60
    instructional strategies for, 60–61
    objectives for, 56–57
    overview of, 56
    planning for, 61–63
    selection of instructional items from actual errors, 58
    teaching in sets of five, 59
    two-part mastery criterion for, 58

Engaged on-task behavior, 36–37. *See also* On-task behavior

Error correction procedure, 82–83, 97

ESCAPE, 183

Escape-maintained problem behavior, 208–209

Evaluation. *See* Assessment

Extinction of problem behavior, 203–204

FACs (functional assessment cards), 179–180, 231

Families
    legislation on involvement of, in special education, 236–237
    parent/professional relationships, 237–240
    person-centered planning and, 240–243, 249–252
    roles and responsibilities of parents in inclusion, 55
    stress of parents, 240
    training parents to implement interventions, 243–245
    trans-situational intervention and, 245–246

FAOF (Functional Assessment Observation Form), 182–184, 233

Full inclusion, 11. *See also* Inclusion

Functional assessment cards (FACs), 179–180, 231

Functional Assessment Observation Form (FAOF), 182–184, 233

Functional communication training, 201–203

General education. *See* Curriculum; Inclusion; Instruction; Teachers

Gestural prompts, 83–84, 87, 93

Goal Attainment Scale, 268–269

Graduated guidance, 87–89, 146

Growth trajectory of children, 22–24

High-probability (high-p) and interspersed requests, 194

Hypothesis development, 191–192

Hypothetical developmental trajectory of children, 22–24

IDEA (Individuals With Disabilities Education Act), 13, 236, 237, 239, 241

IDEIA (Individuals With Disabilities Education Improvement Act), 13, 236

IEPs (Individualized Education Programs), 11, 237, 242, 251–252

Incidental language instruction, 105–111, 267

Inclusion

    arguments for, 13

    in Canada, 13

    cluster inclusion, 11–12

    elements of supported inclusion, 238

    equipment and materials for, 15

    full inclusion, 11

    instructional targets in, 17–19

    legislation on, 236–237

    optimal learning arrangement for children with autism, 15–16

    paraprofessionals for, 15, 55, 147–150, 254–255

    person-centered approach to, 240–243, 249–252

    planning for, by teachers, 15, 54–56

    preschool inclusion, 11–12, 56

    research on, 13–14

    resources for, 15–16

    reverse inclusion, 11, 12

    roles and responsibilities of team members, 54, 55

    social inclusion, 11, 12

    statistics on, 11

    supported inclusion, 14–19, 238

Individualized Education Programs (IEPs), 11, 237, 242, 251–252

Individualized group instruction, 63–65

"Individualized Support Project," 241–242

Individuals With Disabilities Education Act (IDEA), 13, 236, 237, 239, 241

Individuals With Disabilities Education Improvement Act (IDEIA), 13, 236

Inference making, 154, 161–167

Instruction. *See also* Classroom skills; Curriculum; Peer interaction; Teachers; and specific
        content and behavioral skills

    adaptation of commercial curriculum, 71–73

    adaptation of general education class curriculum, 65–71

    classroom routines in, 18

    definition of, 82

    embedded instruction, 56–63

error correction procedure, 82–83, 97
individualized group instruction, 63–65
instructional targets in support inclusion, 17–19
optimal learning arrangement for children with autism, 15–16
participation in group lessons, 149–150
peer incidental teaching, 120
prompts, 68–71, 82–93
reinforcers, 82, 92–97
responding to questions during lessons, 18, 33, 35–36, 48–49
seatwork assignments, 18, 36–37, 50, 150
Inter-observer reliability, 38, 40. *See also* Assessment
Intervention. *See* Applied behavior analysis (ABA); Early intensive behavioral intervention; Families; Problem behavior; Teachers
IQ gains, 3–8

Journal of Applied Behavior Analysis, 9, 10, 11, 54
Journal of Positive Behavioral Interventions, 54

Language. *See* Communication
LEAP program, 14, 56, 63
Learning Experiences . . . An Alternative Program for Preschoolers and Parents (LEAP) program, 14, 56, 63
Least-to-most prompting, 90, 93

MAPS (McGill Action Planning System), 241
MAS (*Motivation Assessment Scales*), 177
Mass-trial teaching of language, 105
Mathematics. *See* Arithmetic
McGill Action Planning System (MAPS), 241
Modeling, 83, 93, 124–126
Modified competing behavior model, 209–211
Most-to-least prompting, 89–90, 93
Motivation Assessment Scales (MAS), 177
MS-CISSAR, 183
MSWO (multiple-stimulus without replacement) preference assessment, 94
Multiple-stimulus without replacement (MSWO) preference assessment, 94

Neutralizing routines, 193–194
Noncontingent escape, 200
Noncontingent reinforcement, 200
Norm-referenced assessment, 22–24. *See also* Assessment

Observation, for selecting reinforcers, 93
On-task behavior
    assessment of, 29–32, 36–37, 46
    data collection form, 46
    engaged on-task behavior, 36–37
    seatwork assignments and, 36–37, 50, 150

Pacing, 68
Paraprofessionals, 15, 55, 147–150, 254–255. *See also* Teachers

Parents. *See* Families

PAS (picture activity schedules), 115–117, 143–144, 146–148

PASS (*Program for Academic Survival Skills*), 254, 255

PBI (*Problem Behavior Interview*), 177–178, 216–229

PBS (positive behavior support), 192–193, 241–243, 270

PDD (Pervasive Developmental Disorders), 2

PECS (Picture Exchange Communication Systems), 102, 103–105

Peer incidental teaching, 120

Peer interaction
    adult-mediated approach to, 118–122
    assessment of, 30, 33, 34, 47
    Ball and Pipe Game, 137–139
    classwide approach to, 126–134
    Classwide Social Skills Program (CSSP), 127–134
    data collection form, 47, 138–139
    direct teaching of, 122–134
    environmental arrangements to promote, 117–118
    as instructional target, 18, 114–115
    peer incidental teaching, 120
    peer mediation, 119–120
    peer networks, 122
    picture activity schedules for independent play, 115, 116, 117
    picture activity schedules for interactive play, 115–117
    recess buddies, 120–121
    self-monitoring and, 160–161
    social scripts training, 122–126, 137–139

Peer mediation, 119–120

Peer networks, 122

Person-centered planning, 240–243, 249–252

Perspective taking, 167–168

Pervasive Developmental Disorders (PDD): Autistic Disorder, 2. *See also* Children with autism

Pervasive Developmental Disorders–Not Otherwise Specified (PDD-NOS), 2

Physical prompts, 83–84, 87, 93

Picture activity schedules (PAS), 115–117, 143–144, 146–148

Picture Exchange Communication Systems (PECS), 102, 103–105

Planned ignoring of problem behavior, 203–204

Planning
    Adaptive Classwide Plan, 274
    curriculum adaptation, 67
    for embedded instruction, 61–63
    for inclusion, 15, 54–56
    McGill Action Planning System (MAPS), 241
    person-centered planning, 240–243, 249–252
    roles and responsibilities of inclusion team members, 54, 55

Play. *See* Peer interaction

Positional prompts, 83, 84, 93

Positive behavior support (PBS), 192–193, 241–243, 270

Preschool inclusion models, 11–12, 56

Preschool Problem Behavior Interview, 216–219

Priming, 196–197

Principals, 55, 256

Problem behavior. *See also* Applied behavior analysis (ABA)
    ABC (Antecedent–Behavior–Consequence) recording, 178–179, 230
    access to desired activities or objects and, 206–207
    assessment of, 38, 39, 51, 177–192
    attention-maintained problem behavior, 203–206
    choice and, 194–196
    clear requests and, 205–206
    data collection forms, 51, 216–233
    descriptive assessment of, 178–190
    differential reinforcement and, 204–205
    direct experimental manipulation of environmental events, 190–191
    direct recording of behaviors and environmental events, 178–190
    ecobehavioral analysis of, 183, 185–190
    escape-maintained problem behavior, 208–209
    extinction/planned ignoring of, 203–204
    functional assessment cards (FACs), 179–180, 231
    Functional Assessment Observation Form (FAOF), 182–184, 233
    functions of, 172–174
    high-probability (high-p) and interspersed requests, 194
    hypothesis of, 191–192
    indirect or anecdotal information on, 177–178
    interventions for, 203–209
    making problem behavior ineffective, 203–209
    making problem behavior inefficient, 201–203
    making problem behavior irrelevant, 193–200
    model of, 175
    modified competing behavior model, 209–211
    neutralizing routines and, 193–194
    noncontingent reinforcement and noncontingent escape, 200
    positive behavior support (PBS) for, 192–193, 241–243, 270
    priming and, 196–197
    scatter plot grid, 180–182, 232
    sensory stimulation-maintained problem behavior, 207–208
    social stories and, 197–200
    teachers' attitudes toward, 172
    transitional warnings on, 194, 195
    triggers of, 174–177
    video priming and, 197

Problem Behavior Interview (PBI), 177–178, 216–229

Problem Behavior Interview: Adolescent Version, 225–229

Problem Behavior Interview: Elementary School Version, 220–224

Problem Behavior Interview: Preschool Version, 216–219

Program for Academic Survival Skills (PASS), 254, 255

Progressive time delay, 90–91, 93

Prompt fading, 87–88, 91–92

Prompts
    adding prompts for curriculum adaptation, 68–69
    definition of, 82
    example of, 82
    hierarchies of, 87–92, 93
    incidental language instruction, 108–109
    most-to-least and least-to-most prompting, 89–90, 93
    for participation in group lessons, 149–150

prompt fading, 87–88, 91–92, 93
time delay prompting, 90–91, 93
types of, 83–87, 93
visual prompts, 69–71
Psychologists. *See* School psychologists

Questionnaire for selecting reinforcers, 93
Questions
data collection form, 48–49
group choral responding to, 64–65
group-directed questions, 64–65
individual-directed questions, 64–65
individualized group instruction and, 64–65
inferential *why*-questions, 154, 161–167
responding to, 18, 33, 35–36, 48–49

Reading
assessment of, 26, 27
curriculum on, 68–69, 72, 73, 76
Reasoning and Writing, 80
Recess buddies, 120–121
Reciprocal peer interaction. *See* Peer interaction
Reinforcers
choices on, 195–196
Classwide Social Skills Program (CSSP), 129–130
definition of, 82
delivery of, 94–95
differential reinforcement, 204–205
noncontingent reinforcement, 200
selection of, 92–94
token systems, 95–97, 255–256
Requests
clear requests, 205–206
high-probability (high-p) and interspersed requests, 194
Reverse inclusion, 11, 12. *See also* Inclusion
Reviews, 68

Saxon Math, 77
Scatter plot grid, 180–182, 232
Schedules
computer activity schedules, 148–149
picture activity schedules (PAS), 115–117, 143–144, 146–148
steps in design of, 144–147
text schedule, 146, 147
visual schedules, 142–149
School psychologists, 55
Seatwork assignments, 18, 36–37, 50, 150
Self-contained classes, 12–13
Self-monitoring, 158–161
Self-regulation, 18, 155–158
Sensory stimulation-maintained problem behavior, 207–208
Sign language, 102–103

Simplified curriculum, 66. *See also* Curriculum

SLP (speech–language pathologist), 54

Social inclusion, 11, 12. *See also* Inclusion

Social scripts training, 122–126, 137–139

Social skills. *See* Peer interaction

Social stories, 197–200

Special education. *See also* Inclusion
    legislation on, 13, 236–237
    roles and responsibilities of special education teacher, 55
    self-contained classes in, 12–13

Speech–language pathologist (SLP), 54 .

Spelling Mastery, 78

Staff. *See* Paraprofessionals; Teachers

Staff training. *See* Training of teachers

Stimulus fading, 85–86, 93

Stimulus preference assessment, 93–94

Stimulus shaping, 85–86, 93

Supplementary curriculum, 66. *See also* Curriculum

Supported inclusion, 14–19, 238. *See also* Inclusion

Systemic changes, 269–270

Teachers. *See also* Instruction; Paraprofessionals
    attitudes of, toward students' problem behavior, 172
    development of training for, in ABA procedures, 263, 265–269
    factors effecting adoption of interventions by, 255–256
    intervention implementation fidelity by, 256–257
    parent/professional relationships, 237–240
    performance feedback for, 257–258
    positive behavior supports for, 269–270
    preparation of, for ABA-based supported inclusion, 254–270
    roles and responsibilities of, in inclusion, 54, 55
    training of, on development of ABA interventions, 260, 263, 264
    training of, to implement ABA interventions, 258–259, 261–262

Teaching Your Child to Read Well, 68–69, 72, 73, 76

Text schedule, 146, 147. *See also* Schedules

"Theory of Mind" study, 154

Thinking Basics, 79

Thinking skills
    curriculum on, 79, 80
    inferential *why*-questions, 154, 161–167
    perspective taking, 167–168
    self-monitoring, 158–161
    self-regulation, 18, 155–158

Time delay prompting, 90–91, 93

To Do/Done board, 195, 196

Token systems, 95–97, 255–256

Training of parents, 243–245

Training of teachers
    administrative support for, 265
    content of, 265
    on development of ABA interventions, 260, 263, 264

development of, in ABA procedures, 263, 265–269
development of training material, 265–266
evaluation of, 268
on implementation of ABA interventions, 258–259, 261–262
method of training, 266
positive behavior supports for, 270
selection of staff for, 266, 268
systemic changes and, 269–270
Trans-situational intervention, 245–246
Transitional warnings, 194, 195
Treatment implementation fidelity, 256–257
Triggers of problem behavior, 174–177

Verbal prompts, 83, 86–87, 93
Video priming, 197
Visual prompts, 83–86, 93
Visual schedules, 142–149

Why-questions, 154, 161–167
Writing curriculum, 80